D0843292

Leaving Home

BOOKS BY ANNE EDWARDS

Biographies

Judy Garland: A Biography
Vivien Leigh: A Biography
Sonya: The Life of Sonya Tolstoy
Matriarch: Queen Mary and the House of Windsor
Road to Tara: The Life of Margaret Mitchell
A Remarkable Woman: The Life of Katharine Hepburn
Early Reagan: The Rise to Power
Shirley Temple: American Princess
The DeMilles: An American Family
Royal Sisters: Elizabeth and Margaret
The Grimaldis of Monaco: Centuries of Scandal/Years of Grace
Throne of Gold: The Lives of the Aga Khans
Streisand
Ever After: Diana and the Life She Led
Maria Callas: An Intimate Biography
The Reagans: Portrait of a Marriage

Novels

The Survivors
Shadow of a Lion
Miklos Alexandrovitch Is Missing
Haunted Summer
The Hesitant Heart
Child of Night
La Divina
Wallis: The Novel

Memoirs

The Inn and Us (cowritten with Stephen Citron)
Scarlett and Me

Leaving Home

A Hollywood Blacklisted
Writer's Years Abroad

Anne Edwards

THE SCARECROW PRESS, INC.
Lanham • Toronto • Plymouth, UK
2012

Published by Scarecrow Press, Inc.
A wholly owned subsidary of The Rowman & Littlefield Publishing Group, Inc.
4501 Forbes Boulevard, Suite 200, Lanham, Maryland 20706
http://www.scarecrowpress.com

10 Thornbury Road, Plymouth PL6 7PP, United Kingdom

Distributed by National Book Network

British Library Cataloguing in Publication Information Available

Library of Congress Cataloging-in-Publication Data

Edwards, Anne, 1927–
  Leaving home : a Hollywood blacklisted writer's years abroad / Anne Edwards.
    p. cm.
  Includes index.
  ISBN 978-0-8108-8199-0 (hardback : alk. paper) — ISBN 978-0-8108-8200-3 (ebook)
  1. Edwards, Anne, 1927- 2. Authors, American—20th century—Biography.
  3. Screenwriters—United States—Biography. 4. Expatriate authors—England—
  London—Biography. 5. Blacklisting of authors—United States. I. Title.
  PS3555.D87Z46 2012
  813'.54—dc23
  [B]   2011043169

Printed in the United States of America

For Catherine and Michael

The two of we three

Without you I would never have been complete

Contents

Acknowledgments

My heartfelt gratitude to my children, Michael Dean Edwards and Catherine Edwards Sadler Grill, who relived and shared with me their memories of the times of our lives chronicled in this book. My pride in them as man and woman has grown steadily through the years. I have always believed I am the luckiest mother I have known. In recounting my life during their childhood and youth, I now know that to be true.

There have been others who shared those times with me, some who were fond friends, others who were the progeny of those who are now sadly gone—I give to them my deepest gratitude. Their personal reflections and the filling in of so many details have contributed greatly to a fuller and more accurate portrait of our "expat" years.

I have been extremely fortunate in having Stephen Ryan as an editor for he has, from the beginning, shown his belief in this very personal book at a time that has not been easy in the publishing world. I also want to extend my appreciation to others who have assisted so well in the final making of *Leaving Home*: production editor Jessica McCleary; the fine copyeditor, April Lehoullier; the proofreader, Annette Van Deusen; and my good friend George Djordjevic, who navigated me through the high-tech seas of the twenty-first century.

Last, but certainly not least, my loving appreciation goes to my husband, Stephen Citron, who came into my life only after I had returned "home," and who has never lessened his support of me or my writing.

Setting the Scene

$\mathcal{T}$he day that would change my life and that of my two children, Michael, almost seven, and Catherine, almost three, is indelibly carved into my memory. A hot California sun burned through the large, arched front windows of my small Spanish bungalow, blinding the familiar view beyond—palm trees towering over like houses on the fringe edge of Beverly Hills, where more expansive, pricey dwellings were the usual, many occupied by movie stars and other well-known denizens of the film industry. This was a fiery day in August 1954. Summer would soon pass and time was running out for "we three." A divorced mother in my midtwenties, my ex-husband gone—no one knew quite where—I had no job (I was an "independent" neophyte screen and television writer), do-piddling in the bank, with only six weeks remaining on an eviction notice to vacate our home.

I had been nineteen in 1947, when I married my husband, who was twenty-one and a seasoned veteran of World War II, having served in Guam. We had been divorced for the past year. In the intervening months I had fought my own war after being attacked by poliomyelitis at a time when the virus that paralyzed and killed was rampant (mostly among young people, although our President Franklin D. Roosevelt had also survived polio, and managed, just dandy, thank you, to get us through the Depression and World War II) and the vaccine not yet available. Oh, yes! I have not mentioned that I was also in danger of momentarily receiving the dreaded pink subpoena to appear before the House Un-American Activities Committee, already apparently having been found "guilty by suspicion and association" of having tangible connections to Communist ideas and their supposed supporters—Hollywood writers mainly—who were being accused of disseminating Russian political propaganda through their screenplays.

A mushroom cloud of fear had hovered over my beloved United States for a number of years, since the fall of 1947, in fact, settling over Hollywood and directing its lethal rays on the movie industry. Its chief instigator was US senator Joseph McCarthy, rabid for power at any cost to his nation and devastation to hundreds (make that thousands) of people, a huge majority of whom were innocent of any crime or malfeasance to their country. (His surname, many damaged lives later, would give birth to the word "McCarthyism," defined in the American Heritage Dictionary as: "The practice of publicizing accusations of political disloyalty or subversion with insufficient regard to evidence [and] the use of unfair investigatory methods in order to suppress opposition.") McCarthy, his cohorts, and his disciples, believed, or pretended it to be so, that Communist Russia was trying to undermine, and eventually take over, the United States through a conspiracy of Hollywood screenwriters, producers, and directors. The attacked moviemakers (excluding the studio moguls whom the Committee appeared to consider blameless) were the creators of stories dealing with the greed of the rich and the oppression of the poor.

What better show trial and media blitz could be had than one that paraded on television (the country's newest diversion) before the Committee some of Hollywood's most famous moviemakers, stars, writers, directors, and producers—as both friendly and unfriendly witnesses; the former siding with the "Committee." One member, congressman, future vice president and president, Richard M. Nixon, made a public statement that he was seriously concerned about John Steinbeck's great 1930s Depression opus about migrant farm workers, *The Grapes of Wrath* (screenplay by Nunnally Johnson) being shown in Yugoslavia. No reason was given as to why our nation might be concerned about how the movie (originally released in the States in 1940) might affect a mid-European country that had broken with the Soviet Bloc in 1948 and at this time enjoyed a varying degree of freedom in the arts. Then, along came Jack Tenney, the inquisitorial state senator from California (and friendly witness), who testified that Frank Sinatra was abetting Communism by appearing in films filled with Communist propaganda. The movies were not listed, but it is difficult to comprehend how Sinatra's appearances in musical films such as *Ships Ahoy!*, *Anchors Aweigh*, and *It Happened in Brooklyn*—all good-feeling, shallow stories—could convey a political agenda.

The first Hollywood hearings began on October 20, 1947. They were produced like a gala Hollywood premiere. (There were jokes about "walking down the Red carpet" but it was too real to laugh at—except perhaps with a wry "he-haw.") Despite what the men who had been called before the Committee expected (no women were called in to this first inquisition), they were not prepared for what met their eyes. A battery of television newsreel cameramen stood side by side, their cameras whirring as the witnesses entered and were led to their seats. Photographers broke ranks and dashed toward them, bunching up, crouching for angle shots, their flash cameras raised like artillery, bursting into blinding light in the men's faces.

Spectators crowded into a bank of seats to one side. Across the front of the room was a platform where the Committee sat, brass plates before them to identify who they were for the cameras. Below the platform was the witness table and flanking it to the right and left, tremendous tables set up to accommodate the press. The room was windowed but sunlight was deflected by the massive broadcasting equipment and rows of control panels. In every corner of the room were loudspeakers for the public address system. Microphones were stationed on both the Committee and witness tables. One of the first of the nineteen accused witnesses to be called (labeled by the press as "the Hollywood Nineteen") was writer, director, and producer Robert Rossen who later told me that his immediate reaction was to search the room for a sign of an American flag as any American court of law displayed. There was none. At the time, Rossen was one of Warner Bros. leading scriptwriters with such dramatic, socially conscious, and critically acclaimed classics to his credit as *Marked Woman, They Won't Forget, Dust Be My Destiny, The Roaring Twenties, The Strange Loves of Martha Ivers, The Sea Wolf, A Walk in the Sun*, and (although uncredited as it was released when he appeared as an unfriendly witness before the Committee—the credit therefore given to the film's director, John Huston) *The Treasure of Sierra Madre*, which won the Academy Award that year for screen adaptation.

The hearings went on for three weeks during which time the nineteen men, one by one, refused to answer questions put to them regarding their political affiliations, religion, or the names of other members of the film colony, who belonged to some of the same organizations as they did, and whose silence lawyers rightly declared a given right of the Constitution. Of the nineteen men brought before the Committee, twelve were writers (including the playwright Bertolt Brecht, author of *The Threepenny Opera*), five directors, one producer (although Rossen was all three), and one actor, Larry Parks, who famously had just made a huge hit in—and for which he received a Best Actor Academy Award nomination—*The Jolson Story*. Together, their contribution to what is often referred to as "the golden age of Hollywood" was considerable. Lester Cole and Alvah Bessie had cowritten *Objective Burma*; Ring Lardner Jr. the 1937 version of *A Star Is Born, Woman of the Year, Cloak and Dagger*, and *Laura*. Dalton Trumbo had been nominated for an Academy Award for *Kitty Foyle*; Howard Koch received the same honor for his stunning screenplay of *The Letter* and won it for *Casablanca*. The remaining screenwriters included in the Hollywood Nineteen—John Howard Lawson, Albert Maltz, Waldo Salt, Adrian Scott,

Richard Collins, Samuel Ornitz, Gordon Kahn, Herbert Biberman—and the directors Lewis Milestone (*All Quiet on the Western Front, The Front Page,* and *Of Mice and Men* for a start), Edward Dmytryk (*Tender Comrade*), and Irving Picket (*The Moon Is Down*) were no less talented, for each brought his special ability to his work. Ten of their number would face a prison sentence of one year for refusing to name others and would become known as the Hollywood Ten. All would have their careers and personal lives torn asunder as would the hundreds of Hollywood's creative men and women who would be dragged up before the Committee or had been made to flee before being cited.

And so the deadly game began.

"Are you now, or have you ever been, a member of the Communist Party?" was the key question asked by the inquisitors, a public query not admissible in an American court of law that included a judge and a jury, neither present in these hearings. But the Committee had been set up as a congressional investigation and witnesses were given fewer rights. In fact, a large number of well-known film folk had been members of left-leaning organizations in the early 1930s—most of which had no connection whatsoever with the Communist Party or its agenda, for this was a time when our country was in the depths of the Great Depression and help was desperately needed by the millions of unemployed as government relief or health benefit measures were not available to the majority.

This was also during the Spanish Civil War, a fight for personal freedom against a dictator. Organizations were formed in Hollywood to raise funds to aid the rebel fighters. Numerous other Hollywood groups joined in to raise awareness of the armies of unemployed in our country and of the workers who were earning substandard wages and living in dire poverty.

World War II followed fast on the heels of the Depression. It was a lot for a country to take during those years and people grasped whatever they could to get through it. An artist's currency has always been ideas. During the thirties, communism seemed a word that meant something like "share the wealth, help the needy." There was a small membership in the American Communist Party, which during the wartime alliance between the United States and the Soviet Union gave it a boost in credibility, causing its membership to grow countrywide to something near fifty thousand. Fewer than one hundred were ever known to be members who had worked in Hollywood movies. Over half of those who were in the business of making motion pictures before the war had become disenchanted and quit the party well before the bombing of Pearl Harbor and a decade before HUAC (the House Un-American Activities Committee) began its investigations. Shortly after the war's end came reports of Soviet repression in Eastern and Central Europe. That was the start of the "Red Scare" in the States, which fueled the fire that drove McCarthy and the

Committee to their own political agenda, thus creating a society in Hollywood that was split in two and then fragmented. The most evil persons in old gangster movies were most often not the criminals but the informers—stoolies, they were called, and loathed. Suddenly, being a stoolie was the only way in Hollywood to hold on to your job.

The televised Committee hearings were difficult to turn away from. One felt like a deer caught in the blaze of oncoming headlights, frozen with fear and awe at a speedily advancing vehicle. If the witness refused to answer, or stood on the Fifth Amendment not to (as was their right as an American citizen), they were in contempt and liable for a jail sentence. Despite this, the Hollywood Ten felt obliged to stand by their colleagues and not feed the Committee names. Others who followed into the witness box, their desperation for the survival of their career pressuring them, were bowed into submission. They believed their only out was to give names—people who they stated had been members of the Communist Party or had belonged to any organization that was suspected of having Communist members. Although they often did not know whether a colleague had been engaged in such activities, the routine was for the witness to identify others, whenever possible, who had already been named. It seemed not to matter if this was true, nor did it appear to cross their conscience that they were further digging a hole for these colleagues, thus ending his or her working days in Hollywood. The majority of the witnesses called before the Committee were into late midlife and had been plying their craft for decades. Few possessed other talents or were equipped with the ability or the means to make an otherwise equitable living for their families. Unemployment benefits were not applicable. Among the named, there were mental breakdowns, divorces, and suicide.

It has to be understood that writing a screenplay does not necessarily mean one so employed can write in other mediums as well. Films are a visual art; literature a narrative one; theater spoken but without the assistance of the great open vista of a camera lens, which in a matter of a single moment or two could eradicate the need for pages of dialogue, explanation, or description. Great novelists like F. Scott Fitzgerald and William Faulkner failed miserably in their attempts to write for the screen and only a minuscule number of screenwriters have made a successful crossover to publishing. They are quite different mediums, each requiring separate skills and training.

The studios were sent lists of people, many under contract to them, whom the Committee deemed questionable. Instead of a black mark, they were given a red one. As one Committee hearing closed and another and still another was held, these lists became lengthy, including those who had been unfriendly witnesses, those named and those who were on what was referred to as a graylist—those whose circle of friends and acquaintances were suspect and/or their scripts had a liberal leaning to them. The moguls who ran the studios, fearful of a backlash and drop in ticket sales if they hired anyone on any of the lists, closed the gates of the studios to them, no matter how great an artist or long a contributor to their studio's critically acclaimed and largest grossing films. Desperately needing writers and directors to replace the artists they had fired, the studio moguls reached out to their young and growing rival—television, just as they once had taken actors from the theater with the advent of talking films, leaving the majority of silent movie actors abruptly without jobs.

These were scary times in Hollywood. People turned their backs on longtime friends and coworkers, panic stricken that they would "catch the virus." My uncle, Dave Chasen, owned a famous restaurant beloved by the Hollywood glitterati. It was a clubby sort of place. Everyone knew each other and mingled, table hopping from one group to another. Then abruptly, that stopped. Guests kept their heads down, eyes averted when a person thought to be on one list or another was being led to a table, or passing by to leave. Someone who had been a frequent guest at one's dinner table and shared holidays, birthdays, and anniversaries—whose children had playdates with your children—were suddenly cut, telephone calls unanswered, notes ignored.

I felt disgust when I heard these stories. It brought images of Hitler's youth movement and the start of the ferreting out and persecution of Jews in the early years of Nazi Germany. A good percentage of the Hollywood film industry, especially the creative artists, were Jewish (as were the moguls themselves). "It can't happen here!" I kept telling myself. But, in truth, I was not 100 percent sure. After all, the moguls were giving in to the political pressures just as the rich and powerful Jews had in Germany—and look where it got them.

Still, this was not Germany. This was the US of A. I loved it dearly. It was the only home I ever knew. My childhood had been a scattered one— here for some time, there for another, constantly moving on to another house, apartment, city, state. Yet, I retained a sense of security, of family with my homeland, for my country seemed the parents of us all. I was (and remain) tremendously proud to be an American. We stood for everything good, didn't we? (Well, every family had their bad moments, their truants, their buried secrets, and those they wished they could bury.) I was a history buff and knew very well that we had suffered some pretty dark times, unthinkable regresses. But there were always those among us who fought and struggled and overcame with amazing grace and strength. I believed that despite the current disease of McCarthyism that had gripped our country, those infected by its virus loved our land as much as I did—each in their own and very personal way.

Those who were blacklisted or graylisted, and could, left for Europe (or hid out in Mexico hoping it would blow over) before their passports were confiscated. They were cinema artists concerned in their occupations with stories frequently dealing with human suffering. Even comedy, more often than not, is born out of tragic situations (and still is). Screenwriters took story ideas from the headlines and from the breadlines. In its early incarnation the American Communist Party (a very small minority when the dark wind of McCarthyism swept in) seemed far less threatening than the Tea Party appeared to liberal groups in more recent times. A great many Hollywood members had left the Communist Party by the time of World War II, disappointed that it was not what they had believed it to be. By then, the great motivation was to bring Hitler down and save the world from his terrorizing despotism. European artists—actors, writers, directors, composers—who had been able to escape Der Fuhrer's murderous madness by immigrating to the States for a chance to continue their careers in Hollywood—formed a new group of film intelligentsia. The pendulum swung in another direction. Still, McCarthyism continued. A new wave, in which I was caught, hit hard in 1951–1952 and continued through to 1958, despite the senator's death in 1957 (said to be caused by acute alcoholism).

The endless harassment and outrage of individuals over strongly held left and right diverging opinions continues to the present time. In those years when I was young, I was filled with a kind of desperate hope, an all-encompassing faith, that left and right could one day manage to join hands in a bold effort for the better good of all people, especially those in my homeland. I don't think I was alone in my thinking.

The writer Arthur Laurents once told me, "The informers were not evil because they informed, and not informers because they were evil." I believed that then and I believe that now. Dalton Trumbo (one of the Hollywood Ten) famously added, "Everyone [who came up before the Committee during those years] was a victim." I believed that, too. Still, when the phone rang on that sweaty, hot August morning, my children's happy voices rising in the background, a cold-blooded snake of fear slithered down my back. This happened whenever the telephone rang, for there was usually a call from someone—agent, lawyer, still-employed studio friend—to warn you that a pink subpoena slip might be heading your way or that you had been upgraded to the flashing red-zone list.

This was my state of mind at the time of my current contretemps. I was scared. You can believe that. But I was a feisty kind of lady. I refused to let the bullies get me. Most of all I had kept my sense of humor (which I value above almost every other human trait). I believed I had what was well worth fighting for. Not only was I an American, I was a woman with two terrific kids, a measure of talent, and an active libido that even the dread polio could not stifle.

• 1 •

Departure

$\mathcal{T}$he electricity off, I stood by the window in my bedroom looking out onto a darkened middle-of-the night street. The previous August day in 1954 had been blistering hot and humid. The coming dawn promised little change. My Spanish-style bungalow was on the fringe edge of Beverly Hills, an area that never appeared on the tourist maps designating stars' homes that were hawked on the corners of the upper reaches of Sunset Boulevard. The house, which I was within weeks of losing, had been my home for the past two years, the down payment made with the money I had received from the sale of an original story my agent had sold to a major studio. It was my first real home, purchased with the hope that owning even such a minuscule piece of God's earth would somehow stabilize my life and that of my two young children, Michael and Catherine, both asleep in their beds, with no knowledge of the fragility of our finances.

A small gleam of light from the corner streetlamp filtered through the partially closed Venetian blinds. The surrounding quiet held me tightly in its grip. There were hard decisions I must make and I felt incapable of making them. It is curious how one can remember with much acuity the silences in one's life. I recall that during one of her many separations from my father, my mother's brother advised her to divorce my father (for numerous good reasons), and her replying: "Maybe that is so. But will you be there when I wake up alone at three o'clock in the morning?" She never did leave him, but they were more often apart than together.

I had no such reservations about having dissolved my own marriage. My husband, I had come to accept, was a compulsive, addicted gambler who, only days before, I had locked out of the house, his personal possessions boxed and left on the front porch for him to collect when I learned that without my

1

knowledge he had signed over the deed of the house (forging my name) to casino owners to cover losses he could not pay and obviously had been in fear of reprisal and possible bodily harm. I understood his dilemma when it came to light. He felt caught between my expected wrath and the gambling syndicate's long arm. But this was after years of difficult times and failed attempts to secure help for him (family intervention and an analyst). I now had only six weeks (given to me out of compassion, I had been told) in which to come up with the money (an astronomical $20,000) or forfeit my home. Unbeknownst to them I had the option of reporting the fraud to the police. (I had dismissed this route as my husband was, after all, the father of my children.) The scenario grew darker when deepened by the other problems current in my life.

Was I stressed out? You bet your ass! And I do not scare easily. A Southern lady once had told me that I had "gumption." I was impressed by this as her grandparents had been born into slavery, and although well educated and successful in her field, she had endured racism at her place of business and in everyday life—as did her children. I like to think that she was right, that I am a fighter, a survivor. After all, we have only one life, no returns or second chances. I had been given some low blows in my short time on earth; I was twenty-six at this time, currently recovering from a year's battle with polio and was also in political hot water, steamy enough to end my career as it was just beginning to take off. But there had been great times, too: unique experiences, loving presences, what I thought had been sexual gratification served up with love, and yes, plenty of laughter. Laughter, I believe, is the best-kept beauty secret in the world.

During my physical therapy treatments to help me walk again (which I now did, albeit with the aid of my hated "sticks") I was taught to just put one foot in front of the other and keep going. That was the only course I knew to follow. Writing was all I ever wanted to do. I wasn't sure how I was going to write myself out of my current situation as I was presently on the studio's "graylist"—considered politically far left due to the themes of my writings and the groups I had supported (the farmworkers in California who were pitifully underpaid, for one, and for whom I had signed a petition for fairer earnings) and in danger of being called before the House Un-American Activities Committee (more often referred to simply as HUAC) in their manic search for writers who might have once belonged to the Communist Party to bring before their body.

I had never been a member, nor can I recall ever having been approached to become one. I knew that made little difference and that just to have been called before the Committee would have made me unemployable in the industry. This was the sinister period of McCarthyism in our country. Led by a thirst for power, Senator McCarthy and the Committee, formed by strong right-wing members of Congress, were out to prove that Communist Russia was engaged in a conspiracy to undermine and eventually take over the country through messages being delivered subversively in motion pictures. A deadly chess game was being played, and I stood a chance of becoming one of their pawns, not because I was famous (which I certainly was not) but because I had close ties to "suspected" members of the Hollywood movie industry who were.

When I was a youngster, the Depression a dark chasm filled with failing banks, unemployment, hunger, and great migrations, Hollywood was a Tinker Bell of hope to families with children (who were a popular commodity in films at that time). I had been one of Hollywood's thousand-some performing children (ages three to ten, "in-betweens" eleven to fourteen seeming to possess the mark of Cain and unhireable). I never was picked up by the movies but I appeared on stage in "kiddie groups" (then popular attractions) where my birth name Anne Louise Josephson had been shortened to Anne Louise in the Meglin Kiddies and then changed to Anne Edwards when I joined Gus Edwards's troupe. At ten, I tap-danced on a radio program hosted by comedian Ken Murray (listeners obviously did not think that curious). My dream was never to be a star (or even a supporting player) but to write. I devoured what books I could get at the library. At night I would go to sleep with a small notebook and pencil beneath my pillow and in near darkness sneak-write stories I made up in my head. Even though my scribbles were nearly illegible in the morning light, the stories had been birthed.

At seventeen, having written a high school play, I was "discovered" by a studio talent scout and hired as a junior writer for Metro Goldwyn Mayer (only two miles from my home). Between interrupted college years, my marriage, and divorce, I had sold two original screenplays (after probably ten or more rejects) and my most recent work, a script for live television which had been aired just hours before my current nocturnal turmoil. I had "family connections" as well. My uncle, Dave Chasen, owned the restaurant Chasen's, perhaps the most famous of all movietown eateries in the 1930s through the 1980s. My early years were softened when my mother and I lived with him and his first wife, my aunt Theo, in a crowded bungalow (I slept in the "dinette," an L-shaped area off the kitchen, my cot in the corner, folding shutters in the archway for privacy) that would eventually back the original restaurant when it was built.

My extended family were the nobs of filmtown's elites, who were Uncle Dave's close friends. To me they were just Uncle Claude (W. C. Fields), Ruby (Keeler), Mr. Baritone (John Barrymore), Jimmy (James Stewart), and Uncle Frank (Capra) and so on down (or up) the list of famous Hollywood players of the 1930s and 1940s. In 1947, my wedding reception (a gala affair) was held at Chasen's. My husband (tall, slim, dazzling green eyes, a movie idol Kirk Douglas cleft in his chin, bright, no hero, but a veteran of the gritty war in the Pacific) was the nephew of Robert Rossen, the brilliant writer-director-producer presently blacklisted after refusing to betray his colleagues by giving HUAC their names as possible "sympathizers of Communist philosophy." Later, he would sadly go back before the Committee and reel off a long list of names that allowed him to work again. Although able to contribute memorable films, among the liberal population of the industry, he would—like Elia Kazan—be treated as a pariah. But during the time of his reticence to give names, he had little other recourse than to leave the country in order to continue to work. During that difficult period, my husband and I had moved into his and his wife Sue's home in tony Bel Air to oversee the care of my son, Michael (Cathy still to come), along with the Rossens' three children while their parents were abroad.

The telephone call I feared receiving that day did come. My agent, Mitchell Gertz, had rung to inform me that a pink subpoena with my name on it commanding me to appear before the Committee was heading my way. An insider had warned him that it was only a matter of short weeks. My close association with the Rossens (Bob having yet to recant his testimony) and their friends as well as my "subversive" script, *Riot Down Main Street*, sold to the great director King Vidor at 20th Century-Fox (to be permanently shelved), were said to be the source of my "suspicious status." My screenplay was based on the true story of an American soldier of Mexican ancestry recently killed in the Korean War after an act of great bravery, whose body, when it was returned to his south Texas birth town, was refused burial at the local funeral home and cemetery which were designated "white only."

The good news was that an original teleplay of mine had just been on view (although attributed to Al Edwards—the first name composed of the initials of my first and middle name—Anne Louise). The story centered on a young man who joins a kibbutz in Israel and is discovered to have been a member of a Nazi Youth gang in Germany during World War II. The members of the kibbutz (including the girl with whom he is now in love) turn on him. In a key scene the Jews have suddenly become the racists. There was one short, violent scene when they attack him, then, realizing what has happened, pull back. The young man tearfully explains that he had changed his name and used a forged passport to get into Israel—not to harm anyone but, in some small manner, to do penance. The girl is unable to forgive and forget and he leaves the kibbutz alone. As one can see, I clearly chose to make a statement: racism is a two-way road.

I have no idea what HUAC might have thought about the last scenario. But as I watched the show with great wonderment earlier that evening, I found it amazing to see people I had created come to life before my eyes and speak the words I had written. Still, I expected little from the telecast other than the pittance I had been paid (and gratefully received) for its purchase. When I finally crawled into bed I had no idea of what I should, or could, do next. The following day, the summer sun blazing high but my head still in a fog, Mitchell Gertz called again. Raymond Stross, an English producer, was currently in Hollywood scouting stories and writers. He had seen the TV show and wanted to meet me the following afternoon in his suite at the Beverly Hills Hotel. I assumed he was interested in the kibbutz story and could see that it might work well abroad in large-screen format. I agreed enthusiastically to meeting the English filmmaker.

I was not prepared for Raymond Stross. Short (about 5'5") and squarely built, he walked like a bantam cock and was dressed (coiffed and costumed, really) to play Brutus in some new-wave-theater camp production—hair swept over his forehead, heavy gold chains around his neck, the top two or three buttons of his shirt opened to display them. He had a noticeable stutter and his cheeks flushed red when the words he wanted to say did not slip out smoothly.

Upon introductions, he stared at me with great alarm. He had thought, not unnaturally, that Al Edwards was a man. He said something to Mitchell to that effect and added, "You sssee, I pr-pr-produce X-rated movies!" He had no interest in buying the kibbutz story but, as the script contained some shocking scenes and showed a marked style, he thought the writer might be the sort he was looking for. He was—and not very slyly—implying that a woman (especially the one standing before him on two canes and weighing maybe one hundred pounds dripping wet) could not be up to writing an X-rated movie script.

My dander was raised. "What does X-rated mean in England?" I asked brusquely.

"Shhhh-shocking! Not for children! SSSSexy!" he stuttered. "And new!"

"What was your last film about, Mr. Stross?" I inquired, expecting to hear it was pornographic and filled with exposed bosoms and leather whips.

"Pr-pr-prostitution on the London streets!" he replied in a raised, nasal, British voice.

His reply struck me as funny. Prostitution on the London streets! That had been going on since Elizabeth I and certainly centuries preceding her reign. I thought—did anyone *really* know if Elizabeth I was a virgin queen? I tried to stifle the laughter gathering in me but could not. Maybe it was a nervous reaction, maybe disdain. But it was uncontrollable. Tears ran down my face.

"Smmmmm-smmmmm-SMART ASS!" he shouted. "You have a better idea?"

I have no clue where the following came from as it was not a subject that I knew anything about nor had I seen it covered in the press or mentioned on the radio or TV. But I snapped back, "Artificial insemination!"

There was dead silence in the room. It was the only time I can recall seeing Mitchell Gertz, the ultimate talking-selling agent, struck dumb. Raymond Stross stared at me with his pink-rimmed eyes (booze or late night, I thought and later learned that Raymond, dear, dear Raymond, suffered terribly from allergies). Then, suddenly, he spoke.

"I'll buy it!" he said without a stutter and walked over to a desk in the corner of the elegant front room of his suite and pulled out a large, leather-bound checkbook. "What is the Writers Guild rate for an outline to a script?" he asked Mitchell.

My agent had not yet grasped what was happening (nor had I) but quickly seized whatever opportunity was being offered. "Three thousand dollars," he replied loud and clear. Raymond leaned over his checkbook, picked up a pen, began writing, and then, done, stepped in closer to Mitchell and handed him a check—a Cheshire smile on his face. "It's drawn on an American bank, no wait, perfectly good," he announced with no hint of hesitation on the second from last word.

Now, in fact, the Guild minimum for an outline such as he was requesting was more like $750, at that time a fair price. However, I could not figure out what script this feisty Englishman was referring to.

"What you want Anne to write is an outline for a story about a woman who has been artificially inseminated and . . ." Mitchell was fishing.

"And it is up to Mi-mi-miss *Smart Ass* here to come up with a story and make it X-rated!"

"How soon?" my agent inquired.

"A fortnight."

We seemed to be in Shakespearean territory.

"That would be two weeks?" Mitchell queried.

"Two weeks."

Raymond shook both our hands and saw us to the door. Mitchell and I walked in silence to the elevator and stood there for a moment. "You'll return the check to him, of course," I finally managed. "I can't write a story about sperm," I added with some disgust.

"You know, he's right," Mitchell declared. "You are a smart ass! Here you stand, held up by two crutches, two kids at home to support, HUAC hotly breathing down your neck, and your home about to be taken from you and you tell me to return"—he shook the check in my face—"three thousand dollars! You are not just a smart ass. You are crazy!"

The elevator doors opened and we got in and rode mutely to the lobby where he sat me down in one of the hotel's elegant, gold-leafed, green upholstered chairs (classified by some as California-French period). "Look," he began, now in a more kindly tone. "You don't have to write the script, just the outline. That's maybe fifteen, twenty pages including a little dialogue and some character development . . . nothing more."

"And if I can't?" I protested.

"You *will*."

He was right, of course. I swallowed my repugnance for the subject and, the following day took myself to the Beverly Hills Library. No books on artificial insemination. Then I went through the more recent newspaper files. To my surprise there was a report of a legal action filed in another state in which artificial insemination was the basis for a divorce and a child custody suit. The husband claimed that although he had approved of the use of artificial insemination, the sperm inserted in his wife's uterus was not his and therefore he was not responsible for the child's support.

I decided I could manage that. Courtroom scenes are great to write. But shocking? X-rated? When I got home the first thing I did was type a title on my Olivetti:

A QUESTION OF ADULTERY

At least adultery had the sniff of sex.

I finished a story outline and character analysis plus a few short dialogue passages (maybe, all in all, twenty-five double-spaced pages) in the allotted two weeks, gave it to Mitchell and promptly put it out of my mind—except when I deposited the $2,700 check (discounted by my agent's 10 percent) in the bank so that I could pay some of my medical bills and put something aside for a rental where we three could have a roof over our heads when the eviction notice came due. Ten days later, with little time to spare, Mitchell was on the telephone.

"You want to fly or take the boat?" he asked.

"What are you talking about?"

"Stross loved the outline, submitted it to MGM—where he has a three-picture coproduction deal—and they just gave him the go-ahead. Stross wants you to write the script, $18,000, payable in thirds over sixteen weeks, the first payment due upon signing. I'm coming right over for your John Hancock. Oh, and here's the extra sugar: he wants you to write it in London. I told him about the kids and he has agreed to pay their passage as well as yours, a nanny in London for their care, and your housing for the term of your contract. Therefore, you can either fly the entire distance with a short stopover in New York, or fly to the East and then cross the Atlantic on a liner. Whatever you choose. He needs you there, however, in three weeks and I have agreed to that!"

I opted for the fly/sail method. I had never previously flown, nor taken a sea voyage (unless the glass-bottom boat from Long Beach to Catalina counts) and, except for a day trip across the California-Mexico border, had never been out of the United States. There had been plenty of travel in my life, back and forth across the country—to Connecticut, Texas, and Oregon—but always by train or automobile. I was, however, more apprehensive about developing my story into a viable screenplay (especially one now agreed to be reset in England) than about my means of transportation to Great Britain. Therefore, I felt the four days on the boat would give me a chance to rework the central characters of my script.

Everyone dressed properly for plane travel in the 1950s, it still being viewed as an important occasion. Several friends came to see us off. I wore a bright blue suit (with skirt, not pants), a gardenia corsage pinned to the lapel of my jacket, a wide-brimmed black straw hat that I thought very glamorous, and spanking-clean, white cotton gloves. The children were dressed in their Sunday best, hair spit-perfect, shoes spotless. We departed from Burbank Airport by TWA (the irony being that Chasen's was now the airline's official caterer). It seems to me there was only one class—what we now know as first class. A rather wide aisle divided two long rows of two seats each. There was a steel staircase close to the cockpit that led to the "Sky Lounge" where drinks were served. Our chairs reclined into a kind of chair-bed and there was a heavy curtain that unfolded for privacy.

Michael was seated directly across the aisle from Cathy (my pet name for Catherine) and me. Next to him, at the window seat—to my absolute thrill and amazement—was the great, and notorious, *New Yorker* and Algonquin Round Table writer Dorothy Parker, who also wrote screenplays and was well known for her sharp wit. (It was Parker who famously quipped when first reviewing a stage performance of Katharine Hepburn's, "She ran the gamut from A to B!") It struck me that Miss Parker might not consider a child a welcome traveling companion. However, the plane was full and I thought it better that I not trade seats and remained close to Cathy, who at almost three, I believed needed closer supervision. I assured Miss Parker that my son, four years his sister's senior, was very bright and I was sure would not be a problem.

They seemed an amiable if curious pair. As we prepared for takeoff, Michael turned and said something in a confidential manner to Miss Parker. She laughed in a truly amused manner and then leaned across him and asked me in a voice with gravel in it, "Are you absolutely sure he is not a dwarf?"

Once in the air, the plane became a bit rocky. There were no jets or real stabilizers at the time. Caught in an air current, planes could suddenly and sharply dip. This occurred shortly after takeoff, and Michael, who was often carsick, turned putrid green. Before I could unstrap him, he had pivoted his head toward the window and vomited right into Dorothy Parker's expensively suited lap. The steward and stewardess came on the run, extricated Michael *and* Miss Parker, leaving my son for my attention as they rushed her off. I did not see the doyen of saber wit again until we landed something like nine hours later. She had spent the rest of the flight in the Sky Lounge, obviously imbibing, and could barely navigate the stairs on her descent, having to be held up by the two aides to make it off the plane.

We arrived at Idlewild Airport, New York (now Kennedy), at about eight that evening. A travel agent, hired by the production company, met we three at the gate and escorted us and our baggage to a waiting car which took us to Hoboken where the Dutch liner *Nieuw [New] Amsterdam* was docked. Departure time was 11:00 p.m. We had two first-class connecting cabins. Michael had been given a small model of a cruise ship as a going-away present and Cathy a lot of coloring books and crayons (her favorite pastime), so I suggested that Michael take Cathy into the adjoining room—the door kept open between the two—and entertain his sister while I got us somewhat organized before we were at sea. Since we were all still on California time, I promised we would go up on deck to watch the ship pull out of port. About a half hour passed when I heard a woman shrieking in the hallway—"We're sinking! We're sinking!" I knew this was madness because we were still docked, but I hurried into the other cabin to grab my children just in case.

They were standing side by side, Michael clenching Cathy's hand. Water was flooding out from the open bathroom door of the cabin and, as the ship was slightly atilt, streaming across the cabin's short hallway and out the opened door into the exterior corridor. They had put the plug in the bathtub, turned on the taps, tossed the toy boat in, and then became distracted by some other idea. Bathtubs on the ship did not have escape drains. You put in the plug and then followed the warning that it was to be filled only to one-third capacity. The crew were all very kind about the incident and the cabin and the corridor were cleared of water and fairly well dried by the time of our departure.

I remember feeling a great swell of emotion as the ship's horns blasted and I felt the forward motion of the boat as it moved out into the open sea, the light of day having given way to night, the starry skies and the flickering lights of the buildings along the shore looking a bit like fairy dust. I had been given a reprieve but I still had no clear picture of what our future would be. Sixteen weeks can pass pretty fast—then what? Still, for now, I was determined to enjoy the time and the exceptional experience that I had been granted.

The *Nieuw Amsterdam* had been converted to a troop ship during the war and then repatriated a year and a half after the war's end, a backbreaking task that had overtaken all the grand oceangoing vessels postwar. We were traveling in great luxury as all the reclaimed liners were competing in service, perks, and comfort for their share of the traffic—Great Britain's Cunard White Star ships, the *Queen Mary, Mauretania, Caronia,* and *Aquitania;* France's *Île de France* and the *Liberté;* and the United States' *President Coolidge* (downed in the South Pacific), among others. Our ship had reemerged (along with her sister ship, the *Rotterdam*) into passenger service in all her prewar finery, her two funnels stripped of their drab gray paint were replaced with Holland America's bright yellow hallmark (later the yellow would become a more subdued, but not drab, gray). All her original furniture, paintings, and appointments, which had been stored in San Francisco throughout the war, had been restored and returned to their rightful places on board the ship. The *Nieuw Amsterdam* was not the largest liner in transatlantic service, but she was called "the darling of the Netherlands." I fell in love with her and the grandness of ocean liners from that very first night.

When we returned from seeing the boat set sail on its ocean crossing, there was a note under my door informing me that arrangements had been made for the children, as of the following day, to eat all their meals in the children's dining room at special hours and that there would be staff to supervise them. I was to dine at the captain's table in the first-class dining room (it seemed that women traveling without a companion were mostly so honored). There followed a list of the hours meals were served and a dress code. Several of the evenings would require formal wear.

With all I had to think about before I left, the dress code for dining had not been a priority. I had not packed (nor purchased) any such items. There was a shop aboard where a selection could have been found. But then, how could I wear such a garment in London when I would either be working or taking care of the kids? Back home, I had not worn an evening gown since my high school prom! No gown for me. Therefore, I ate my daytime meals in the grand dining room and the evening ones, listed as "formal," in my cabin. I recall that a ship's officer took Michael on a tour of the radio room and other areas of interest to young boys. I worked on notes for my script in a comfortable deck chair or in my cabin. I did not feel too steady walking around the boat's slanting decks on my sticks.

On the sunny morning of our fifth day we docked in Southampton. A travel agent met us at the dock to help collect our baggage and to settle us in the boat train that would take us to London—a short journey of about two hours. Vendors came by the aisles with baskets of sandwiches and drinks. The moving view outside the train's windows was a magnificent slide show of all the great British landscape paintings I had ever seen. I loved the crooked houses and small villages we passed, the Gothic churches with their sky-piercing spires. Sheep grazed on hillsides. And many, many people rode bicycles along paths and through narrow lanes. This was a country I was sure I was going to like.

When we arrived in London, a porter helped me with my hand baggage and the children as we stepped onto the platform.

"Miss Edwards!" a male voice shouted.

"Yes, here," I replied, expecting another travel agent.

Suddenly, there were several flashes of light. I dropped my sticks and held the children close to me before I realized that a band of photographers were taking pictures of us but why, I did not know. By late afternoon, we had settled into our hotel suite at the Cumberland Hotel on Marble Arch, an elephantine establishment that—although grand—looked as though it had been mummified for the last four decades without making a single change to its pre–World War I decor. There was a newspaper on a table (along with some messages). Within, was a featured photograph of me and the kids . . . under which was printed:

"MISS Anne Edwards has arrived in London from Hollywood with her two children to write the screenplay of her story, *A Question of Adultery* about artificial insemination, soon to be a Raymond Stross production."

No doubting the implication. MISS Anne Edwards—two children—artificial insemination. "Oh, Lord!" I thought. "What have I got us into?"

Never did it cross my mind that London would be our home on and off for nearly twenty years. Wherever I had lived within the borders of the United States, my ties had always been to country, not four walls. America was my world. When I stepped onto English soil the first time, I did so, perhaps not as a tourist, but as a working writer—an American writer, at that. Home seemed behind me—across the vast sea I had just traversed. Yet, really, what had I left? An unfulfilled career, an incomplete and troubled life. I know I thought about it, because I wrote in my journal, "What on earth am I going to do when this gig is up?" And then added in parentheses: "(Will there ever be a man—and SEX—in my future?)."

For now it would have to be just one foot in front of the other.

An American in a Queen's Land

$\mathcal{R}$aymond met us for lunch in the restaurant of the Cumberland Hotel where we were to stay until our new home was ready for occupancy. He was dressed, sans chains, in a business suit, shirt, and tie. However, his thinning hair was still combed, Brutus fashion, across his forehead. There were, I now realized, two Raymonds. Hollywood had only temporarily shed him of inhibitions carefully inculcated by exacting parents and Britain's rigid public schools. I had advised him that I would have to bring the children with me to lunch and he had graciously accepted their inclusion. As we entered the massive room with its dark-wood-paneled walls, white starched linen, and rather starchy-looking diners as well, I silently prayed Cathy and Michael would remember their manners. They did. Still, I had overlooked Michael's knack of feeling free to express himself.

An explanation might be necessary here. My son has a very high IQ. This was ascertained when he was three, and preschools refused to enroll him, citing his ability to read at a highly advanced level, adding that his vocabulary was extensive. The same thing occurred when he was set to enter first grade. The principal insisted that it would be better if he went directly into second grade. "Children who are too advanced become bored when the work in no way challenges them," he told me, adding, "The fact that they seem to know all the answers is disturbing to the other youngsters." I did not approve, mainly because I felt that being physically younger (and smaller) than his classmates could be a problem for him. I never discouraged him from reading what he wanted to read—books on my shelves, the daily newspaper—and enjoyed our conversations about them.

"Would you like to see the changing of the guards at Buckingham Palace?" Raymond asked him in what can only be called a condescending manner (that voice that is often used when an adult, who is uncomfortable with children, is talking to a child).

"I'd rather go to Parliament," Michael replied.

Raymond was taken aback. He smiled indulgently. "They don't allow ch-ch-children in Parliament," he countered. And then, obviously curious about the request, asked, "Why do you want to go there?"

"That's where they make the laws."

"Yes, but it's not like a courtroom."

"Law courts pass sentences. Parliament and the American Congress pass laws," he replied in a matter-of-fact manner.

Raymond said he would arrange for a car to take us to the changing of the guard and then drive by the Houses of Parliament. Michael shrugged his shoulders and said, "okay," and then got busy with his dessert. With much relief, Raymond turned back to me and to the main purpose of the lunch: advising me of what my schedule would be. He had obtained a working permit but I still had to appear at the Home Office to finalize the arrangements and sign some papers. His assistant, a young man named David Deutsch, would accompany me. A house on nearby Albion Street would be at my disposal in two days. It came with a resident housekeeper, Mrs. Barnes. An agency would be sending several applicants to the hotel for interviews for the position of nanny.

We briefly discussed the script. I told Raymond how I planned to adapt my story to an English setting. He seemed pleased but leaned in close across the table to speak to me in a confidential voice. "Don't forget the sex," he admonished.

Back in our rooms, the newness of it all set in. On parting, Raymond had handed me an envelope containing one hundred pounds (in a variety of rather large-sized notes) for out-of-pocket expenses. It also included a list typed up by his secretary with some "helpful hints," and a request that I record expenditures in regard to my work.

I sat down with Michael at the desk in the room and spread out Raymond's expense money, along with the bills I had exchanged for American dollars at the foreign exchange on the boat. The British monetary system in the 1950s was nondecimal and more than a little confusing. Twelvepence was one shilling; twenty shillings made a pound ("It's called a quid," Michael popped up). There were many more coins than we had in the States: the penny (one pence), twopenny (tuppence), threepenny (thrupence), each coppery colored and of a different size; the silver sixpence, a one shilling, two shilling; and larger half crown. Biggish, colorful paper notes in denominations of ten shillings, one, five, ten ("a tenner," Michael smiled), twenty, fifty, and one hundred pounds. To add to these, there was the "guinea," a currency without a coin or note. To figure any item marked in "guineas" you added one shilling to the pound to the selling price (if, for instance, the item was selling for twenty guineas, you would be charged twenty-one pounds). To further the complexity of my money expenditures, Mitchell Gertz had made it clear in my contract that I was to be paid in American dollars. As the rate of exchange varied daily so did the amount of my paycheck—which upon receipt I had to take to American Express and exchange my dollars for pounds at the going rate (often higher or lower than what it had been moments earlier).

One "helpful hint" from Raymond's secretary had to do with tipping: "In a restaurant ask if service is included. If not add 12½ percent." I was to figure a fraction of a fractional currency. How daunting does that get? A shilling tip was adequate for a local taxi ride; a half crown "if going across town," and a shilling more per mile for any "lengthy journey." I was certain I would never get the money system straight and probably would overtip in order to reach an even amount. Somehow that seemed fair to me as the cost of living, from what I now observed, was at least 30 percent less than at home. I had not factored that in when Mitchell made the deal. But now I realized I could squirrel away a good sum, if careful.

The list continued: "When crossing a street remember to look right, then left. Our motor cars have right-hand drive, the reverse of yours."

"Banks open at 10:00 a.m., close at 3:00 p.m. American Express closes at noon on Saturday." (In the fifties, with tourism just regaining its prewar numbers, and communication and banking transactions a long way from being computerized, Americans abroad used American Express for a multiple of needs—banking, mail, a meeting place. It was one's "home away from home.")

"In dialing a telephone, note that O shares the last finger slot with "zero" and Q. If using a public telephone make sure you have a threepence coin. For information dial DIR. For use of a public toilet you will need a penny." Aha! Now I knew the genesis of the phrase, "I have to spend a penny"!

In a handwritten note at the bottom of the page, most certainly added by Raymond, was the advice: "Do not use the word 'fanny' in conversation. Here it means a woman's c—t!" And, in case I did not get that, he added, "It rhymes with front."

We had arrived in the first week of October. The often reluctant English sun shone. Hyde Park was aburst with brilliantly colored autumn flowers and filled with Londoners sunning themselves on rented lounge chairs or stretched out on the dazzling green grass. The body count was amazing. Sunshine is a rare commodity in London. I would soon be aware of the gray days that dogged the city for months on end and the need, for nearly ten months of the year, to carry an umbrella. Coming from Southern California, I never quite got used to it.

Our new abode was only two blocks from Hyde Park, situated on a handsome street of large town houses, mostly of late Victorian and Edwardian vintage. At the corner was a massive, deep dirt cavity surrounded by a fence where once—a sign proclaimed—a church had stood and would soon be rebuilt. It had been demolished by the Germans during the war. Similar devastation remained visible in many sections of the city, especially the East End (we would be living in West London). Although this was now the 1950s, Britain remained a long way from putting World War II behind. Bomb sites were not the only reminders. A wartime approach to daily life prevailed. One queued for everything and remained patient about it. After my successful (if exhausting) day spent at the Home Office, I was issued a ration book for myself and each of the children to be used for small portions of dairy goods, meat, butter, and sugar. Restaurants made up for the lack of these staples by the use of substitutes (cereal in sausages, meat pies, and loaves were to be avoided at all cost). On the first morning of our residence on Albion Street, two half pints of milk were delivered on our doorstep (and all those where children under the age of ten were known to reside). We were also issued temporary health cards.

The house was like no other I had ever inhabited. When I stepped through the door I was suddenly in Victorian England and where the rich and mighty probably had lived privileged lives. Our landlord was a member of the peerage who chose at present to reside in his country estate. Many titled families with stately homes found themselves strapped financially at the war's end and were happy to rent out their former London town houses (others of the landed gentry had recently opened the marble halls of their country estates and castles for paying tours). One entered our new home on the ground floor into a grand hallway—marble floors and vaulted ceilings held high by dark-wood beams. The reception rooms with their brocade drapes and polished wood floors on the right; dining room, butler's pantry, and breakfast room on the left. At the rear, its windows overlooking the gardens, was a library with shelves filled with aging leather-bound volumes. A sorely out-of-date but handsome globe on a mahogany stand occupied one corner, and a huge library table was placed in the center of the room.

The decor of the house, almost as it must have been a century earlier, evoked the cultured and moneyed lifestyle of the previous inhabitants, obviously an educated and aristocratic family. I could not help but wonder how many ghosts of those past dwellers might be occupying the rooms with us. There was the distinct smell of oiled wood and well-worn leather. An impressive, dark-wood staircase was situated halfway down the entrance hall. At the end of the hallway, concealed behind a door, a narrower stairway led down to the basement where the kitchen, supply room, laundry, and staff quarters were situated, with little access to natural light. A dumbwaiter brought food up from the kitchen in covered dishes to the butler's pantry. We did not have a butler. Mrs. Barnes, a no-nonsense widow in her sixties, managed these duties plus her own and was the sole occupant of the below-stairs accommodations. A charwoman came daily to help her in the upkeep and cleaning. Twice weekly a laundress (her Irish brogue so thick I had a hard time understanding her) did the laundry one day, the ironing the next. As there was no washer or dryer, on those days the under-stairs area was exceedingly damp as clothes and linen were strung out in the back washrooms. A groundsman (fee paid by the landlord) attended the garden and hedges weekly. As—less than a day after our arrival—it had rained in London almost on a daily basis, there was no worry as to watering the plants.

On the floor above the ground floor, there was a comfortable sitting room that adjoined the master bedroom, both of which would now be designated (by Mrs. Barnes) as "milady's apartments." My bedroom enjoyed the garden view, an Italian marble fireplace (every main room had a fireplace—there was no central heating), and a large bed that is unforgettable. Four richly carved, mahogany bedposts propped up a canopy of heavy, fringed, gold-tasseled green velvet (faded in streaks by its age and where light had fallen upon it) that cascaded from the corners to the floor (think of that green velvet, gold-tasseled gown Scarlett O'Hara fashioned from her late mother's portieres to meet Rhett Butler). The velvet drapes could be pulled shut—sealing out the cold once the coals were ashes in the fireplace. (Coal was the fuel Londoners depended on for heat, and the coal trucks with their blackened delivery men were a common sight.) There was also a connecting dressing room with a cot covered in scotch plaid, there—I was told—for the husband's use when his wife had her "monthly."

A hallway led from these "en suite" rooms (a sitting room, big, old-fashioned, white-and-black-tiled bathroom included), to two guest chambers. The top floor was described as "the children's wing." It also contained staff quarters, as once there would have been at least one upstairs maid and a nanny. A good-sized, sitting-playroom centered the children's rooms and off it a tiny kitchen for the nanny to prepare the young ones' tea. The nanny I had hired, Fiona Ffife, a lanky, good-natured young Scotswoman with carrot hair, a ruddy complexion, and a strong scent of heather about her, was to have the entire upstairs staff quarters, giving her a bedroom and sitting room, albeit neither of them very commodious.

The house had seen better days. Still, evidence of those times remained. It came furnished and that included crested silver cutlery, trays, toast racks, tea set, and a fine china dinner service for twelve, as well as a few truly remarkable antique chests and tea tables. Framed portraits and landscapes, mainly eighteenth and nineteenth century, hung on the flocked, wallpapered walls, fadings on it indicating the removal of perhaps the most valuable of the owner's collection. Raymond's company was paying thirty-two pounds a week for all this grand old-English luxury (rents in London were almost all due weekly in the 1950s), approximately $400 a month. Mrs. Barnes's weekly salary was seven pounds ten, Fiona's eight pounds, and the daily char a small hourly rate. I was, of course, responsible for feeding the members of my household staff, and for the telephone, utilities, and coal required for the stove and fireplaces. One of the first purchases I made was a number of portable electric heaters as the house often had a definite chill. In the bathrooms there were heating rails for towels, a small luxury but one I came to love. There is nothing like the cozy feeling of wrapping a toasty towel around one's naked, shivering self when stepping out of a bathtub onto a cold tile floor.

Grocery shopping was not an easy task but it was a great adventure. There was one "supermarket" on the nearby Edgeware Road. It was not comparable in any way to the supermarkets back home. It seemed most of whatever you thought you needed, the London store did not stock. One quickly learned the art of substitution. Shopping was better done in the individual shops—and there were many of those clustered along the busy high streets of almost every neighborhood: greengrocers, fishmongers, butchers, bakeries, chemists, dairy, charcuterie (prepared foods and jarred items like pickles, olives, "gentleman's relish," and marmite, the latter two requiring a cultivated taste). Flower stalls brightened many corners.

Shopping for food was time consuming, there being queues for everything. People bought fresh foods in amounts that would be used in a day or two (refrigerators were not yet in every home and easily spoiled food was often left to keep cool on windowsills). My American training had taught me to buy more than one tin of something if it was at a reduced price. My first time out I purchased three cans of baked beans, planning for them to be stored in the larder. You carried a fishnet bag (or two or three) to hold your purchases. Some things were wrapped in paper, but grocery bags were not generally given and it was a juggle to fit your items into these bags without them poking through the holes. One could, of course, order from the few top department stores (Harrods, Fortnum & Mason, and Selfridges, etc.) who had food floors stacked with the best quality of available provisions and offered accounts and delivery. That was, however, an expensive way to go and I only used these outlets when absolutely necessary.

I never stopped thinking of the short time I would be enjoying the bounty I had reaped of new experiences and steady pay. Soon I would be returning to the States, unable to use my identity in my chosen career. And there was still the possibility of being subpoenaed to appear before the Committee. Raymond's generous contract, I now realized from Mitchell Gertz's first letter (wherein he boasted of his great negotiating powers), had been due to his desperation to make a deal with MGM which required his ownership of three viable properties. He had two—mine was the last needed to finalize his negotiations. When I completed my contractual obligations and went home, there was no chance of my receiving my current handsome fee. To make things scarier yet, I had earned my living from the age of seventeen as a writer and knew no other way to seek gainful employment. At university I had studied theater and Russian literature. Small chance for that to help me. The future looked cloudy at best. I was determined to make the most of this glorious reprieve while saving what I could for what—it seemed only natural to believe—would be tough times ahead.

Adjusting to a new culture and surroundings was not easy for the children. I tried to make our time together as sharing and as learning an experience as possible. They had been through a lot in their short years what with our moving about, their father's neglect, the divorce, my illness, and now being thrust into an unfamiliar world. I went to work almost immediately. But they were used to my having "writing-can't-disturb-Mommy-except-for-an-emergency" hours. Fiona made the children afternoon tea (more like a light supper) in the upstairs kitchen.

For the first weeks, Mrs. Barnes cooked our remaining meals (cold meat left in the larder for Sunday night dinner when she was free). I would bring the provisions home and she would whisk them away below stairs. Her pride in her culinary abilities was estimable. She served us in the dining room—arms folded as she waited to be congratulated after a meal. This was not an easy matter. Mrs. Barnes was a hard worker and a lovely woman. She was also a terrible cook, and my children were not always able to conceal their displeasure of what was on their breakfast and dinner plate. The fine vegetables I had handpicked at the greengrocers all came out a mash and unattributable. The lack of eggs during the war had caused her to guard those I brought home as if they were golden. After three consecutive mornings of being served the tinned beans on burnt toast for breakfast (toast seemed always to be charred as it was made in an antiquated—antique, really—toaster), I rebelled. Eggs for everyone tomorrow morning, I insisted. They were set before us the next day scrambled in fat drippings, their volume inflated by gummy, cooked cereal. It was my difficult problem to tell her that she could do the preparing, chopping, and washing, while I would handle the cooking. In terms of the unwritten laws of English household staff members, this was a demotion and she did not take it kindly. I was stiff lipped by her for a good week. Finally she relented and became interested in how and what I was preparing for a meal.

Cooking had always been one of my favorite pastimes and I liked to think I was good at it. My mother, Marion, was a talented cook, self-taught and creative. The two of us had lived with my uncle Dave for several years of my early life. My parents were separated and in that era—the early 1930s— a woman resided with a member of her family during such unfortunate circumstances. Uncle Dave was a well-known vaudevillian who was brought to Hollywood to appear in motion pictures. The Hollywood offices of the studio that hired him had not been informed by their New York arm that he was a mime. This was the beginning of talking pictures. Mimes—even famous, comic ones—were not wanted. A few years later Harpo Marx came along, but he had brothers and a musical instrument to do his talking for him. Still, Uncle Dave had a contract that the studio had to fulfill and an income for the length of it. Most other former vaudevillians were not that lucky. They came to Hollywood looking for that big break which had not happened and were unemployed and broke.

My mother and my aunt Theo (Uncle Dave's first wife—whom I greatly loved) took to cooking large quantities of inexpensive recipes—stews, chili, and something my mother invented called "deviled bones" (made from the remains of the roast she had made the previous day) to feed the hungry theater and out-of-work vaudevillian performers who gathered at our dinner table. Uncle Dave filled in with hamburgers from our backyard grill. "Chasen's" was born of that beginning (and constructed on an adjoining lot). The scents of all this home cooking, so rich with spices and glowing with the warmth of those gatherings, comprise the happiest times of my childhood. I have always associated food and cooking with them. Therefore, I was quite pleased to have decided to take up the reins as cook to my household. My nemesis was not Mrs. Barnes, but an enormous old black stove (circa 1910) that dominated the kitchen and was fed by coal.

"The stove is your problem," I told Mrs. Barnes, "the food made on it mine." So she fed it and kept the temperature at least near where I needed it, and I cooked.

The char prepared fires in all the rooms before she left so that they could be lighted early the next morning. Keeping the house warm once London was awash in daily rain was no easy task. Dampness crawled into the very center of one's body and splayed outwards to one's extremities. After breakfast with the children, I retired to my bedroom, doors closed and knees raised; as I reclined on the bed, yellow lined pad and sharpened pencil at hand, my portable Olivetti nearby to transpose my written words, I started my work day. (This was a regime I had developed during the onset of polio.) To keep my hands from becoming numbed from the cold, I often wore gloves as I worked on my Olivetti or pushed my pencil along the lines of my yellow pads. I had regular office hours, usually nine to four, lunch on a tray, Monday through Friday. Saturday was shopping time, Sunday exploration of London and the outskirts with Cathy and Michael. I met with Raymond and David Deutsch for a story conference every two weeks and saw them both socially as well.

Raymond was married to a beautiful young woman, twenty years his junior, who he adoringly called "my angel." He had a teenage daughter, Larain, from his first marriage. Larain was going through great angst at the time. We bonded and she often came by for supper or joined us on an excursion (later, when Fiona was no longer in my employ, Larain would be a big help as a "childsitter"). Claire was blonde and looked a bit like the fair Elaine—pure and innocent. Raymond never tired of telling the story of how he fell in love with her upon first sight, how he arranged secret meetings with her, and how her brawny brothers nearly killed him when they discovered they were lovers. He had the scars to show for it—and did.

The Strosses lived in a handsome flat on Connaught Place, a short walk from Albion Street. Residing in the same building was an American family, Gerry (Gerald) Adler, his wife Kit, and at that time their two children, Nancy (Cathy's age) and Steve (still an infant). Gerry was a lawyer and the British director of international enterprises for NBC. There were only two television channels in Great Britain at the time, and they went off the air before midnight, often way before midnight. Scheduling was haphazard. Programs started at ten minutes after the hour, six before the hour—however long a show took. And there were no commercials. Viewers mostly rented sets and paid a fee for a television license. Radio was the best free ticket in town. It was excellent. I quickly became addicted to a program called *A Book before Bedtime*, on which well-known theater actors read a chapter from a classic each weeknight.

American film and television production was booming in England as budgets could be slashed dramatically from what they would have been had they been shot in the States. Gerry was a towering, gentle man. Standing, he would always bow his head to talk with you, as most people were at least a foot shorter. He was extremely sympathetic to the plight of HUAC's victims. Kit Adler, formerly a puppeteer who had starred in her own television kiddie show in upstate New York, was a delight. When we met at dinner at the Strosses' we immediately hit it off.

David Deutsch was a constant presence and escort on my evenings out to the theater or cinema. I was not lonely, nor was I looking for romance. My current physical condition made sex something to be avoided for the present. God knows I would have welcomed a bit of loving but my body was still in the healing process. I had been lucky to have had a fairly mild case of polio. My lungs were clear and the paralysis had affected only my right leg, the inner thigh, and a bit of necessary plumbing, the last creating private doubts that I would ever be able to reveal myself to a lover again. During the past year, after a rather lengthy hospital stay, I had been in intensive outpatient therapy care and had shown considerable improvement, mentally and physically. On my last visit to my doctor in Los Angeles, I had agreed to see a London colleague of his. I put off doing so as there were just too many other things that seemed to have first call on my time. Also, I greatly welcomed my reprieve from medical services. I promised myself to make the call the day my script was completed.

I never discussed my physical condition with my new friends, and everyone was too polite to ask. After several evenings with David, I realized he had taken a more romantic approach toward me. He brought me, and the children, small presents, put his arm around me in the theater, and kissed me on the cheek rather lingeringly at partings. One night he asked whether my "situation" was permanent (meaning, with the glance that accompanied the inquiry, would I always need canes).

"No," I told him, more hopeful than sure. "My doctor at home says I am progressing well. But it will be a while. . . ." I hesitated.

"A while for what?"

"Until I fully recover."

"Look," he said with great serious concentration, his hand tightly grasping my shoulder. "We here in Britain have been through a long, painful, costly war. I don't have a friend who has not lost a member of his family or suffered from serious wounds—physical and emotional. We Brits may appear unromantic by American standards, but I can tell you honestly we can love and deal with situations that require great understanding as deeply as any of your countrymen."

I was greatly moved. That night, before we parted, he held me in a tight embrace and I did not pull away.

A few days later, he asked me to join him for tea with his mother at her home. (He had his own flat in a section of the city called St. John's Wood.)

"David, what is this about?" I prodded.

"I would just like you to meet my mother. She greatly admires women of independence and talent."

So I went.

David was an earnest fellow about my age, of average good looks and height. He did not stand out in a group and was not a talented conversationalist. However, he was bright and good natured. What he lacked in charisma he made up in curiosity and conviviality. We enjoyed many of the same things—films, theater, history, and—oddly—art deco design (a big passion of mine). We did not, however, laugh over the same things. David had a very British sense of humor, which had a way at times of being sophomoric—a lot of scatological and bathroom jokes bred, I assumed, in the all-boy boarding schools in which well-born British males were raised.

Raymond had told me a great deal about David's background (he, on the other hand, was reticent about it). His father, the late Oscar Deutsch, had developed and owned the Odeon cinema chain, the largest in Great Britain, and was responsible for the proliferation during the twenties and thirties of the fanciful art deco movie palaces in both America and Great Britain. These, in turn, inspired the art deco design in films like the Ginger Rogers/Fred Astaire musicals. It had obviously not been easy for David to be the son of a strong personality such as Oscar Deutsch was said to have been. Although unharmed in the war, he was, nonetheless, a wounded soldier in life. I cared for him as a good friend might, but I was not in love with David, nor did I think—in view of the shortness of our relationship and my imminent departure—that he had any long-range feelings for me.

The moment I entered Lili Deutsch's elegant sitting room, I knew I had made a grievous mistake in accepting the invitation. As Lili did not rise to greet me it seemed obvious this was not to be a simple social visit. David took my arm and advanced toward his mother. Her smile was obligatory as he made the introduction. Groomed impeccably in a gray tea gown (long, elegant, and simple), ropes of real pearls (how could they be anything else?) about her neck, Lili Deutsch looked very much the "grand dame" as she nodded for me to be seated on a chair opposite her. Her first words to me after "How do you do," offered not as a question but as a statement, were "I understand from David that you are an American and a divorcée."

I admitted to both crimes.

"And you have two children."

"A son and a daughter."

She poured tea from a magnificent silver pot into fine china cups without a single drip. "Milk or lemon?" she inquired.

"Neither."

There were in Lili Deutsch vestiges of Oscar Wilde's Lady Bracknell in his *The Importance of Being Earnest*, who, when confronted by the young woman her nephew has brought her to meet, asks about the girl's parents. She is informed that they are both deceased. "To lose one parent is tragic," Lady Bracknell responds archly, "to lose two, careless." David's mother could have forgiven me many things. However, never that I was both a divorcée and American (shades of Wallis Simpson, I suppose). She had been hostess to Britain's most famous stars, political figures, and, as the silver-framed photographs on display in the sitting room revealed, members of the royal family. One, in a prominent spot, was of her standing beside the sweet, jolly-faced Queen Elizabeth, recently widowed consort of George VI and mother of the current, young Queen, also named Elizabeth. At the bottom of the photograph was a handwritten inscription (which I could not read). There followed about twenty minutes of strained conversation. Mainly Lili addressed David—who called her "Mum"—testily chiding him for being rather inattentive during the previous weeks, and then relating to him her current complaints. David had morphed into a different man than the one I thought I had come to know in the past three months. He seemed suddenly to have regressed to truant schoolboy, be it one about to enter his third decade. He was not wholly in fear of Lili. "I already told you that, Mum," he said with a decided edge. Still, he was noticeably anxious for her approval and clearly experiencing some pain that it was not being extended and that her attitude toward me was frosted with disfavor.

Not able to endure David's discomfort, his mother's pompous attitude, and my own awkward situation, I rose to say that I was sorry but I must leave. This was obviously a social gaffe, for David jumped immediately to his feet and chimed in with a fictional excuse for my abrupt departure. Lili, unperturbed, walked us to the door of the sitting room, no farther. David leaned over and gave her a glancing kiss on the side of her pale, bisque-like cheek—his lips barely touching her pale white skin. I was conscious of the click-click of my canes as I cautiously walked down the highly polished hallway floor to the front door where the uniformed maid stood at attention to see us out.

Once on the street, I could not control the anger that was rising inside me. I'm not sure if I felt more fury toward David for placing me in such a wrongheaded situation, at Lili for her arrogant rudeness, or at myself for not making it clear to David before it got this far that I was not in the least interested in marrying him—or anyone else for that matter—as that was what I had suddenly realized he had in mind. Once out on the street as he prepared to hail a taxi, the anger in me seeped out. He had placed me and himself in an ugly situation and done so without consulting me or asking my views.

"How could you? You brought me here on a fraudulent premise!" I accused. "She admires independent, talented women, does she! My God! Your mother looked at me as though she were interviewing a highly unacceptable, prospective daughter-in-law! Well, she is damned right!" A taxi had just pulled over to the curb. I got in and closed the door before he could join me.

My anger toward David cooled rather quickly. I had, in fact, after meeting Lili Deutsch, greater empathy for him. He apparently was desperate in his wish to change things between his mother and himself, for her to see him as a grown man—a married man. I was going to leave in a month's time, if he didn't stop me. Therefore, his rush to move things along between us. I told him what I felt and he seemed to take it well enough. We vowed to remain friends. And we did.

A few days after my tea with David's mother, Raymond informed me that he was going to need my services for another two months to do further work on my screenplay. The rent on the house would still be covered, as well as the other perks I had been given, but my salary was cut by a third (no Mitchell Gertz to negotiate for me, sadly). I accepted, with relief. Fear of what I would do after my stint abroad had been nagging at me. Now I had been given another reprieve, however short, and I was grateful to have it. The children had settled in. Michael was attending school, Cathy was in a playgroup organized at the American School, and I had made an appointment with the doctor suggested to me by my stateside physician.

David and I never spoke about that disastrous tea party again. When I gave thought to it, I realized that Lili had freed us both. David had made his first bold move in cutting the cord that held him to Lili. And I had realized that I needed help to deal with my problems. Still, I knew that divorcing the children's father had freed me on one hand and brought me more responsibility on the other. Neither was David really free. He might one day soon revolt. But my instinct was that he would win that battle and still face a long, difficult war.

Believing I had only two more months abroad, I put in many extra hours in my pursuit of all things British. I was obsessed, and being obsessed with anything other than my own condition felt extremely good. My greatest pleasure was in wandering about London on my own or with the children. I had fallen in love with Great Britain—the people, the country, and its history. Once the Russians, with all that drama and melodrama in their history and fictions, had fascinated me. My mother, however, was a dedicated reader of English literature (she had studied to be an English teacher) and she was entranced with British royalty. We spent a lot of time alone during my growing-up years—my father moving in and out of our lives for such long periods of time. I read the four Ss at her request (Shakespeare, Shelley, Sheridan, and Shaw), and listened to her stories about "that scandalous Mrs. Simpson." She possessed some talents as an actress and her recitations were always entertaining. Of all the royals, I had been drawn most to the commanding image of Queen Mary, George V's consort, mother of the infamous Edward VIII, who had abdicated the throne to marry Mrs. Simpson, and of his brother, poor, stuttering George VI, who—nonetheless—got his country through a terrible war. As I was now living close to Buckingham Palace—just across Hyde Park from Albion Street—my appetite for more information about the history of the country that was my present host was spurred.

Reality soon invaded the peace I had negotiated for myself. A letter arrived from Sue Rossen alerting me to the possibility that Bob would recant his initial stand in a second hearing before the Committee. It would be the first of Sue's letters to me in which she opened her heart, out of character for this seemingly iron-strong woman. She and Bob had not agreed that this was what he should do. In the end she had relented. True, Bob could work again, the money would once again flow, but she feared what this would do to their lives, how the children would be affected, how many friends would now turn their backs on them. She asked me if I had been in touch with any of the blacklisted members of the industry who were now in England.

This last query unsettled me. I had been so involved with my own good fortune and my wonder at being abroad that I had not contacted one person who I knew was in London trying to reconstruct a life after McCarthy had robbed him of his old one, although I had brought with me ways to reach several of them. The first name on my list, along with a telephone number, was Lester Cole, one of the original Hollywood Ten who had served a year in prison for courageously refusing to give the Committee names of friends and associates who might (or might not) have belonged to the Communist Party (or a left-wing organization) at one time, even if they had rejected it in recent years. I had met Lester and his wife a couple of times at the Rossens'. He answered the phone. Yes, of course, he remembered me. His wife had divorced him while he was serving time—"a betrayal, beyond betrayal," he bellowed. He had heard rumors about Bob—and pressed me for an update. I told him what Sue had written me.

"Sonofabitch, lousy bastard!" he hissed.

I changed the subject and suggested maybe we could meet for coffee.

"Sure. Are you working?" he added.

I told him the story of my first interview with Raymond and how I now happened to be working on the script here in London. He laughed heartily.

"What are you going to do when the job is done?" he asked.

"I don't know, Lester," I said honestly. We set a date to meet.

After I hung up, I felt like a tsunami wave had flooded over me. Not only did I not know what I would do once I was off Raymond's payroll, lately I had been avoiding any thought of it. Time was ticking away fast. I knew I had to find a reasonable course to follow.

· 3 ·

In a London Kind of Fog

*L*ondon continued to intrigue me, especially the royal family. One could not escape their omnipresence. The pages of the daily newspapers (London had a lively press, at least eight dailies and five Sunday editions) were filled with the comings and goings of not only the Queen, Prince Philip, Duke of Edinburgh, young Prince Charles, and Princess Anne, but with the Queen's rebellious younger sister, Princess Margaret, and the royal sisters' host of cousins. I would, at a later time, form a friendship with one of the cousins, the effervescent and extremely bright Lucinda Lascelles, who would kindle in me an even greater interest in the royal family. My friendship with Lucinda would be augmented in the future by a closer relationship with Margaret's great love, Group Captain Peter Townsend. But that would be after the current flurry. Right now, their wish to marry dominated newspaper headlines and caused members of average British families to take sides—should Princess Margaret and Townsend be allowed to wed and Margaret keep her title?

As a romantic and an unrelenting feminist, I could not fathom why a young woman over twenty-one (Margaret was twenty-three at that time) should not marry whomever she choose? I came to understand that church and state are not separated in Great Britain as they are in the United States. The ruling monarch takes on the oath as head of the Church of England— a religious institution that did not at that time recognize divorce. It appears that I had not understood the full extent of the power of monarchy or of its subjects' obeisance to it.

Everywhere I went, tributes to royal ancestry permeated the great buildings, shrines, and museums. Squat center of the West End of the city spread the massive Buckingham Palace (known familiarly as Buck House) with its twenty-four-hour watch by the palace guard in their tall, black bearskin hats and gold-trimmed scarlet uniforms, their changing a popular rite for the influx of tourists to view. Buck House looked strangely like a government building rather than a palace. In fact, about one-third of its three hundred plus rooms are given over to offices of staff members, and numerous other areas are delegated for state matters and state occasions. There was the fabulous Ball Room where investitures and banquets were held, the impressive Throne Room, State Dining Room, the Ball Supper Room, and the Balcony Room overlooking the front of the palace with a view down the Mall. At times of great occasions the members of the royal family came out on the room's wide balcony to wave to their subjects. The "royal wave" was an art form learned early in life by them—hand no higher than one's head, palm open, hand moved as though caught in slow motion—small nod of the head to the one side and then the other.

Unlike American presidents (who, after all, had only from four to eight years of power), whose relatives mostly lived ordinary lives greatly lacking the luxury of the White House, many of the reigning monarch's extended family had for years lived in regal splendor and shared occupancy in the various state-owned great houses and palaces in the city—St. James's Palace, Kensington Palace, Marlborough House, and Clarence House.

By the time I arrived in London, the Windsors (formerly the Saxe-Coburg-Gothas) were already the longest running soap opera in the history of the world with an aura of both melodrama and scandal. Mrs. Barnes was proud to confide to me that her grandmother and mother had worked as kitchen maids in the households of Edward VII and George V, regaling me with some amazing and fairly scandalous stories (as heard through the soap suds and re-told to her). These tales did in no way diminish her love and respect for the monarchy. I found, generally, that the British were in awe of their sovereign but viewed that person as human with foibles that all people experience. They also possessed a curious double standard. It was acceptable for Edward VIII, like his grandfather, Edward VII, to keep a married mistress, but not for him to marry a divorced woman. There were antiroyalists, but not in any great number; the vicissitudes of the Depression, then World War II, and now the work of moving forward into the second half of the twentieth century had bound the people of Great Britain together. In a sense they were all survivors. I held them in great respect—awe, really. When death and destruction had stalked them during the war they held fast. What David had said—that few families had not lost at least one parent, son, daughter, or close relative—I found true. The British had looked to the late King George VI for guidance and felt a great love for him, his wife, and his two young daughters. When, quite suddenly, he died in 1952, it was a severe blow to his subjects. London was almost entirely draped in black, whole buildings covered burka-fashion with only their window-eyes exposed. The extent and length of the mourning nationwide was all-encompassing.

One bright spot eased the pain of the country's loss. Young Elizabeth's coronation was set for June 2, 1953 (she was actually Queen from the moment of her father's death; this would be the official crowning). Buildings shed their shrouds and were scraped of years of encrusted black coal dust. Storefronts were freshened. The many parks and squares in the city were planted lavishly with brilliant, summer-blooming flowers. Then Queen Mary, Elizabeth's grandmother, consort of George V, the very symbol of majesty and much beloved by the people, died. By arriving the following year, I had been catapulted into a historic time in Great Britain purely by a set of circumstances I could never have predicted. I found the British a most dependable, stalwart people, and at one point I wrote home to a friend, "In case of sudden catastrophe, fire, flood, earthquake, rise up and shout, 'Is there an Englishman in the crowd!' for even if there is only one, I'm certain he—or she—will lead you and all others to safety." Still, for all their cool courage, the British could not control the weather. England endured rain and grayness for great expanses of the year. Yet, there was a sense of buoyancy about the people, a good dose of panoply and parades to lift one's spirits, and royal scandal to titillate and amuse.

The divorced man Margaret loved, Group Captain Peter Townsend, was a former fighter pilot, one of England's most decorated war heroes and equerry to her father, King George VI, throughout the final eight years of his reign. Peter was fifteen years Margaret's senior, tall, slim, exceptionally good looking and possessed a memorable face, the kind that stood out in a crowd. It had more to do with an attitude than anything else. As I was relatively soon not only to make his acquaintance but to consider myself his friend, I came to understand Margaret's attraction. Peter's flinty gray eyes had a directness that took magnetic hold when he was engaged in conversation. And, unlike most other members of the court, none of the usual stiffness and arrogance of their honored posts existed in his makeup. Peter was not an outsider or of questionable reputation (he had been the injured party in his divorce and had custody of his two sons) as Wallis Simpson had been when Edward VIII chose to give up the throne in order to marry her. During the war Peter had led flight squadrons into what he knew could be harm's way and staunchly fought to bring them safely through. His wartime heroism, in fact, had made him a national legend. This posed a serious problem for the Queen as many of her new subjects were in favor of her sister's marriage to one of their country's great heroes despite the dictates of the Church.

"That Margaret!" Mrs. Barnes bleated to me. "Got a sure streak of her uncle Edward VIII, she has! My mum saw it in her when she was a young girl of maybe eight or nine and come to visit her grandmother, Queen Mary, may the saints take good care of her! She'd come down to the kitchens in the palace for cookies. The whole downstairs would be in a flap, I'll tell you! She weren't supposed to be there. And my mum and the others were not dressed proper for a royal visit—even one from such a young one! 'No good will come of her,' my mum told me." Seldom did Mrs. Barnes, while she lived with us, say a kind word about Margaret. But she did speak well enough about Townsend. "A man can't help but be took by all that pomp," she once said. "A man's just a man, after all."

The "affair of the princess and the pilot" remained a topic for discussion and in the press long after I arrived in London. It was a terrible time for the royals and their subjects. A royal soap opera, really. Sister was pitted against sister. The Queen was at a standstill with the Church. There could be no concessions. If Margaret chose to marry Townsend, she would lose her title, her position in the line of ascension to the throne, and her state income and possibly be excommunicated from the Church of England. The young, beautiful princess was in despair, blaming her powerful sister for her adamant stand against the marriage, looking—in the flood of media photos of her—wan and as if she had spent a good deal of time crying. Which, indeed, she most probably did.

I was facing some dilemmas of my own, although none of them newsworthy. My first draft screenplay was completed and my tenure in London appeared to be coming to a close. The news from the States was not promising. HUAC was still swinging its executioner's ax, decimating families and careers. Among people I knew there had been one tragic suicide and several unexpected divorces caused by the investigations and the blacklist (where husbands and wives had strong differences on positions a mate took before the Committee, or could not deal with their newly demoted and insecure future caused by the blacklist). Mitchell Gertz sent me a terse, three-word telegram:

DON'T COME HOME!

A letter followed explaining that two of his clients had their passports confiscated upon reentering the country. This meant that they could not leave if work was offered abroad. How was I to support "we three"—the kids and me—once the money from *A Question of Adultery* was depleted if I opted to return home? This was a question that was not often out of my thoughts.

I had not squandered the money I had earned. Still, what remained could not sustain us for more than six months if we continued to live on Albion Street. I needed to secure an assignment in London or come up with a story that could be filmed in England, both options a definite challenge. From my struggles with my script on *Question* I had learned that the English spoke English (or about a dozen curious versions of it—cockney, etc., etc.) and

Americans did not speak English—or write it. They spoke sometimes with a Southern drawl, a Brooklyn dialect, or a nasal Boston twang. It might take time to secure work and I would have to radically change our current lifestyle, and also hope to get an extension on my work visa.

With these troubling musings rattling around in my head, I set off, on a particularly gray day, for Wardour Street in the heart of the district where most of Britain's film production companies were located (the studios were in outlying Shepperton). I had completed work on *Question*, but before a film could begin shooting, the screenplay had to be approved by Britain's Film Censorship Board. I was thus on my way to an appointment with Raymond and some representative members. There appeared to be problems that had to be fixed before the board would grant approval for filming to commence.

After twice rereading the script (once that very morning), I decided that the Censorship Board might have had an objection to one fairly graphic scene that I called "sex on the sand," which Raymond had insisted I include, against my better judgment. He had just viewed the American film *From Here to Eternity*, that contained a highly erotic scene where Deborah Kerr and Burt Lancaster appear to have sex at the ocean's edge in wet sand, the waves lapping up on their feet and the lower halves of their bodies. I was indignant. Using another writer's creativity was highly offensive to me. Also, such a scene would be difficult to place in the script without slowing down the thrust of the story. After all, this was a couple who had been unable to conceive due to the husband's problem (it being broadly hinted that he was impotent). The audience was surely going to be confused when they saw the two of them going at it like dogs in heat. Additionally, the story was set in London and the surrounding countryside. No ocean, or residual breezes, close at hand. By using the technique of flashback, I finally managed to weave a similar scene up front—taking them on a holiday on the Costa del Sol in the beginning of their marriage. I never liked it and had little regret if it had to go. I also thought the board might be objecting to the use in a clinic scene of close-ups of test tubes supposedly filled with sperm. That had also been Raymond's contribution, and I knew I could rewrite the scene avoiding the offensive test tubes.

Raymond, David, and the director, Don Chaffee, an animated, young-ish man with an intriguing goatee, arrived at the meeting before me along with three members of the board—two men in black funeral suits, looking like aging clerics, and a woman of indiscriminate age who bore an uncanny resemblance to Margaret Hamilton in full makeup as the Witch of the West in *The Wizard of Oz*. The woman had an unfortunate mole on the side of one nostril which moved up and down as she breathed. I had a difficult time averting my glance.

To my surprise, neither the Spanish scene nor the test tubes were mentioned. It was the language in the courtroom scenes. The word "panties" had been used four times, "intercourse" five times, and "climax" twice. I could not believe what I was hearing. At the end of an hour of haggling I agreed to substitute "underwear" for "panties," and to cut three mentions of "intercourse" and one "climax."

The meeting had already lasted the better part of two hours when I left Raymond, David, and Don still talking to the censors to finalize our compromises. That evening I was attending a dinner party at the Adlers' and I wanted to spend some time beforehand at home with the kids. When I reached the lobby of the building, it being only 5 p.m., I was startled to find it was pitch black beyond the glass windows at the front of the building.

"One of a'r black fogs, I'm afride. No taxis," the cockney doorman told me, holding his hand up as to stop me from leaving the building.

"I have to get home," I insisted.

He shook his head but he lowered his arm.

"Which way to the tube?" I asked.

"Left. 'Bout five streets. But I'd sty 'ere if I was you."

Disregarding his warning, I opened the door myself and stepped out onto the street and into a thick, soggy blackness. There was an acrid smell that burned my nostrils. Streetlights were dimmed to tiny bug-like specks and did nothing to illuminate one's path. Silence buzzed in my ears. There were no moving vehicles on the street. I put one stick in front of me to balance myself and probed with the other to make sure there wasn't an obstacle to trip over. I then took a small step forward, continuing in this mincing manner for several minutes until I saw a beam of light advancing toward me.

"Stand still," a man's husky voice called out. "I've got a flashlight. I'll help you if I can."

I froze, and in a moment a rather large face streaked with black soot was staring down at me from a distance of about two feet, the brightness from the arc of his flashlight blinding me for a second or so. He had, during that short time, taken note of my sticks.

"You shouldn't be out in this," he scolded gently. "Where are you going?"

"To the tube stop."

"That's a bit of a walk—and in this muck . . ." He came alongside of me and put his arm in a supportive way under mine. He was a stocky man, probably in his midyears, dressed in a proper overcoat, a bright red scarf about his short neck. He did not appear to have been drinking, although with the sour taste of the air, alcohol would have been hard to detect.

"We'll take one step at a time in rhythm," he instructed. "One . . . two . . . one . . . two."

I placed my trust completely in him and concentrated hard on keeping a straight line within the beam of his flashlight. When we came to the first curb, he placed his arm protectively around my waist and made sure I was steady on my feet. We continued like this for maybe twenty minutes. Both of us so concentrated on what we were doing that no conversation passed between us. Finally, we reached the tube station and he opened the door and guided me inside. I stood for a time and looked around me. The place was packed. When I turned back—my guardian angel was gone, vanished into the impenetrable darkness outside. I never had a chance to thank him, or even to ask him his name.

The trains were not running. I stood in a long queue to use one of the public telephones so that I could call home. I had forgotten to keep that thrupence in my pocketbook as Raymond's secretary had advised, but the person next in line handed me one.

The children were home and safe.

Almost the entire night passed before the fog began to lift and we were informed that the trains would be moving. Queues for boarding immediately formed. I could not help but imagine that to some degree this must have been what Londoners had experienced during the war when the Underground had sheltered them during the German Blitz. Not all of those who sought its safety made it down the steps as I had. I recalled a memorial plaque on the entry to Bethnal Green Underground Station in memory of the "173 men, women, and children who lost their lives on the evening of 3 March 1943," while seeking shelter from a German air attack as they descended the steps just moments before entering. This night there was no threat, just precaution. A cheerful mood existed. A man was playing jigs and old English tunes on a harmonica. People were singing along, taking it very much in their stride. Babies cried. The toilets had ten-minute waits. Food vendors were serving free hot tea, but doing a fair business with their snacks. Almost everyone had black smudge on their face and clinging to their clothes. An acrid smell had swept down and through the area. I learned later that Raymond, David, and Don Chaffee had been stuck half the night in the building where we had our meeting along with the Wicked Witch and her companions. I did not envy them.

What I had experienced was what Londoners called "the black fog," caused by the use of coal in heating their homes, offices, and public buildings. This had been happening since the days of Jack the Ripper but was becoming more frequent. Eventually, Parliament passed the Clear Air Act and coal was forbidden to be burned in the city. Time was given for the conversion to other heating and cooking methods. When the bill was finally put into law, I thought about my nemesis, the coal stove that commanded the kitchen on Albion Street. A fitting end for that brute, no doubt. Still, it marked the passing of an era. But that was yet to come. Right now my greatest problem would be to find less expensive lodgings for we three. My decision had been to remain in London, at least for the present time.

I had come to feel a bond growing between myself and the British. Also, I did not have a job, family, or home to return to in the States. My parents were once again separated, my mother living for the time with her mother, sister, and brother-in-law in Hartford, Connecticut, my father somewhere (I had no address) in Texas. The Rossens were moving to New York and my chances to get a writing assignment in either Hollywood or New York were slim to zero.

What I knew was that writing constituted my very being. Since youth I had not aspired to be anything else but a wordsmith. In truth, it was the literary path I most wanted to travel, not scriptwriting. I had many ideas for a novel that I started and put down as they never seemed good enough. I worked on character, profiles of people who I might develop. I began one short story after another and, displeased with the results, threw them away.

My problem, I reasoned, might be that all my stories were set in America, and the people in them, Americans. I tried another approach and began working on sketches of the people I knew, or had observed in England. Meanwhile, I was grateful for a paying assignment given to me by Gerry Adler. My children seemed happy. We three could certainly make it through for the next six months. I decided to remain on Albion Street for a time so as not to disturb their current routine. Mine was also well established. Daytime, I worked on my assignment (a half-hour television adaptation based on the character of the Scarlet Pimpernel). Finally, I came up with an idea that I thought could be developed into that novel I was so anxious to write. Set in England by the sea, it owed a lot to Daphne du Maurier's *Rebecca*, if one considered the setting and the story, which was a love story and a mystery. My burgeoning work was, however, about an older woman and a younger man (no drowned or suicidal former wives or lovers involved). I did first drafts on several chapters but the underbelly of emotion that I needed was missing. I had to dig deeper into the English psyche which was in a separate place from my own. This time, I did not trash the pages. Some day, I reasoned, I might want to return to the story and try again.

I was reading and rereading all the classic English novels I could manage with women as their main characters. I had met through the Adlers, Doris Cole Abrahams, an American woman and theater producer, married to a wealthy English businessman. She had a house in Worthing by the sea, and she lent it to me and the children to use during a school break. From the front windows was a view of the water—so different in color and nature than the ocean off Santa Monica Pier in Los Angeles where my childhood friend

Greta Markson and I used to bicycle to on Saturdays when we were in our teens. The water had huge crested waves that started far off at sea and rolled in with beautiful symmetry, all frosted and foaming onto the white sands of the beach. The sand at Worthing was composed of pebble rocks, and the sea, much less ebullient, was the color of twilight. It seemed this was the perfect place for me to go back to work on the novel. I wasn't any more successful with the second go.

Could be I was feeling homesick. More likely I was not yet comfortable in my current surroundings. I certainly was not longing for a particular place back in the States. There was nowhere that I could honestly call home. I had never given in to the kind of wanderlust that so many American writers of earlier periods had harbored. I was content for the time to be wherever fate had taken me and had made the best of it, found the things that would make it a special place for me. I was doing that in London, as well. Still, something deep in me was fighting its way out for air.

• 4 •

A Dream Is Born

I am well trained at making order of my life once I have put a plan into action. At the moment I had no viable answer as to what I should do next; indecision made me nearly manic (or perhaps I already was!). Then Raymond called to say he would like me to remain in London another six months. Production on *A Question of Adultery* was delayed and he wished to engage me to work on a breakdown of *The Angry Hills*, a best-selling book by Leon Uris (author of *Exodus*), about the resistance forces in Greece during World War II. He was going to be in Hollywood for six to eight weeks to meet with studio heads and to hopefully sign some American stars to appear in both productions (the need of an American star on an Anglo-American film planned for release in the United States being of utmost importance). I could stay on at Albion Street at his company's expense, and he would continue to pay me, in pounds, the diminished amount I was currently receiving. If I did not accept the offer, my funds would be cut off in a fortnight. Of course, I agreed. I had been handed another six-month reprieve and at least my rent would be paid.

Things appeared to be looking up. Then, early one morning, the sky not yet having lost its darkness, I awoke feeling a terrible chill. I tried to rise from the bed but my legs refused to move. I recall struggling to lift them over the side and falling back onto the bed. I called out for help but the house was too solid for my shouts to reach the floors above or below. A telephone sat at my bedside table. I rang David with great apologies for the early hour, and he arrived in maybe fifteen or twenty minutes, aroused Mrs. Barnes with the sound of the doorbell, and moments later the two of them came bursting into the room. I still could not move my legs and I was taken by ambulance across Hyde Park to St. George's Hospital.

I received immediate attention and great care. None of the doctors were able to diagnose the cause of my sudden paralysis or if it was related to my early illness. One doctor thought it might have been brought on by an emotional upheaval. I insisted that I had been concerned about my situation (to stay in England or return to the States) but I did not think I was unduly disturbed (vastly untrue!). "The past might just now be catching up with you," he told me and ordered an electric shock treatment which he said could affect my recent memory—but that it would return. At first I fought submitting to the treatment, but finally, after speaking with a psychiatrist, decided to go along with it. What I remember is the distinct smell of garlic—strong—like in highly seasoned cooking. For my safety, I was bound to a gurney. I understood why moments later for, once the electric currents began, I shook until I thought the gurney would overturn with me on it. The experience was so fraught with fear and repulsion that I refused further treatments and accepted the cost of the doctor who I had ordered to call my physician in Los Angeles for an overseas consultation, who thought it might be something newly named and seen to recently occur called post-polio syndrome.

I was in the hospital for several weeks. Kit Adler stepped in to help with the children along with Fiona and Mrs. Barnes. By the time I came home, I was actually in better shape than I had been in many months. The most amazing part of the entire ordeal was that within six months I was able to walk without sticks. I felt like a suddenly freed prisoner. I had been able to do the work Raymond had engaged me to do and was looking forward to being a complete "me" again. To celebrate, one of the first things I did was to go shopping for a new dress. I taxied over to Sloane Street where there were some lovely shops. In the window on display was an emerald green, eye-catching evening gown, off the shoulder, wasp waist, full skirt. As my hair was dark auburn, the color had always been flattering to me, and the gown reminded me of that dress I had worn to my high school prom and had long ago discarded. I marched inside, tried it on, and purchased it without questioning the price (over fifty guineas! A huge outlay in England in the 1950s and a considerable dent to my budget)—or considering when or where I would ever have an occasion to wear it!

The other amazing thing that happened during the time that Raymond was in Hollywood and I was in the hospital and then an outpatient, was that David and Claire ("my angel") Stross saw a great deal of each other and apparently fell in love. On Raymond's return, Claire had already packed up her bags and left their apartment with plans to divorce Raymond and marry David. It boggled my mind to visualize how Lili Deutsch might react to that. But I was pleased that David could also shout, "Free at last!" (at least from Lili).

Raymond wasted no time in coming over to see me upon his return; confronting me would be a better description. The sight of him was terrifying.

He was in a state of disarray. His clothes looked as if he had slept in them for days. His eyes were red and swollen. His hand kept furrowing through his hair so that strands of it appeared electrified.

"It's y-y-your f-f-fault!" he stuttered.

"My fault?"

He managed to explain that David had seduced (his word) "my angel" and would not have done so had I not rejected him. I found it too ridiculous a notion to contradict and, anyway, he was far too distraught to listen to reason. "Empty! Empty!" he shouted. "When I arrived home it was empty! Sh-sh-she was g-g-gone!" Claire had left him a note telling him that she was in love with David and that she wanted a divorce.

"I can't understand it. Why? Why? Why?" he cried.

I thought I did. Both were obviously unhappy and lonely and turned to each other for companionship. Man being man, woman being woman—the obvious had occurred. And David was a lot younger and a lot richer than Raymond.

I tried to calm him. I poured him a glass of brandy, which he didn't drink. He paced up and down, talking compulsively, retelling the story of their love affair and all he had gone through with her family. Then he sank down onto an ottoman, covered his face, and sobbed, looking suddenly shrunken and pitifully defeated.

"Raymond, look, these things happen," I offered limply. A few minutes passed before he had controlled his emotions and bounced up onto his feet, head high.

"I ap-ap-apologize," he managed. "It was not your f-f-fault." And then he departed. He never spoke of Claire to me again, not once during the period of the divorce and her marriage to David, who left his employ immediately and went into production on his own to become very successful. I did not envy Claire her new mother-in-law, but years later (after David's death in 1988), I was happy to learn that their marriage had stood the test of time.

Kit and Gerry Adler and their children (by now there were three) were going to the States for the summer and, as my arrangement on Albion Street had finally concluded, they offered their grand apartment for our use (to maintain the flat and to walk Gerry's beloved dog). The offer included two members of their staff (a nanny and daily maid, whose services they did not want to lose). Not only did we three have a glorious place to live for the next three months, Gerry had hired me to write a pilot script for a planned NBC television series, *Captain*

Blood, based on the swashbuckling pirate story by Rafael Sabatini, which in 1935 had been adapted by Warner Bros. and starred the dashing Errol Flynn. I had neither seen the film nor read the book. The only pirate with whom I had any literary acquaintanceship was Captain Hook in *Peter Pan*. Still, Gerry had great faith that I could pull it off (or, at least, convinced me he did), and so I went to work doing a breakdown of characters, their background, and the history of the period in which the stories were set. I thought it would be daunting. It turned out to be great fun. I also learned much from the undertaking. One, that I had a talent for taking a book and breaking it down to find the visual elements and characters that would transfer well to screen. Two, that almost every good theme or morality tale could be told within the framework of a classic adventure story, be it pirate, historic, or western. Actually, this was something I previously had discovered without realizing it, for the first original screenplay I had sold, *Quantez*, was a western with a strong moral theme. It was (so I read in the English edition of *Variety*) currently being filmed at Universal Studios in Hollywood, starring Fred MacMurray and Dorothy Malone.

By the time the Adlers returned I had connected with many of the HUAC expats living in London. A few who I knew had gone to France (those who spoke the language well) and Italy (who were high on American-style westerns at the time). But the majority of expat film writers chose England for the obvious reason—they could write in their own language. Also, the British film industry was just reviving itself after the difficult years of the war in which so many of their talented writers, directors, artists, and technicians had sacrificed their lives. At the same time British television, which had a late start, needed a knowledgeable, creative workforce. There were more than thirty expats, wives and children added, whom I knew fairly well. Although several American film and television companies (Columbia Studios, NBC, and Screen Gems Television leading the pack) now had active representatives working in London, most of the expats chose to remain close to each other, forming a small, exclusive social clique. I was accepted in this group, but I had also formed friendships and working alliances with newly arriving American movie folk—future gay activist Larry Kramer, in his twenties at the time and a prodigy honcho at Screen Gems who had not yet embarked on his successful writing career, and the Adlers, who were established in England before the influx of the expats.

In Hyde Park there was a large patch of grassy field that on Sunday afternoons became a baseball diamond where many of the expat men could engage in their favorite American sport. There were enough players for two teams and several reliefs. Wives and children cheered them on from the sidelines. Except for a severe downpour, nothing canceled these games. After, there were group picnics, or—if it was too cold and damp—they broke up into smaller groups and spent the afternoon at one or another's home. News was exchanged: what was happening "at home," who had come before the Committee, had they taken the Fifth or been an informer, what was being produced in England, and where could any one of us find employment? People helped each other with leads, loans, encouragement, or just by sharing their anger for how their lives had been upturned. There were among this self-exiled circle some of Hollywood's most talented moviemakers, recipients of numerous Academy Awards, and younger players who had just started to see their star rise when it was pulled out of the sky.

The death in 1952 of John Garfield of cardiac arrest while having sex with a young woman—not his wife—was a personal and continuing sorrow to me. Jule (as he was known to his friends) was only thirty-nine at the time. Before Warner Bros. canceled his contract due to the blacklist, he had been one of the top stars in Hollywood. Jule, and his wife Robbie, were close friends of the Rossens and had been supportive of me during the time my ex-husband and I were living with Bob and Sue in their Bel Air home, the blacklist having just begun. Jule had read whatever story I was attempting to develop, discussing it with me and encouraging me to press on. He had a terrific story mind and a deep understanding of the world condition and people's motivations. Robbie was a very special and intelligent lady of whom I was extremely fond. Jule's death, and the circumstances, had been a great shock to her. The media attention it received became more than she could bear. She came to London (the media in this instance, being kinder to her than they had been in the States) to get away from it. I was grateful for her presence.

One woman, Hannah Weinstein, was more responsible than any other person in London to help the Hollywood expat writers find work (Larry Kramer ran a close second). Hannah was a former American journalist and left-wing political activist who had come to England in 1952 a step ahead of being summoned to appear before HUAC. She became a mother hen to the flock of expats whose numbers kept increasing, offering her home, her counsel, and her heart to them. She rather quickly established her own movie production company, Sapphire Films, solely for the purpose of aiding them.

Until 1954, Great Britain had only a government-sponsored television station (the BBC). The first commercial network was ITV. Hannah sold them on the idea of adapting as a series, *The Adventures of Robin Hood*, and secured Richard Greene to play the lead. Greene had been a dashing young star in Hollywood during the 1930s and 1940s. He returned to England when his career in the States started to ebb. His being known to both English and American audiences contributed to Hannah making a deal. Blacklisted writers were almost exclusively hired under pseudonyms (as was I). Without doubt, Hannah's writing staff consisted of some of the most talented scenarists that

Hollywood had once employed. I, therefore, felt quite honored to accept a "Robin Hood" assignment to follow *Captain Blood*. There were 137 episodes of *The Adventures of Robin Hood*, written over several years. To my recollection, I scripted four or five of them.

I now came to accept the fact that London would be home to we three for an extended period as news from the States indicated the dark days of the blacklist would not brighten any time soon. When the Adlers returned, for less than half the rent on Albion Street, we three moved into a charming row house on Markham Street, just off Kings Road in Chelsea, a popular shopping area, burgeoning with youthful clothing establishments. Accessible at one end of Kings Road was Peter Jones Department Store, where afternoon tea in the vast, top-floor restaurant, surrounded by windows that looked out to an exhilarating view that stretched across Sloane Square and down elegant Eaton Place, was a must on Saturdays for Cathy and me. Around the corner from our house was an intriguing, cluttered bookstore that became a frequent rainy-day shelter for me and from which I would lug home an intriguing sackful of books by contemporary and classic British authors. Our street was lined with attached row houses that all looked much the same—three stories stacked one atop the other, just wide enough for one large and one smaller room on each floor, bedrooms and baths above, kitchen, small dining space, and staff quarters (a closet-sized bedroom and a poke-hole toilet) under stairs. The joy was the kitchen as it had an electric stove with a grill and a refrigerator with a small freezer that held three minisized ice trays that produced circular cubes the size of an American nickel (iced drinks were an American, not an English custom). To add to our good tidings, Mrs. Barnes came to work for us on a daily basis. The house on Albion Street having been sold, she had moved in with her sister fairly close by.

On Albion Street, with its grand houses, one could hear Big Ben ring out the hour and from the window in the children's wing on the top floor see the rooftops of Buckingham Palace across Hyde Park. Chelsea was another world, middle class, younger in mood, attractive to artists and to tourists who came to shop there. English cozy had its charm, but I wanted to make our new home reflect more of my own style. I had not brought anything much of a personal nature with us when we three had left the States. Now, I wandered about the many flea markets in the city searching out inexpensive items that caught my eye. Collectors' fairs flourished and each usually featured different categories and periods. Nothing aged less than a century was considered an antique. Victorian items—unless very early Victorian—were plentiful and reasonable. Least expensive were articles made in the 1920s through the 1930s, the art deco era. I was drawn to the vivid colors and began collecting pottery, dishware, statues, small tables, and books with hand-tooled bindings. Many large homes and estates had been sold, broken up, or lost during the years of the Depression, the war, and their aftermath. There was a surfeit of exquisite used monogrammed table linen (kept pristine, no doubt, by the laundresses in the fine homes from whence they came)—the monogram believed to diminish the value. The same was true of silver serving pieces. I bought what I could afford, the initials making me no never mind. When I realized what I had stacked on shelves, I planned some small dinner parties.

Not only did I love to cook, it seemed a good way for me to get into the social swing. Restaurant food had not yet improved to any recognizable degree, even as supplies became more plentiful. Rationing had ended, but the English home cook or chef remained entrenched in their old methods. Meat was either roasted or potted (unfortunately the customers most often were not), well done, and heavily sauced; vegetables—generally of the gaseous sort—were overcooked, puddings soggy or drenched in treacle. The Grill at the Savoy Hotel was excellent (meat grilled, pink and tender), but terribly pricey. Ethnic restaurants were the best alternative for dining out—Chinese, Indian, Hungarian. Iso's catered to Jewish staples (as did a few places in Golders' Green)—salt beef, chicken soup and matzo balls, and a savory brisket with onion gravy.

The most elegant restaurant was French (or claimed to be). I have forgotten its name, but it was outrageously expensive and pretentious to the extreme. One evening Jules and Bea Dassin (a talented cellist) hosted a dinner for six there—very extravagant for the usually conservative Jules. He was both a writer and director who had just found his stride with the slice-of-life drama *The Naked City* (1948) when he was blacklisted and with his family left hurriedly for Europe, settling in Paris (as he spoke French) where, after a difficult four-year dry patch, he had finally signed a contract with a French company for a film to be called *Rififi*. He was ebullient and the trip to London and the dinner was a celebration (I recall that Sidney Buchman and Carl and Estelle Foreman were the other guests). When it came time for the main course, a battery of six waiters approached our table, one standing to the side of each chair. A plate covered with an ornate dome was set before each of us. With the precision of a Rockefeller Rockette, the waiters lifted the domes and whisked them away. We were served French-style food, overcooked by an English chef. Jules, spouting excitedly in French, made a terrible fuss. The chef (who seemed untutored in the French language) came out and shouted back in cockney English. I don't believe either one of them knew, or cared, what the other was saying and I thought for a few moments that fists would fly, for Jules, a rather slight and not very tall man, had pushed himself up and away from the table with energetic force and had taken a stance that was surprisingly threatening. Nothing was done about the food. However, as soon as the fracas cooled, our table was presented with a chilled bottle of champagne. Jules glanced at the label and sent it back.

Clancy Sigal, a former Hollywood agent (and Beverly Hills neighbor, and coworker of my ex-husband) was now a published writer living in London. I thought he had enjoyed the glitzy experience of being an agent, lunching with pretty starlets and all that. But, at heart, Clancy was a far more serious sort with strong roots in social activism and a driving ambition to become a critically acclaimed author. He had won a contest for new writers sponsored by an American publisher and with the money departed California and the States to start a new life abroad, settling in London.

The first time he showed up on my doorstep on Markham Street, I hardly recognized him. He had shed weight and traded his sharp Hollywood wardrobe for weathered, well-worn garments, layered sweatshirts, and sweaters. His hair was no longer barber trimmed. Round granny glasses had replaced his former large airman's tinted ones. He had fought with his lady friend and landlady, the writer Doris Lessing, and needed a bed for the night. This happened periodically and as Markham Street had an extra bedroom (the one below stairs), it was fine with me. He shared some of his current problems—the writing was tough but he was determined to turn out a work of literary and social significance (although he did not use those exact words, that was the implication I got). Doris Lessing was an amazing and talented woman. "Older, you know," and—after viewing me dressed to go out for the evening—"rather stout," which made buying clothes difficult. She had a son who Clancy very much liked. He took to Michael, as well, and I believe enjoyed the idea of paternal relationships. Earl's Court, the area of London where he and Doris lived, was a more working-class neighborhood than Chelsea, a bit scruffy in places and for now I assumed Clancy liked that along with the local pubs and the Bohemian lot who filled his lodging with impassioned debate. He made it clear that he did not think much of my current "guy" (it turned out I would shortly agree with him). "A bit too much of a toff, don't you think?" and then added—"Why are you wasting your time writing for television?" I reminded him that I had a family to support.

Although an intellectual dreamer, Clancy was also a realist when it came to the plight of the working man and the poor. He was, even in those green days, an exceptionally gifted writer as his early books, *Weekend in Dinlock* (about coal miners) and *Going Away* (a more autobiographical book), proved and his social commentaries in England's left-wing press solidified. I invited him to a few of my small dinners. He declined, I assumed because he wanted to experience what the working-class English experienced. He hinted that Doris was the jealous type. If so, she had no reason to be jealous of me as Clancy was a good friend, nothing more. However, she might have wrongheadedly feared that he would discard her world for mine if exposed to more of it.

Certainly I had not given up sex; my libido was too strong for that. I was also now more of a whole woman, the sticks kept at the back of my closet, my plumbing problem seen to and corrected by a fine British doctor. I had not shed all the side effects of my long illness, but I felt almost newborn. In truth, Mr. Right had not yet knocked at my door. I turned my bottled energy into my writing. Though I had not discussed it with Clancy, I did not want to write for television forever. Not that I believed it was in any way demeaning. I loved the medium for what it was. However, like the short story, I felt that thirty-minute segments were not long enough for me to develop the characters as I would have wished. To write so concentrated a story and characters takes a certain talent, one that I did not fully have confidence I possessed. The strengths I had sharpened through the years were the ability to visualize a story, capture voices, write dialogue and scenes of confrontation—all prime in working in film. I had studied theater with the great Margo Jones (Tennessee Williams's muse) during my two years at Southern Methodist University in Dallas, Texas (when I was married to my ex-husband). Now, as I struggled with my attempts at a first novel (still set in the English seaside), I regretted not spending more time studying the contemporary novel. After my third attempt at a novel failed to come together, I turned my attention to the play form, attending the great theater being presented at the Royal Court, walking distance from our house, and usually easy to pick up one seat. A play finally emerged from this. Titled *Sally Sunday*, it was set in a seaside town and centered on a young Englishwoman's one-night-weekly affair with a doctor who would not allow himself to become emotionally involved. Then, Sally attempts suicide in his flat and the doctor is crushingly unable to deal with this sudden appearance of reality in his life.

I knew only one person in the British theater, Doris Cole Abrahams. Doris was still in the embryonic years of her long career as a theater producer, known primarily at this time for her considerable help to new playwrights (including Tom Stoppard). I wrote her a note and asked if she would read *Sally Sunday*. She rang back (that metallic, high-pitched, mid-Atlantic voice—so memorable and irritating). "Send it right over," she ordered.

I traveled by bus across town to the block of flats where she lived—the palatial Bryanston Court, where Wallis Simpson had once served up dinners and herself to an ever-hungry King Edward VIII—and left it with the concierge. I felt so good about it that I splurged on a taxi home, not that I had any great hopes that a production might be in the stars for *Sally Sunday*. It was simply that I had made a move that could mark a change in my life, provide a new avenue for me to follow (while I held on as tightly as I could to my current means of support—writing for the small screen and breaking down books for possible adaptation for the large screen). I had not given up my dream of eventually writing a publishable novel. That time, I told myself rather convincingly, would, *must* come.

· 5 ·

Gentlemen Don't Always Prefer Blondes

It was no accident that Los Angeles was often referred to as "movietown." Movies, and everything to do with them, were at the heart of the city. Fantasy was manufactured there, and celluloid, rather than flesh-and-blood people, formed the basis of its culture. Oh, there were multiple subcultures—black folk in a seething slum section known as Watts; legal and illegal Latino immigrants struggling to make enough to just put food on the table. Fantasy from the dream factories supplied little nutrition. However, in areas like Beverly Hills, where I had spent so many years of my life, for its rich and famous film colony (not fully representative of the incorporated city's twenty thousand or so residents), dream and fantasy *had* overtaken reality. The current movie that looked like a blockbuster was the "must see" on most people's agenda. If you wanted to attend new plays with their original casts, you had to go to New York City—a journey only a privileged few could afford—or wait for a successful show to be dehumanized for the screen. I was as much a dreamer as anyone. Still, I grew up with vaudeville in my genes and always felt starved for the electricity of live performances.

There had been (and remained) a dearth of theaters devoted to stage works in the Los Angeles area. Touring companies occupied a few venues from time to time. Young hopefuls studied the craft and appeared in tried-and-true vehicles at the Pasadena Playhouse with the dream of being discovered by a studio and placed under contract. On the other hand, London theater was a magnificent feast with no taste excepted. There were over one hundred venues where Shakespeare, drawing-room comedy, music hall, pantomimes (great for the children and young at heart during Christmas holidays), straight drama, musicals, and burlesque (where actors dressed in drag and seasoned their acts with salty humor) were available. I loved every form and would quite often attend by myself. With so many stages, it seemed a new playwright would have more of a chance to secure a production in London than anywhere in the States, including New York City. I was hopeful (make that "giddy") with the prospect of possibly getting a play produced.

My approach to *Sally Sunday* was influenced to a large extent by what was currently happening in British theater, specifically at the Royal Court on Sloane Square. The premises had a long significant history, first opening as a theater in 1870 where several of William S. Gilbert's early plays had been staged (before his collaboration on comic operas with Arthur S. Sullivan). In that era there had also been a stage adaptation of Charles Dickens's *Great Expectations*, and of Arthur Pinero's *The Magistrate*. The building was demolished in 1887, rebuilt a year later, and christened the New Court Theatre, becoming a leading venue for works by George Bernard Shaw. Badly damaged during the Blitz in World War II, it reopened entirely refurbished in 1952 once again as the Royal Court, bringing with its rise the rebirth of a great theater history and reputation under the artistic directorship of George Devine, who was determined it would be a "writers' theater," a place where new authors could produce serious, contemporary works. He formed the English Stage Company and was constantly on the prowl for new writers with fresh ways of saying things.

The Royal Court was an easy walk from Markham Street but located a distance from London's heavily populated and thriving theater district, set apart not only by its position but by the plays it elected to produce. *The Mulberry Bush* by Angus Wilson, which premiered in April 1956, was the impetus for the new wave that soon overtook much of Britain's mid-twentieth-century theater. John Osborne's *Look Back in Anger* followed one month later and created a storm of outcries among most critics and theater stalwarts but was a clarion wake-up call of what they could expect would follow. (Only the acerbic, young critic Kenneth Tynan thought it a worthy play and I agreed, returning several times to see it.)

Look Back in Anger was a social drama, real down to its dilapidated kitchen set, a bucket to catch leaks from the roof center stage while the beleaguered female lead ironed away on a rickety board for a good part of the action. This new play style was swiftly named the "Kitchen Sink School," and presented its audiences with an image of abject poverty not previously showcased in the twentieth century. Audiences took note. Osborne's play did for English theater what Tennessee Williams's and Arthur Miller's works had done for the American drama. Major numbers of theater audiences were now exposed to a present-day world most often alien and very far from their own.

Doris rang me a few days after I had left *Sally Sunday* with her concierge. Although it needed work, she liked it. Would I have tea with her? Of course,

I agreed. Doris thought the play would be better set in Miami Beach where such ambition for a doctor was perhaps more understandable than England—a country that had converted to a national health plan. I did not entirely agree with this as I had met during my medical sojourns some very ambitious English doctors who also had private practices. Still, after serious consideration, I went along with this idea. She optioned it for her company, Albion Productions, and I went back to revise what I had written. Doris always sounded on the edge of some major emotional collision. The need to succeed, to prove herself a real theater person, was palpable. Her New England family was moneyed, and everything in her youth had pointed to a marriage to some rich, Jewish scion. She wanted to be an actress, went to New York, and was unable to get past first auditions, but worked hard at any theater-related experience and ended up on the production staff of a black musical called *Blue Holiday*. She met Gerald Abrahams (both rich and Jewish) when he was in Manhattan on a business trip and shortly thereafter followed him to London where they were married. After the birth of two daughters, she joined London producer Oscar Lewenstein's company raising money for many of his productions, while furthering her career as a producer.

With an agreeable husband, generous with his support, a luxurious flat ideal for large social parties, and the money to throw them, Doris's festive gatherings usually included local and visiting celebrities, wealthy potential theater backers, and a hungry young playwright or two. Her parties were often the starting place for a deal to be struck and a play to be born.

I liked Doris. She was honest and straightforward as well as intelligent and feeling. I know she financially helped many young playwrights during their lean days. It took a long time for her to gain the respect of her peers, partly I suspect because she was a woman—and a rich one, at that. However, she possessed a strong sense of what good theater could be and the ability to recognize untested talent as promising. She mounted a regional theater production of one of Tom Stoppard's early plays, *Enter a Free Man*. Young playwrights were her shining prizes, the theater—her life's spark. At times her wound-up personality could be trying. She had a nervous laugh and a speaking voice that was often grating. Besides its high register, she had trained it into an eccentric accent that was a cocktail mix of Boston nasal and Knightsbridge head cold sieved through a mesh strainer. In all fairness, Doris Cole Abrahams was not the only American living in England who had adapted a form of spoken English that they considered tony. It was an affectation I did not admire. Despite the dark period of McCarthyism at home, I felt proud of my nationality and determined to hang on to my American speech. I found this equally true of most of my compatriots in the expat society, mainly, perhaps, because they clung together and did not mix often with the Brits on a social level. Twenty years later, taxi drivers would assume I was a tourist! It always amused me. I understood that Doris needed to belong, while many expats, including myself, were mainly fighting to survive. I also realized that her part in our friendship was driven somewhat—curious though it seemed—by envy. She would often remind me that she could not be as free as I was. Lack of a specific talent or position and a moneyed husband held her back.

"In what way?" I once asked her.

"Well, you create. I have to wait for a writer to do that for me. You don't have to answer to anyone, nor are you always reminded that you have a name or position to uphold." The last was a reference to my being able to have an open affair if I so wished, for Doris was more than once strongly attracted to the young male playwrights she sponsored.

I cannot count the times I had either read the book or seen the various film adaptations of Charles Dickens's *A Christmas Carol*. My favorite movie version was British and starred the veteran English actor Alastair Sim (he of the most unique physiognomy) as a memorable Scrooge. In all versions, snow fell upon the streets and rooftops of London Town and goose was served for Christmas dinner. Dickens seemed to have taken literary license regarding the arrival of a white Christmas. Mostly, during the early days of my residency, it had rained, skies were grumpy gray, and the houses in which I dwelled (and visited) damp despite wood-burning fires and multiple electric heaters. The dampness in London during the winter months penetrates to, and through, one's bones and is the reason those with some resources, however slight, holiday abroad during that season. Others of us who could not go off to sunnier climes for whatever reason, pulled an extra sweater over our heads and drank a lot of hot tea. For Christmas 1959, flakes—if not a full snowstorm—had been forecast and I decided to prepare for the holiday in Dickensian fashion.

As my family never celebrated Christmas, this would be my first and I wanted it to be something special: one that would erase all the public Christmas images during my previous life in Southern California where the sun was guaranteed to shine, snow was something unheard of, and street Santas at Yuletide wore sunglasses. The fashion in Beverly Hills for years had been to spray a magnificent evergreen, cut down for a holiday tree, blue, pink, white, or silver, the scent of pine overcome by the lacquer in the paint. These freak specimens—frequently towering and adorning front lawns—were then decorated in a fantasia of ornaments that carried out a theme—often of a current movie. There were Mickey Mouse trees, cowboy trees, bow-bedecked trees, and butterfly trees. Houses had huge lighted displays: Santa and his reindeer riding a sleigh over the red-tiled roof of an adobe bungalow; Snow White and the Seven Dwarfs guarding a painted white tree covered with apples; Peter Pan and Tinker Bell topped another that I remember.

Holiday gifts had been a big deal in the Hollywood that I had left—those for the A list, B list, C list, and so on. In the movie colony, what you received for Christmas often defined where you stood socially and the successful work you had done the previous year. Before my onset of polio, I had been the story editor for a television anthology program called *Schlitz Playhouse of the Stars*. One Christmas, I received a huge record player, set in a handsome, tall mahogany chest, that not only played the records, it turned them over. The next Christmas, spent in the hospital, I received a letter of kind apology from the producers stating that my services were no longer required. With the forecast of snow glistening like sugar icing on the white streets of London, I planned my first real Christmas dinner. When I was a child this had been a nonholiday in our house. My religious training had been scant—actually overlooked. My mother was born into a Jewish family but became a devout Christian Scientist when a severe, lingering illness struck her directly after my birth (cured by her belief in Christian Science, she declared). Still, she could not bring herself to honor Jesus on that occasion. My father was also of Jewish heritage. However, his family had immigrated to Sweden from Spain during the Inquisition and there had been about four centuries of intermarriage. I don't recall that my paternal grandfather, Big Charlie, followed any religion. However, he was never united with us on any holiday. My ex-husband's grandparents (on the Rossen side), although not strictly orthodox, considered the celebration of Christmas a corruption of Jewish belief and I had respected their belief. Now I thought we three should free ourselves of the persuasions of others. In doing so, I was determined to go with Mr. Dickens.

A Christmas tree lot had been set up near the old soldiers' home that backed on King's Road just a few streets from our house. I purchased a huge one, branches outstretched like a lover's open arms and a tip that reached at least seven feet. Two ruddy-cheeked teenage boys working there delivered it and had a terrible struggle getting it through our door. Finally, after they hacked off about a foot, it stood erect and commanding in a corner of the sitting room. I gave each of them a pound and whatever change I had, much to the annoyance of Mrs. Barnes who deemed it far too generous. I organized Michael and Cathy to string cranberries and popcorn (that we made and ate gobs of as we worked), which we draped over the tree's limbs along with silver tinsel and red and silver balls purchased from Peter Jones along with some cotton batting to cover the base. At the top was a beautiful angel with golden hair and flecks of silver on her wings that glistened in the ceiling light when it was turned on. We three stood back and viewed our work. It was, we agreed, the most beautiful Christmas tree we had ever seen.

Then came plans for Christmas dinner. I invited five of my English friends who were familyless—making us eight in all. In Mr. Dickens's

Christmas story, dinner was a roast goose. Now, I had never eaten or cooked a goose (I don't believe they were easily available in the States where I had lived). But how difficult could it be? They were fowl like chicken, turkey, and duck and I had roasted my share of them. I marched over to Harrods' giant food halls (a terrific extravagance—but this *was* to be we three's first real Christmas dinner).

Harrods' food halls were a wonderland, vast and filled with individual stalls devoted to voluptuous displays of every variety of food—cheese (the strong aroma announced its presence), fruits, vegetables, pastries (sweet and savory—always looking much more appetizing than they tasted), smoked fish (kippers, salmon, herrings, and eel), meats (cured and fresh, butchers standing at the ready with an array of gleaming knives and hatchets), dozens of fresh-caught fish (small eyes, big eyes, eyes glassy in death, yet staring—I zipped past this stall as quickly as I could), seafood (cockles, whelks, periwinkles, prawns, and limpets), game (during hunting season a colorful mélange of feathers and fur), and of course every creature with wings, most still feathered, from the tiniest bird to the larger species, many I had never seen before—and certainly had never consumed. This is the stall at which I stopped. A ruddy-faced man in a huge white apron, slightly blood splattered, came forward and asked if he could serve me. I told him I wanted a goose large enough for eight people and some leftovers. He stepped back behind the marble counter and then disappeared through a rear door, returning with two dead feathered creatures that I assumed were geese, each clutched in a hand by their spindly yellow feet. He suggested I might prefer the larger one if I was thinking as well of lunch on Boxing Day (the day after Christmas and a national holiday). I asked to have its head and feet cut off.

"The feet, madam?" he inquired disapprovingly.

"Yes, also plucked clean and delivered." I did not know what the British cook did with the feet of a fowl, but I knew seeing them on a serving plate would turn me off.

The only cookbook I owned was an American volume. No recipe for roast goose was included. So I ambled over to our neighborhood bookstore and bought an English cookery book that contained not one, but several, methods to roast a goose. Christmas morning, after we three had opened our presents, I went down to the kitchen and started my dinner preparations. Mrs. Barnes was off for the two-day holiday. I was on my own. I baked two pies and many side dishes with proud results. Then, carefully following the recipe that seemed the simplest in the volume I had purchased, prepared the goose, placed it in a roasting pan, and shoved it into the oven.

Nose-tickling aromas floated up to the ground floor where I was setting a festive table while my goose roasted. The BBC program on the radio issued forth cheerful Yuletide music. The children were upstairs in their rooms involved with their new gifts. I was a most happy woman.

When I took the goose out of the oven at the appointed time, I knew something was decidedly wrong. A probe with a fork released a gusher of fat and had been a struggle to pierce through the skin. I stepped back with a touch of horror. Surely this could not be the same bird I had placed in the oven. It now swam in a sea of fat and had shrunken horridly, reminding me of the scene in the film *Lost Horizon* where the ever-youthful Margo, having dared to leave the land of never aging, morphed into a shriveled hag of a century-old lady. Whatever was I to do?

I remembered holidays past (not Christmases) when my mother made a Thanksgiving turkey and in removing it from its roasting pan, had let it slip out of her grasp—turkey and gravy splattering all about on the floor. The door to the kitchen had been open and the scene visible to the expectant diners. But Marion did not lose her cool. She had thrown some dish towels on the floor, so as not to slip, then taken pot holders and lifted the turkey onto the counter, placed it on the tray she had already prepared (with sliced oranges and parsley for decoration), pressed the severed joints of the bird where they anatomically belonged, and then with the help of some of us carried the tray into the dining room and went on with slicing what she could and serving it. No one had said a word. (However unhygienic, the turkey was—to my memory—delicious.)

Then there was the time that Sue Rossen's cook made a huge standing rib roast for my family engagement party (I believe there were twelve of us) and let it rest in the pan on the opened door of the oven while she and an aide went into the dining room to remove the dishes from our first course. There was a mighty crash that came from the kitchen and the sudden appearance of Leo, the Rossens' massive, bearlike dog (part St. Bernard I believe, and generally the gentlest of God's creatures), the huge roast clasped between his large jaws as he dragged it across the dining room and into a corner where he dropped it and squatted down, contemplating his kidnapped meal. Bob had risen from the table and ordered us out into cars where we continued our celebration at a local restaurant.

Although equally disconcerting, my situation was not comparable. I could not afford to take us all out to dinner—and most probably could not find a restaurant to accommodate eight walk-in guests on Christmas Day. I had the choice of disposing of the goose and serving a vegetarian meal from the side dishes I had made, or adapting my mother's attitude and just get on with it. So I lifted the goose from its lake of viscous yellow melted fat, patted it as dry as I could with a clean towel, and placed it on a silver platter. The monogram HRH had intrigued me when I bought the tray, even though I knew it could not stand for His or Her Royal Highness. More likely it had belonged to someone with a name like Horace Rippington Hugglesmith. I garnished the platter with holly and crab apples, made a quick white gravy of flour, milk, and butter, spiced it up a bit (the pan drippings were just too loathsome to use), filled a silver gravy boat (with still another monogram), and with some assist carried it upstairs and set it down on the table to a burst of applause from my guests. There was very little flesh on the bird and what there was proved to be so tough that it was almost impossible to carve. I was somewhat saved by the tastiness of the rest of the food and the good manners of my guests (or perhaps the English liked their goose tough and greasy!). To my puzzlement, they left on their plates no remnants except the bare bones of their scanty servings.

Doris rang to tell me that she was entertaining the following Sunday night (theaters were almost all closed on Sunday) and wanted to be sure I would attend. She was having some theater people from the States as well as those who were local, and the American actress Donna Reed and her husband, the agent, Tony Owen, who she knew were friends of mine. Donna had won an Academy Award for Best Supporting Actress in *From Here to Eternity* (but probably was best remembered for her role as Jimmy Stewart's wife in *It's a Wonderful Life*). We had met in Hollywood when I was story editor for *Schlitz Playhouse of the Stars*. Her career had not been going too well of late. She had recently arrived in London to film *Beyond Mombasa* (years later she would re-gain stardom on American television with *The Donna Reed Show*).

"It's Sunday," Doris added. "Not too dressy. Black cocktail dress, something like that. Come in a taxi, but our chauffeur will drive you home."

The little black dress was almost a uniform in London and New York in the fifties, brought to popularity I believe by Coco Chanel. Unfortunately I did not own one. I had taken to wearing silk evening pants with an attractive, and a bit dressy, blouse which I could alternate to make a new outfit when needed. Despite Katharine Hepburn's and Marlene Dietrich's penchant for them, pants were an avant-garde fashion and seldom (if ever) worn at the time in the salons of London. I felt extremely comfortable in them and they looked good on me so I had included them in my limited wardrobe. I was the only woman in pants that evening—deep purple ones with a cyclamen-pink blouse that was sashed around my waist. Doris wore a midcalf, black taffeta Dior with one blazing diamond pin. She had hired a pianist and he was playing a set of Cole Porter songs, which no one in the crowded room appeared to be listening to as they chattered and laughed and mingled while a uniformed maid and a butler in tails walked among them with drinks and cocktail bits on silver trays with DCA's very own monogram.

Suddenly, I felt a man's arm around my waist. I turned. "Jule Styne," he announced.

"Anne Edwards," I replied.

"Do you belong to someone here?"

I laughed. "I don't belong to *anyone*," I emphasized.

"Why are you here?"

"I'm a writer. Our hostess, Doris Cole Abrahams, has an option on a play I've just written."

"I'd like to read it."

"Why?"

"Well, you are obviously an American who has written a play optioned for English production. That interests me. You interest me. You are the only woman in the room in trousers, purple at that."

I laughed again.

"And I like your laugh."

I recognized the name Jule Styne, popular Hollywood songwriter and Broadway composer (*Gentlemen Prefer Blondes*), who probably had composed as many standards as any of his contemporaries. He was in his early fifties, short but well built, dark hair, and winning smile. In no manner an imposing presence, but definitely vital. He was in London to see about a possible British production of one of his more recent shows and, he proudly told me, he was also producing. He was asked to play a song or two of his own composition and he refused. "They hired a pianist," he said to me. "It's his piano tonight, not mine."

Donna and Tony entered, and I excused myself and went over to greet them but soon found Jule once again by my side.

"Let's get something to eat," he said.

I looked around nervously.

"Come on. They'll never notice we've gone."

We went to Iso's. He liked deli-style food. His office in New York was over a Broadway theater, and Lindy's Restaurant was around the corner. He ate lunch there every day—or had them send over sandwiches—corned beef or pastrami with sauerkraut. He was born in London, Jewish, working-class East End. His family immigrated to the States when he was eight. They settled in Chicago. He always loved the piano and was good at it—naturally. He was a child prodigy, did some concerts when he was still a kid, nine or ten. The classics. That pleased his mother but not him. He liked the popular music he heard and started composing his own. He just had never stopped. "Hardly a day goes by," he laughed. His real first name was Julius (like John Garfield, I thought). He asked me a host of questions about myself, and I answered as squarely and honestly as I could.

"Your uncle is Dave Chasen!" he exclaimed at one point. "That seals it. I always eat at Chasen's when I'm in Hollywood. Dave's a great guy."

He was in London for about three weeks, and we saw each other almost daily. I fixed dinner for him and he met the kids. A divorce from his now ex-wife had been bitter. She had the custody of his two sons and they lived in California. More recently he had broken off relations with a French woman, an heiress. "Two worlds," he explained. "It didn't work."

Two days before he was to leave for New York he asked me to meet him at Iso's for lunch. He talked about his production of the musical version of *Peter Pan* that had starred Mary Martin. Some of the lyrics had been written by Carolyn Leigh, a young woman he thought was very talented. He went on to say that he had optioned a book by James Thurber, *The Wonderful O*, which he planned to turn into a musical. His idea was that Carolyn Leigh could write the lyrics and I could write the libretto.

"How about it?" He had brought along a copy of the book, a very slim volume I noted, and handed it to me.

"You want to produce the show here, in London?" I asked.

"No, in the States. I'll take care of everything if you'll agree to come to New York and give it a try. So far there's no official blacklist in the Broadway theater," he added. Jule knew a lot about many things, music, Broadway, baseball—but he was not politically inclined—or knowledgeable. I wasn't sure he was right, but it did seem that Broadway had not been hit in the way the movie industry had. Playwright Arthur Miller had been caught in the crossfire. However, had he not been so famous and therefore useful for propaganda, I was not sure that would have been the case. And there were those like the great tragicomic actor Zero Mostel who were still in limbo, along with my good friend Jack Gilford (who had been a regular at Uncle Dave's home table when he was a young, struggling performer), who had been singled out. There was no guarantee that theaterites would not be brought before HUAC if it was to strike again.

There was also my commitment on *Sally Sunday* to be considered. I had just finished a rough draft of the new version before my meeting with Jule. However, Doris was presently deeply involved with a play about to be mounted and *Sally* was not prime on her agenda. Jule said he would fly me back to London if meetings should be required. He was so earnest, so persuasive in his attempt to convince me to join him in New York, that I found myself being swayed. The blacklist remained but the media mania had quieted some. Still, the chance existed that I might have my passport confiscated, and I was wary of being cut off from what I had achieved in England. That was so, I argued with myself, but it might not be a bad idea for we three to return stateside for a time to test the waters and for us to see my mother, who remained separated from my father and was living with my grandmother in Hartford, Connecticut. Marion was the one person I sorely missed and our weekly exchange of letters and occasional overseas telephone conversations (never lasting more than three or four minutes, due to the cost), had not filled the hole our being at such a distance created. Marion had never interfered with my personal life or my choices and her pride in whatever I did always bolstered my spirits. Also, she was a unique and quite wonderful woman despite her weakness where my father was concerned. More importantly, I loved her very much.

"I have to think about it," I hedged.

He put his smallish hand—small for a pianist, I thought—over mine, grasping it tightly.

"One other thing you have to know," he said.

"What's that?"

"I'm crazy about you."

This was the summer of 1960 and the children were on a school break. Within six weeks we three flew to New York. I was in a nervous state (well concealed, I prayed) until we successfully passed through passport control, with it neatly stamped and returned to me. Jule met our plane at Idlewild Airport and took us to a building on East Eighty-Second Street, near the corner of Fifth Avenue, where he had secured an apartment for we three, owned by playwright Samuel Taylor (author of *Sabrina Fair*—the "*Fair*" deleted for the title of the two subsequent film adaptations). Taylor was somewhere in Maine or Vermont or New Hampshire—Jule could not recall exactly where—working on a new play. We were guaranteed the premises for the next six months. There were enough flowers in the flat to have pleased a diva on opening night. Jule's secretary, Dorothy, had seen to the practical things—food in the fridge, information about the nearest school, and anything else we needed, we were to just call her.

He kissed me lightly as he left (the children were close at hand) and with a light step, flashed a wide smile before heading down the corridor to the elevator. We had been intimate on several occasions during our time together in London and had meshed well. It seemed our bodies had known each other for a long time. Jule was a man with a great deal of love to offer, and I was well aware and accepting of the knowledge that my coming to New York at his request meant we were at the start of an affair. For me this would be newly explored territory as I had not had a sustained sexual relationship for a long time. I felt well loved and most beholden to this talented, spirited, warmhearted man who had given me back my feeling of once again being a complete woman.

We were not living together. Jule had a garden apartment a short distance down and off Fifth Avenue. Mine had only one bedroom (which Jule had not realized as Taylor had assured him it was "plenty big enough for a dame and two small kids"). The rooms were spacious, and it had a bath and a half and a terrific eat-in kitchen. The living room contained a couch that pulled out into a bed. I took the sofa bed and gave the kids the bedroom, which had twin beds. When I opened the closet door in the bedroom the first time, there hung a ranch mink coat—almost full length. On the hanger was attached the note:

"To keep you warm when I can't. Jule."

The added bonus to the apartment was that it was situated directly across the street on Fifth Avenue from the Metropolitan Museum. Michael immediately became obsessed with the armor room and the mummies. Our building was also around the corner from 1010 Fifth Avenue, where—by exceptional coincidence—the Rossens now owned an apartment, having permanently departed California.

Late one night, just after we had settled in, children asleep and I just beginning to doze off on the sofa bed, I heard the turning of a key in the lock of the front door, then someone swearing and pounding as I had put the chain in place and it was holding. I grabbed a robe, shut the door that led to the bedroom, and picked up a poker that stood by the fireplace. "Who is it?" I called out, firmly grasping my weapon and edging close to the telephone to call for help if needed.

"Who're you?" came an alcohol-blurred voice through the narrow opening. "Thish is my apartment."

"You must be wrong. I'm calling the police." I started to dial the operator.

"My apartment! I'm Sham Taylor," the intruder slurred.

I cautiously approached the door, phone in one hand, poker in the other. "Sam-*u-el* Taylor, the playwright?"

"Yeshhhh, fur God's shake!"

I put down the phone but held on to the poker as I undid the chain. The man reeled in, almost landing flat on the floor. "Omigod! I almosh furgot! Jule's girl!" He stumbled over to the sofa and collapsed.

"I am nobody's 'girl,'" I protested, "and you are a sorry sight for a landlord!"

He refused to get up and certainly was not considering departing. "I furgot," he kept mumbling. "Shurry, I furgot. . . ." Then he went off to sleep—soundly with a snore and a snort. I searched in his jacket pocket for his wallet. He was, indeed, Samuel Taylor. There was little I could do at this late hour about his invasion, so I went into the children's room, jammed a chair in front of the closed door, and crawled into bed with Cathy. My intoxicated landlord was apologetic the next morning, explaining that he had planned to drive north late in the afternoon of the previous day. Then he had stopped to have a drink, then another, and obviously too many more to count. By then, he was too inebriated to consider driving for three hours up the East Coast. He claimed he had forgotten all about renting the premises to Jule—"Chrisssakes, don't tell him about it!" he insisted.

I gave him some coffee and scrambled eggs, which he ate along with the children, who were simply told "this gentleman is a good friend of Mr. Styne's." He left directly after breakfast. I never saw Sam Taylor again, but I did tell Jule what had happened. He was furious. I'm not sure that Jule confronted him, but Dorothy called and assured me nothing like that would ever happen again.

Jule and I soon fell into a routine. I hired a part-time maid-sitter. Several nights a week after dinner, the theater, or an evening with friends we would go back to the garden apartment. The place was quite attractive. I called it "the hideaway" as we never had others in for drinks or dinner. It was always just the two of us . . . and a piano in the front room where he would play songs that he was working on for his new show.

Adapting *The Wonderful O* into a musical was not easy. The story was more of a cautionary fable, something the brothers Grimm might have relished if they had come back to life. The story was simple: A pirate has committed (by accident) matricide by pushing his mother out of a porthole window in his ship (the porthole thus representing the *O* in the title). He is overwhelmed with grief and remorse. He captures an island and rules ruthlessly over its people—making them take the letter *O* out of every word—ah! But when they bring up the word "freedom" they realize they must revolt—and do. Freedom triumphs over dictatorship in the end. I told Jule it really was the Hitler legend—I believe Thurber agreed with that theory. We decided the story had to be lightened and I made more of a satire of it. Cy Coleman was composing the songs, Carolyn writing the lyrics, and Jule acting as producer. One day he came up with what he thought was a terrific idea. As the story progressed, each musical instrument in the orchestra that contained an *O* (like violin, oboe, piano, saxophone) would be removed. I hated it and Cy was adamant and refused to do it, and that was that.

Carolyn Leigh was an exceptionally gifted lyricist. She was also going through some form of emotional distress that was making working with her almost impossible. A pretty woman in her mid to late twenties, she was borderline obese and a compulsive eater. She insisted that at least once a week, Cy and I work with her at her house in Long Island, a two-hour train journey from the city. Her husband was a successful lawyer and seldom around (I saw him briefly only once as he was leaving). But he had been a great help in boosting her career. As Cy and I traveled by train to and from her home (quite a charming place) we had to leave at a certain time to make the last one that would get us back into town at a decent hour. Carolyn would insist she needed us there just one more hour, then another, and finally we would have to stay overnight. So when we traveled out to the island, I left the kids with Sue. Carole, the Rossens' older daughter, was now a teenager. Ellen, their youngest, was just a year older than Michael, and Stevie—their only son—in the middle. In many ways it was nice for my kids to have cousins—for their father had totally opted out of any contact before we three had left for England and had not been in touch since.

The nights we remained on the island, neither Cy nor I, occupying the two upstairs guests bedrooms, found it possible to sleep. Carolyn haunted the hallway and staircase—back and forth by our doors, up and back—back and down the staircase. She seemed never to sleep and she carried food with her each time she returned to her bedroom. (Later, when we were left alone in the house for a time, Cy went on a hunt for what she did with all that food—for it seemed impossible that she could have consumed such quantities as we had seen her with. He found a cache of it under her bed: a whole salami, a bottle of pickles, boxes of cookies, pretzels, and heaven knows what else.)

One night my phone rang about three in the morning. Carolyn was calling from the road (or at least that's where she said she was). She was sobbing, hysterical. I had a hard time calming her down so that I could follow what she was saying. Since she could not sleep, she explained, she had decided to drive into the city. An officer in a police car had pulled her over to the side of the road. He made her get out of the car and walk a line to make sure she was not intoxicated (all this was told through sobs). Then when she was ready to return to her car, he had thrown her down in the grass by the roadside and raped her. It did not sound plausible. But then, such horror stories about good-cop-bad-cop did hit the papers from time to time.

"Where are you calling from?" I asked. She told me she had walked up the road to a gas station, which was not open but had a pay phone. I did not hear any clicking for more change but I accepted what she said on the slight chance that she was telling the truth. I told her I would call the police.

"No! No!" she shouted. "They're all in cahoots."

"Where's your husband?"

"In San Francisco."

"Did you call Cy?"

"He's not home." She made some rude remark about "that aging former movie star, Veronica Lake," who had been having severe drinking and money problems and who he had befriended.

I told her to stay where she was and somehow I would get help to her. So where exactly was she? At that point we were disconnected. I called the help line and gave them what little information I had. There was nothing more I could think of doing. A few moments later, I decided to call her house and see if her maid knew how to reach Carolyn's husband. Carolyn answered the telephone and I hung up.

It was obvious that the project was not going well and would never find its way onto a stage. It never did, although Carolyn and Cy did write one marvelous song for the stillborn show, "Witchcraft," that would later become a popular standard.

My relationship with Jule was fulfilling. He had taken to the children. I'm reminded of the line in a song in *Gypsy* (for which he would compose the music) that goes "I'm a man who likes children." Jule did. One night he took Cathy with us to Sardi's after we had been to the theater. Ethel Merman stopped at our table on the way to her own and made a big fuss over Cathy. "Would you like me to send you an autographed picture?" she asked in her inimitable to-the-back-row voice as Merman and her party were moving on.

"I don't collect autographs," my seven-year-old daughter replied to one of Broadway's greatest musical stars.

It wasn't long after this, however, that both Jule and I found ourselves in a stressful situation. On my side, I was not really comfortable in the city. I had never spent any time there and the tempo and the people—especially Jule's friends—seemed more foreign to me than my life abroad. The Rossens were having serious marital problems, which was upsetting. I was totally detached from the liberal political scene and members of the movie industry. The children were attending PS 6, walking distance from our apartment, and one of the best public grammar schools in New York. But my life was so tentative and I was plagued with questions as to how that would affect them. Also, there were the strange working conditions on *The Wonderful O*. Carolyn's bizarre behavior continued. Cy pulled back and detached himself. No more working days in Long Island. We met at Jule's offices on East Fifty-First Street where there was little privacy or quiet space. I could only see failure for the project. Then what would I do?

Although our relationship had not cooled, and Jule was most attentive, he had his own pressures with the writing of his next show and the plays he had taken on to coproduce. We saw each other at least three nights a week ending up back at his apartment. It was an arrangement that made me feel as though I was living a divided life. Then, when we were together, he began receiving late-night telephone calls of a threatening nature. He would hang up the receiver, having turned pale and looking terrified. He kept telling me not to worry. I wanted to help him but he refused to discuss the subject of the calls with me. One night, after receiving such a call, he sank down in a chair, his face ashen. "I think these guys are serious," he said. He now explained that he owed some gamblers a very large sum of money that he did not have and they had threatened to break every finger on both his hands if he did not pay up.

Jule was an addicted gambler (the horses, baseball games—you name it). I could not understand why I had not seen the signs, having had a father and a husband who had both been addicted gamblers. I was at a loss at what I could do to help him and so I did nothing. Our relationship took a dark turn.

Shadows of the past. I knew I could not relive the trauma I had gone through with my children's father, nor could I place Jule's problem and how to solve it above the safety and well-being of my children. A week went by, then another, and another. The situation grew more tense. He had managed a down payment on what I now knew was an astronomical debt. The threatening calls continued. Jule was sure gangsters were going to take control of the royalties from his music. It was hard for me to be as empathetic as either of us would have wished. How could he have allowed himself to get this far into debt with people who were obviously dangerous? I didn't understand gambling or men, I was told. Oh? Didn't I?

We had our first real fight and it was a lulu. It would be our last. He needed my sympathy and support; I could not rein in my anger that he had not let me know early on how involved he was in gambling (or, perhaps at myself for not recognizing, and dealing with, the situation earlier). The children had a school break coming up soon. They were doing well, but I knew life in New York as a single mother and a writer was not for me. I could not return to Hollywood as I remained unemployable there, at least as far as movies or television were concerned. And as there was no other reason (or person) to go back to, I made arrangements for us to fly to London.

"If you do this, there's no way back," Jule furiously warned me.

Two weeks later, after a warm and emotional weekend in Connecticut to see my mother (my father, she told me, was still somewhere in Texas), I packed up our belongings and bought our return tickets to London. I took the mink coat with me—but I left an envelope at Jule's office with Dorothy. It contained a diamond bracelet Jule had given me for Christmas. Maybe it would end up on another woman's wrist—but it could also be returned or sold and perhaps help him in some small way (it being somewhat more conservative than bracelets worn by the eponymous blonde in *Gentlemen Prefer Blondes*).

I felt a huge sense of guilt at leaving Jule with such hard feelings on his part and at a time when he needed support. I told myself that I was fighting for my children's and my own survival. Yet, I knew deep down, that maybe—just maybe—I had not loved him enough.

· 6 ·

My Kid Seems to Like Your Kid

$\mathcal{H}$ow was it, I pondered, that in New York I had felt like an alien and as our plane set down in London, I was overwhelmed with an emotion of homecoming? Part of the reason could well be that in London I belonged to a community—and a large one at that. I never counted how many of our American expats currently lived in England. We had arrived like sheep, one following the other bringing our American customs, dreams, and resentments with us. Being survivors had bonded us. There were degrees of separation, but they mattered little. Some of our group had been famous and secure before HUAC; some too embryonic to have made our names and fortunes yet; and some had neither garnered fame nor fortune, but a livelihood that kept the wolf away from the pantry and their dreams intact. All of us were, however, like-minded in our liberal viewpoints and none, that I recall, were Republicans.

Resentment ran high. Companies hired blacklisted writers for payment far, far below Hollywood standards and their names did not appear in the credits, except in the form of a pseudonym. Anger festered over their Hollywood colleagues who had recanted their former position and had given names. These things distressed me as well. But, I was convinced that the only way to survive was to concentrate on present needs and not on past abuses.

In Great Britain a seriously ailing Sir Winston Churchill had stepped down as prime minister in favor of the elegant Conservative, Sir Anthony Eden, his former secretary of war. Eden had ordered British forces to occupy the Suez Canal Zone ahead of the invading Israeli army, and Great Britain was in the grip of a bitter controversy caused by his action, which had been condemned by the United Nations. The prolonged dispute was so acrimonious that Eden resigned the premiership in January 1957, to be succeeded by Harold Macmillan, a Conservative and scion of the publishing firm, Macmillan. Although English politics were complicated, we expats could not help but get involved, at least in the hard issues that were current. Nonetheless, what was happening in the States remained our top concern.

General Dwight D. Eisenhower had been reelected president for a second term in November 1956, defeating yet again the intellectual liberal Democrat Adlai Stevenson. The whole colony of us had voted at the American embassy, giving Stevenson the largest percentage of votes in any "precinct." For one of us not to vote was considered a cardinal sin. We gave Eisenhower points for sending federal troops to Little Rock, Arkansas, to enforce the integration of black students. Still, it seemed incredible that the nation could not see the damage that Senator Joseph McCarthy had done to our Constitution, nor how cowed during his first term Eisenhower had been by McCarthy's growing power in the early 1950s over the Senate. The more recent Army Investigations Hearings when McCarthy had gone over the line and abused and threatened Senate members finally spelled the end of McCarthy's grasp on the government. Censored, ridiculed, and robbed of power, he died in 1957 of diseases caused by alcoholism. But for those whose careers had been mined and their rights to free speech trampled upon, the blacklist outlasted McCarthy's life and would remain in existence for many more years.

Before my departure from New York, I had been brought sharply up to date by Ted Ashley, a major agent, as to my chances of finding work in television. He advised me that I would do better to distance myself in England and continue to write under an assumed name. With children to support, I had to have a reliable income to cover our living expenses. Hannah Weinstein was producing a new adventure series so I sent off a letter to her. She would see what she could do, she replied. In the same post was a letter from my dear friend (and elder statesman) Sidney Buchman, written in his minuscule handwriting (Sidney could get on one piece of thin, blue airmail paper what others needed three sheets to accommodate). There was a project he wanted to talk to me about. Sidney had championed my career in my early years in Hollywood when he had been second man to Columbia Studios' mogul Harry Cohn. Mitchell Gertz had sent him my screenplay, *Riot Down Main Street* (that Gertz later sold to 20th Century-Fox). Sidney was all for buying it, but Cohn turned it down. Sidney had been one of the first expats I had contacted in London as he was working on a project, coincidentally being produced by Raymond Stross.

The evening before our return flight to London, we three had dinner with the Rossens. The hostility between Bob and Sue was tangible. Bob was in an extramarital relationship with a young female assistant, Elise, at least half his age. Sue was determined to keep their marriage intact. These were tough times for the Rossens. Old friends, still loyal to their beliefs, turned their backs on them. Bob was able to work and had formed his own production company. Most of his projects had to be made in Europe and Sue seldom accompanied him. He was in New York during a break in his shooting schedule.

"Look, kid," he said to me privately after dinner. "I need a reader, a scout, someone with story sense and good taste. You're determined to go back to England with the kids—okay, check out what's being published there for me. Maybe, you'll find a good story. I'll put you on the payroll, fifty bucks a week. It's only a part-time job and you can do it on your own time. It shouldn't interfere with any writing you may be doing and it'll come in steady. Deal?"

He was sitting on the edge of a desk, looking down at me, his gaze penetrating, his forehead furrowed, concentrating entirely on what I was about to say. I could easily imagine him in the same pose making a deal with an actor he wanted to hire. Although short and stocky, Bob's piercing blue/gray eyes, his attitude, the use of his hands (quick jabs for emphasis, thumbs-up fist when he knew he had scored a point), and his carefully measured speech—most times low and personal, his breath seeming the only barrier between himself and the listener—were mesmerizing. Bob possessed a powerful presence and he knew it.

"This is a professional offer, not a family handout?" I asked.

"Strictly."

"Deal," I replied.

We shook hands (dry palms, hard grasp).

"You're doing a great job with the kids," he added. "Ever hear from that sonofabitch nephew of mine?"

"I'm afraid not."

"You're better off. I washed my hands. I did what I could to straighten him out. His mother's my sister. Blood counts with me. I always treated him like a son. But a man doesn't take care of his kids—he's shit."

On arriving back in London we three stayed for two weeks at the moderately priced Basil Street Hotel in Knightsbridge. The place was like a setting for an Agatha Christie novel. Built in 1910, it appeared untouched by time. The guests were mostly frugal, English country folk in the city for a week's holiday and shopping. Afternoon tea (served in a mahogany-paneled room with paintings of sporting dogs on the walls) contained the only edible food their kitchen served. The toast at breakfast was presented burnt and wrapped in a white linen napkin. The eggs were overcooked, the coffee bitter. Yet, I loved the very stodginess of the building, the narrow, winding corridors, and the windows of tinted amber glass. I could write a good mystery here, I thought!

I found an apartment for us in a small building on Elvaston Place, just off Gloucester Road, and enrolled the children in the American School to insure a continuity of the studies they had been having at PS 6 in New York. The school (actually two branches—lower school for Cathy, upper for Michael) was across town near St. John's Wood, where they were taken to and collected from by private transportation. Without the additional two hundred dollars a month I was regularly (and gratefully) receiving from Bob, I would have had to squeeze things to handle the school fees and transport. At the same time, I was enjoying the task he had given me, and had made contact with numerous publishing houses. Books and manuscripts arrived so regularly, I no longer found time to listen to *A Book before Bedtime.*

Our new home was on the top floor of a small, four-story building. Each of the lower floors were divided into two flats, whereas ours occupied the entire top floor (however, I am not sure one could call it a penthouse!). A narrow lift with room for two (if on lean daily diets) was situated in the small lobby. By clasping the children close to me, we three could ride to the top together. Once there, it seemed well worth the cramped (and sometimes halting) ride. Windows on all sides afforded some light even on the gloomiest of days. The children each had their own bedroom and mine connected with a dressing room large enough for me to use as an office. The living room was divided by an archway to a dining room that led into—great wonder of wonders—a large kitchen with American appliances that worked on transformers (left behind by the previous tenant, said to have been an employee of the American embassy).

The first thing I did was go out to Hammersmith (a ten-minute tube ride from the Gloucester station near us) to collect the things I had left behind in storage. The apartment was comfortably furnished but the small knickknacks, paintings, photos, art deco ware, kitchen equipment, and our personal treasures (all items on English current, plus toys, books, and files) that I brought back in a taxi (amazingly stackable in the great old black English vehicle) made the place our home. The area was not as fashionable as Markham Street, but I loved the ethnicity of the food stores and small restaurants on Gloucester Road. There was a public library and a post office (the latter in a paper shop) within walking distance, and Kensington Gardens was at the top of the road (with Kensington Palace close by in case one should want to drop in for tea).

Next, I rang up Hannah and Sidney, who both seemed hopeful that there would be work for me. Sidney Buchman was a wonderful guide and mentor. Before the blacklist, he had been one of the most powerful men in Hollywood, and considered "the golden boy" of Columbia Studios. Many people compared him to the late Irving Thalberg who had been equally revered at MGM in the 1930s. He was both a brilliant screenwriter and an impeccable filmmaker with the ability, sensitivity, and intelligence to deftly handle drama and comedy (often blending the two). A list of just a few of his screenplays reveals the caliber of his talent: *Theodora Goes Wild, The Awful Truth, Lost Horizon, Mr. Smith Goes to Washington, Here Comes Mr. Jordan,* and a particular favorite of mine, *Holiday,* the delightful Cary Grant and Katharine Hepburn comedy (with strong anticonformist overtones). In addition, for over ten years, he had overseen the production of most major Columbia films as vice president of the studio.

Called before HUAC in 1951, he had admitted a membership in the Communist Party twenty years earlier but refused to give names. The ten men who had preceded him on the witness stand had been found guilty of contempt of Congress for refusing to admit anything, and sentenced to a year in prison. Sidney duly expected the same penalty. Miraculously, he had been spared prison, fined $150 and given a year's suspended sentence. Harry Cohn's intervention on his behalf was believed to have been responsible for the "leniency" given him. Immediately blacklisted, he came to England in 1952 and would commute back and forth to a home he owned in Cannes (being one of the more affluent of his fellow expats and having had a French mistress, film star Simone Simon, for many years).

In his youth, Sidney had been a strikingly handsome man. Now, well into his fifties, he had retained a strong presence: well built, a perfectly carved profile, and possessing the most amazing china blue eyes. He walked with innate authority. There was an aura about Sidney that Scott Fitzgerald could have best described—for he seemed to carry with him a lost period in time. He was old world in his manners, a poet in his heart, and a ready captain when a project or a person needed one. In the twenty-five years I would count Sidney as a close friend (only his death would inactivate our friendship), I do not recall him ever using swear words (at least in my presence). He possessed a gentlemanly regard for women and a respect for their intelligence. He remained on good terms with his past lover and his divorced wife and loved and worried over his only daughter who lived in the States.

Sidney was happiest when working in collaboration with other writers. He enjoyed the give-and-take of ideas and the company of fertile minds. He never gave me the feeling that he felt anything of a sexual interest in me, and I regarded him with the fondness one might feel for a close relative. When in London, he was always on his own. We went to the theater together and discussed books, films, and the world condition. On one of his London trips, he asked me to read a Romain Gary book that he had optioned. He did not yet have a production company, nor did he know if he could find one that might commit to a film deal. But the story haunted him—and he was, above all, a story man. I worked on it with him for a time until we both finally concluded that it was better as a novel than a movie. (Titled *Curtain at Dawn*, it would be filmed in 1970 by Jules Dassin as *Promise at Dawn.*) His much-loved daughter lived in the States, and with her at such a distance, I suspect I became sort of a substitute, for his attitude toward me was quite paternal.

On the surface, Sidney could seem a cool, controlled man, always in command of a situation. But he also could be highly emotional. Once he sobbed openly when he began talking about his childhood. He had a younger brother, Harold, and a sister. They lived in a rural area outside Duluth, Minnesota, and his father enjoyed the sport of hunting. One day when the three children were alone, Sidney (eleven at the time) had taken down his father's hunting rifle, which he had never been allowed to handle. The gun went off and killed his sister. Family life was never the same. He had left early and had always felt the weight of his childhood misaction and the tragedy he had caused.

With shocking duplicity, Sidney's home studio, Columbia (who had fired not only Sidney but all employees who had tangled with the Committee, leaving many destitute) was the first Hollywood studio to make use of the tremendous talents of the expat population living in England and had sent over executives who had clean bills from HUAC to inaugurate foreign productions for film and television. Many in our community were hired to write scripts under assumed names (at a rate of pay often as little as one-twentieth of what Columbia would have had to pay their Hollywood staff). All such deals were done under the table and with the use of pseudonyms. Of course, it was not moral, but it was a living and a means of survival.

The commercial feature films being made for American production companies were in quite a different category from those being produced by British filmmakers. The English theater's "kitchen sink realism" had led to the birth of "new wave cinema," which dealt with formerly taboo subjects (still taboo stateside) like homosexuality and abortion. Working-class dramas had overtaken English country-house frolics. A new breed of young actors lit up their screens, many with regional accents that were incomprehensible to the American ear. The "wicked witch" on the censorship board had been ousted. The new rule seemed to be that no film, excluding those of politically controversial nature, could be too intimate, while in the States the proven box-office winners were epic movies like *The Ten Commandments*, teenage romps, or beach parties. Comedy was apparently not universal. Hollywood broke box-office records with the zany clowning of Jerry Lewis, later to also take France by storm, but never England. What caused laughter in Great Britain was of a subtler nature like the Alec Guinness comedies, *The Lavender Hill Mob* and *The*

Ladykillers, or the more ridiculously outrageous ones made by the Boulting brothers that pilloried national institutions (the forerunners of Monty Python).

Clearly, filmmakers in Britain and the States marched to different drummers. This was where the expats came in. Here, in London, was a large pool of American-trained film writers all desperately needing work. The system was corrupt, and yet it allowed writers to engage in what they did best while putting food on their family tables. Did any of us refuse to work under these inequitable conditions? Not any I know of. Were we also corrupting our ideals? My answer is: You can't feed your kids ideals.

Although eminently gifted, by the mid to late fifties, several of our community had risen to heights they might not have achieved had HUAC never existed. Jules Dassin, whose work as writer/director/actor evoked a European spirit, had made the right decision in settling in France where he was well received and able to work under his own name (later in Greece, as well). *Rififi* (*Du rififi chez les hommes*), a prototypical caper movie, was a huge success in its American release (for the US version Dassin had to use the pseudonym Perlo Vita). He won the Best Director Award at Cannes, and *Rififi* at the time became the most profitable film ever made in France. With the Cannes Award his new career as a writer/director of foreign films took flight. Cannes also ended his marriage to Bea, as it was at Cannes that year that he met and fell in love with the Greek actress Melina Mercouri, whom he would later marry. That merger eventually produced the internationally successful film, *Never on Sunday*.

Joseph Losey, the Harvard-educated, blacklisted American director, now living in London, had never become an integrated member of the expat community. His distancing of himself from his peers was replicated in his films where it produced a Brechtian alienation—"a deliberate denial of audience involvement, intended to make spectators think rather than feel"—surely a more European than American approach to film. He had paid his dues. One of Losey's first films made in the UK was *The Sleeping Tiger*. The credit was given to the English producer Victor Hanbury. For a time he assumed the name of Joseph Walton. But by 1957, he was credited under his own name (the brilliant films *The Servant* and *Accident* would later be among his best work).

The expat who was on his way to achieving the greatest financial success and power in London was Carl Foreman. This had not yet happened when I returned from New York but soon would. He had been something of a golden boy before leaving Hollywood, having received an Academy Award nomination for his script of the Kirk Douglas film *Champion*. His original screenplay, *High Noon*, on which he was also the associate producer, was in midproduction when he was called before the Committee. Once blacklisted, he and his wife, Estelle, came to London where for the next six years Carl worked without credit. Recently, he and Michael Wilson (a fellow blacklisted writer) had cowritten the adapted screenplay for the acclaimed *The Bridge on the River Kwai*. The screen credit was given to Pierre Boulle, the author of the novel, who had contributed very little to his book's adaptation. *River Kwai* was the turning point for Carl. A feisty Jewish guy who grew up in a Chicago working-class family, he began to fight for his life and his career.

Estelle, blunt and often militant, was not an easy woman to be with. But she was a friend of Sue Rossen's and had called me several times to join them and their young daughter Katy for dinner. Carl looked a bit professorial behind his large, horn-rimmed glasses but was, in fact, fiercely ambitious and a bit of a rough diamond. As a young man he had worked as a circus barker. I could see that was entirely possible. He liked to talk and was good at it. Any subject, you name it, he had something to introduce, add, or contradict. Sometime late in '57, he had returned to Washington to meet behind closed doors with members of the Committee. There would always be speculation in the community about what happened in that room when, a short time later, he inaugurated Open Road Productions where he would write, direct, and produce under his own name (rumors circulated that he had made a deal and had secretly named names—an accusation never proved). Despite his ability to work unencumbered, those expats he hired to work for him could not use their name and were paid far below established minimum wage, an action that did not endear Carl to me, nor have I ever been able to excuse it.

I remember Carl once saying to me, "You're no one in the film industry unless you are a hyphenate: writer-director, writer-producer. But when you are a triple hyphenate—writer-director-producer—then, and only then, do you have real power." Carl was making sure he had it. In contradiction to this, Sidney had told me, "Any filmmaker who wears three hats—writer/producer/director—is a three-headed monster. Sometimes lines have to be cut. If they are your lines, you might not do it. And sometimes if you are the director, an entire scene needs to be scrapped, and if you feel it contains something you like, you might [foolishly] retain it."

Delayed by casting problems, filming had finally begun on *A Question of Adultery* starring the American singer and actress Julie London. The movie also had a distinguished English cast that included her British costar, Anthony Steel, and fine supporting actors Basil Sydney, Donald Houston, Anton Diffring (actually German), and Andrew Cruickshank. Since censorship had been eased, the sequences that Raymond had originally wanted were returned to the script with added melodramatic flourishes not writ by my hand. Nonetheless, it was being made and as it was now an English production my name would be up there on the screen.

Raymond wanted me on the set, although I don't know why because hardly a word from the screenplay they were shooting was changed during production, except perhaps Julie's husky moans and sighs as the muscular Tony Steel made love to her. Handsome as Tony was, he lacked sexual chemistry on-screen and off, but was a "jolly good fellow" liked by all his coworkers. Julie and I hit it off. She was open, frank, caring, and down to earth. The last few years had been difficult. Her divorce from *Dragnet* actor Jack Webb, worse than bitter. She needed to talk about it and I was a willing and sympathetic ear. She claimed he was often violent, and that even separated by so many thousands of miles, she found herself looking over her shoulder, fearful he would appear. We spent Thanksgiving and Christmas together (turkey and ham—no goose!). She had two young girls, one who was having emotional problems. Friendships during the filming of a movie are tentative at best. Yet, they can be more intense than outside friendships. A film company is like an island unto itself. The members spend fourteen hours a day together. They share experiences and secrets. Then the movie is in the can. Most go on to make other movies, join with other crews, and might never see a colleague from a past endeavor again. Julie and I exchanged Christmas cards for a few years. I was pleased when she remarried the musician Bobby Troup. But our lives never again crossed.

Dalton Trumbo was in London, and Sidney was hosting a small lunch for him at the Ivy and had invited me. There were nine of us: Dalton, Sidney, me, Adrian Scott, Ring Lardner Jr., his wife Frances, Lester Cole, Kate Simon (the American travel writer who was dating Lester at the time), and Harold Buchman, Sidney's brother. The Ivy catered to the before-and-after theater folk. We arrived as most of the customers were leaving for a matinee performance and had the place almost to ourselves for the rest of the afternoon.

I had not previously met Dalton. He was a well-sung hero among the expats, silent before the Committee, having served prison time for it and, although blacklisted, turning out one excellent screenplay after another from Mexico under an assumed name. The previous year his screenplay for *The Brave One*, which was credited to Robert Rich, won the Oscar for Best Original Story. The Academy had not known that Dalton Trumbo and Robert Rich were the same man. Dalton never showed up in Hollywood to collect the award and so a mystery was born: who was Robert Rich? The expats knew but weren't talking. (The credit, as well as the Oscar, was given to him years later.) Dalton was well loved, a small, vigorous man, dapper in appearance.

Four of our group—Dalton, Lester, Ring, and Adrian—had been members of the Hollywood Ten and had spent a year in prison for contempt of the Committee by refusing to give names. Lester had achieved less success in Hollywood than the others and was of the strong opinion that his best work was on the horizon when HUAC dropped the ax. He was a very angry man. Fortunately he was warmhearted as well, loyal to his trusted friends and giving. He often was a guest at my table and each time he would bring with him a gift, however small, that represented my taste, or the children's—not his. A true talent. But he did have this combustible anger inside and when fired up, his face flushed dark red, and his voice took on a hard, cutting edge. Someone at the table made a passing remark about the director Edward Dmytryk, one of the Hollywood Ten who had been sentenced to prison and then cooperated with the Committee to give names to earn an early release. Lester bristled. "I hate that sonofabitch!" he said as he put down his knife and fork and edged his plate away.

"Calm down, Lester," Kate advised.

He instantly turned on her. "I hate that man!" he repeated.

"It doesn't help to hate," she cajoled.

"What do you know about hate?" he asked in a raised voice. "Hate is when a little Napoleonic chairman can sit in judgment of you and your government allows it. Hate is when you live in subhuman conditions for a year in a state institution that your countrymen permit to exist!"

Sidney rose from his chair and came around the table and placed his hands on Lester's shoulders.

"We know, Lester. We know," he said gently.

The room had suddenly chilled. There was graveside silence. Then, Frances Lardner, whose husband had also been incarcerated, began to talk to Kate who had grown pale—just a casual conversation, inquiring about Kate's long stay in Paris, people they both knew. Sidney remained with his hands in place for a few moments and then went back to his seat.

Ring and Frances were a great couple. He had won an Academy Award in 1942 as coscreenwriter with Michael Kanin of *Woman of the Year* and had written many fine movies before his world had crashed. It would not be until 1965 that his name would reappear on new works for the screen—*The Cincinnati Kid* and *M*A*S*H* being two of his later screenplays, the latter bringing him a second Oscar.

At one point, Adrian (who had kept his ear to the Hollywood scene) leaned across the lunch table to tell me that he understood someone at MGM had bought from Fox the rights to my script *Riot Down Main Street* in a trade-off deal. There was a rewrite being done, changing the reporter's race from Mexican to black as a vehicle for Sidney Poitier, who was a fast-rising star.

"But it's based on a true story," I protested.

"What does Hollywood know about truth? You've heard the axiom 'Never let the truth get in the way of a good story'?" he laughed. "They have a black actor bringing in the coins and a lack of stories for him that Southern exhibitors will accept."

[Flash forward to 1961: Sidney Poitier had not made the movie. I get a call from a man who tells me he is a representative of Pennebaker Films, Marlon Brando's independent production company. Mr. Brando, he informs me, has recently purchased the rights to my script from MGM and is in London and would like to discuss the story with me. He added that Mr. Brando would not be appearing in the film if it was made; he would be acting as producer and director. I made an appointment to meet with Brando the following afternoon in his suite at the Savoy Hotel.

I had been around so much celebrity in my life that I was not usually awed in one's presence. Marlon Brando was another matter. I had seen *A Streetcar Named Desire* four times and *On the Waterfront* twice. I considered him America's finest screen actor. He was both an artistic and a social force. I arrived on time, and a bit nervous. He stood up when his assistant led me into the drawing room of his suite, but he kept his hands buried in his pants pockets. No handshake. His dress was casual—a blue cashmere sweater over a white shirt—hair slicked back in place.

The assistant departed. Brando freed his hands, motioning for me to sit down on one of the two sofas that faced each other in the room. He lowered himself carefully on the sofa opposite where I was now seated and picked up the receiver of a telephone from the end table beside him. "Tea, coffee, maybe something stronger?" he asked.

"Nothing, thank you."

He replaced the receiver. "I'm told you're a blacklisted writer." He leaned forward and lowered his voice to a more intimate level. No mumbling, however. He had beautiful, melting eyes. "It fucks," he said. Then he spread his legs and leaned back against the cushions of the sofa. "I thought you might want to take a look at the script. I got two versions—yours and another one. Yours is pretty damn good. I'd like to preserve what I can. The basic premise. You're writing about racial bias. The Mexican situation in Texas? Fucks. We know that. You ever think about real Americans—Native Americans. The country's injustice to them. That fucks. Nobody writes about them. Unless they're riding hard on their way to scalp a party of white usurpers. It was their land, after all." He pulled himself slowly together and up and walked around the back of the sofa and leaned on it as he stared directly at me.

"You never see an Indian hero in a movie. I know a few Navahos. They fought in World War II, the Korean War. They live like shit and are treated like dogs. Now ya know, you can stick to the same story. The minority guy, this time a Native American, getting a bum rap. He was a hero. Fought in the war, fuckin' died, and now they want to ship his remains to a reservation and bury him without all the rat-tat-tat that a white soldier would get. Like the government doesn't want the country to know that there's been an Indian who helped save American lives."

"Mr. Brando," I interrupted, "I have no doubt that what you say about our Native Americans is correct. They are treated shabbily. They live in poor conditions. But my story is based on a true incident. The dead hero was of Mexican descent. From Texas. There was some historical truth to MGM's recasting the story with blacks. There is, as we know, color restrictions in parts of the States where cemeteries are repugnantly segregated. Maybe there's a story in your Indian—"

"Navaho."

"Navaho—hero. I don't think the story I wrote works with your premise."

"Ya don't?"

"It's a different story. I don't know if a Navaho Indian in Arizona—or whatever state there's a reservation—has been refused burial outside his reservation. I sincerely doubt it."

"Why?"

"Well, a lot of research would have to be done."

"It could happen. It could happen," he mused, ignoring my answer.

"And the reporter?" I asked. "He is really the major player. The soldier is dead from the opening shot."

"Big league. Comes to town—desert shit-place. Sand in your teeth when the wind blows. He comes into town ready to fight for one of his own."

"The reporter is an American Indian?"

He looked upward as if the movie was being projected on the ceiling. There was silence for a few long moments. Then he lowered his gaze and smiled at me, not a big, wide smile, one that twitched at the side of his mouth. "It could happen," he repeated.

I rose from the sofa.

"I'll keep in touch," he said as I spoke my farewell and headed for the door. He followed me there and held it open. "It fucks. Really fucks," he said and patted me on the shoulder.

That was the only meeting I ever had with Marlon Brando. *Riot Down Main Street* was never made as a movie.]

Sunday mornings a lucid stillness descended on London until the sound of church bells echoed across the city. Pubs were closed. Many stores locked their doors at one p.m. Saturday and did not open them until Monday morning. One paid a penny a day for an overdue book from the library, but as it was closed on Sunday there was no charge. The museums generally did not open until two p.m. Tourists tended to go out of the city, weather permitting, to places like Hampton Court where the famous maze was a popular attraction. We three took the train there one Sunday that began with moderate sunlight then darkened into a threatening storm. I have never had a decent sense of direction. The children had run ahead in the maze, Michael leading the way dexterously when I suddenly found myself separated from them by thick shrubbery and descending black clouds. Everywhere I turned took me farther away from the clear sound of their bright voices. I was quite terrified, so I stopped and began shouting to them. Suddenly, there was Michael's grinning face as he pulled Cathy behind him and called out, "Here we are!" He believed I thought they had been lost.

One similar thundershowery Sunday afternoon, Kit Adler called to invite we three over to her apartment where she was planning a puppet show for the children (she now had four) and some of their small friends, tea to follow. It struck me as a jolly way to spend a dreary Sunday afternoon and off we three went. The show was a happier, less slap-me-down version of Punch and Judy. Kit was wonderful with children—old and young ones. There was one little girl, about three, accompanied by an au pair. The child's name was Laura. The young woman seeing after her was a friend of Kit's helper. Laura did not let go of the au pair's hand for a minute and was not really happy to be where she was or to join in with the other children when the puppet show ended. By the time tea was served (highly diluted with milk) along with cookies and small sandwiches, Cathy, always the hostess even when she wasn't, had made a small inroad in gaining Laura's attention and she sat down beside her. About an hour later, her father came to collect her and the au pair. Laura was clinging to Cathy's hand, not wanting to let go. The father introduced himself—sort of.

"My kid seems to like your kid," he said, a Brooklyn cadence to his voice. "You live near here?"

"Off the Gloucester Road."

"Oh, uptown."

"That depends on which direction you are coming from."

"Audley Street."

"Uptown."

"Maybe we can make a date—your kid—"

"Cathy."

He grinned at her. Strong, even, white teeth, big smile, black wavy hair—carefully coiffed, the scent of a familiar men's cologne.

"Cathy. Hi. I'm Sy Stewart, Laura's dad." He turned to me. "And Cathy's mother?"

I nodded and added, "Anne Edwards."

He went over and lifted Laura in his arms. He was not a tall man—maybe five foot seven, tops. A little heavier than Tony Curtis, but there was a distinct similarity in their looks and manner. Never could Sy Stewart be taken for any other nationality than American, even if he was silent.

"I'll call you," he said as he was leaving. "I got your number from Kit. Okay?"

"Okay."

In movie-talk, this would be called "meeting cute." But I gave little weight that he was actually interested in me in anything other than to organize a playdate between his daughter and mine and, as Cathy was four years older than Laura, I was not sure that would work out satisfactorily.

· 7 ·

Everything in Life Is a Gamble

If I had known more about Sy Stewart at the onset, I might have seen the danger signals and averted them. I later told myself that I should have been prepared for what was coming. It was not as though I had never found myself hoodwinked by a man's flattering attention or my hungry libido.

His full name was Seymour Stewart Schwartz. He grew up in New York wanting to be rich and famous. The problem was he did not have a great talent that might fulfill his ambition, although he did have style and a certain charisma. He was enamored by the entertainment business—music and films, by the lifestyles of the movers and shakers, the stars, the winners. The world according to Sy was made up of only two groups—winners and losers. Winning was important. He was good looking, quick thinking, and when he finally came to think about it, did have one talent: an ability to sell almost anything—especially himself. He had some early success in the music publishing business, which in the forties and fifties was centered in the Brill Building at 1650 Broadway where something like three hundred music publishers had offices, most with cubbyholes overcrowded with a piano, a bench, and maybe a chair. In these, songwriters performed their pop tunes to a publisher. If the song was bought, it was published. A song's popularity was judged by how many sales the sheet music of it sold. Song pluggers were responsible for upping sales, getting bands and singers to promote them. In earlier times, the street the Brill Building was on was nicknamed Tin Pan Alley, as had its predecessor in lower Manhattan. Sy was able to make his way to the top people. "Always start with the big brass" was his motto. For him, it worked. What he hated about what he did was the stigma attached to the profession. Song pluggers were perceived as being "not too classy." If there was one thing that Sy really wanted to acquire, it was "class." Innately he did possess it. He dressed expensively but never looked flashy. He had an inbred instinct for what was good and admired, not just people who had made pots of money, but those who had achieved something of worth. His education had not included a college degree, but he was a fast learner, recognized knowledge that would be helpful, quickly processed it, and dispersed it with much authority. By the midfifties the song plugger had become outmoded. The recording industry had taken over. Now it was how many records were sold. Sy decided to take a crack at movies one-two-three: 1) find a script (a property), 2) get someone with a name (sales value) involved, and 3) pitch it to a backer (and end up with a fair percentage of the deal). What he was engaged in—promoting—was not exactly a profession. Still, he had the talent and the instinct for it and developed it into a profitable enterprise.

He was not political, although he was a liberal steeped in American values and the godlike memory of Franklin Delano Roosevelt by his Jewish immigrant parents. He had come to London because England was the place where films were able to be made much cheaper than in the States, a pool of talent was ever available, and Hollywood credentials were not required. Promoting on this high a level was not done in an office but during an expensive luncheon or dinner in a four-star restaurant (where the owners and headwaiters knew you as a good customer and big tipper). A clever promoter dressed well, had manicured nails, and was up to the minute on current film transactions and transgressions.

Two or three days after we had met at the Adlers', he called. It was the au pair's day off and maybe my kids could go somewhere with him and Laura. "Cathy doesn't get home from school until after three, and Michael not until five," I told him, adding, "Look, why don't you bring Laura here about 3:30. She can stay for the afternoon and have an early supper. You could pick her up about seven."

"I don't want to just drop her on you."

"It's fine. Really. Three fifteen. Okay?"

They arrived twenty minutes early. "We had lunch and did some shopping and were through early," he said, handing me a Fortnum & Mason bag. "Did I interrupt anything?"

"I usually work when the kids are in school. I'm a writer. But I was just set to quit for the day."

Laura had already found, and was hugging, a giant teddy bear that Cathy had left in a chair, more as a decoration, having passed the stage of playing with stuffed animals. "Pooh Bear," she said. I went over to her. "Not Pooh. A relative, like a cousin. Do you have a cousin?" She shook her head. "Well, like a friend. He can be your friend until Cathy comes home and then you'll have two friends." She seemed pleased with that idea and became involved in a low-voiced conversation with the bear. "Why don't you leave Laura here with me and come back at seven?"

"I'll stay for a few minutes to make sure she's okay," he decided, and sat down in the chair the stuffed animal had just vacated. "Kit Adler told me you are divorced."

"That's right."

He craned his neck for a quick glance toward the front bedroom. "No one . . . you know."

"I'm unattached if that's what you're getting at."

"Yeah. That was what I was getting at. What are you writing?"

"A television script."

"No real profit in that. An original pilot, yes, maybe. You'd get a cut of that."

"Well, it's just a television assignment and I'm glad to have it," I said with an edge.

"Sorry. It's just that with your kind of talent . . ."

"How would you know about *my* talent?" I interrupted.

"Kit Adler."

Laura picked up the teddy bear and placed it on his lap. He put it back on the floor and scooped her up on his knee. She slid back down and dragged the stuffed animal a short distance away. "I'm a little new to being a single parent," he smiled. "Laura was in New York with her mother, my ex-wife, until a month ago when they arrived in London. Her mother left her with me for an evening and was gone. No explanation. No forwarding address. So I have Laura." He sat watching the child—a pretty little thing, very feminine. "I love the kid," he said with great feeling. "She got a bum break and somehow I want to make it up to her." He suddenly changed his mood. "So this television script you're writing—who's it for?"

I told him.

"Second team!" he snapped. "What you need to do is come up with a big idea, one that can appeal to a star, fill a movie screen. I bet you have a dozen of them buzzing around in your head. You should grab hold of one and go with it. Natalie Wood's in town. I saw her the other night at the White Elephant. Bet you could write a helluva script for her. Poor little rich American girl runs away to England and falls in love with an East End Alfie-type guy. The two worlds crash."

Cathy came waltzing in none too thrilled, I suspected, at having a three-year-old to entertain. Like the good sport she always was, she pitched right in and led Laura to her room to show her some of her toys. Sy rose from his chair.

"Seven, you said?"

"Yes, that's fine."

"Stretch it to eight. No, eight thirty. The au pair comes back about eight. I'll bring her here. She can stay with the kids while we go out to dinner."

"Wait a minute! I didn't say—"

"You have another date?"

"That's not the point."

He was at the door. "Eight thirty. You been to the Tiberia? Best Italian in town."

He opened the door then stepped back in. "It's better if Laura doesn't see me leave. Tell her I went on an appointment and will be back later."

"You tell her."

"Father knows best," he said and closed the door after himself. I stood and listened as the lift could be heard descending.

That was how my affair with Sy Stewart—confessed promoter, part con artist—began. Oh, and by the way—gambler, big-time. I was asking for trouble and was likely to get it. But there was something about Sy that was genuinely appealing besides the sexual attraction. There was my incurable need to try to understand what made people tick, to get to the heart of the person. With all his bravado, Sy was a needy man. He was also fun, and that quotient had been missing from my life for a long time.

By 1959 a new wave of Americans had arrived in London and not for political reasons. London was fast becoming a hub of commerce for the international film and music industry. New restaurants were opening every week, it seemed. Italian trattorias were now all the rage. London's nighttime scene was also glitzed by the number of high-end, glamorous gambling clubs that had opened or been refurbished. Yearly membership was required at a cost of anywhere from five hundred to two thousand pounds. The city had always had shops where bets could be placed on almost anything—horses, cricket games, election results. A gambling club was different. They were handsomely decorated, had splendid restaurants and pandering service. Patterned after the casinos in Monte Carlo and the South of France, they had rooms featuring roulette, chemin de fer, 21, and baccarat. The croupiers wore tuxedos. Chips clinked, dice rattled, and the smoke was thick. The clientele were well dressed. Mostly the men gambled while the women remained in the restaurant or sat quietly at the gambling tables as they were plied with drinks and food by the waiters in order to keep them happy.

Crockford's, around since the mid-eighteenth century, had been a favorite of Edward, Prince of Wales. The Curzon Club boasted the best restaurant and highest fees (which would indicate wealthier customers). The White Elephant and the River Club (the two in which Sy had a membership) leaned toward a film and entertainment clientele. There were no singers or acts performing as in the French casinos. People watching was the divertissement. When dignitaries arrived from abroad, they were given guest privileges at the Curzon. When Hollywood personages of note were in the city, they were welcomed at the White Elephant.

I was not blind to the fact that once again I was involved with a gambler. On my second date with Sy we went to the White Elephant. The restaurant was downstairs. After dinner, Sy escorted me upstairs to the gambling room. What took place here would not have attracted the gamblers who had previously played important roles in my life. Horses had been my father's undoing; dice (or craps) my ex-husband's; and Jule—sports. The common link between them had been the slender thread of secrecy that held them to their obsession. They were secret gamblers (or thought they were), much as some people are secret drinkers. For them, gambling was not a social experience.

There were, of course, those in the room who were simply having a good time, "a bit of a go at it," able to win or lose a few hundred pounds at the tables and call it an evening's entertainment. They were seldom at the tables with the serious gamblers, Sy among them, who placed a mound of chips (each worth no less than ten pounds, and often were of one-hundred-pound value) on the 21 table and left them, plus his winnings, for the next deal. This kind of gambling was open, and often a display of confidence, bravado, or "swank" as the British called it—exhibiting that win or lose would not affect your bank balance. This last was not true for Sy, and probably three-fourths of the players. The perception was apparently worth the cost.

I discussed this later with Sy. "Everything in life's a gamble," came the same old routine reply gamblers gave. "You gotta know how to take the ups and downs if you ever expect to win."

Shortly after our relationship began, I saw a psychoanalyst once a week. I needed to find out why I was drawn to gamblers before their addiction was revealed to me. Well, that was one reason. I also had other problems that required some counseling. My analyst, Phil, a wise older man in his midsixties, helped me to sweep out some of the cobwebs in my head, but I continued to see Sy.

Sidney Buchman was the other person on whose intelligence I relied. He never pontificated. Sidney cared, not just about me, my kids, his family, but about why we did things, patterns, the people who could not help themselves, those who made a mark in the world with a little help. "In real estate it's location, location, location," he insisted. "In life it's education, education, education." He was always helping someone out. Perhaps his guilt was a result of his little sister's death. If it was, I hope it eased his pain, for Sidney Buchman was one of the finest men I ever knew. "You can't really be in love with this Sy Stewart," he told me over coffee in the apartment, after we had spent a good part of the day working on a story proposal. "You must see that you are living two quite separate lives. He is not a part of your family life, any more than he is of his own. Nor are you sharing with him what means most to you—your writing. Does he even know—or rather did you tell him what you were currently working on? What is on your mind? In your heart? You see *his* friends. How many of *yours* have the two of you spent time with?"

"The Adlers." I stopped there. Sidney's words struck deep. I had made no effort to combine our worlds assuming, probably correctly, that it would not work.

"Women have hormones, men a sex drive. They equate to much the same thing. I don't say deny them. But, sweet girl (a name he sometimes used, which did not seem demeaning to me), don't confuse sex with love." He smiled broadly. "Of course, if you have both, cherish it."

Within a short time, Sy's ex-mother-in-law arrived in London, a lovely lady of middle-European background. She took a flat near Hyde Park and Laura moved in with her grandmother.

Sy and I were seeing each other two or three times a week. If we stayed together, it was at his apartment on South Audley Street. He was often surrounded by a small entourage of men who viewed him as a leader and were always trying to be helpful or discussing "deals." I left as soon as they arrived. Often on a Sunday we would plan something that involved all three children. Meanwhile I saw my old expat friends on my own whenever I could. What had begun to disturb me was how many of us no longer were socially conscious—that is, to the point of doing something active about it. This seemed especially curious as we had all been so hepped up about the chaos at home, in England and abroad in the first years after we had arrived. Many of our members had turned their original anger at the Committee and Hollywood into self-pity, which I found especially troubling. Sidney called it "a transient madness." None of us had forgotten the violation of our rights we had experienced, so why weren't we more concerned for others who were now in the same place? That is not to say that nothing was expressed or done, it simply did not go deep enough.

I had not been rich and famous in my Hollywood years. However, I had been young enough to start anew. Where, though, had I lost my zeal for protest? As a young woman I had carried picket signs in labor disputes, organized letters of protest to Congress decrying the conditions of our farm laborers, and lobbied in passing bills to aid the veterans of our wars. I had put my pen to paper to develop stories that pointed up injustice and man's inhumanity to man and woman. Maybe that was one reason I clung to, and so admired, Sidney. Every script he chose to work on seemed worthy (his current project, *The Mark*, dealt with England's harsh laws against practicing homosexuals).

I could not speak for the others, but in my case there was a living to be made and there was no market for idealistic stories, even if I did carve out time to write one. More devastating was the cold truth that no such story had fired my imagination. I had folders filled with starts and spasms, but none that I was able to bring to completion.

In the spring of 1960, Judy Garland came to London to recuperate from a serious and mysterious illness that for three weeks had put her on the critical list at New York's Doctors Hospital. She was experiencing severe pain, her body had swollen monstrously, and her voice become a raspy whisper. Her condition was finally attributed to hepatitis, but I don't believe that was ever a proven fact.

Judy's life had been reaching the extremes of up and down from her youth. Now only thirty-eight, she was in a severe state of depression. Her marriage to producer/promoter Sid Luft—her third husband and father of two of her children—had become a living nightmare. Though few outsiders knew it, Sid had encouraged her dependency on pills to keep her performing. He would withhold them before her entrance on stage, and stand in the wings, refusing to give them to her until after she took her bows. ("Like a trained dog who does tricks," she once told me.) Despite the critical acclaim for her "comeback" film *A Star Is Born*, it had not been a financial success. ("Whaddaya mean, comeback? I've always been here!" she cried one time.) Sid did not curtail his lavish expenditures, and Judy was deluged with bill collectors and pressed on all sides for money she did not have.

She was led to believe that her time in London would be work and stress free. Luft had collected a $35,000 advance from Random House on the promise that Judy would cooperate in the writing of an autobiography. However, he had been privately negotiating for her to return for an engagement at the Palladium where, in 1954, she had been a sensation. The deal he made was for her to do two solo concerts called *An Evening with Judy Garland*. When she found out there was little she could do to stop it, the advance from Random House had been spent and no work had been done on the autobiography. Bills were piling up daily and there were Sid and their two children to support.

The media coverage of her presence in London stirred up strong memories in me. As a child of five I had been a member of the Meglin Kiddies, a booking agency for child acts. Judy and her two sisters were also Meglin Kiddies. Luckily, I did not have a stage mother. In fact, Marion had been extremely vocal against my pursuing a career at such an early age. This was, however, in the darkest days of the Depression. Mother and I were living with my uncle Dave and aunt Theo in a small house on the fringe of Beverly Hills. My aunt Theo convinced my mother that I should at least be given the opportunity to try it. Child performers were the current rage on the stage and in the movies. I sang (I was not very good, but I sang loud, a definite advantage as few theaters had microphones), had a good memory for lines and lyrics, and—if not beautiful, was eye catching with my red hair and long legs that looked good in tights (especially for a child of my tender years). Aunt Theo's best friend from their "chorine" days was the tap dancer Ruby Keeler, now married to the star performer Al Jolson and on her way to movie stardom. Ruby came over and gave me tap lessons in the kitchen of the house (I had to dance around the old wood icebox and learn how to bow with one leg behind me—as if I were being presented to a king). Aunt Theo thought I should use the stage name Anne Louise, my full name being Anne Louise Josephson and a bit of a mouthful. My mother agreed and it made little difference to me. I thought dancing was fun, took to it naturally, and was happy to believe that I was pleasing the people I loved.

Judy was five years older than I and when we were together at auditions or at the Meglin studio, she was extremely protective. I quit show business at age nine, after going from the Meglin Kiddies to Gus Edwards Kids (which is when I was renamed Anne Edwards), and ended up tap-dancing on a radio program (how crazy was that!) where the host was Jan Murray. Judy had been signed to an MGM contract. In 1943, at the age of sixteen, I auditioned for a role in the film musical *Best Foot Forward*. I did not get a speaking part but was hired as one of the two dozen or so young students attending the school that was the setting for the movie. A show was planned when a visiting star (Lucille Ball) shows up on campus (too complicated to explain why she was there!). Judy, now twenty-one, was on the lot shooting *Presenting Lily Mars*. She had just divorced her first husband, the considerably older composer/arranger David Rose. At lunchtime in the commissary one day, I noticed her seated alone at a table in a far corner of the room and went over to speak to her.

"Remember me? Anne Louise."

"Anne Louise! My, how you've grown!" she laughed. "Sit down! Sit down!" She seemed genuinely glad to see me and asked me all about myself. I told her I had given up performing but was working on *Best Foot Forward*, as kind of a one-off experience, never having been in a movie before. I told her I saw most of her movies and asked about her two sisters and her mother. She leaned across the table and in a lowered, rushing torrent of words filled me in on all the difficulties in her current life. Her mother was stealing from her. The studio overworked her and had people sneaking around behind her. Her life was not her own. I felt a deep empathetic pain for her. She still looked as vulnerable as she had when we were children; the throbby voice, trembling with emotion, had not changed. Finally, I rose to go. She grabbed my hand and held it tightly. "No! Don't go!" she said. I sat down again, and she leaned back in her chair and started to tell stories about our younger days. She was very funny, suddenly, a changed person until two men came over and told her she had to go back to the recording studio with them.

MGM was like a small town with many buildings and streets that led to them. There was a lot of walking done, from office buildings to structures for makeup, cutting rooms, stages, sets, recording studios, wardrobe, and the back lots where city streets, foreign and domestic, had been constructed. In the next three weeks that I was on the lot I saw Judy a number of times. She always stopped, no matter who she was with, and talked to me, hugging me to her before we separated.

I would never appear in another movie. However, two years later, having just graduated from high school, I had the incredibly good fortune to be chosen by an MGM scout who had seen a school musical that I had written the book and lyrics for (Mark Sandrich Jr., a school friend and son of the director of the Astaire/Rogers musicals, composed the music—later he would write the score for the Broadway show *Ben Franklin in Paris*) and asked me to join the studio's newly instituted Junior Writer Program. It was a dream come true, as by then I knew that writing was what I wanted most in the world to accomplish. Judy was now remarried to Vincente Minnelli and was on the lot making the nonmusical *The Clock* under her husband's direction. (Fred Zinnemann had started as director and Minnelli had taken over after a disastrous beginning.)

Judy and I met again on the lot, and she displayed the same graciousness and affection toward me. Once she took hold of my hand, pulled me aside near the Writers' Building, and in a dead serious voice said, "Anne Louise, don't let them own you!"

She had thought I was acting in films, not writing, so I explained to her what I was doing.

"Oh! How wonderful! That's something I always wanted. To write. I do write sometimes—poetry." She invited me to come on the set whenever I had time. I never did, thinking it might be an imposition. Now, here she was in London. No one could escape the tons of media coverage of her illness, her depressions, her weight and financial problems. There had been no mention yet, however, of a return engagement at the Palladium. I decided to write a little note to tell her I hoped she was feeling better after her hospital stay. I signed it—Anne Louise (Edwards)—and wrote my address and telephone number beneath my signature. A few days later my telephone rang and when I answered it Judy said, in a dramatic, declaratory voice, "Anne Louise, I hope to hell you followed my advice!"

She called often, not always at the best hours. She was having an ugly time with Sid Luft. I don't know if everything she said was true, but if only

10 percent was, Luft was pretty much a villain. She kept talking about writing her memoirs herself. "But you know, Sid owns everything. I can't die without his permission!"

She did two concerts and left tickets for me at the box office for both. Sy was in Paris, so I took Lester for one performance (we were working together on a first draft script for Carl Foreman) and Doris Cole Abrahams to the second. Judy was superb at both performances. The audience went wild. As much as she believed that Sid owned her—onstage, on those nights, Judy owned the theater and everyone in it. When Doris and I went backstage after the last performance, there was a gaggle of people in the hallway outside her dressing room. From inside came loud voices. Sid and Judy were engaged in a terrible row. Doris and I decided to leave.

Around Christmas, I had one last call from her. "I'm leaving Sid," she cried. "He's going to kill me if I don't." She departed for the States on New Year's Eve, flying back alone almost immediately after a record blizzard— snow and wind like London had not experienced in over fifty years. Later, on air, she would tell TV talk show host Jack Paar, "I went for a walk in the snow [during the blizzard]. Suddenly, I realized I didn't give a damn about him [Luft] . . . for a few hours it was difficult—like being shot out of a cannon. It was really terrifying."

"The blizzard?" Paar asked.

"No, leaving Sid. I thought he might come after me."

Sy had returned. I remember that he brought me a huge bottle of my favorite perfume from "Freddie's," the duty-free shop in Paris that everyone with a passport and air ticket visited before leaving Paris as the prices were so good. We went to the River Club after dinner. It was late, maybe eleven p.m. The River Club, which was on the shore of the Thames, was not the best place to be in the freaky, freezing weather and winds that January. The wind howled, the premises shook, and the lights flickered, but it did not seem to impede the gamblers at the table where Sy was playing.

At first he was losing but he kept on playing. It got to be three a.m. I considered calling a taxi and leaving. "Not when I'm behind," he whispered in my ear and then ordered the waiter to bring me a chicken sandwich. Suddenly, his luck turned. He was winning big. Pale light came through the seaside windows. The storm had passed and it was almost morning. By five a.m. a large mound of chips were stacked beside him. I made a rough guess that he had won something in the neighborhood of fifteen to twenty thousand pounds. When the next hand was dealt he pushed the entire pile into the center of the table. He was betting all he had on one draw. He lost the game, giving no evidence in his attitude that this affected him in any way. At the start of the evening he had given me chips that amounted to one hundred pounds. He now asked for their return and handed them to the dealer as a tip, made some small talk with the other players, and had the staff call us a taxi. We rode in silence for a few minutes. Then he said, "Keep the weekend open. Maybe we'll go to Paris."

I called him the next day to say I wouldn't be going and that it would be best if we didn't see each other for a while (my decision made after a session with Phil).

"For a while? You mean you want to break up?"

I told him it just wasn't working. There was too much disparity between our lifestyles. I needed mental stimulation, perhaps more than sexual satisfaction. I loved the theater, ballet, the opera, the concert hall, not celebrity gathering spots and gambling casinos. And maybe, I loved him. At least felt strongly about him, cared for him—and Laura. I added that this was not an easy decision for me. But my kids came first before anything or anyone else. And most important, I needed to be in control of my life, to keep my identity as a working writer, and somehow in our relationship I was losing ground and feeling more like an attachment than a separate person.

"This is it, then?" His voice had hardened.

"Yes."

"Your spin," he said. "It was good while it lasted."

"Yes, it was," I agreed.

"I guess there's nothing more to be said."

"Nothing."

He cleared his throat and after a moment signed off.

I had not told him that I was pregnant.

I needed some time to think. So, instead of Paris, I flew to Switzerland and boarded a train for Klosters to visit my friend Salka Viertel. I first met Salka when I was a junior writer at MGM. She had been a noted actress in Poland in the days of silent film. She married the Viennese director Berthold Viertel and they both immigrated to Hollywood in 1929. Salka would find fame in American films, not as an actress, but as a scriptwriter, whereas Berthold would not do well in the transition. Salka was quick to learn to speak English and would write the screenplays for many of Greta Garbo's most celebrated movies—*Queen Christina*, *Anna Karenina*, and *Conquest* among them. She and Berthold led separate lives. She had a house in Santa Monica where she hosted a fabulous French-style salon every Sunday afternoon where intellectuals and well-known artists comingled.

I had been introduced to Salka on the MGM lot by William Fadiman, the head of the story department and my boss when I was a junior writer. He said some small complimentary thing about my talent and writing potential. Salka made a passing remark that I should come to one of her Sunday afternoon gatherings. This was followed up with a note that requested my presence the following Sunday. I was honored and in wonder at being invited. I was, after all, only seventeen years old.

One particular afternoon remains vivid in my memory. Gathered in Salka's front parlor and dining room, furnished in grand European style were Greta Garbo, Charlie Chaplin (Salka's great friend), writers Thomas Mann, Lion Feuchtwanger, and Stephen Spender. Chaplin came with his elder son, Charles Jr., just two years older than I. Being the youngest in a group of about thirty people, we naturally gravitated toward each other. I would have two or three dates with him after that. I recall him as being a highly emotional young man, not very happy although creating a facade of being so. Salka knew I was an ardent admirer of Thomas Mann, and she made a point of carting me over to where the great writer and his wife were standing and then introducing me. For I believe the one and only time in my life, I was tongue-tied. He was kind and said a few words to me and must have been relieved when someone else approached to demand his attention.

Rumors proliferated in Hollywood (squashed by the ever-vigilant studio publicity corps) that Salka and Garbo were lovers. I do not know that as fact. I was often in both their company in Klosters in the fifties and sixties where Garbo was the frequent guest of Salka. They were most certainly close, dear friends—to that I can attest. They put on no airs with each other. Lesbian lovers? Quite honestly that was beyond my ken to discern. Even at the age I was during that time, I had little knowledge of lesbian relationships beyond what I had read in books of fiction. I pretty much thought what I still do today: physical love between two adults is a private matter and a love strong enough to bond them, whatever their race, color, religion, or sex should be respected. Also, when I visited Salka in Klosters, both women were in their sixties and I saw nothing of a romantic nature pass between them. They were two women of a certain age who had mutual interests and had shared important events of their lives.

Wherever Salka lived she established *une maison Cocotte* of the most interesting and celebrated of artists living or visiting Switzerland who eventually made their way to Klosters. This visit was my third or fourth. Later, I would have a chalet in Klosters. In earlier times, such as followed my breakup with Sy, I stayed at the Chesa Grischuna and brought Cathy with me as Salka had a grandchild, the daughter of her son, the writer Peter Viertel. She lived with Salka when she was not at her Swiss boarding school. Michael had remained in London as a guest of the Adlers.

The Chesa was a special hotel, set well, looking up to the awesome crest of the Gotschna, the Swiss Alps. It was January and the height of the skiing season. The small town was crowded with skiing groups moving in a solid parade to and from the slopes. If warmly dressed I got used to the cold, which was much dryer than London winters, and on most days shafts of sunlight would cut through the clouds and I could sit on the terrace of the Chesa drinking hot chocolate and feel the warmth of the sun lay its hand on my back.

The interior of the Chesa smelled sharply of the fragrant wood used in its construction. There was a great fireplace in the wood-beamed dining room. Meals were included, and you had the same table for the duration of your stay. The rooms were small, cozy, low ceilinged, the beds covered in thick down quilts. Despite the season there were geraniums in the outside window boxes in full bloom, a phenomenon that never ceased to fill me with wonder.

Salka had been blacklisted. She was, it seemed, no longer writing, her life for the time being wrapped around her granddaughter, whose mother had tragically died in a fire caused when she had fallen asleep on a couch with a lighted cigarette. Salka's house was across the road from the rear of the hotel. I recall Garbo and the writer Irwin Shaw (who lived in Klosters for part of the year) being at Salka's the first afternoon of my arrival. Garbo was very relaxed around Salka, dressed in a heavy sweater and wool pants. Salka's secretary, Marian, was also present. The two young girls had gone off into another part of the house.

A French couple were also visitors, as was Irwin who was speaking to them in their language but was receiving puzzled looks. "Speak to them in English, Irwin," Salka demanded. "No one can understand your French!"

Garbo left Klosters the day before I was to depart. "Something's troubling you," Salka told me on the telephone. "Come for lunch."

Marian took charge of the girls and we lunched alone. I took Salka into my confidence about my current condition and that I was considering going to an abortionist.

"That is a very personal decision," she said, pausing for a moment. "Tell me, are you a member of any organized religion?"

"No. I don't believe in them."

"How do you feel about this man? Do you love him?" she asked feelingly.

I thought carefully about it. "Not deeply." I remembered Sy saying one night after we had spent the evening with the Adlers, "We have much more together than they have." I knew that we did not but kept silent. "I would never marry him and I cannot even contemplate the idea of having a child at this time in my life," I finally replied.

"Well, darling, you seem to have made up your mind."

"Yes . . . yes, I have. There is one thing, however." She leaned in closer and took my hand. Her deep-set eyes were fixed on me. I could see how beautiful she must once have been, those amazing eyes, the fine-carved bones of her face. One could not help but note the grace with which she used her hands. "I'm not going to tell him either that I am pregnant or that I plan to have an abortion," I finished.

"Do you think he would stop you if he knew? Or maybe wish to do—the right thing?"

"No. Neither. I just want the relationship to be cut clean. Nothing left open for further discussion. Do you think that's wrong?"

"Who can say what is wrong or right in such cases? A woman's body is her own to do with what she chooses. If you were married it would be another matter—perhaps. Or, perhaps not. I think, perhaps not. It is not my business, of course, but how are you going to pay for this?"

"I have the money. I've been working steadily for the last few months. I was saving it for a trip back to the States to see my mother. But this seems more pressing."

"You must promise me—no back-alley operation?"

"No, no. A good doctor. Not ethical—but reliable and used by the studios."

"Ummm. I know the kind. We had one like him at MGM. Married to Louella Parsons, I believe."

When Cathy and I were leaving, Salka gave me a fond hug. "You'll call?"

"I promise."

Within a week after my return from Klosters, all the arrangements had been made. Since the doctor's name was not a secret in the industry, I called and made an appointment, citing another minor ailment, and went to see him.

His office was on Harley Street where most of the private practices (those not a part of National Health) were located. There remained numberless British citizens of the upper brackets who could afford private care and desired to do so. It could have been a class issue. But I had so far found the National Health excellent and could not have hoped in my past experiences for better care. National Health, however, did not pay for abortions, nor could a doctor in the scheme perform one unless the mother's life was in critical danger. I was perfectly healthy.

When I arrived at the doctor's suite in an elegant Harley Street building, I was led into a private anteroom to wait. The magazines in the rack left to amuse patients while they waited were *Majesty*, and others to do with horses, cricket, and golf. I did not have to fill time for I was almost immediately ushered into the doctor's private—and extremely well-furnished—office. The doctor was of tolerable good looks, extremely fit for a man of his age (I assumed he was in his midfifties) and possessing considerable charm. His hair (dyed dark) had begun to thin and so he combed it forward, much as Raymond did. He wore a well-tailored, expensive business suit and sapphire links on the French cuffs of what appeared to be an expensive Sulka shirt.

The story I had heard about him was that not being from an affluent family, he had been performing abortions while attending medical school to help with his tuition and lifestyle. He had a definite pride in what he did, believing himself to be something of a humanitarian as well as an expert. Someone high up in the Rank Organisation had found need for his discreet services, and so his career had taken wing. He also performed such services as procuring pills for addicted patients—performers, sports figures, and scions of famous or titled families. A recurring rumor was that he supplied the former Duke of Kent (King George VI's youngest brother who died in an air crash in 1942) with drugs for his habit.

He verified that I was seven weeks pregnant, asked a few questions about my past health history, and then in a faintly condescending manner added, "I am in private practice, you know. There will be a fee. Is the gentleman . . ."

I interrupted. "I will be responsible for the cost. How much will it be?"

"Five hundred pounds. Cash," he said, very straight and clear. "Before . . ."

"I understand."

"Fine. Fine." He looked through an appointment book on his desk and suggested a date and time for the following week. I asked him questions on how long the medical procedure would take, what were the possible complications, and what should I do before and after.

"You will be able to go home directly after. But you should have someone of a discreet nature to accompany you. If you change your mind, please ring and simply state that you have to cancel an appointment." He walked me to the door and placed his hand on my shoulder. "Not to worry. You're in good hands now," a declaration that did not entirely reassure me.

I took my time to decide who I could ask to accompany me. Not Sidney, nor Kit, nor Doris, each of whom might try to dissuade me. No one from the expat colony, either, for news was shuttled between them with amazing speed. And certainly not Raymond, who was the only Englishman I knew whom I would not turn to in an emergency. I finally decided on Stanley Mann, an American film writer who had come over with the new wave of Americans and Canadians. He was currently working with Sidney on a screenplay (*The Mark*) on which Raymond was one of the producers. We had met socially and rather hit it off. Stanley was a capable and sympathetic person. Very sensible. I called and asked if he could meet me for lunch at a Chinese restaurant on Kensington High Street. Over a Mongolian hot pot we discussed the situation—or rather, I talked and he listened.

"This is rather new to me," he said, hedging.

"I would understand if you don't feel you can do it."

"And the guy? Where is he in all this?"

"It's over and he doesn't know."

"Have you told Sidney?"

"No. I've told only one friend and she lives in Switzerland."

"What do I do if things—well—if you need . . ."

"I guess at that point you could call the Adlers."

He agreed to take me, but I could see he was not pleased with the idea.

The procedure took no more than a half hour. I rested for a while and then Stanley drove me home. The whole thing had transpired between the time the children had left for school and the time that they returned.

On a Saturday afternoon about two weeks after the abortion, Cathy and I had gone food shopping at Harrods as I was planning to cook Sunday lunch for some friends. The clouds were gray, rain constant by the time we came out loaded with packages. There were no taxis at the taxi rank. We stood under the canopy waiting for the doorman who was trying to hail one for someone ahead of us in the queue. Suddenly I sighted a free taxi coming toward Brompton Road (where we were) from a side street. Switching to a "New York mentality," I grabbed Cathy's hand and took off at a run for the cab, hoping to reach it before the doorman saw it. The street was slick with rainwater. I made it just past the curb, let go of Cathy's hand, and went flying through the air having totally lost my footing. I landed badly, my right leg (my weak one) underneath me. The pain set in immediately. The doorman came running, cars to a screeching halt, whistles blew, and a crowd was gathering. Cathy leaned in close to me.

"Mommy," she said softly, "pull down your skirt."

That day I had decided to wear a dress (I was going to Harrods, after all, and must look proper), and in the fall my coat had flown open and my skirt beneath it risen to my hips, revealing my undergarments. What could I do but laugh? At least two things were certain. I had been raised as a genteel young lady and heeded my mother's oft-said advice, "Always wear a clean pair of panties when venturing out."

An ambulance was quick to the scene. I was taken to St. George's Hospital, about five minutes or less away. My leg was broken badly in two places. After a week in the hospital (the children had stayed with the Adlers) with my leg in a cast from groin to toe, I was brought home in a wheelchair by ambulance. Two burly paramedics got me into the lobby of our building and then were confronted by that narrow, boxlike lift. There was no way that even one of the men could ride up with me. They tried fitting me and the wheelchair in, the idea being that I would ride up alone and they would walk up the four flights of stairs and take me out when I arrived at the top. However, I could not bend my leg because of the cast and had to extend it straight out. The door would not close. No way to go but for the men to carry me up the four flights. They decided it would be a lighter load if I was out of the wheelchair and so up the three of us went with Michael heading the progression by walking backward and holding up my leg.

It took several months before the cast came off. During that time those same two paramedics came twice a week to take me to St. George's for x-rays and therapy, carrying me up and down the stairs. Once the cast was removed and I was on crutches, they picked me up and delivered me with the same gentle care.

The children were so wonderful. I know there cannot be better kids anywhere in the world. I hired a lady to come in for a few hours a day during the week, but Michael and Cathy insisted on doing the cooking and serving of meals. The first efforts were rather disastrous. I remember a charred-almost-to-cinders stew that Michael (now twelve and quite a young man) cooked (he would not let Cathy touch the stove), toast for breakfast that made the burnt toast at the Basil Street Hotel pale by comparison, and eggs that were like small curds. Nonetheless, every meal was served to me on a tray with a pretty doily and a flower in a glass.

By mid-May, I knew I was not well and must make some sort of plan to get myself back on my feet—literally—for my leg was healing slowly and I was seriously anemic. Summer break was coming up, which meant no school. My parents had reunited (at least they were living together part-time) in Miami Beach, Florida, where they had a small house near the beach. Decision made. We three would fly to Miami and stay with them for the summer. With Marion in charge, I knew we would all be well taken care of. I made all the arrangements, bought our flight tickets, contracted the movers to pack up our things to be returned to storage in Hammersmith, and gave notice to my landlord of the date we would be departing. We would simply have to relocate on our return in September. Finding a flat in London was never difficult and this time I wanted a place with either no stairs or a proper lift.

Two days before our departure, Cathy ran a high fever. The morning we were to leave she was covered with red spots. She had the measles. That was a harrowing morning; I did not want Michael to catch them so it seemed the sensible thing was to have him take the flight as planned, and as soon as Cathy was better (the pediatrician said that in ten days she would be fit for travel) we would follow. I changed the tickets, called my mother, and then asked Doris Cole Abrahams to take Michael to the airport and see him off (which she seemed pleased to do and as she had a chauffeur it was no problem). My landlord, a terrible prig, was another matter. The flat had been let, the lease to begin the weekend following our originally planned departure. He had a contract and could not change it. Desperate (and not high on funds) I offered to double the rent for that week's extension and he finally agreed.

All did not go great. Michael's plane hit severely bad weather and had to turn back and land in Shannon, Ireland, where he was put up in the airport hotel for the night, quite an adventure for a twelve-year-old. More telephone calls back and forth to the States and to Michael, with long-distance calling steep in those days.

Came the day that Cathy and I were scheduled to leave and she was still covered with red dots—slightly faded, but quite visible. What to do? Even though the doctor had assured me she could no longer pass on the disease, I doubted that the airline would let her board if they thought she had a communicable disease, and I just could not figure out how we would manage another delay. So I sat her down at the dressing table (which I had used as my desk), got out my makeup bag which contained my old faithful Max Factor pan(chromatic) makeup that I had used since I was a child performer. It was a staple for most performers as it covered up any blemish that might suddenly develop. A singular blemish was one thing. Cathy must have had twenty or thirty marks on her face and neck. I carefully applied a thick covering of Max Factor on each one. Then I took regular makeup and smoothed it over her face and neck, and lastly powdered them. She looked extremely odd for a child her age. But the spots were hidden. I pulled some colored stockings of mine over her legs and held them in place with rubber bands so that no spots on her legs would be visible. The intrigue of it had gotten to Cathy, and she was quite enjoying herself.

We received some strange looks as we boarded the plane but I was certain no British Airways employee would dare such a comment as, "Madam, your child looks odd." Indeed, we made it past passport inspection and onto the plane. Now I had to worry about our landing. It was the law then that a health inspector would come on board an overseas plane's arrival and go up and down the aisles. It had always seemed ridiculous to me before. Now, I understood. I took Cathy into the toilet and once again went to work reapplying my Max Factor. We made it through inspection and customs. We were home free.

Within a few days all of Cathy's measles spots had vanished and both children were enjoying the beach. On the other hand, I took an immediate dislike to my environment. Miami Beach was as unreal as those recreated towns on the back lot of MGM with facades and nothing behind them. I adored my mother and was relieved that my father was not around all that often as his presence always changed the atmosphere into one of stored-up hostility. There was no work for me until I gained back my strength. London and the close community of friends I had left behind were always on my mind. Still, I was not at all well and was most grateful for Marion's tender, life-restoring care, and was especially forbearing in listening to her Christian Science homilies.

· 8 ·

A Time for Dreams—and Norman Mailer

I had arrived in Miami Beach at a time of great chaos. Relations between the United States and Fidel Castro's government in Cuba had hit an impasse. As one of the last acts of his administration, President Eisenhower had closed the American embassy in Havana and severed diplomatic relations between the two countries. Cuba was a small island republic, about the size of Virginia, and just ninety miles south of Key West, Florida. Castro had formalized his alliance with the Soviet Union. Thousands of Cuban exiles fled their homeland, many in rickety boats, and made it to Florida, which already had a sizeable Cuban population.

Non-Cuban residents of Miami remained fairly detached, a feat that truly amazed me. Life simply went on as usual for non-Cuban elderly retirees, the divorcees scouting for husbands, the very rich building beach estates, and the tourists who blew in from winter sodden states up North to loll in the sun, tanning to toast perfection on the beaches, and pumping up their stomachs from the sumptuous buffets served in the splendiferous hotels on Miami's golden shores. Current entertainment stars appeared in their glittering club rooms and lounges. The single missing indulgence were gambling houses which, before Castro's takeover of Cuba, were unneeded as all one had to do was board an inexpensive tour boat over to Havana where hotel rates were low, alcohol cheap, and gambling open—as was prostitution.

My mother was not oblivious to the plight of the Cuban population or their families stranded in their homeland. She would sigh or whisper something of an empathetic nature when she read the newspaper reports or watched the news on television. But Marion had always been otherworldly. She lived in the past—the faraway romantic and historic past. I believe that is how she survived and also it was a part of her charm. Born into a large, upwardly mobile, Jewish family in Hartford, she had been "the beautiful sister" (there were three). Never a part of her postwar, jazz generation, she had graduated from college with a degree to teach English and had married my father, Milton Josephson, instead.

Most people called my father Merk, short for Mercury, as he had been a football hero at New York University where his swiftness down the field to score for his team was almost legendary. He had a dynamic, seemingly invulnerable presence: broad shouldered; strong chin; dark, smoldering eyes; and a hearty baritone voice. Despite his dark, good looks, his parents were Swedish and both looked very much of that stock, as did his blond, blue-eyed older sister, Beatrice. However, the family's Jewish ancestors had escaped the Spanish Inquisition in the fifteenth century and made their way north, finally settling in Sweden. There had been a great deal of intermarriage during the passing centuries, and my father had seemed to have singularly carried the Sephardic gene.

His mother had died, age twenty-one, in childbirth (his lifelong claim for sympathy) leaving his twenty-three-year-old father with two infants under the age of two. But Big Charlie Josephson, an inventor, was a millionaire by then, holding the patent for the first plasticized cloth and for the snap fastener (hooks and eyes had been previously used). Milton was raised by nurses until he was six, when he was sent away to an elite boarding school. After university, he joined the marines and was shipped overseas in the last months of World War I. On return, emotional problems, which lasted throughout his life, plagued him. He never spoke about the war to me, but my mother once told me that he had been only a short distance behind two buddies when they were blown to pieces by a grenade.

Movie-star handsome and very rich, he had a cold, distant father who by then had remarried for the third time, a beautiful war widow younger than his son, and had six children, two from each marriage. With an abundant trust fund, Merk did not have to work for his living, and chose not to. Manhattan in the 1920s was a playground of pleasures for a rich young bachelor. Merk had a noted affair with a stage actress and was engaged for a short time to a scrap-metal heiress. Money slipped like fool's gold through his fingers. Big Charlie came down hard on him with an ultimatum: if he did not settle down within a year, his trust fund would be revoked. An aunt suggested he visit her in Hartford, where she knew just the right young woman for him to meet. Marion was beautiful, bright, and receptive to the idea of such an introduction.

Merk was twenty-eight when he married my mother, thirty-two when, with the advent of the crash, his world collapsed. His trust fund was wiped out, his father's fortune almost entirely swept away. (Big Charlie, strong immigrant survivor that he was despite the Depression, took himself and his young family across the country to Portland, Oregon—a new frontier—and made his way back up in the business world.) Merk had a wife who had taken ill, and a small child of two—me. He had never worked a day in his life and had no clue as to how one earned a living. He was angry and he would remain angry until death did they part.

Marion—who took "till death do we part" seriously—remained a strikingly handsome woman, tall and willowy, with a slender face, flawless complexion, cameo profile, deep-set, dark brown eyes, and remarkable auburn hair that prematurely turned a lustrous, whitish gray by the age of thirty and seemed to enhance rather than detract from her beauty. Yes, she was vain (I often caught her looking at herself in a hanging mirror as she passed it—"Just as always," she would say in a proud manner). It was amazing how little makeup she used. Most often, just a light pencil to her finely arched brows and a carefully applied rose red to her lips. Occasionally, if dressed to go somewhere special, she would powder her face and add a blush of rouge. Lack of funds for a wardrobe (after my father lost all of his money) was never an obstacle for her to look stylish. Added to her small collection of sample dresses—my father contributed from whatever line he was representing on the road at the time—were purchases from the store Mode O'Day, where few items cost more than $2.95. She wore them proudly, a simple, coordinated silk scarf tossed over one shoulder, her posture always aristocratic ("Shoulders back, Anne Louise. Chin up," she would instruct me). Walking through a room, she seemed to float, the verbena scent she always wore trailing faintly behind her. Her vocabulary was curious, studded with the least common words to express herself in a voice that was a bit Brahmin—broad *A*s—prevalent among her peers in West Hartford where her family had lived in her youth (across the street from Dr. Hepburn, his wife, and four children, Katharine among them), before they moved into Hartford proper. A dedicated reader, there was always a book by the side of her bed (wrapped in brown paper if she thought it might be too "mature" for me), fiction mostly, French and English classics quite frequently, and slim volumes of poetry—which she herself wrote and kept in a folder with "POEMS BY MARION" boldly written on the cover.

It was not uncommon for an acquaintance of my mother's to say to me, "Oh! You're Marion's daughter! Your mother is so beautiful!" I felt pride in her beauty, not envy, for Marion was as full of love and warmth and pride in me as my father was in anger and disappointment that I was a girl and, like my mother, not a fit companion for a man who preferred football games and boxing matches to concert halls and books.

To say my parents were mismatched is a monumental understatement. Still, they had managed to remain married all those years (albeit with long separations!). I did not understand it during my youth and really have never done so. Maybe their marriage was good sexually. When together, they always slept in the same bed with the door closed. My father seemed to be a prim man, his bathrobe tightly belted, jacket and tie always worn when he stepped outside. The few times he took me to swim at Santa Monica Beach, a white undershirt covered his chest (although, to be honest, this was somewhat the style in those times). I had little doubt that he much resented the fact that his only child was a girl and one, at that, who showed no athletic inclinations. Once, when I was four or five, he carried me over the hot sand down to the sea's frothy edge, wading in with me until the water reached his waist. Then he pushed me hard from him and shouted, "Swim! Kick your legs! Move your arms!" I can still feel my terror when my head went under and I gagged on the salt water I had swallowed. He pulled me out and held on to me under his arm like some errant domestic animal. Marion came quickly to me. I recall that he said something like, "Even puppies by nature are able to swim!"

My mother spoke lovingly to him and of him, defending him at every turn. Yet I never saw them exchange a kiss or hold hands. He brought home gifts for me from his trips—a small Brownie camera and a tin bank painted like a log cabin. Otherwise he evidenced little affection for me. He was always able to ooze charm to outsiders and to make friends: broad smile, hand in his pocket ready to pay any check that might be placed on a restaurant table. There was a distinct duality in his persona. The man at home was not the same as the public saw. I attributed his paternal coldness to his Swedish heritage, as Big Charlie was so cool to his children and grandchildren. I have considered that he might have been bipolar. Certainly, his wartime experience had a dramatic effect on him as had his motherless childhood and the loss of his money and status. Some time after we had gone to California he had begun to earn a living as a traveling salesman. He never said a good word about any job he ever held. I had the impression that he disliked what he was doing and thought it far below him. Away a good part of the time, when he was living with us there was always a packed suitcase in the corner of some room and his car shined to mirror perfection, ready for a speedy takeoff. I have no idea what he did on his extended absences. In later years I wondered if he might have had a second family stashed away somewhere.

His presence in the house was like waiting for a bomb to ignite. I never knew him to be physically violent, but he was verbally abusive, his booming voice rising like the yowl of thunder. Marion would rush around the room they were in, closing windows as she called out, "Milton! Modulate your tones! The neighbors!" He would then slam doors, finally leaving with his packed suitcase.

He had collected Michael from the airport upon his arrival in Florida then departed two days before Cathy and I arrived. "Your father had to go back on the road," my mother explained. "A man has to work." She sighed and then shifted quickly into a welcoming, celebratory mood.

Marion was a joy to be with. She loved the radio, listened to the soap operas, and sang along in a modestly trained high, coloratura voice with the music programs. She was a fabulous cook, and the small house we were in was tantalizingly redolent of the spices she used. Each plate she served was a work of art. She did most of her cooking without the help of a cookbook, a feat I considered quite amazing as she tended toward complicated dishes, cakes, and pastries made from scratch. Within a week, I began to gain a few pounds and also to relax. Mother would read to me from Mary Baker Eddy's book on Christian Science. She was as devout as ever. "I know you don't believe as I do," she told me. "But just do me a minikin favor and listen to this passage." "Minikin" was one of her favorite words. It meant minimal or a little bit and was archaic. "Just eat a minikin for my sake," she would plead when my appetite wasn't up to where she thought it should be.

Michael was a happy kid. The house was across Collins Avenue and one of Miami's smaller hotels, the Beachcomber. He went there every morning, and finally the owner asked if he would like to earn a few dollars (and tips) at the pool by fetching lounge cushions for guests. I was not in favor of the idea. Still, he put up a convincing argument. He thought he might not be able to continue going there if he did not take the offer, and he liked the people and being able to swim in the pool. He was an extremely strong-willed boy. He was also rather short for his age and picked up the nickname "Stretch" as he managed those lounge pillows which were about six feet long.

Cathy was a vivacious, very pretty child, not fond of swimming, or enthusiastic about anything too athletic. Extremely social, she made young friends easily and won over adults. She was thriving beautifully with the attention she now had from both me and her grandmother. I did not know how it would all work out once my father returned from the road. Also, Marion was managing on next to nothing and my abortion, the move from the apartment, and our airfares had eaten up most of my reserve. A month into our stay in Miami, my health considerably better, I answered an ad for a model/salesperson for H & J Blitz, a jewelry store in the Americana Hotel. Model for jewelry? The idea was intriguing. I was hired. It was surreal. Every two hours, the elderly Mr. Blitz, a delightful Dutch gentleman, would drape me with jewelry—bracelets, necklaces, broaches, and rings on my fingers. I would then walk around the pool area, stopping at the cabanas and poolside lounges, a security guard a few steps behind me. I was paid a smallish wage, but if any of the merchandise I wore sold, I got a hefty commission. I did surprisingly well. This would be the only job I would have in my life that was outside the world of entertainment and publishing.

Marion decided that I needed to meet some people my age (a euphemism for eligible men). One of her friends had a bachelor son who was a doctor (every mother's dream for her daughter in those days). Ben was a heart-and-lung specialist with a successful practice. Obviously prompted by his mother (who had been prompted by my mother), he called and asked me out to dinner. He was a well-dressed man about thirty-two, a bit plump ("Hardly plump," Marion had countered when I described him. "A bit adipose, perhaps") with a small, trim mustache beneath a rather large nose. However, he took me to one of Miami's best restaurants—so at least he was not a skinflint. My smoking became the central topic of conversation for the evening. Did I realize it could kill me? First, though, I would become addicted. In fact, I probably was already addicted. My heart and lungs would become diseased (if they already were not). I might have to live out my life reliant on an oxygen tank. He refused to let me smoke after dinner. "You have children. Do you want them to get a life-threatening disease as the result of your smoking?"

I was not a heavy smoker. Maybe three or four cigarettes a day smoked during breaks in my writing, and one after dinner. "It's your body, fine," he said. "But you are poisoning the atmosphere every time you exhale."

I took great offense at his turning our evening into a lecture.

"Look," he finally said when driving me home. "You may not like me, but I want to see you break this habit."

"Why me? You hardly know me," I asked.

"It has to be done one by one until the cigarette companies are stopped. It's my mission," he asserted. Then he made me agree to accompany him the next morning to the clinic where he was on staff.

He arrived at our door promptly at seven a.m. What I saw that day in the clinic was a wake-up call. Wearing a white doctor's jacket, he had me walk beside him in a ward. There were patients unable to speak, a hole surgically made in their throats so that they could breathe, their speech sounding robotic. Yet some were inhaling from a lighted cigarette, the smoke entering and exiting through that hole. I never dated Ben again. I did, however, eventually stop smoking, that image of the people in the clinic unable to erase.

Marion did not give up on her matchmaking. Another friend had a son who was a dentist (perhaps not as "select" as a heart-and-lung specialist, but guaranteed not to have as many emergency calls late at night and on weekends, she counseled). His name was Jerome and I was most resistant. "Just meet him, darling, for me." She suggested I make an appointment for either myself or Cathy. Since Cathy's teeth had not been checked for quite a while, I made an appointment for her.

Jerome was youngish—in his thirties. Nothing special, but not unattractive. The office was not child friendly, leading me to believe that he did not have many children as patients. I stood by my daughter as she sat down warily in the dental chair. Jerome and I exchanged a few words. "I met your mother recently at our house," he said. Aha! He still lived at home. "Beautiful woman." Not too tactful. Then he turned to concentrate on his young patient.

"Open wide—there's a good girl." He leaned in close with a small metal tool and a dental mirror to see better into her gaping mouth. He probed deeper, toward her back molars. ZAP! Cathy bit down hard. He let out a very unprofessional, "SHIT!" as he swiftly withdrew his hand the moment she opened her mouth again. There was blood oozing all the way down the starched white sleeve of his medical jacket.

Forget Jerome.

Miami did not offer a great deal of intellectual stimulation. But what it lacked, the nearing presidential election, covered on television, supplied. The race was between John F. Kennedy and Richard M. Nixon, the latter an incomprehensible choice for any liberal. In my free time, I was glued to my parents' small TV set watching the debates and the commentaries. Kennedy was young and inspirational, a war hero, married to the intelligent and most attractive, Jacqueline Bouvier Kennedy. They were a couple who could proudly occupy the White House.

Physically I was doing well, walking with a minimum of discomfort and, best of all, an even gait and was able to handle the job at the Americana Hotel without much strain. Still, the money I was paid was not enough to refill my coffers so that we three could return to London—which I was determined to do, especially after my father returned from the road and an uneasiness settled like thunderclouds over the house again. I knew I had to find myself a writing assignment. I contacted Ted Ashley in New York, and he came through a few weeks later with an offer of two television segments of a series being shot in New York. Still skeptical about the credit, Ashley drew up the contract in another name. That was fine with me. By now, television was a means for survival. It was not what my heart and mind told me I should do for the rest of my life. Yet, neither did it prevent my writing short stories or a chapter or two of that novel that was still brewing in my head even if very little of it was being transferred to paper.

As September approached, the children were enrolled in Miami schools, and I felt compelled by that (and finances) to leave them with my parents for the eight to ten weeks I would be in New York (coming down to Florida for weekends whenever possible). I was not happy about them living in the same house with my father for such an extended period, for it had never been helpful to me as a child. But, as it turned out, two weeks after he returned, he went right back out on the road again. Marion was thrilled with the prospect of having Michael and Cathy in her care, and I would be earning enough to send her funds and still stash some away. From what I could glean from my mother, my father was having "some problems" in Miami. There never had been a problem that my father could not run away from. He was an expert at it.

Early autumn in New York can be a place of extraordinary beauty— and it was. The fairly low-priced Adams Hotel, where I had a small but comfortable room (and a closet with a hot plate and a minisize fridge), was on East Eighty-Sixth Street off Fifth Avenue and just a few steps from Central Park. The place had a rather clubby feel to it. Many visiting theater people and playwrights stayed there. Arthur Miller had a two-room accommodation on a higher floor while I was resident (I can't remember what play he was working on—but he pretty much locked himself in and was seldom seen in the lobby). A few of my California friends now lived in Manhattan— writer Vera Caspary (probably best known for *Laura*), who had been one of my mentors in my Hollywood days; Greta Markson, my closest childhood friend, now an actress appearing on Broadway in a supporting role in a Joseph Cotten play; and, of course, the Rossens, who had moved from 1010 Fifth Avenue to a building on the corner of West Eighty-Sixth Street and Central Park West. I had seen Bob and Sue in London several times. Bob had gone through much emotional stress. His affair with Elise was over and had not ended well. Sue had been forgiving. But he was not in good health, due to diabetes and other complications.

I was still reading for him. Two years earlier I had come across a softcover edition of a Walter Tevis novel, *The Hustler*, which had not been a best-seller and had been passed over by the studios. Before coming to Hollywood in the 1930s, Bob had written *Corner Pocket*, a play set in a pool hall about pool-hall hustlers. Never produced in New York, he had tried to get studio interest when he was under contract to Warner Bros. They found the setting—a dingy, smoke-filled lower East Side, 1930s pool hall—too seedy and the tough, beer-swilling characters not likeable enough. *Corner Pocket* remained Bob's one lost, but favorite, work. Tevis's novel, updated to the 1950s, had brilliantly managed to bring more action, better characters, and suspense. Bob took an option on the book and, with an excellent adaptation by Sidney Carroll, directed and produced the film. I am sure he was a close advisor on the screenplay. But Bob, like Sidney, believed that taking on all three top tasks on a movie was riding a slippery slope. The film was enjoying excellent reviews. It would play a major role, along with *Body and Soul* and *All the King's Men*, in cementing Robert Rossen's legacy as a filmmaker.

The Rossens' new apartment was on a direct route through Central Park to the Adams. One night I joined them for a small dinner party that included

Shelley Winters, Charlie Katz (a powerful left-wing lawyer), movie producer Bernard Smith and his stylish wife, Frances, and Norman Mailer, the controversial young novelist known as much for his macho public behavior as for his early World War II literary sensation *The Naked and the Dead*. Bob was interested in Norman's satiric novel of Hollywood, *Deer Park*, published a few years earlier to dismal reviews. Despite the book's muddled plot and mainly unsympathetic characters, the novel contained one major, interesting figure (at least to Bob)—an informer during the early years of the blacklist—through whom Bob might have thought he could channel some of his own emotions.

Shelley Winters, recently divorced from the actor Anthony Franciosa, was more Raphaelesque than I remembered from her movies. Her frankness was a revelation. The evening was lively. Hollywood was skewered. Bob was in especially sharp form, throwing words like a veteran boxer's precisely aimed left-hand jabs, his cool, blue eyes never missing a move of anyone within his sight range. His smile was more of an appraisal than an expression of pleasure, but it seemed clear he was, indeed, enjoying himself. Many people found Bob difficult to like. But, through the years, I had been drawn to a warm and magnetic side of him. He had a strong belief in family bonds, a sentiment which probably had weighed in against continuing his affair with Elise.

Watching Bob at a gathering of like, bright people was always fascinating. He was expert at engaging them in controversial issues. He was not a man who could tell jokes or relate stories of his colorful past history. He spoke in a low, confidential manner that demanded attention, and doted on one-to-one confrontation. At times, a conversation with him was somewhat of a sparring match. A kindred spirit was evident between him and Norman. Both were keen wordsmiths, short, weighty, but vital, ego-driven, Jewish men with a pulsing need to prove themselves right and to come out on top in any debate or competition. Even Shelley—who could throw a pretty good verbal punch herself and whose voice was a sharp, ragged-edged knife—was no contender.

Norman paid scant attention to me except for those moments when he thought he had shot a zinger—at which point he would glance slyly over to where I was seated across the table from him and raise a bushy eyebrow. After dinner, when I rose to leave, Bob said he would have the doorman hail me a taxi. Norman jumped to his feet. "Where are you going?" he asked.

"Crosstown. East Eighty-Sixth."

"I'll take you," he offered.

Sue was quickly at my side. "Stay awhile longer," she insisted with unusual urgency.

"No, I should have an early night," I declined. "I have a breakfast meeting."

She took me by the arm and steered me toward her bedroom. "You can't go with Norman! You know, he knifed his wife!" she said, eyes wide, back stiff.

That had been last year's news. Adele, although seriously injured, had recovered and had not pressed charges. Norman had received a suspended sentence—no jail time. The Mailers were living apart and Adele was petitioning for divorce. She was his wife, his domestic partner, someone with whom Norman had a troubled history before what was surely a vicious and unforgivable attack. Still, I did not see him as a danger to me, a woman he hardly knew. I thanked Sue for her counsel and rejoined the group, where I accepted Norman's offer. After all, we would only be alone during a five-minute ride through Central Park.

The road was brightly lit on this warmish, autumn night. Norman asked me many questions. What was my relationship to the Rossens? I told him he was my children's uncle through my ex-husband. How did I feel about his being an informer?

"At first I was furious, disappointed. I wrote him a very nasty letter. He replied, 'Sorry you feel that way, kid. Someday, maybe you'll understand.'" I thought about it a moment before adding. "It's complicated."

He let it go at that. "Rossen seemed primed to make toast of me," he laughed. "I gave him the edge. He was buying dinner, after all."

"I think he admires you. I'd guess he's even a bit fascinated by you—the young genius, the macho man, hell-bent for destruction."

"That your opinion?"

"I have no opinion. We've just met. I'm seeing you through Bob's eyes and sifting tabloid headlines. I know him pretty well and think he sees pieces of himself in you—say twenty years ago. He's been writing that character for decades. All those John Garfield movies he made for Warners. His own film— *Body and Soul*—the moxie fighter who sells out for money and possible fame. He's drawn to tough guys who fall and then become heroes. He would have loved to have gone to war and written a novel about it like *The Naked and the Dead*. He didn't fight because of the diabetes and was 4-F'd and never wrote a novel because he was too much in awe of literary works to chance failing at it. Failure is not in Robert Rossen's vocabulary."

When we reached the Adams, he pulled up in front and turned off the motor. For about a half hour we continued our conversation. He asked if I had read *Deer Park*. When I said that I had, he wanted to know what I thought. I was honest, but not unduly harsh in my criticism, which centered on what I thought was an unsatisfactory plot and flawed characters. He immediately changed subjects and asked what I was presently writing. When told, he inquired, "Why?" in a disdainful manner.

"I have two children who grow hungry three times a day and require a roof over their heads," I explained.

"What do you really want to write?"

"A novel. I've started several. Lately, I've thought it should be about Hollywood and those of us who found ourselves in Europe after the blacklist went into effect." This had actually been occupying my thoughts all the time I was in Florida.

"Any time you have something on paper, I'd be glad to read it."

"I've never been too crazy about that idea—having a work read before I feel I have given it my all. Readers, no matter how well intentioned, at an early stage can often sway you into rewriting and then you are in danger of losing the original impetus of the story."

He slammed his hand hard against the steering wheel. "I think that's what happened to *Deer Park!*" he exclaimed. He went into some detail as to how he had insisted the early manuscript (which had been rejected by his editor) be read by an outside reader and when that opinion proved negative, passed it on to someone else. The novel had been rejected multiple times before finding a publisher. He was quite emotional about this whole episode. Accepting harsh criticism was obviously not one of Norman Mailer's better character traits.

He asked if I would have dinner with him the next night. I agreed.

"Eight, okay?"

"Fine."

There were three messages from Sue. "Thank God, you're all right!" she said when I rang back. "But my advice for you is not to see Norman again," was spoken as an order. Sue could be both abrasive and self-righteous at times. She had been raised in a tough New York neighborhood where a girl had to fight for respect and independence. It had been a struggle to secure an education, and she had achieved it and, before she married Bob, succeeded to get a job as one of the first editors on the newly formed Literary Guild Book Club.

Sue had believed in Bob's talent as an unproduced playwright and supported him during their early years of marriage. His success had not mellowed her, but she had been a concerned friend to me, her advice—although often unsolicited—always offered with good intention.

The next evening I dressed and was ready by eight. When a half hour passed and no Norman, I figured that he had changed his mind. I was about to settle in for the evening when the telephone rang. "There is a *very* drunk man asking to see you, Miss Edwards," the front desk clerk said sotto voce. "*Very* drunk. What shall I do?"

"Tell him I'll be right down," I responded in a bit of a panic. The last thing I wanted was a scene in the lobby of the hotel.

Norman was standing stage center in the small entryway. He was well dressed, but his thick head of dark, curly hair was in disarray and he was unsteady on his feet. I quick-stepped to his side, took a strong grasp of his arm, and walked with him out the front door to the street. The question was, what should I do next? He had come in a car and I thought it a bad idea for him to get back in it and drive—with or without me.

"There's a seafood restaurant around the corner on Madison called the Captain's Table. We can go there," I said in an authoritative voice and, holding on to him in a tight grasp, headed him in that direction. We were given a table close to the front of the restaurant (which turned out to be a good thing). When we were seated I took a hard look at Norman. His remarkable blue eyes were bleary but he appeared somewhat more sober, perhaps due to the short walk in the evening air. He ordered lobster dinners and drinks and talked in a constant stream. I can no longer recall what he actually said as it seemed to have no relevance to me, to him, or the evening. His voice began to rise. The maître d' nervously hovered around our table.

Finally, our dinner plates—each holding a large, glaringly red, boiled lobster, giant claws rubber banded as though to keep the monster from rising from hell and jumping up to attack—were placed before us. I glanced up to thank the waiter. The man's expression suddenly changed from servility to one of shocked horror. I looked back toward Norman. He had collapsed facedown on his plate, melted butter sputtering and splattering onto the table. The maître d' immediately reappeared. My first thought was that Norman had suffered a heart attack, and I asked the man to call the paramedics. "I don't think so, madam," he whispered to me. "The gentleman has simply had too much to drink and has passed out."

I told him to get me a taxi, took out what money I had to cover the bill, and with his help and that of the waiter (Norman only showed a slight sign of awareness) got him out of the restaurant, onto the street, and finally into the backseat of the cab, a feat—since Norman was a man of some girth—not an easy task. It dawned on me at that moment that I did not know where he lived. Also, I had given the restaurant all the cash I had. We could not return to the Adams. No way could Norman remain in my room for the night. I reached inside his jacket and found his wallet (shades of Samuel Taylor!). Inside was his driver's license with an address in Brooklyn, which was a long ride from Eighty-Sixth Street. I retrieved two twenties from it, handed them to the driver, and told him to take Norman to that address and to see him to the door and make sure someone took him in. "If there is any problem, call me," I added. I gave him the number of the hotel. Then I slid the wallet back in Norman's jacket pocket.

After the taxi disappeared, I felt acute apprehension. I had no idea what I would do if no one was at the address the driver had been given. And what if the man did not take Norman to Brooklyn? There had been quite a large sum in his wallet. I was up the entire night with visions of Norman being thrown unconscious out of the vehicle into a ditch off some dark road. I had not taken the taxi's license plate number. I did not know any of Norman's friends, or how to reach Adele. There was no one I could call (I supposed Sue as a last resort). My phone remained silent throughout the night. That could be good—or it could be bad. Midafternoon, Norman rang.

"Do you know where you sent me last night?" he shouted into my ear.

"No. Where?" I replied weakly.

"To my mother's house." Then he burst into raucous laughter. It seemed that he and Adele had been in California and Mexico for an extended period before his attack on her and the breakup of their marriage and, when he returned to New York, his driver's license had expired. Not yet having a permanent address, he used his mother's. Fanny Mailer had given him a tongue-lashing for appearing on her doorstep in such a drunken state. I later learned the control Fanny had over Norman. His father had been powerless in family affairs. Fanny had run the house and made the decisions for Norman and his sister Barbara. Her only son was everything to Fanny. She fought like a tigress for him during his youth, defended him to the world once he was an adult and a celebrity. Privately, Fanny Mailer was, at least at that time, the one person in Norman's life to whom he felt he had to answer to.

He appeared at my hotel an hour or so later, intending to collect his car. By this time, however, the traffic police had towed it away. No explanations for what had occurred the previous evening were offered, none requested, no apologies rendered (he did, however, insist on repaying me for the uneaten dinners). I never had the courage to revisit the Captain's Table. But I did see Norman quite often while I worked on my assignments. One night we went to an Italian restaurant in Spanish Harlem where he apparently was a frequent customer. Norman's choices for dining, companions, or entertainment were unusual. He invited me to a boxing match and I refused. We went to some off-off-Broadway shows. We had a few peppery exchanges. I accused him of being antifeminist. "The hell I am!" he shouted back. "No one loves women more than I do!"

"Only in the bedroom!" I countered. Actually, Norman liked women and subscribed to Momism. But he could become venomous toward women who he felt were militant or defiant of men. Following the contentious discussion we had previously had about *Deer Park*, I did not mention his writing again—although we extensively discussed the work of other writers.

Norman was a great fan of Ernest Hemingway. I don't think he deliberately tried to emulate him—either in his writing or his creature habits. From the back history of his life that he revealed to me (and it was difficult, as he was a consummate storyteller, to know what was real, embroidered, or borderline lies), I gathered that he had possessed a combative nature since early youth. There were two Normans, really. One was the short, feisty son of a dominating Jewish mother, who more than anything courted her approval. The other saw himself as a younger Hemingway: adventure loving, shock provoker, new-world writer. Hemingway was his unique idea of the macho, intellectual man. He was also obsessed with the idea of the writer as celebrity.

Hemingway's shotgun suicide in July 1961 and the media follow-up in years to come, which asserted that he was bisexual, was a major jolt to Norman, for he had considered him to be the symbol of masculinity with an almost mythological fixation. After all, the man was a big game hunter and was mixed in the intrigue of foreign wars. He was hard drinking and endured embattled marriages. That fatal shot left an impact on Norman. Still, as long as I knew him (and we would remain friends for many years) he never let go of his need to be considered Hemingway's literary descendent.

Norman was a person of great warmth and sensitivity. He could also be light and fun. I much enjoyed his company during those short months in New York. He loved to hear Hollywood stories (and to tell them) and was deeply interested about life among the London expats and, most curiously, pressed me for what I knew (that the world might not), related to members of the royal family.

When I had finished my work in New York (and collected my check) I flew down to Miami and made immediate plans for we three to return to London. We arrived in time for me to cast my ballot for Kennedy in the presidential election. Letters to and from Norman hen-pecked their way across the Atlantic for a time. He considered himself a soldier in the "New Left," an ecumenical, political, and ethical mixture that avoided narrow ideological labels, and complained that other New Leftists refused to see him as "a comrade in arms." He sent me copies of articles he had written for the *Village Voice*, which was not obtainable in London. In one letter he joked that I would not believe "how respectable" he was getting. He sent along an open letter to the president that the *Voice* published in which he addressed him as "Dear Jack," and then chided him in seeking advice about Cuba from the CIA when he would have been better served by artists like himself.

[Flash forward: In the early '70s, after I had published several novels, I wrote a profile of Norman for the *Atlantic*. He read it, of course, and wrote back to compliment me on "the best writing you have done."]

A year or so after my return to London, Norman married Lady Jeanne Campbell, daughter of the Duke of Argyll, granddaughter of the powerful British newspaper magnet, Lord Beaverbrook, and quite a formidable woman. They had a daughter, Kate (Norman's fourth child), and then divorced. We remained friends through the years and he never tired of telling the story of the night I sent him home drunk in a taxi to his mother.

It is strange about England. One can be away for long periods and when you return nothing seems to have changed. By 1961, most of the bomb sites had been replaced with new-era buildings (of questionable architectural value). Still, the queue mentality remained. The obsession with the royal family was just as fervent. There was always a royal celebration to look forward to—the spectacle of the Queen's arrival for the State Opening of Parliament, her birthday celebration (held in June and not on her birth date), the family's seasonal peregrinations from Buckingham Palace to Sandringham to Windsor and on to Balmoral in Scotland—all covered by the press. Rain was a frequent and accepted inconvenience. The Chelsea Flower Show was the bright spot each spring as it had been since 1862 (time out for wars). There was a monotony to the sameness along with the sense of continuity. Yet, something seemed afoot, an inkling of a new period. Jet planes flew the Atlantic in seven hours. Heathrow Airport had expanded and there were moving sidewalks to take passengers from high-numbered gates into the distant terminal to collect their baggage. The British theater was alive with left-wing plays. British musicals were competing with Broadway, and Anglo-American films were a thriving industry.

Until we located we three stayed at the American Hilton Hotel, a twenty-eight-story, towering eyesore on Park Lane (the hotel advertised "509 beautifully decorated rooms all with American-style comforts," apparently meaning central heating, constant hot water, and a small drinks cabinet in each room). The children were delighted with the hotel's three disparate restaurants—a Swedish open-sandwich cafe, Trader Vic's Polynesian-style restaurant serving pupu platters, and mysteriously, on Sunday mornings, bagels and smoked salmon—and the elegant rooftop dining room featuring expansive windows that gave diners a view that included the Queen's private gardens and the windows of Her Majesty's own apartments at Buckingham Palace. The latter remained a controversy and scandal ("those gauche Americans!") for the year it took for the palace to relandscape the gardens so as to block the intrusion. The incident did not help Anglo-American relations. I don't think the name of the hotel was actually the *American* Hilton, but that is how it was always described in the tabloid press, obviously a bit of a slur.

Behind the hotel was Shepherd's Market, a warren of narrow streets with a jumble of unusual, small shops. Michael was allowed to take Cathy there. His favorite stores sold lead soldiers as he collected whole, miniature regimental military bands. He played the trumpet amazingly well and fortissimo and could not wait until we settled someplace so that he could blow as loud and bluesy as he wished. I was impatient to find us a home. London's rumble of change ahead had awakened me. For too many years my career had been ruled by financial need. I had gone down the path of quick and easy. Now I was determined to concentrate on what I wanted to achieve, not only in my career but in my personal life.

· 9 ·

Love and Other Emotions

$\mathcal{A}$side from Kit Adler and Doris Cole Abrahams, I had few close women friends in London. I attribute this, correctly I believe, to the fact that I was a working single mother, earning our keep in a pretty much male-dominated industry and that the majority of wives in the expat American film colony were a good deal older than me. With scant exceptions, preblacklist and back in the States, they had been housewives, dedicated to social functions and to their families. Only a small number had been as political as their mates and now, their children (in most cases, at least a decade older than mine) fairly independent. They sought to find activities to fill their free time that involved lunches with other women in similar circumstances, and shopping. We met at largish social gatherings or film showings. I attended dinner parties at their homes—but an extra woman was not as convenient as an extra man. I, perhaps, was not as sociable as I might have been, as I had to scrounge for any small bit of free time. I did not find their activities objectionable. Our priorities just happened to be at odds.

I would like to think that none of those women saw me as a threat. Being a considerably younger single woman might have rung bells. I was always careful to keep my friendships with married men with whom I worked on a strictly business basis, a decision made long before when I had chosen films as a career, well aware that it was a male-dominated industry. Actresses and secretaries often became involved with Hollywood's married men—creative and executive. I wanted no part of such arrangements. Morality had some part of it. However, I was too self-motivated, too prideful, to place myself in such a compromising and demeaning situation. I viewed myself as a businesswoman and always did my best to transmit this message to the men I worked with—many of whom did become good friends, but that was all.

It is said that men almost always have sex on their mind when in the presence of women and that most women dress to be sexually attractive to men. I cannot claim I know what is at any time in the mind of a man. I can attest to the fact that in my business dealings with men, I never made an effort to be considered sexually attractive. I dressed to be comfortable and in the best taste I could afford. I had only two unpleasant experiences of sexual harassment in my long career, and they had been in my early days in Hollywood. When I was nineteen, one producer—who was interviewing me as a prospective writer for television, chased me around his desk and then attempted to block my leaving his office. As I was near the door, I threatened to scream loudly so that everyone in the building could hear. "Come, come, dear," he cajoled and advanced closer to me. I let out a deafening scream (as a child, I had, after all, not required a microphone to be heard up in the far reaches of the balcony), which brought instant pounding on the door. He scurried back to his desk. Several employees were standing on the ready when I stepped out into the hallway.

"What happened?" someone asked.

"I saw a rat!" I replied and rushed past them to the elevators in the building.

The second incident also occurred in those early Hollywood years. A well-known actor at the time, Scott Brady, whom I knew from the television show that I worked for as story editor, had volunteered to drive me to an industry meeting, which he said he planned to attend as well. He headed into the Hollywood Hills where he lived instead. When he parked the car (after a lively argument), legs agape, he grabbed hold of my shoulders and started to pull me to him. I still had hold of my pocketbook and slammed it smack center, hard on his rising manhood, got out of the car, and walked all the way down the mountain to Sunset Boulevard, a mighty hike, where I could get a bus.

He did not follow me.

When the occasion presented itself, I had friends, couples and singles, over for dinner. I remember small gatherings with William and Betty Graf (new arrivals, he would produce the Academy Award–winning *A Man for All Seasons*), the Adlers, Lester Cole, the blacklisted film composer Sol Kaplan and his wife, the actress Frances Heflin (sister of actor Van Heflin), Frances and Ring Lardner Jr., Sidney Buchman, whenever he was in London, and of course, whatever friend was over for a visit from the States. At least once a week, the harmonica virtuoso Larry Adler, blacklisted and recently divorced, would, uninvited, ring my front doorbell at about seven p.m., just as we three were settling down to dinner. I called him America's guest as I could hardly avoid extending an invitation for him to join us. He never refused. We three were happily ensconced in a well-appointed Victorian row house on Hasker Street, which bordered Chelsea yet was also near Brompton Road and Harrods, Coopers' supermarket, and a huge Boots pharmacy that carried everything one needed for bath, beauty, and beyond. There were also new, intriguing specialty and antique shops around the corner from us on Walton Street. Somewhat larger than our former home on Markham Street, we enjoyed a modern, remodeled kitchen, adequate dining room—with room for eight chairs, if a bit crowded, and a bright living room. There was a service area under stairs but I turned it into more of a family room as it backed the garden. The master bedroom was on the first floor, two additional bedrooms above.

Michael was attending Central High School in Bushey Park, situated on an American army base in Hertfordshire. Despite it being a fifteen-mile daily commute back and forth by bus and tube, the selection of the school, after some objections on my part, had been agreed. Due to his advancements, Michael would in two years be going off to college. He was very clear in his decision to obtain his degree in the States. The University of California, Berkeley, appealed to him—most certainly due to its current wave of much-publicized student political action. As certain subjects not in the British curriculum—American history and civics, mainly—would be required for him to pursue his chosen major, political science, an American school was necessary. Nothing I could say re the inconvenience of the distance (and my own concern of him traveling back and forth alone—sometimes in bad weather and dark days) deterred him. Michael was mentally mature for his age. I often said that he was born with a fully developed brain. By now, he knew exactly what he wanted and had well-honed skills in reasoning and debating. My pride in him was enormous.

Cathy's current school, Glendower, on Queen's Gate, was a ten-minute bus ride from home. To attend she was obliged to wear the school uniform, the purchase of which was a yearly ritual in Great Britain where a large percentage of young people from middle- and upper-class families were entered in private schools, perversely called "public schools." (I don't know if they offered scholarships to low-income students. I hope that was the case. But I have to admit that I did not pursue the matter as I might well have done back home.) Each school uniform had a unique color combination and style that set them apart. Department stores of size had school uniform sections. With Cathy in hand we made our way to Peter Jones. About half of one floor was entirely devoted to school uniforms, girls' and boys' in separate departments. That day it was bustling with mothers and children, ages six to twelve; uniforms for upper-grade students were sold on another floor. Racks jammed with jackets, skirts, and trousers, short and long, lined the walls divided by a card that had a school's name on it. Tables were covered with socks, mitties, shirts, ties, hats (for the girls), and caps (for the boys). To be a part of this rite was to understand a great deal about Great Britain's class system. Children at free, government schools (except for orphanages) wore no uniforms and therefore were looked upon as being from families of lesser means. School colors created a further classification. Schools were not always considered socially equal. I had no idea how Glendower rated on England's social scale. We chose it as 1) it was close to home, 2) it had a high scholastic standing, and 3) Cathy had a friend who also attended. The Glendower uniform was striking: deep-plum-and-mauve-crested jacket, gray skirt, and a perky gray hat with a plum ribbon. My daughter loved clothes (I recall most vividly a particular yellow dress she desperately wanted for her fourth birthday), so the attractiveness of her uniform augured well for our choice of a school for her. Michael, being at a school on an American army base, wore whatever he wanted. He was, however, a meticulous dresser—and remains so to this day (clothes color coordinated in his closet, shirts hangered and smoothly ironed). He loved music (as did Cathy), was sports oriented (which Cathy was not)—but being slight in build chose relay racing, and was a top performer in the school's wrestling team–welter division—and was keen about his work on the debating team. We three all missed Sidney Buchman, who was entrenched for the time being in his home in Cannes working on the troubled screenplay for *Cleopatra*, to star Elizabeth Taylor. Sidney was always energized by Michael's living room debates with him on various topics. I remember a spirited one on China (Michael was all of twelve) and its position in the world's current power scheme that lasted well over an hour and only broke up when I called a halt for dinner.

Cathy was the social one with many friends, a developing artist, and amazingly sensitive to others—especially to me. I could easily imagine that her friends confided in her and trusted her comments or advice. She also had an unusual grasp of language for one so young. Without a male figure in the house to share her attention, we were perhaps closer than many mothers and daughters. But it was her understanding heart—and her ability to express what she felt—that bound us (and still does).

The American film colony in London now consisted of both expats and recent arrivals—probably in equal numbers. Many of the newcomers were associated with Columbia Pictures. The two groups commingled, and I found new friends and colleagues. Columbia had gained the upper hand in Anglo-American production for two major reasons. In the 1950s, when the rise of television all but mined many Hollywood studios, Columbia embraced it by establishing a major television subsidiary, Screen Gems. The profits from this enterprise were then channeled into the company's film productions. While MGM, Paramount, and 20th Century-Fox had turned their backs on television, Columbia, who had trailed behind these movie mammoths for years, was now solidly entrenched at the top. Not only was the company making its own films and television series, it was a distribution company for independents.

Relationships were not always amiable between the men working in the film colony. Often one man's success was a thorn in another's ambition. Also, for reasons not revealed (or rather, kept secret), some expats had begun receiving credit under their own name and others had not (a disparity that continued for too many years). Sunday baseball games in Hyde Park continued, but hostility prevailed and bitterness bred among the expats who believed that others of their group had made covert deals with the Committee, held behind closed doors, and had named others. There remained a large segment of the expats who were working as writers for "slavery pay" as Lester termed the low salaries of the expats. Also, selling an original screenplay was extremely difficult. The studios owned a library of literary works—plays, short stories, books, and a backlog of old films that could be remade. The same was true about the music, which studios had bought for earlier movies and reused for current productions.

The expat community was not limited to actors, writers, directors, and producers. Some of Hollywood's finest cameramen, sound engineers, cutters, and composers had been blacklisted and forced to find work and make deals for themselves. For those who had ambitions to be producers, the added pressure was that of putting a deal together. This involved packaging, distribution, promotion, and selling. Carl Foreman, foremost among those artists who had gone beyond their original career choices, writing in his case, to branch out into independent filmmaking, had started Open Road Productions. His first movie under that banner—*The Guns of Navarone*, from a novel by Alistair MacLean—had been a huge box-office success. Carl was extremely gifted at self-promotion. Whatever movie he was shooting quickly became identified in the media as "Foreman's film" or a "Carl Foreman production."

The recent years had found Carl less interested in writing than supervising a script's development and being engaged with all the other facets of his productions. He had reached out to the expat colony and surrounded himself with an extremely talented and cohesive team to whom he paid below-scale wages. Open Road Productions at the time was a leading independent overseas production company with grand offices on Green Street off Park Lane in fashionable Mayfair. One fine day in May, nearby Hyde Park abloom in golden daffodils and flaming tulips, I made my way to their offices for a meeting with Carl's associate producer, Leon Becker. Carl had optioned the best-selling book, *Born Free*, and was considering me as a candidate to "crack the back" of it as a first step to screen adaptation.

Leon was not a man comfortable in conducting a conversation across a desk. The hour was late for lunch and as he had not had his, he asked if I might like to join him. We went around the corner to a small sandwich shop that had a few tables set out on the street. I had read the book and offered up some ideas. He seemed to like my suggestions. Obviously ill at ease, he then set forth what the company would be willing to pay me for my services. It was low even as a sub-rosa fee.

"You might very well get the job of adapting the book," he added quickly, I suppose as a sweetener.

"I feel like a former headliner being asked to come in to test for a bit role!" I laughed. "I am not interested in auditioning," I added. "I am working on my own project [meaning the novel that was still in flux] and really am not sure I would want to take the time out for the length of time an adaptation would take. Sooooo . . . you tell Carl that I will be happy to do a twenty-five-page breakdown of *Born Free*, if he is willing to pay me twice what you have just offered."

"I'll give him that message," he said, averting my glance.

After lunch, he went his way and I went in a different direction.

The concept of a breakdown of a book purchased for films was to find the main thrust of the story and major characters, to cut the chaff from the wheat without compromising the author's intention. Characters that do not contribute to the continuity of the story have to be cut. The trick was to find others who might be developed in a manner that would be more filmically dramatic. As example, in Margaret Mitchell's famed book *Gone with the Wind*, Scarlett O'Hara had borne two children before she married Rhett Butler. To make her "more desirable" and amplify the dramatic power of the death of their daughter, Bonnie Blue, Scarlett's two older children were not acknowledged in the movie although her two earlier marriages were included.

Often, two characters can be combined into one, scenes reset to allow for available and less expensive locations, or camera shots created that will both lower the budget and intensify the impact. Perhaps one of the most memorable examples was the Atlanta railway depot scene in *Gone with the Wind* where the depot had been turned into a field hospital for thousands of wounded and dying Southern Confederate soldiers just before the Northern Union troops ravage and occupy the city. This scene had been movingly evoked in the novel but would have cost a fortune in extras to film. Cinematographer William Cameron Menzies (who won the Academy Award for his work on the film) had handled this problem by pulling the camera farther and farther back, widening the shot to show up close the terrifying numbers of moaning, writhing, fallen Confederate soldiers as they lay stretched out on the open, parched field, crying for aid that was not there and would never come. The farther the camera pulled back the smaller and more distant the "men" at the far end of that field could be distinctly seen. Dummies designed in various positions were substituted for the extras, and the camera swept high and over their forms. This dramatically cut cost and sped up the action. Menzies then went in with his camera for a close-up of Scarlett, horrified at the carnage she was witnessing, that one shot giving total motivation for the ensuing scenes of her desperation to escape Atlanta before the Yankees had captured the city.

A good breakdown also gave a producer and director a guide as to the necessary locations and the number of characters needed to be cast. It was a starting point for a production. Many producers, directors, and adapters did their own breakdown. Still, having one in hand early in a film's development was an aid to the production team and could save considerable money in the long run. I had discovered that a unique part of my creative abilities in these early years was to visualize written scenes and to see the narrator as a camera. It had just come to me naturally.

Wishful thinking had combined with the truth when I once had confided to Norman Mailer that I was planning one day to write a novel about the McCarthy period and the expat community in London. For years, I kept journals, notes, character sketches, before I came to the realization in the early 1960s that many (make that most!) of our lives remained in flux and that no one yet, including myself, knew the result and certainly not how history would record the period. Due to that conclusion, I felt the novel would have to wait a time before I could write it. Meanwhile, I was quite happy to do the breakdown of *Born Free* (once Carl settled on a better deal) to support we three, while in whatever spare time I had I went to work on another novel. The crux of everything I ever wrote had been a story element that stressed a guiding principle, what the French call *idee-maitresse*. Mine was simple. Survival, a common drive of almost every sane person—and insane ones as well. One variation intrigued me—guilt at surviving an experience that inexplicably killed many others and left you alive.

Joined with this was the horror of the Holocaust. And, lately, a phenomenon of unlikely mass murders, which kept appearing on the front pages of the press. I began to research these. Somewhere during this process, my two major characters for a novel (to be called *The Survivors*) started to take life. This would be a suspense-love story involving two people who are drawn together by the mutual guilt of being alive when so many others had not escaped extermination. The woman would be the lone survivor of her murdered family; the man, a war correspondent, spectator to the power, greed, and intolerance that led to the cold-blooded massacres of World War II. There would be love and suspicion that brings them together and yet pushes them apart, and a cunning mass murderer to be caught. I wanted the story set in locations I knew intimately. Therefore, Klosters, Switzerland, and London, but which part of that great metropolis? I wondered. London is a city divided not only by sections and the river Thames, but by dozens of dialects and class divisions. Where my heroine lived before the murders would be an important element.

On weekends, I put aside my work for Open Road and, with the children, investigated the various areas of London for my book-to-be. There were shopkeepers to talk to, small cafes for lunch or tea, old homes that were open at certain hours to the public, parks to stroll through, churches to attend. One Saturday afternoon it would be Regent's Park (too conservative), Mayfair (too upper class), Swiss Cottage (possible), St. John's Wood (also possible), and then—finally we spent a day in Hampstead. That was it.

I remembered how fond my friend, the American travel writer Kate Simon, was of Hampstead. After my third visit, I understood why. Kate had described Hampstead as having streets "extraordinarily fanciful, yielding houses for Ushers [the family in Edgar Allan Poe's famous tale of horror] to decay in, for rotting loneliness and people administering slow poisons to their loved ones." How delicious! How creepy! How apt!

Hampstead wears almost as many disguises as it has corkscrew, eighteenth-century alleys (outdoing all other sections of London, I think). Never good at mazes, I easily got lost as there seemed no specific route to follow to reach a high street (main thoroughfare). There were narrow paved and cobbled roads, jagged with cottages from pre-Victorian days. Go around a turning and you were faced with stately brick and gated homes where Queen Victoria's son, Edward VII, had visited friends and lovers. The area was a delightful hodgepodge of architectural style and, happily, the modernists had not yet torn down the old shops and replaced them with cement-block buildings.

Hampstead Heath delighted me. The rambling, curving paths of this massive public park were covered in autumn leaves, the gently rising and falling slopes of its hilly grounds in magnificent bloom in spring and summer. Children's shouts and laughter echoed as they ran through the woody, leafy trails playing games of tag or hide-and-seek. On rainy days, there was the heady scent of wet wood and damp moss and, on sunny ones, the sweet fragrance of new blooms. One could quite easily become lost, or could experience pure communication with nature. My young woman was a dreamy sort, somehow isolated from the outside world, only comfortable before the murders when in her home among family and a small domestic staff. She often would have gone to the Heath to paint or write or just to surround herself with what the ancient poet Milton called "beldame Nature." Her house would not have been one of the great houses but, more likely, a large Victorian cottage, neatly kept yet badly in need of modernization.

I cannot recall when it was that I realized Leon Becker's interest in me had become personal.

He was always the gentleman and not prone to discuss his private life. I knew he was a widower, his wife, Kathryn, having died of an overdose of sleeping pills the previous year. He intimated the dosage had been accidental. I was shocked to learn (not from Leon) that she had been having an affair with

Carl Foreman and that her death had been recorded as a suicide, a note having been found beside her body. It could well have explained why Estelle Foreman had returned to the States and filed for divorce. I was amazed that their affair had been kept so quiet in a community that loved to share the current gossip. More so, that Leon continued to work side by side with Carl under such devastating circumstances. When I considered the masochistic elements involved, I was truly confused, for Leon did not seem to be a man who hated himself. Nor was he self-effacing.

I was thirty-four, Leon fifty, a stretch, yet no more than the age difference between Jule Styne and myself. Leon was not anything at all like Jule or Sy (or my ex-husband, for that matter), either in appearance or personality. He was on guard, conscientious, yet there was a touch of the poet in his deep brown, expressive eyes and often in his speech. Of Russian heritage, he had been born in Canada and raised in the States and yet seemed a foreigner to both those cultures. Tennis was his game of choice, and he played as often as his schedule allowed. His step was brisk, his energy fully charged at most times. He was also highly intelligent and spoke seven languages—five of them fluently, a great help when Open Road was shooting a movie abroad (Spain, Yugoslavia, Italy, Greece being the locations that film companies mostly used). As time went on, I came to understand the moodiness that shadowed some of our early meetings. As our relationship progressed, his dark attitude decreased. It was as though he had stepped out of the shade and into the sunlight. His sense of humor (especially in the use of wordplay) was exposed. He was warm, loving. A complicated man, he could display a childhood delight in such simple things as a dish of ice cream or the brilliance of late Turner paintings, his favorites at the Tate.

Of many things, Leon was a man of refined tastes and of consummate knowledge, not only of paintings but of music, especially music. Our transition from casual companion and business associate to dating took place after we had attended several operas and concerts together. No romantic overtures were made on his part, so I assumed we were good friends and nothing more (I also knew that he was seeing Joseph Losey's ex-wife, Mary, at the time) and I was quite content with the status quo. We shared a deep interest in music—opera, concert, classic, and modern. Our first dates were to see live performances, which I had hitherto not been able to afford for myself, and since most of my friends preferred films, theater, dinners at good restaurants, and gatherings at people's homes, I had accepted these entertainments as a fair exchange.

I had, in fact, never heard opera live in an opera house, and it was a wondrous world that Leon made possible. Covent Garden, home of the Royal Opera, is a world of its own—and I loved it. From the sixteenth century, the area in the yawning hours of the morning was an open market, which I did on rare occasions venture to, and there might still be a flower lady extending an almost empty tray of violets and asking "'Ows about it, luv? All 'alf the price?" The market porters would be packing up their crates of unsold vegetables and the ground would be strewn with waste. Came evening, everything had been whisked clean, and taxis and elegant cars deposited gowned·and tuxedoed patrons at the curb. Umbrellas would snap open as the operagoers ducked beneath them and carefully navigated the slippery steps to the open doors. By the second or third time that Leon accompanied me to the opera, I wore that green gown that I had bought on Sloane Street and felt very grand, for attendees did dress formal for the opera in those days!

I recall hearing Joan Sutherland sing the "Queen of Spades," and excellent productions of *Aida* and *La Traviata*. The most thrilling experience for me—seated in the fifth row center—was the night Leon had tickets for *Tosca*, sung by Maria Callas. There was no disputing the diva's brilliance. Callas had more than a superb voice. The opera critic Andrew Porter called it "something else which cannot be defined—it has to do with bearing and gesture and timbre, and phrasing, and utterance of the words, and combined—the mysterious qualities which not only make her Callas, but also make every heroine she portrays distinct and indelible." For me, that was *Tosca*, never to be forgotten. (Years later, the occasion still vivid to me, I would use the quote from his review in my biography of Maria Callas.)

Leon had an insatiable passion for Russian opera, as well as great piano music and the songs of Handel. One cannot deny Handel's genius, but he was definitely not one of my favorites. Joan Sutherland always liked to tell the story of being invited to sing at the conductor Sir Thomas Beecham's home in St. John's Wood. Asked what she was to sing, she replied, "Handel's 'Let the Bright Seraphim.'" Beecham exploded, "Oh! Not Handel!" I felt much the same way.

Leon knew many of the performing artists, so after a concert we would go backstage where he would be greeted warmly. One night, after a Yehudi Menuhin concert at Royal Festival Hall, the world-famous violinist threw his arms around Leon. "He was my earliest accompanist," he told me. "My good friend. We were children together. Prodigies together."

That was how I learned that Leon—before his engagement in film—as a young boy and adolescent had a short career as a concert pianist. Rather reticently in the days that followed that meeting, he revealed to me more of his past. His parents were from a small town in Russia where, before his birth, there was pogrom where many Jews had been slaughtered. His father managed to get his pregnant wife out of the country. She found refuge in Germany (this was 1911) and then, taking the name of her protectors, continued on to America, where she was in hopes of her husband joining her. He never was heard from again. The pregnant Mrs. Becker had been put on a boat that docked in Canada, not the United States. She was, by then, nearly nine months with child. A contact found her a place to stay and a job as a domestic with a family in Montreal. She gave birth to Leon with the help of passengers and a porter on the train journey there, in a car named Sagamore (therefore, his middle name—Leon Sagamore Becker).

Very early on, Leon showed extraordinary musical talent. He and his mother lived in her employer's home, which had a piano. The story goes that he had wandered into the music room when he was about four and sat down and played some Mozart piece that he had heard being executed by a guest of the family the previous afternoon, and did so with surprising adeptness and a good ear. He was given access to the piano and lessons with a local teacher. At age nine, believed to be a prodigy, arrangements were made for him to study with a well-known piano teacher in Los Angeles who was a friend of his mother's employer, and for him to live with Paramount Studios' head of production, Benjamin (B. P.) Schulberg and his wife, Adeline, who had a son, Budd, close to Leon's age. Not until the end of her life would Leon, then in his late thirties, see his birth mother again. During the formative years of life, he became the Schulbergs' de facto second son.

The Schulbergs were an unusual family. Benjamin was "a political liberal in the reactionary world of [Louis B.] Mayer and [William Randolph] Hearst." Adeline, however, was the true political activist. She visited the Soviet Union in the late twenties and brought back for Leon scores of Russian operas, which he had kept with him throughout the years. The boys shared a room with bunk beds and read as late at night as they could. Budd was a frail child and as a young man suffered fainting spells. He also had a speech impediment and, as one close member of the family said, "stammered his way from therapist to therapist." There was a concert Steinway in the living room of their palatial home on which Leon practiced and under which Budd Schulberg claimed he hid "in the darkest corner" to write poetry to give to his mother for "various holidays [including] Mother's Day." Although not actually brothers, it would seem that Budd had strong pangs of sibling rivalry that matured with him. Once the boys were grown, and graduated from universities, Adeline became an agent. It was always her goal to push people as far as she could toward fame.

Leon made his first public appearance at the age of eleven, accompanying the nine-year-old Yehudi Menuhin on the piano. Leon soon developed a case of stage fright whenever he had to appear before an audience (although he played magnificently, otherwise). He explained to me that he was terrified of playing a piece entirely by memory as he was expected to do. He needed the music as a prop and was forbidden by his teacher to use it. "If you do not have it in your fingers and in your heart, you will never be a great concert pianist," he was told. He, therefore, decided at seventeen to attend Caltech and study to be an expert sound technician—badly needed in those early days of all-talking films. When in his twenties, both he and Budd became politically active and joined the Communist Party. This was during the darkest days of the Depression (although they wanted for very little). Both dropped out of the party a few years later.

Leon advanced fast, being placed in charge of the Warner Bros. sound department (he also played the piano on tracks for several films). He was greatly sought after in that capacity and became director William Wyler's associate on four films. Then came Senator Joseph McCarthy. Budd was called up before the Committee and, turning informer, rattled off a string of names of people he had known who had been in the party with him, Leon among them. Blacklisted, unable to work and still holding Canadian citizenship, Leon was one of the first of Hollywood's HUAC victims to move, with his wife, to London. A valid Canadian passport was accepted in Great Britain, and he was able to work immediately without restrictions.

We had been dating for a time when, a week or so after my meeting with Yehudi, and after a dinner out, Leon invited me for the first time to come back to his flat at 25 Lennox Gardens (which faced one of London's charming squares). The four-story house, occupied originally in Edwardian days by a well-to-do family, had been converted into flats, as had most of the other houses on the square. Leon's apartment was on the top floor. There was no lift. To reach his aerie, one needed to first take the marble steps that led into the building, then walk up three long flights of stairs (ceilings being eleven feet high), to reach his door. When opened, one was faced with still another staircase, steeper and narrower than the others. By this time I had left my breath on the floor below. Mounting this staircase for me was akin to the challenge of climbing to the peak of the Gotschna in the Swiss Alps! But I took it.

When I retrieved my breath, I was quite taken with what I saw, not that the apartment was grand in any way, but it was unique. Before Leon's occupancy, walls had been removed to make larger rooms than in the original. You entered partway into a long, rather wide hall, the living room visible beyond via two more steps. It contained a marvelous high-arched window overlooking the square that on fair days cast streams of light through multi-panes. A grand piano occupied one entire corner and dominated the room. At the other end of the generous entrance hall was a galley kitchen and to its left, a door to a large master bedroom and bath. Another door, and two steps midway in the hall, led to a second bath and bedroom (used by Leon for an amazing collection of sound equipment and tapes—operas, concerts, film scores).

I asked Leon after we had settled in if he would be kind enough to play something for me. He sat down on the piano bench in the manner of a concert performer. There were several tall, neat stacks of music piled up on the floor beside him. Immediately, without reclaiming a score from the stacks beside him, the most beautiful and full sound filled the room. Leon was not the least bit rusty. What I got was a professional performance, as moving and well played as many that we had attended together. I was confused. He had told me why he had not continued his concert career—but not why he had chosen not to be involved in the music world. Nor did he ever play at people's homes when we were there for an evening and they were good friends—with a piano just waiting to be brought to life. He gave me private concerts (well received and welcomed) often making for a warm, intimate evening. He practiced diligently and daily. Nonetheless, I always felt he was happy with the work he was doing, involved and giving himself entirely to it. Carl once told me that Leon could hear things on a sound track no one else could, and that he was a true artist when it came to sound and music recording. He seemed to mask any bitterness toward the McCarthy period and the end of his Hollywood career, with one exception: the betrayal of Budd Schulberg.

Although I had a house for we three, I was spending a lot of time at Leon's flat. Very vivid to me is the time Adeline Schulberg (who Leon called Addie), while visiting London, rang up to ask if she might come over and speak to Leon. I had answered the telephone. He looked more tortured than I had ever seen him when I passed the request on to him. After a long moment of consideration, he agreed. Addie, now a widow, was no longer a young woman and she took the stairs with great difficulty. I sat her down in the hallway, where there was a dining table and chairs, and brought her a glass of water. It must have been about five minutes before Leon came out of the sound room to greet her. She got to her feet and threw her arms around him. When they moved apart they were both crying. He helped her into the living room and I went into the kitchen to make tea. When I returned with a tray, Addie had Leon clasped by his sleeve.

"You must see Budd. Talk to him. He'll make you understand. You were brothers—*are* brothers. I raised you both. . . . I . . ." She let go of his arm and sank down into a chair. She was once again suffused in tears. Leon was not. "We will not discuss Budd, is that understood?" he said in a strained voice. She nodded her head. The remaining hour or so she was with us was not easy. Budd's name was not mentioned again. Leon held on to her arm as he helped her down the staircases onto the street. I watched from the front window as he walked slowly with her up Lennox Gardens. Thank God, he was going to make sure she was safely deposited in a taxi. He returned fifteen minutes later, sat down at the piano, and played for a long while—Rachmaninoff and at a furious tempo. That was the only time I saw Addie Schulberg and the last that Leon ever spoke of either Budd or his mother.

The lovely Marion. My mother's engagement photograph, 1926.

A rare togetherness: my father and me in Hollywood, 1933. By then, I was on stage and dancing and singing.

Anne Louise, 1931, before we left New York, bankrupt by the Depression, and headed for California on an unforgettable journey.

Dinner at The Algonquin, 1929. Left to right: Uncle Dave, Aunt Theo (his first wife), Harold Ross (editor of *The New Yorker*), two friends, and Joe Cook. Hollywood was calling.

Seaside, Connecticut, 1929, the year of the crash. Left to right: Marion, me, Grandma Pauline, and Uncle Dave (Dave Chasen).

Left to right: Frank Capra, Uncle Dave, Joe Cook (unidentified fourth man), on the set of *Rain or Shine*, 1930.

The children's father (right), serving in Guam at the end of World War II with fellow naval friend.

Michael, 7, and Catherine, 3, about to leave for England and a new life.

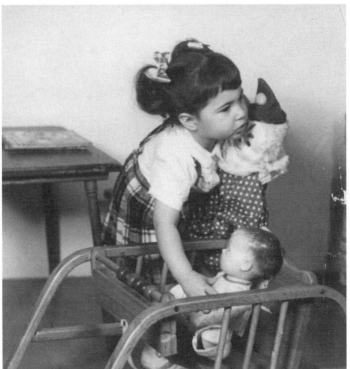

Dancing the tango: Michael and Catherine in Florida, 1961.

The children's uncle and aunt: Robert Rossen and his wife, Sue Rossen, in London, 1963. Rossen had just racked up a major hit, *The Hustler*.

The Hollywood Ten, minus one: Lester Cole, balding member, center; Dalton Trumbo, third from right rear; Adrian Scott, far left end; Ring Lardner Jr., second row, far right end; Albert Maltz, second from left (with pipe). *Associated Press*

Sidney Buchman, 1966. Good friend and great filmmaker.

Michael at 12. He and Sidney had lively political debates.

Sy Stewart and his daughter, Laura (c. 1960–1961).

Leon Becker in one of his happier days.

The newly married Anne Edwards Becker in the Lennox Garden apartment with film composer Sol Kaplan.

Leon with my friend and confidant, writer Vera Caspary, at an outdoor café in France (that's the back of my head seated across from them).

Always on Sunday! Brunch at Carl Foreman's boathouse on the Thames. Carl was the cook.

Me, exchanging kitchen chatter with Carl's wife, Eve.

Leon takes time out in front of the humble abode.

Jay Schlein, Gstaad, 1968. He had just "come out" and was one happy fella!

Gstaad, 1968. The always amazing Dale Witt, architect and adventurer.

Swiss Interlude, 1968–1970: Chalet Fleur de Lis. I thought I had found a home at last.

On the terrace: Jay, Catherine, and our poodle family.

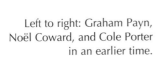

Left to right: Graham Payn,
Noël Coward, and Cole Porter
in an earlier time.

Sandy waiting at the window for Catherine to return from school.

Sunning with Sandy, the patriarch of his dog family.

Catherine, now a young woman
in her teens.

Michael with mustache and goatee about to depart for Berkeley and his return to the States.

Catherine during her short spell as a flower child.
And back to her gamine look!

Rod Serling: a not-so-brief encounter.
Photofest

Chicago, 1968: On tour for the publication of *The Survivors* and appearing on the Irv Kupcinet television show. Elia Kazan, left end; our host with cigar, second from right. I'm the sole woman, center. Kazan and I clashed, a most unpleasant incident.

Actress, comedian, and childhood friend, Joyce Jameson, in my apartment in Beverly Hills, 1969. The photograph on the bookcase (this portrait of me) was the back cover photo of my book *The Survivors.*

Judy Garland and Mickey Deans in their London mews flat shortly after their wedding.

Jay Schlein and Robert (Bob) Jorgen in Gstaad. It was a difficult time. Judy had just died and her husband was trying to con me into something I did not want to do.

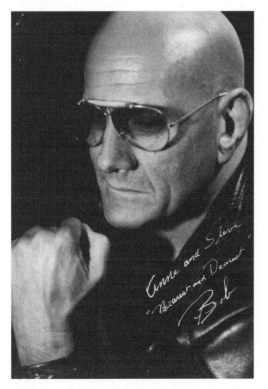

A macho portait of Bob, who also happened to be my uncle and Mickey Deans' lover.

Gstaad. From left to right: Me, Bob, Catherine, and Mickey Deans.

Returning home.

· 10 ·

Funny Girl

$\mathscr{F}$or personal use, overseas telephone calls were expensive (and difficult due to the time differential). Cablegrams were also seen as an extravagance by my penny-saving mother. Therefore, she sent me an express letter to inform me that my father had been diagnosed with rectal cancer and would need an immediate operation if he was to prolong his life. The tone of her letter was infused with fear. This was the summer of 1963 and my parents, still in Miami, had little money. It was obvious from her words that Marion did not feel capable of handling the urgency or the nuances of the situation.

Right or wrong, I was more concerned about my mother than my father. Marion could always be relied upon to dispense loving care, nursing skills, and nourishing meals and to create a degree of harmony in uneasy times. In the advent of a real crisis she went to pieces (and often to her bed). There had been a legion of grave happenings during her marriage to my father, mostly having to do with his comings and goings and the sea of troubles he brought with him and left behind in rough-water waves for her to navigate. Several times during my adolescence I had to go by myself to make a payment to a beyond-the-law creditor who she was too ashamed and fearful to approach. (Boom-Bah! for football heroes!) There was a period when he had written a series of bad checks and was being threatened to be turned over to law enforcement. Marion collapsed. I was twelve years old, yet very adult in many ways. I understood the seriousness of the problem and the consequence if something was not done right away. I had a friend whose father was a top lawyer in Los Angeles and called him. I can no longer remember (or perhaps was never told) how the gracious gentleman mediated this potentially disastrous situation. Charges, however, were not pressed against my father, and my

121

mother's brothers paid the outstanding debt. That time, it had taken months for Marion, even with her daily readings of Mary Baker Eddy, to recover.

My mother was weak where my father was concerned. Somewhere it is written, "Beware of the weak," and I believe that to be true. My mother's first responsibility should have been to herself and to me, a maxim she never adopted. If her gentility and expansive love had not been so seductive, I might have, when younger, seen her inaction as the iniquitous force that it was. I lived with the knowledge that I was the adult in our lives and that I was somehow expected to take the responsibility that she could not bear.

I rang her immediately (damn the cost!). Her voice was imbued with gratitude. I told her I would wire her some money and arrange for two tickets to take them from Miami to Hartford, where she and my father could stay with her mother (my beloved Grandma Pauline, a Hungarian lady of lively temperament, who I knew would welcome them in a time of emergency despite her intense dislike of my father). Dr. Hepburn, who had been the family doctor since Marion was a child, had recently died. I suggested she should call the physician who had taken over his practice and ask him for the name of a colon cancer specialist then make an appointment for my father to see him. I also reminded her that he was a war veteran and that some part of the medical expenses might be absorbed if he went to a veterans' hospital. Thirty-six hours later my parents were on a plane to Hartford.

After further medical tests, it was decided that my father should be operated on in New York by a specialist. This was early August; the surgery was scheduled two weeks hence. We three flew to New York on "cheap end" tickets. (Airlines like Air India or Pakistani, who stopped in London on flights to New York from their countries, offered cut rates for unsold "end of flight" seats the day of a scheduled flight.) Good friends, who lived in New York, were planning a trip to England and I made a trade—they use Hasker Street while they were in London and I would occupy their apartment on East Seventy-Ninth Street while I was in Manhattan. My position was to stand by my mother and be there to help her with any decisions that might have to be made.

Ever the iron man that he was, he survived the operation and began a course of radiation. On a Friday afternoon on November 22, my father still in hospital, we three and my mother were at the apartment when there was a loud banging on the door and a neighbor burst in, shouting for us to turn on the television. We did and, horrified, watched the vivid coverage of the shooting death of our young president John Fitzgerald Kennedy in Dallas and the swearing in on Air Force One of vice president Lyndon Baines Johnson— the former first lady, Jacqueline Kennedy, standing beside him still dressed in the blood-stained clothes she had worn in the motorcade when the assassin's bullets had killed her husband.

The tragedy of John F. Kennedy's death was a deep, deep wound to our country and country folk. I don't think any of us old enough at the time to comprehend what had happened will ever forget that day and those of national mourning that followed. The scenes of the assassination, the swearing in of Lyndon Johnson and the funeral procession with little John, a child of three, saluting as his father's hearse and riderless horse passed by, were played over and over on television—so that those images became branded on one's heart and mind. Never before had I so profoundly felt my sense of being an American. John F. Kennedy had symbolized hope, a new prospect for our country.[1]

This was the first time since I had gone abroad that I considered the idea of remaining in the States, no matter the circumstances. Finally, I decided against it for a market basket of reasons—my work, finances, and my unsettled relationship with Leon. When my parents returned to Hartford, taking a small apartment of their own, my mother now in the comfortable role of nurse Marion, we three flew back to London and continued our lives. I found not only the American community but the British mourning Kennedy's death. He had been greatly admired throughout Great Britain, especially in Ireland, the homeland of his ancestors.

I was spending more and more time with Leon and his friends, largely the more recently arrived members of the film colony. The expats were now spreading their wings a bit—moving to the South of France, or able to work again and so returning to the States. The new American embassy, which now dominated Grosvenor Square, had recently opened. Designed by noted architect Eero Saarinen, it had been loudly decried by the British (especially Londoners) who found the building "an impressive but decidedly embarrassing building," due in a great part to the large golden eagle, standing eight to nine feet on the top, its thirty-five-foot wingspan displayed against an open sky. Also, because Saarinen's precedent for the outside of the building had been the Renaissance Doge's Palace in Venice, the context of the Georgian and pseudo-Georgian character of this, one of the grandest squares in London, seemed heresy. I had to agree. Still, there was something comforting to an American to enter the square and look up to that overwhelming symbol of our country. Despite controversy ("the Americans have taken over Grosvenor Square!"), or maybe because of it, the American embassy became a favorite visitor site, and there were always groups of people standing about in the square staring at it.

Cathy had passed her eleven-plus exams with honors. In England this means that the student must matriculate to an upper school (like middle school or junior high school in the States). Cathy wished to attend a Swiss boarding school (as Salka's granddaughter was presently doing). I was not immediately in favor of this for both financial and personal reasons. We investigated schools in London without much enthusiasm. They were mostly elite and class structured and not inexpensive, either. Cathy and I went to Klosters, from where we trained about to various nearby schools. The one she favored was Professor Buser's Voralpines Tochter-Institute in Teufen, near St. Gallen by way of Zurich and a little over a two-hour train journey from Klosters.

The school was located in a bucolic setting—fields of wildflowers—the magnificent Swiss Alps as a backdrop. There was a barn with cows that supplied the school with its dairy products. There was something very "Heidi-ish" about Buser's, but it also boasted a high scholastic standing. The staff was most accommodating and the students we met, friendly. "But it is German speaking," I complained to Cathy. "Lessons are taught in German, which you don't know. I can't imagine how that would work for you." She was determined, as only Cathy can be. "I can learn it," she insisted. I could only think that there was something about those cows' melting brown eyes that had gotten to her. I finally agreed and rented a house in Klosters—Chalet In-sidina—so that I could spend large blocks of time near enough for her to come home for weekends. It helped that Salka was also in Klosters. I brought down our new family member, a large, three-year-old apricot poodle we renamed Sandy, who had been given to me unexpectedly as a gift by the producer of the film in which the dog had appeared. I had been a visitor on the set and, always a dog lover, was smitten by him. He was, I was told, to be retired as his handler was in poor health. Trained for movie work, he did a multitude of clever tricks on cue: go to sleep, pick up and carry items, jump over bushes and hedges, limp, cry, howl, and many more that I never did learn the commands for him to respond to. There was something eerily human about Sandy. He sensed when either I or Cathy was sad and he had an uncanny ability to tell the time. Cathy always came home on the same train every Saturday. Five minutes beforehand he would stop whatever he was doing to stand staring out the front window. Just moments before she appeared, he would race through the house to greet her at the door. I remained puzzled at how he knew it was Saturday, as well as the arrival time of her train and his instinct (or whatever it can be called) that timed her approach.

The first month new students at Buser's were not allowed to leave the premises of the school. Cathy shared a large room with three German girls who spoke no English. The reason for this, I was told, was for her to become totally immersed in the language. "It will work, you will see. She is a smart girl," the headmistress assured me. After I deposited her in her room (which was in charming, Swiss-cottage decor) I took her aside and told her that if after the first week she was unhappy, she should come home anyway and we would look for another school. "But that would mean you have to pay for this one as well, doesn't it?" she came back.

"Whatever it is," I replied, "I'll work it out."

She called me after the first week, sounding truly miserable. "I'll come get you," I insisted.

"No! I won't quit!" and she hung up.

The second week, she sounded no happier but still refused to give up. By the third week she said the girls in her room were not friendly to her. "Please! I'll come get you!" I pressed.

The answer was another loud, "No!"

My daughter was not a quitter and never would be. She learned German—and some French as well—in record time, came to like the girls in her room and the others in her classes very much, and remained entranced by the cows. I was flying back and forth between London and Switzerland and beginning to love the beauty of the country, the food, the people, and the orderliness of all things Swiss. Cathy once told Salka, "Everything works in Switzerland, even Mommy." This was true. My writing went well in the peaceful ambiance of Klosters and I was able to further develop my work on *The Survivors* by living in one of the main settings.

Leon and I were now a couple. I had come to care deeply for him. Yet there were many signals of problems ahead in our relationship that gave me pause. For one thing, Leon had a great melancholy within himself. I understood the causes—the sense of abandonment and betrayal he had endured and how this had diminished his sense of self-worth. What I found puzzling was his refusal to seek help. And I was uncomfortable with his friendship with Carl—apart from their business relationship. Carl, after all, had been his wife's lover and from what I gathered had ended the affair in an abrupt manner that was somewhat responsible for her final action. I was unsure if this unorthodox friendship was not wantonly self-destructive of Leon.

On Sundays, when I was not in Klosters, we would go to Carl's weekend cottage, a humble one-story abode on the Thames, river scent and dampness pervading. He would scramble eggs with onions and smoked salmon, turning the dish into a fishy jumble with a fulsome, unpleasant aroma. It was a ritual missed only when Carl and Leon were on location with a film. The conversation at the kitchen table where we ate would start off casual and end up with a intense discussion pertaining to their current work. Carl possessed a talented ability to switch moods, almost like an actor who must do so in a scene. He would squint up his eyes behind his large-framed glasses, his chin set resolutely, his voice taking on a measured tone. Fun time was over. I resented this intrusion in the one day of the week that Leon and I had together when in London, as Leon always worked on Saturdays. It did not help that I had a strong aversion to the implacable menu. A year later, Carl fell in love with Leon's secretary, Eve, whom he married. Sunday brunches continued until after the birth of their first child, Jonathon, but gratefully the menu improved.

Our most divisive problem was Leon's apartment in Lennox Gardens. We were sleeping in the same room, on the same bed where Kathryn had taken her life. When I moved in, her clothes—shades of *Rebecca*—still hung in the closets and were stored on shelves. I packed them up and had Oxfam (a charity organization) collect them. I bought a new mattress and springs and placed some of my favorite things about. I discussed this with my therapist and am sure that I was not jealous of Leon's lost love. Rather, I could not get past the thought of what those last hours had been for her—walking up and down the long hall that connected the two wings of the flat—finally closing herself in the bedroom. I felt I was sharing our home with a restless spirit. Also, I could not help but wonder how Leon, after a marriage of twenty years, had not sensed the seriousness of Kathryn's despair and tried in some way to help. He had been on location in Greece with *The Guns of Navarone* when she committed suicide, returning the morning after to find her body and the note. Her desperation and unhappiness had to have started long, long before then. How was it, I wondered disheartened, that neither Leon nor Carl had been aware of her pain and acted with attribution? Had they both simply ignored the signs of her acute distress? Or had they been so involved in their own worlds that they saw nothing beyond them? I would never have an answer, because Kathryn's plight was not to be introduced into any of our conversations at penalty of Leon withdrawing into a silent, melancholy funk.

We were happiest in Switzerland or when I accompanied him on location, at separate times to Poland and Yugoslavia (later to Copenhagen and Madrid). The change in him whenever we were abroad was amazing. We laughed a lot, shared our impressions, and made passionate love. He loved the idea that I was comfortable with the crews and casts of the productions he worked on. On our return to Lennox Gardens from these junkets, the old Leon would emerge, the glumness seep slowly back. He asked me to marry him sometime during the summer of 1964. I thought it over carefully and earnestly believed we could have a happy life together on one condition: we move out of the apartment into one that we both liked. I brought up my feelings about living in the same rooms where Kathryn had taken her life and, although quite a separate issue, the difficulties I had with the long climb up and down the stairs (even delivery people would leave packages on either the first or second landing for us to trudge down to collect). Leon finally agreed after taking a good part of a day thinking about it. We first set November 22 as the date for our wedding. Cathy was out on school break, so we two went on an expedition looking for flats.

I found a lovely ground floor and garden apartment in a section of London near St. John's Wood, called Venice due to the canal that trickled through it. Property values were not as inflated in this area as they were around Lennox Gardens which was in Knightsbridge, and so one got much more for one's money. The flat was newly renovated, fresh and bright with a lovely, small garden. There was a bedroom and bath on the lower level (you entered on the ground floor) that Leon could use for his home office and sound equipment, and three more bedrooms on the main floor plus a bright living room, generous dining room, breakfast room (which could serve as my office and had steps leading down to the garden), and a remodeled kitchen. The building was Belle Epoch, the street lined with well-tended greenery, and the rates (fees that occupants on leases paid each year) less than on Lennox Gardens. After he looked at the flat and met with the real estate people, Leon signed the lease. We were to take possession in thirty days. I then turned my attention to our wedding plans.

We both wanted a nonreligious ceremony with a few close friends— thirty at most. The ceremony took place on November 27, a Sunday afternoon, in a small, elegant reception room on the mezzanine floor of the Carlton Towers Hotel, off Sloane Square. Betty Graf was my maid of honor, Stanley Mann (who was a mutual friend of Leon's and mine) was best man. After the ceremony there was a reception with champagne and a bountiful early supper-buffet table. Sidney came up from Cannes along with his brother Harold and Harold's wife, Ruth. Carl, Walter Shenson and his wife, Bill Graf, Sol and Frances Heflin Kaplan, Lester, the Adlers, and the director William Wyler and his wife Talli (Margaret Tallichet) were present along with others.

Leon and Willie Wyler had a long history together—having made five movies in Hollywood before the blacklist took Leon to London: *Wuthering Heights*, *The Best Years of Our Life*, *The Heiress*, *Detective Story*, and *Carrie*, and unofficially on several others. The Wylers, in London for a short stay, took us for dinner the night before the wedding. I loved both of them. Talli had come to Hollywood from Texas in the late 1930s as a Scarlett O'Hara hopeful. She had not found a career but a husband and such a wonderful man. Willie had a hearing problem quite early in his life. Born in Alsace, he had been a Swiss citizen before coming to Hollywood in 1921 at the age of nineteen, and was employed in low-level jobs in silent pictures. Within four years he had worked his way up to becoming a director. He developed hearing problems during those years, but as this was during the silent era, it had not created a serious block to his success. I believe one of the things that had drawn Willie and Leon so close was Leon's brilliance as a sound director. Hearing aids were not technically developed by the early thirties when talkies replaced the silent film. Willie, with great seriousness, once told me that Leon had been his ears.

After the wedding we spent four joyous weeks in Klosters. Leon did not ski, but Klosters was alive in December, filled with people we knew. We did a lot of socializing with Salka, Irwin Shaw and his wife, as well as author Elaine Dundy, separated from her husband, the critic Kenneth Tynan, and spending the holidays at the Chesa Grischuna on her own. There were also warm, intimate evenings by the fireplace at Chalet Insidina, and more family-oriented times when Cathy joined us. Leon was relaxed and in high spirits. Not until we returned to London did he tell me that he had changed his mind about the move from Lennox Gardens and was going to renege on the signed lease. He tried to assure me that he was not being obstinate. He heard what I said about my reasons for the move. And, yes, the Venice apartment was attractive and had some added advantages over Lennox Gardens. But he felt comfortable where we were, hated change, and had decided that in the long run Lennox Gardens was a more valuable investment. In England, one generally buys a leasehold on a flat for a number of years. You actually do not own the premises although you are responsible for its upkeep. Yearly rates are paid and when the time on your lease—which can run many decades—has elapsed, the property returns to the owner. One could, with their approval, sell the existing number of years left on your lease. Lennox Gardens had twenty-five remaining years, the Venice flat only eleven, which could greatly deflate a future resale price.

We forfeited our binder fee on the Venice flat (I believe it was about five hundred pounds). Some difficult weeks passed between us. I considered his action grossly unresponsive to my concerns. I seldom allow myself to get pushed to a wall. But when it happens, I can be a fierce contender. I threatened to leave and was prepared to do so, even going so far as to search out a suitable accommodation for myself. Leon was in a state of despair. Still, he declared his decision to keep Lennox Gardens was unassailable. Finally, I came to a compromise. I would spend more time in Switzerland and he would join me there whenever he could. Our primary residence (for tax and business reasons, he claimed) would still be Lennox Gardens—which I was free to redecorate in any way I chose. Obviously, our marriage had made its first step on slippery ground.

Night had not left the sky when the telephone next to the bed in Lennox Gardens rang ominously. The room was in total darkness. Leon stirred. The telephone rang again. I turned on a light. It was about four a.m. I picked up the receiver. It was my father, sounding in a panic. "Your mother is seriously ill. It's cancer. She's in the hospital," he managed. He began to sob. "It's that damned Christian Science," he cried. "She's been in pain for months and refused to go to a doctor."

Due to the time differential, I was on a plane by noon and in Hartford at my grandmother's house late that same evening. By morning I was at the hospital. I had been asked by my mother's sister not to let my grandmother, who was ninety-four and failing, know the gravity of her condition.

When I reached the visitor's desk on the hospital floor where my mother was, I was requested by a nurse to wait a few minutes. It seemed Marion, when told I was on my way, had insisted on coming from her room to see me. The nurse leaned in close to add, "Your mother wants to look her best and for your meeting to be in a more congenial place than her room, which she is sharing with another patient." This did not seem strange behavior for Marion—always the impeccably dressed, gracious hostess. But for God's sake! She was a dying woman in a hospital!

The nurse led me partway down a corridor at the end of which was a turn and on the wall, at an angle, one of those circular mirrors for the staff to monitor any undue activity by ambulatory patients. Then, there she was, painfully thin, dressed in a wine-red, velvet hostess gown, the kind that zips all the way up the front, coming around that turn, a nurse on either side of her, practically lifting her off the ground as they guided her. Her hair was a soft gray cloud as she drifted closer to that mirror. There was a blush of red on her lips and cheeks, noticeable because her skin was so pale. She came to a halt at the mirror, the nurses forced to do so with her, and cocked her head. "I never was photo-gee-nic," she said in that inimitable Hartford twang of hers. Then she started up the hallway to me. "Anne Louise, can it be truly you?" There was a catch in her voice.

I rushed up to her. She drew one trembling, skeletal hand free from her holders and placed it on my cheek. There it was—the scent of verbena. She insisted we go to the visitor's room and, when carefully placed in a chair, wanted to know about the children and Leon. "Is he a good man?" she asked. I wasn't quite sure I knew what she meant by that, but I answered positively. "And the wedding?"

"Lovely. Really lovely. The only thing missing was your presence."

"Oh, well, sweetheart," she smiled wanly, "I was at the first."

We sat there for about five minutes while she held my hand. When she let go, I realized she might be in pain. The nurses suggested she return to her room. I insisted on going with her and remained by her side as the morphine she was administered finally took effect.

For the next two weeks, I spent a good part of every day and evening at the hospital. She had cancer of the spleen, which had spread throughout her stomach and body. She had refused radiation and it had taken several doctors to convince her to have shots of morphine to ease the pain. There was nothing more anyone could do.

"How long?" I asked her oncologist.

"No telling. She seems to be holding on. Six weeks—three months at the most. I've ordered that she be moved to a nursing home. She'll get good care there. The object is to keep her out of pain as much as possible."

A difficult decision had to be made. Either I sat out the death watch or I returned to London and then came back when things looked imminent. I spoke to Leon, who was in favor of my flying home. "Right now she has your father and her sister," he reasoned. Then, there was spring break for Cathy coming up in a few weeks.

"It means two trips—double expense," I said.

"I'll take care of it. Come home."

And so I went without any long good-byes to my mother, for by then the morphine kept her pretty much unaware of her surroundings.

Three days after my return, my father called. "Your mother died an hour ago," he said. "I don't know what I'll do." There were no sobs, but I felt a deep honesty to his words. He had always had Marion to come home to. What now?

There seemed no reason to fly back, for my mother had left instructions that she did not want a religious funeral. She was buried in a small, simple service in the cemetery where Big Charlie had a large family plot. Along with my father, there were seven members of her family present. My grandmother was told that her daughter remained in a nursing home. She passed away less than a year later, never knowing the truth. Or, perhaps, wise woman that she was, did and preferred to accept what was told to her.

The early sixties in England were a time of extremes. At Ascot, the Queen and the racetrack's elite attendees all wore these extraordinary hats. Skirts were midcalf. The Queen, still a young, pretty woman in her midthirties, dressed in coordinated colors—hat, dress, purse, all matching—as did all the women in her party, although the colors the ladies of the royal family wore could not be replicated by others. If the Queen wore pink, no one else could. That stood for the Queen Mother's and Princess Margaret's choice of garment shade as well. The Queen and her mother were ardent horse fans while Margaret enjoyed the side pleasures, for Ascot was the high point of the "social season," a time that had little effect on the rest of the Queen's subjects. Prince Philip and the other attending gentlemen wore top hats, their unfurled black umbrellas (with handsome silver, ivory, or gold handles) giving them a three-legged look. If a dribble of rain fell—as often occurred—there would be an orchestrated opening of the umbrellas to cover milady's plumed and flowered hats (almost a whole garden of flowers it seemed of some).

On the streets of London, in the clubs and chic establishments, designers like Pierre Cardin had shortened women's skirts to heights that displayed a less-than-discreet section of a thigh. Dresses were designed in tents, triangles, and discordant (or just plain splashy) colors. Hair was so bouffant that it was difficult (except in royal circles!) for a woman to wear a hat. I personally believe that the bouffant hairstyle spelled the beginning of the end for milliners around the world. There was even a madcap fad (very short lived) for paper dresses. The new British musical had come into its own with Anthony Newley's and Leslie Bricusse's *Stop the World—I Want to Get Off*, and their follow-up, *The Roar of the Greasepaint—The Smell of the Crowd*, while the previous season's *Oliver!*, music and lyrics by Lionel Bart, went on to become a smash Broadway hit. The new international male film star was dashing Scotsman Sean Connery as James Bond, perfect martini in his hand, a sharp-titted beauty at his side, as he prepared to save the world from destruction. Cockney accents and bastard English heroes like Michael Caine's *Alfie* were in. Reversing the trend, the very English *Mary Poppins* and *My Fair Lady* became Hollywood's top grossers in the same year.

And the music! Let us not forget the music. Sure, Mozart and Schumann were reliable choices at Royal Festival Hall, and the overforties spun Frank Sinatra on their home phonographs. But the most-played music, the sound that would change popular music, that singularly everyman, pop phenomenon, were the Beatles. Strange bedfellows that they were—Walter Shenson and Leon were part of the producing team that made the Beatles' first film, *A Hard Day's Night*, directed by Richard Lester, who was a nonconformist. With *A Hard Day's Night*, he broke radically with the established precedent of performance-based musical sequences. The Beatles came alive, popping right off the screen as they tore through the inexplicable action of the film, the songs ofttimes having little to do with the story (which was nominal, at best). They were a force that could not be denied.

At one point, *A Hard Day's Night* was about to be dropped from production. The studio could not find a director with substantial credits who wanted to make the movie. Lester, who had directed *The Mouse That Roared*—also an oddball film, starring a hilarious Peter Sellers—stepped in. Then the original producer backed out. Walter Shenson, the producer of *The Mouse That Roared,* literally got the movie thrown into his lap. Leon, his associate producer on that film, came along with him. Walter, with little interest in, and almost no knowledge of, music turned to Leon to provide it. I had great respect for Leon, who certainly was one of the first older folks (in his fifties at the time) I knew who saw the brilliance in the Beatles' music and performance and the potential of its effect on popular music. In music terms, the film was historically significant. It spread a new sound around the world. Without it, the Beatles might not have become as globally popular as they did, certainly not with such shocking rapidity. Leon also went on to produce for British television episodes from an animated Beatles twelve-part series. Lennox Gardens was alive with the sound of the four Liverpudlians, and I liked it.

London, it seemed, had come out of the gloom and glory of the past into this strange new world. It was no longer an isolated island but a lifeline to the future—at least in the arts. Nothing, of course, changed in the manners and customs of the royal family. And when occasions arose for ancient pageantry to be displayed, no country could do better than Great Britain. So there you had it. If you lived in London as I did in those years, you were observing (and were often part of) a schizophrenic culture: the staid traditions of the past and the antitraditional movements of the present.

Early in the spring of 1966, Bob Rossen took seriously ill. He died a few months later from complications due to diabetes and other organic problems. His last film (1964) had been *Lilith*, an adaptation of a book by J. R. Salamanca about a troubled woman (Jean Seberg) in a mental home who falls in love with a young therapist (Warren Beatty). Earlier, Bob had been interested in adapting John Fowles's book, *The Collector*, also about madness and obsession, and lost out in the bidding process. *Lilith* was its replacement, so to speak. Although artistically interesting, it did not turn out to be one of his great films. The scrappy fighter, so often the protagonist in his work, was supplanted by a moody, indecisive antihero. I would have wished Bob had gone out in more of a blaze of glory.

I was in London when he died in a New York hospital with Sue and his three children by his bedside. I felt great sadness in his passing but never could discuss it with Leon or Sidney. To them, he would always carry the stigma of an informer. I knew and judged him on a personal level. Bob had always been good to me and the children. There was, I had to admit to myself, a definite double standard. Bob had never turned his back on me and so I could never turn mine on him.

In April of that year, I had received a call from Sidney, who was in Cannes. He asked me to work with him to co-adapt for screen the musical *Funny Girl*. The show had been a success on Broadway, without doubt due to the phenomenal performance of a young woman, Barbra Streisand, as Fanny Brice, former star of the Ziegfeld Follies. It had just opened in London to mixed reviews. "One of the most nonsensical plots in the history of American musicals," the *Times* reported. However, Streisand's personal reviews were extraordinary. "She sings and there are saxophones, trumpets, and violins in her throat," one newspaper wrote. London, in fact, was *en fete* with Streisand's success.

Still, it is hard for one performer to make a film a box-office hit, never mind one who had never before made a movie and did not look like a Hollywood star. It would be doubly difficult when the story was as weak as *Funny Girl*. New York theatergoers had loved Streisand, and it looked like the same would be true in London. She *was* Fanny Brice and then some. Casting someone other than her would be a huge gamble.

Sidney was coming up to London and wanted me to see it with him. "I'd like you to work with me on this one," he said. "I don't feel I can go it alone." (This was a reference to the fact that he had been having some recent medical problems.) He told me that his agent—who would act on both of our behalves—thought he could get a substantial offer. Sidney would be the senior writer. Therefore, the projected fee would be split 65 percent for him, 35 percent for me—but he would pay the agent's fee of 10 percent of the whole. He had not seen the play on Broadway, but he had heard Streisand sing on record. "She's a powerhouse," he confirmed of the reviews. "And she is set to star in the movie." This was a chance for me to gain back my identity on-screen. If he accepted the deal, I agreed to whatever terms he thought fair.

Sidney arrived in London in time for Saturday's matinee. We returned in the evening to see it again. Sunday was spent poring over the play scripts we had been given, making notes—mainly on trying to get a take on the characters and the thrust of the story and how they could be enhanced on film. The male lead was Fanny Brice's gambler husband, Nicky Arnstein. In the play his role was underwritten, and not interesting, save for the good looks of the actor (Sydney Chaplin, Charlie's younger son, in New York) who was cast to portray him. Ray Stark, the executive producer and cofounder of Seven Arts Productions company, was also in London. I am not sure where he was staying, but he took a two-room suite at the Dorchester Hotel for Sidney and me to use as our workplace. One morning, a few days after we had begun, Sidney—always an early riser—picked me up at about eight a.m. We sat downstairs in the Dorchester's coffee shop for some breakfast before heading up to the suite. Sidney had the key, opened the door, stepped inside, and then put his hand up for me to stay where I was. Beyond him I could see Ray Stark and a young, barely covered woman.

"Close the door!" Stark called out.

I stepped back. Sidney went in, to return moments later to me, idling in the hallway. "Can we work at your place?" he asked.

Leon was on location, but in the city. "Sure," I assented, as he hustled me down the hallway and into an elevator. We rode down in silence. Once in the backseat of one of England's commodious black taxis, glass window between us and the driver closed, I asked, "What was that all about?"

"The only thing I can say is that you better keep Cathy away from that lecher," he said, his mouth becoming tightly drawn.

I would not call Sidney a prude. And certainly he was in the front line fighting for free expression. He had, however, his own code of morals and rules that he lived by. One did not swear in front of a lady. One never drank hard liquor before five p.m. Debts must be paid on time. A certain decorum must be upheld in dress and manner. And—most certainly—a man must never, ever, have sex, or even foreplay, with a woman under the age of consent. He felt strongly that Ray Stark had desecrated the last two and refused to return to the Dorchester. We retreated to Lennox Gardens and so the convenient thing seemed to remain there for the work that we had to do. Leon was extremely good about this and was to prove most helpful. We had acquired reel-to-reel tapes made by Fanny Brice shortly before her death in 1951, with the intent of working with a cowriter on her autobiography. Leon transferred them to more easily accessible tapes playable on a small recorder. Fanny's honesty about her own missteps in the marriage—and the intonation of her voice—added much to her character and more depth to the story; especially to a better understanding of her love affair and marriage to Nicky Arnstein. Nicky became more human—whereas in the play, he was no more than a plot device or a lead-in to a song.

We hired a secretary named Roxanne (I have forgotten her last name—but it was of Scottish derivation), who set up her "office" in our hallway on the dining room table. Sidney hired her, not just because she was a fast typist and could read both his microscopic and my sprawling handwriting, but that she laughed at all his jokes (which were usually more witty than jokey). She was an attractive young woman (although no beauty) in her midtwenties. A few days after she started work, she asked if she could discuss a matter of some importance with us. Yes, of course. What was it? Well, she was first an actress and *then* a secretary, and she hoped we would not mind if she received calls on the telephone from her agent. Sure, okay, we agreed. Also—uh-oh! They would be asking for Ruth Bernstein. That startled us somewhat. Why? we asked.

"You know better than anyone how popular—because of Barbra Streisand—Jewish actresses are right now. So I have changed my name—just for the stage, of course."

She did not leave our employ to go upon the stage—so I don't know what her career was after she departed our services several months later. However, I never saw the name Ruth Bernstein on a theater marquee.

Summer was upon us. Michael was back from his first year at Berkeley where he had truly found his niche, was doing academically well, and had become involved with campus politics which were of national note at the time. I don't think he had seriously considered another school, although he had been offered scholarships to numerous ones. Robbie Garfield, now remarried to Sidney Cohen, a theatrical lawyer, had pushed for his going to Brandeis University, where she had donated a large sum of money. She wrote a wonderful letter to the board. When accepted, Michael turned the offer down. President Lyndon Johnson (the connection through my aunt Mary, who was his sister-in-law at the time) extended him an invitation as a presidential scholar. He refused in a letter to the president, citing his views on the president's continuation of the Vietnam War. Summer holidays in England and Europe do not correspond with those in American schools, so Cathy joined us somewhat later from Buser's.

It was about this time that Robbie and John Garfield's son, David—in London to attend the Royal Academy of Dramatic Arts—came to stay with us. Lennox Gardens was filled with the youth and the vitality of music other than Leon's daily practicing. He was not a totally happy camper. Not that I could blame him. Streisand's recording of the show was played over and over—her unique voice a constant trumpet in our ears. Mixed with Beatles' music and mania as well as Fanny/Barbra, Nicky Arnstein, and Jule Styne's marvelous score, the place had suddenly become a set for a revival of a 1930s Frank Capra or Preston Sturges madcap movie.

Ray Stark was married to Fanny Brice's daughter Frances. This created story problems for us. We were strongly warned that certain true incidents must not appear in the script—or should be fictionalized to gain Frances Stark's approval. It did not help that Nicky Arnstein was also alive and promoting his interest—mainly financial. This made the time frame difficult as Frances had actually been born before their marriage. The play had in an earlier rendition been a film script written by Isobel Lennart, for which Stark had not been able to make a deal. Lennart then adapted her screenplay for the theater. According to the play's director, Garson Kanin, he did a considerable amount of uncredited doctoring. We had all versions—but it was those reel-to-reel tapes and Fanny's own voice that had most inspired us.

We never consulted Isobel, whom both of us had previously known. She had been a lethal informer during HUAC, her testimony severely damaging the lives of many numbers of our close associates. Since then, she had adapted many lighthearted scripts from book or theater to film, mostly with great success (*Please Don't Eat the Daisies* and *Two for the Seesaw* among them). Apparently, her testimony before the Committee had saved her career. Still, informing had cost her dearly. She battled alcoholism and a fractious marriage, and had lost most of her old friends.

Sidney and I had concurred in making Nicky Arnstein's role much stronger. But, of course, we would keep the story Fanny's. On the tapes, Fanny had revealed that she knew a great deal about Nicky's gambling and was not in any way the innocent that she appeared in the stage version. Also, she had made these tapes with a plan to publish an autobiography based on them, so why not incorporate the stories she told as long as Frances's birth date was protected? Our first script opened with Fanny—already a star and married to Nicky—dressed elegantly, rushing down a prison corridor, stopping at the cell occupied by Nicky. She expects to see him ravaged. Instead, he is impeccably dressed and involved in a card game with his fellow inmates in which he was winning. She departs after a difficult exchange between them and marches out of the prison. We then flashed back to her early days on Henry Street and followed through with the story, obliging Frances Stark's request for altering time lines. We created the Georgia James character, the Ziegfeld showgirl who befriends Fanny, the relationship allowing us to use integral incidents Fanny described in her tapes to be included in their heart-to-heart discussions.

Just before the Baltimore Railroad scene ("Don't Rain on My Parade"), we inserted one with the Ziegfeld Follies' great black star, Bert Williams, pointing up the harsh racism that existed at that time (Williams was not allowed into the same railway car as the rest of the Follies' cast, although he was one of its major stars). We thought Fanny would be wobbly and funny dancing on roller skates (Jule had a new song that we could use) and that it would emphasize how far she would go to be a funny girl, and replaced one of the show numbers with it. Having the jail scene first seemed to work—as it added the suspense of wondering when "the shoe would drop" and the honeymoon would be over. When this happened, near the end of our version, there were harsh accusations on both sides. Then came the final in-performance scene of Fanny singing the great torch song, "My Man," that had been her signature song in real life. As the song was composed by Maurice Yvain, not Jule Styne, rights had to be secured, an extra cost Stark was not keen to incur.

Writing of the script extended over a lengthy period with Sidney traveling back and forth from Cannes (and in one instance in my going there for several weeks). When we finished the first draft, Sidney flew alone to New York with it to confer with Ray Stark. Their meetings were rife with differences. Calls from Sidney in the first few days of his meetings became lengthy story conferences. He wrote me two extensive letters, both six pages long and written in minuscule script on onionskin paper. I had to use a magnifying glass to read them. "This is a new one on me," he wrote, "having story conferences across an ocean. How are you holding up? I'm fighting for what I believe could be a good movie. . . . Never in all my years as a screenwriter have I known a player to have the control that has been given to Mrs. Gould [Streisand]. . . . I can't even talk about Isobel's sudden interference. She has become an alcoholic and Johnny, too [Isobel's husband]. . . . Take my notes that follow and see what you can do about incorporating them into the script."[2]

Sidney was back in London a week later, and we worked on the script every day for about a month. A revised draft was completed on November 7 and sent air express to the agent in New York.[3] The good news was that William Wyler was being positioned as director. Willie had never made a musical and so Herbert Ross would be brought in to direct the performance scenes. We trusted in Willie's story integrity. Ray Stark, I'm sure, had chosen him for his other strength. Willie worked wonders with his female stars: Bette Davis in *Jezebel* and *The Little Foxes*, Merle Oberon in *Wuthering Heights*, Greer Garson in *Mrs. Miniver*, Olivia de Havilland in *The Heiress*, and Audrey Hepburn in *Roman Holiday*. It seemed that if anyone could handle the willful Streisand in her first movie, Wyler was the man to do it (he was known during standoffs with Davis, a most difficult star, to turn off his hearing aid and wait until her mouth had stop moving before patting her on the shoulder and then turning it back on).

The bad news was that Stark wanted further changes that Sidney felt would compromise the story. He left Cannes and flew to New York. After several contentious sessions with Stark, Frances present at one, Sidney rang me in London.

"It's impossible! Frances insists on having Fanny [her mother] air-blown into an unblemished heroine with no culpability for the breakup of her marriage. I'm told Streisand hates our script because Nicky Arnstein's role has been too expanded. She has the power of veto, something I would never have given to one of our tried-and-true stars at Columbia."

"What do you want to do, Sidney?" I asked.

"If you agree, bow out. Let them hire another writer or writers."

This was Sidney's call. I had no choice but to agree.

Isobel was called back in. I have no knowledge of how much she actually contributed to the final rewrite. Willie later told Leon that other writers had been involved but never revealed who they were. In the end, she received sole credit for the adaptation of the screenplay from her play. Sidney said he had accepted these terms as 1) he doubted that much of our original material in our screenplay would be used as Stark was planning to return to the story line of the play script (although some of the characters—Georgia for one—and a few of the scenes we had contributed remained) and 2) Stark was willing to pay us the full price that the agent had originally negotiated (money that I certainly needed). With *Funny Girl*, Barbra Streisand proved that she was a star and could carry a film. Her performance and her singing were outstanding. Also, although unanticipated, she had a memorable, exotic beauty that shone when the lights and the camera were exactly right. However, the screenplay was no better than the play script, the love story trite, the character of Nicky Arnstein, hollow, more a model for a shirt ad than a brought-to-life portrait of a man. Streisand shared an Oscar for Best Actress with Katharine Hepburn. Her stardom was assured.

Willie Wyler took the brunt of the bad reviews for the script which, one critic wrote, caused the film to be "the nadir of his great career." Within the industry, his status was not impaired. William Wyler in his long career had won three Oscars for Best Director, and had many more nominations. (In 1976 he would be awarded the Life Achievement Award by the American Film Institute, where he was lauded as having "made films of lasting value with a frequency virtually unmatched by his contemporaries.")

To William Wyler's credit, *Funny Girl* (although more credit might be due to Streisand's knockout performance) has lasted. Whatever the failings of the screenplay (and I have no way of being assured that ours would have fared better), he directed a young, unlikely woman in a performance that benefited greatly from his experience and artistry and brought to the screen a radiant new star who might well have been a miss, not a hit, under a less talented and less patient man.

As soon as we were off the script, I settled down in Klosters for a lengthy stay. I had a completed my first draft of *The Survivors*. Now I wanted to go back and do some diligent editing. Within no time my characters began to take over my life. Some days I rose at dawn, so beautiful in any season in Switzerland, the surrounding mountains protecting the small villages, the air always fresh—and went to bed with the moon high and bright in the dark, night sky—without ever bothering to dress or undress. This was a good thing for me, but not for Leon, who was working in London and had little time left over to join me in Klosters. Our telephone calls were not always pleasant. My fault, I fear. I just could not agree to spend more time in the flat on Lennox Gardens at a time when I was writing on my own and would have to be there alone for long periods of time.

NOTES

1. As a curious personal addendum to this historical happening, the new president, Lyndon B. Johnson, was tangentially related. My mother's former sister-in-law

(my aunt Mary, married first to her youngest brother, Albert) had remarried Lyndon Johnson's brother Samuel Houston Johnson and so was the sister-in-law to the new president. During my youth and first marriage, I had spent many years in Texas (Alice, San Antonio, and had attended Southern Methodist University). Mary had been a close ally as I went through many vicissitudes. We remained close until her death in 2006. President Johnson made her the American counsel in Geneva at a time when the children and I lived part-time in Switzerland. She was a remarkable woman. At the age of ninety-one she went back to university for a PhD. She sadly passed away a year short of receiving it.

2. Letter from Sidney Buchman to Anne Edwards, Anne Edwards Archives, UCLA Special Collections, Young Research Library.

3. Copies of both of these Sidney Buchman/Anne Edwards drafts of the screenplay of *Funny Girl*, dated September 26, 1966, and November 7, 1966, are in the William Wyler Archives, UCLA Performing Arts Library and at the Margaret Herrick Library, Academy of Motion Picture Arts and Sciences. An additional copy is also in the Anne Edwards Archive, UCLA Special Collections, Young Research Library.

• 11 •

Hollywood Calling

$\mathscr{M}_{y}$ revised manuscript of *The Survivors* was ready for submission. The next step was to find a literary agent to represent it. As the novel was set in England, and as I was presently in London, a local agent appeared to be the most logical choice. On the recommendation of Alan Sillitoe, author of *Saturday Night and Sunday Morning* and *The Loneliness of the Long Distance Runner* (both made into films), and his wife, the poet Ruth Fainlight, I sent my manuscript to the attention of Mr. Hilary Rubinstein of A. P. Watt Ltd.—an old, reliable literary agency known for their prestigious list of writers, past and present. Three weeks later Mr. Rubinstein rang and asked if we could meet. As he had not been forthcoming, I could not help asking, "Did you like the book?"

"Oh, yes!" he replied with much enthusiasm. As he was only the second person to read the novel, Leon being the first, I felt greatly relieved. "Shall we meet for lunch?" he asked.

"I never have liked the rattle of dishes during a discussion," I replied. "Why not come to my flat?" We set the time and day and I gave him the address.

"I hope it isn't rude of me," he said, "but until we spoke, I thought you were British."

"I'm American," I replied. "And I consider that a compliment."

"Amazing! You've got it just right! The voices and the tone. I was certain you were English or of English background, before we spoke."

His British voice, filled with youthful animation, was educated but not of the "old chap" variety. On the agreed date, he rang the front doorbell not a minute early or late. I stood at the top of the stairs and watched as he puffed and panted his way up the last flight. His so-English-schoolboy face was flushed ruddy red with the exertion. Still, he shook my hand eagerly as he

140

entered the flat, his sun-tipped, wheat-colored hair bristling with electricity, his bright blue eyes alive with anticipation. I assumed, correctly, that he was about my age, not fond of sports unless others played them (if not true, he was certainly out of condition), and was devoted to the work that he did (it was all there in his presence and attitude). I sat him down on a dining hall chair to catch his breath (as I did most of our arriving guests) before guiding him up the last two steps to our living room.

Straightaway, no pause upon being seated, he began to discuss the book. "I believe it could be called a contemporary gothic." A beaming smile accompanied his words. "Suspenseful, but not Daphne du Maurier, although I am sure it shall be compared as such, and absolutely not crusty old Agatha Christie. Not that either likening would be a bad thing. But your novel is fresher and meatier. Mass murder, thankfully not Jack the Ripper stalking London in a fog, a surgical knife concealed under his cloak." He then made some insightful suggestions, phrased in a most polite manner—"You might consider . . ." "Perhaps, it would . . ." Finally, he sat back and took a deep breath. "If you wish to have A. P. Watt represent you, the company would be pleased to do so."

He was certain he could find a publisher for the novel in Great Britain. Of course, book advances were not in the league with those paid by American publishers. But there was good reason to believe the foreign rights on the novel would do well because "suspense, crime, and gothic novels are read avidly by readers in many countries." A. P. Watt did not solicit to the States. They did, however, often work in tandem with Curtis Brown Ltd. in New York. He thought Martha Winston of that firm would be a good choice to represent *The Survivors* in America.

I offered tea. "No, no, I never touch a drop before four," he chortled. English humor. I managed a small laugh and led him back to the endless staircases and watched him take the first flights two steps at a time and then disappear around the bend on the second floor, his step sounding a bit slower as he made the next two flights to ground level.

Our next meeting, to sign an agency contract, was at the offices of A. P. Watt, which was in a great, old early-Victorian building behind the Savoy Hotel on the banks of the Thames. Hilary, glowing with pride, took me into a large back room lined with dark-wood files, the brass pulls shined to glistening. A card adhered to each drawer contained engraved names listed in alphabetical order. He pulled one drawer open. "Arthur Conan Doyle was one of our early clients," he said, beaming, as he showed me the great writer's name on a folder. I was much impressed. Before I left, he warned me that publishers were notoriously slow and that he would be sending a copy of the novel to Curtis Brown in New York, "where publishers don't seem to respond any faster." Upon receipt, Martha Winston wrote me an enthusiastic letter adding the same bromide.

About six weeks later, small suitcase in hand, I made it down the steps on my way to get into a waiting taxi to the airport to take a flight to Switzerland, and was met by the postman on my way out. He handed me the mail, which I quickly sorted through, leaving Leon's letters on the table in the front hall and stuffing mine into my shoulder bag as I hurried out to my taxi. Not until I had settled into my seat on the plane as it prepared for takeoff did I extract the mail from my bag before I slid it under the seat in front of me. One letter caught my attention. It was from Martha Winston, Curtis Brown Ltd., New York. I immediately opened it.

Holt, Rinehart and Winston (the latter no relation to the sender) were pleased to be offering me a $5,000 advance to publish *The Survivors* in the United States and its territories. Would I accept the offer? I turned giddily to the gentleman strapped in beside me and shook the letter. "They want to publish my novel!" I cried. He just looked at me in puzzled wonderment. It turned out he spoke no English.

A week later, Hilary rang to say that W. H. Allen had also made me an offer for rights to publish in Great Britain and its territories. My editor was to be Jeffrey Simmons, stepson of the publisher, Mark Goulden. This meant that whatever editing had to be done could be achieved in London. I wasted no time and hurried back to begin work. My editor was about my age, a handsome man, good looking enough to be mistaken for a film actor: rather a larger-framed, Tyrone Power type, not in the least bit bookish appearing (often a clichéd concept of a literary editor). Extremely down to earth, helpful, and respectful of my manuscript, he only had me change a word here or there, and cut some redundant sentences and passages. I had already known Jeffrey's sister, Shirley—it was she, with the German actor Hardy Kruger, who had double-dated with David Deutsch and me when I first arrived in London. Shirley, possessing coppery hair, delicate features, and a petite figure, was presently married to John Van Eysen, a leading English film agent. Along with Jeffrey and Shirley's mother, Jane Goulden, and their stepfather, Mark Goulden, a lifelong friendship with the family was forged as it had been with Hilary Rubinstein and his wife Helge.

Amazing things happened with *The Survivors* while it was still in galleys in both countries. Blossom Kahn, the film representative for Curtis Brown Ltd., submitted the yet-to-be-published book to the director Alfred Hitchcock, who made a credible bid for film rights. Eventually, Richard Zanuck and David Brown, then producing at 20th Century-Fox, upped the price to an overwhelming six figures (overwhelming to me, at least!). Holt, Rinehart and Winston wanted me in the United States for the publication of the book and for a book tour to follow. Zanuck and Brown also wished to discuss the adaptation with me. It meant being in the States for a period of at least three months. This became a serious bone of contention between Leon and me. He felt I should remain in England and do what was needed to publicize the book from there. And what was I to do about Cathy?

We spoke at length about this, and Cathy decided that if I was going to the States for an extended period, that she wanted to go with me. "After all, they have schools there as well!" she reasoned, sensibly. Leon had just completed his work on the animated Beatles series. Why couldn't we all go to the States? I asked. Maybe it was time for him to return, for he had not been back in fifteen years. True, his US passport had been taken from him. But he was a British citizen now. He need only show his current passport. He was reluctant, but we made plans for the three of us to leave and made reservations at an apartment hotel called the Croydon, in New York, where I would see my American editor and agents before starting a tour. Two weeks before departure he changed his mind. That fortnight was the most fractious of our marriage.

In the midst of all our back-and-forth bickering (something I deeply detest), Doris Cole Abrahams came to call. Leon had always expressed a distinct dislike for Doris, based solely on the sound of her high-pitched voice, which he found an irritant, and her perennial state of near hysteria, which he claimed unsettled him. He always asked me to meet Doris elsewhere—unless he was not home. This one time, Doris rang our bell without calling first, a clue to her state as she was always proper about such things. I told her to come on up. No sooner had she entered the apartment than she broke into sobs. Gerald wanted a divorce. He had fallen in love with another woman. Leon sequestered himself in his sound room until she had left, a bit calmer although still visibly upset.

Cathy and I, along with Sandy and another poodle, a toy-sized, likewise apricot-colored, lively little bundle that Cathy had named Biba after her favorite clothing store in London, departed for New York. Biba was trained by the same man as Sandy, but ostensibly to sell to a circus, not to perform in films. She had failed "her test" at the end of her training for, although she could do dozens of clever tricks (whirling about at a dizzy pace on her two hind legs was one), she had a mental block when put in front of an audience and refused to budge once the lights came on and there was applause. The trainer (the same gentleman who had been Sandy's handler) called and asked if I would like to buy her. Biba immediately became part of our family.

While I was correcting the final galleys of *The Survivors* for publication, the book sold to the Literary Guild Book Club as an Alternate Selection and to Dell Publishing for a future paperback edition. It was early summer and

I planned to remain for three months. Michael joined us in New York for school break and we three were a family again. I moved from the Croydon to a sub-leased, twelfth-floor apartment on East Eighty-Third Street. It was not really a penthouse, but the kitchen opened onto a rooftop terrace that was perfect for the dogs to bask in the sun. My marital situation was in limbo. Leon and I needed time to sort things out, a decision with which we both agreed.

I did not see the publication of the book as a major consideration in that decision. I knew that one book—even if it were a success—did not necessarily establish an author's career. Also, a book could be written anywhere. Hadn't this one been conceived and written in England and Switzerland? The time was still not right for me to begin my book on the blacklist. My years abroad had put me out of touch with current American themes and issues. Arthur Miller, in 1953, had with *The Crucible* made the Salem witchcraft trials of 1692 a parable for McCarthyism. Still, not enough time seemed to have elapsed to write about it in real time. Civil rights in America was the burning issue (literally and emotionally). Had I never left the States, I am sure I would have become an activist for that cause. The plight of blacks in America, especially in the South, tore at my senses. Still, I had not been a part of the action and knew I could not do justice to such a story.

Angry letters flew back and forth between Leon and myself, Leon's displaying a depth of bitterness I had not perceived. He had not accepted my decision that we should be separated as a trial period to see if we could avoid divorce (or had simply reneged as he had with the apartment in Venice). Finally, in a long overseas call, I told him that I was not at all sure we could work things out.

"If it's the apartment . . ."

"That's part of it."

"What else?"

"Why have you been so reluctant to move out of a place that has such an ambiance of sadness about it?"

"I've told you my reasons."

We ended up back where we were.

Whatever the outcome in my marriage, I was certain that I would return abroad, perhaps at the end of the summer or, if Zanuck and Brown wanted me to work on an adaptation of my book, whenever that assignment was completed. One enormous dividend was the personal freedom the money I was presently making would afford me. There would be no need for me to accept an offer of work unless it was truly of great interest to me. I had never expected, or permitted, Leon to take on my responsibilities (my children, my parents). Maybe that had been wrong. I did not know then and I don't know now. But I did not think my suddenly coming into a generous sum of money would affect any decision either Leon or I would make about our marriage. I could not help but remember the difficulties in my parents' disunion. I always felt my mother would have been happier, freer, if they had divorced. The difference was she truly loved Merk. I was not at all certain of my depth of feelings for Leon. Having admitted that to myself, I felt that anything less than separation would be unfair to both of us.

I am a member of a somewhat complicated, extended family. On my father's side, there was his older sister, my aunt Bea (Beatrice). Big Charlie's second wife, whom he later divorced, gave him two more daughters, half sisters to my father. My aunt Edith, Big Charlie's beautiful third wife and half his age, had presented him with another girl, Joy, and a son, Robert, always referred to as Bobby in the family. We two were only a month apart in age and had been close since childhood. Bobby had been a frail child, a confused adolescent, and a resentful adult. He had known since his youth that he was homosexual and did not keep it a secret from either of his parents. Aunt Edith considered it a passing fancy and insisted on pairing him with the daughters of her good friends. Big Charlie knew damned well that he had fathered a homosexual and could not stand the sight of him.

Although plagued by childhood asthma and, later in life, a blood disease, Bobby had grown into a man with a strong, macho appearance. He had been the one to inherit Big Charlie's height and the ice-carved profile—sharp bones, strong chin. His blond hair had recently begun to thin and he shaved it all off, giving him an even bolder appearance that was at odds with his sensitive nature. He was an intelligent, self-reliant man dedicated to a career in social services and was now a well-respected, top executive in that field for the city of New York, a good friend of the mayor, often appearing on television news and talk shows. He had changed his name from Robert Josephson to Robert Jorgen to negate his father, and perhaps his Jewish heritage. I believe it pleased Big Charlie, who wanted to have nothing to do with a homosexual son. His current live-in partner was Mickey Deans, a good-looking young man who was, at present, working as a night manager at one of the city's most popular disco clubs, Arthur (founded by Richard Burton's ex-wife, Sybil), in the building that had formerly housed the famous El Morocco, a mecca for celebrities. Arthur had inherited that reputation.

Unlike Bobby's previous partner, whom I liked and admired, I did not take to Mickey Deans. He was too slick, too in your face, too enamored with celebrity. Whenever I did see him at Bobby's, he would be spewing with scandalous gossip picked up in the club. Bobby's three-room apartment, at the rear of the fourth floor in a run-down, prewar building on East Eighty-Eighth Street and Lexington Avenue, was far from glamorous. Dark during the day (when he was at work), it came alive at night, for Bobby had a great sense of style and an instinctive talent for how to use light to its best effect. There was a living room, bedroom, narrow bathroom, and galley kitchen. The living room had recently acquired a small, upright piano, rented by Bobby for Mickey's use.

Bobby was very much into his work and was forever finding and helping "almost lost causes" whom he was certain he could save. Whatever extra money he had went into these efforts. He was a good person, and I hated seeing him taken in by so obvious a user as Mickey Deans. I have to admit that Mickey possessed a disarming boyishness that he had honed to near seductiveness along with a calculated charm. Slim and vital, he seemed never to be static. He paced a lot, drummed his fingers (the nails well manicured) on the arms of the chair in which he sat, doodled whenever he had a pen and paper close at hand, and gestured animatedly as words shot out of his mouth rat-a-tat-tat. He sang in an untrained voice to his own simple piano accompaniment. Being of Greek American background, his true name was Michael DeVinko. He had made his way on his own from the age of sixteen playing gigs in small-time New Jersey clubs. It had taken him fifteen years to make it to Arthur and the "big time." Bobby was clearly in love with him. What Mickey got from this relationship can only be speculative.

As Mickey told it, he had met Judy Garland while acting as courier to deliver pills to her suite at the St. Regis Hotel; an act of friendship for an acquaintance, he said. Judy had been unable to get herself together to fly to a performance in Chicago. The pills had been delivered to him at the club in an envelope. His agreement to do what had been asked of him, he explained, was because he knew how important they were to a troubled performer like Judy and because he, himself, often needed ups to keep going and downs to sleep. They had seen each other frequently since that time and she had been coming into the club to wait for him to finish his shift.

Early one morning, Bobby called me with an unusual edge of panic to his voice. Mickey had brought Judy Garland, in a near coma, back to the apartment at dawn. She was asleep or unconscious in the bedroom—he had been unable to ascertain which. He was terribly worried about her condition. Could they come right over? What he was suggesting was that they wrap Judy up and transport her in a taxi to my apartment (about ten blocks away) for her to stay until she came out of her stupor as both Bobby and Mickey had to go to their jobs and I was working in my apartment and so could watch over her. Although furious at Bobby, I was greatly concerned about Judy who, from what I had been told, appeared to be in need of professional care, not a watchdog. I also had Michael and Cathy to think about, and I was damned sure I would be one of the last persons that Judy, once conscious, would choose to see her in such a condition. Whatever the consequences, I told Bobby that Mickey, being the responsible party, should call a legitimate doctor or paramedics. I offered to come right over and wait until either one of them arrived as long as Mickey waited with me. Bobby hung up angry but, in the end, the two of them remained with her until late that evening when she became fully awake. Mickey then took her to the club with him, sequestering her in his office with a compliant employee to help him get her through the night when they returned to Bobby's small apartment. And so her romance— and her dependence on Mickey Deans (who saw neon marquees and residual fame attached)—began.

Judy had been in London during the summer of 1964, her health failing, her life a wrenching tangle of drugs, bad decisions, and endless court cases—divorce proceedings with Sid, as well as a custody suit that he had filed against her, debt collectors placing liens and suing, and her agents claiming unpaid fees. During that time, she had met and married her fourth husband, the considerably younger Mark Herron (not at all sure that her divorce to Sid was final), a film hopeful whose only professional appearance had been as a bit player in the Federico Fellini film, *8 1/2*. She had been hospitalized almost immediately upon her arrival with cuts on her wrists, which she claimed were caused accidentally by a scissor that she was using to open a trunk. Not long after, Herron disappeared from her life (Judy would later say that Herron conducted their relationship "from a moving telephone booth").

I was in Switzerland most of the summer of 1964. When I returned to London, Judy was in the hospital again, this time with "an acute abdominal condition." I visited her twice. Her frailness shocked me. She looked pitifully small and could not have weighed more than ninety pounds. I was, therefore, alarmed to learn only a few weeks later that she had accepted an engagement at the Palladium, then relieved when Liza, teenage and adult in many ways, joined her mother in London and agreed to appear with her in the concert. I did attend a performance, but did not go backstage afterward. Judy had been puffed with pride as she shared the stage with her daughter. I think I just wanted to carry away that image with me.

Now, just two years later, she was back on pills (more probably never cleaved of them), placing herself in the control of a man who seemed inadequate for the kind of support and care that she required. She was dead broke, further in debt, unable to pay her hotel bill, and had no place to go.

She remained at Bobby's, occupying the bedroom for a week or more while he and Mickey shared the pullout sofa in the living room. Then Bobby borrowed money so that she could check into a hotel. I have no idea what (or if) Mickey contributed.

The situation grieved me. It was not easy to walk away from a seriously troubled Judy Garland. Still, I felt I had to keep my distance. My concentration and resources had to be on my kids and my new career. Truth was, I felt relieved when Dick Zanuck and David Brown asked me to come to Los Angeles to discuss the screenplay of *The Survivors*. My feelings were bolstered when my publishers suggested that I coordinate a book tour, to kick off with an appearance on a popular nighttime West Coast television show with the publication day of the book, and then cross the country—East, South, Northwest, the upper Pacific Coast States, and back to California. Such an expansive publicity campaign, especially on a first novel, was not always the case. Irwin Shaw had even decried the lack of publicity on his most recent book, as had Vera Caspary, and both of them had been well known. I was informed by author friends that I was very lucky.

Cathy and I flew to LA, while Michael headed for Berkeley. We went directly to an apartment on South Spalding Drive in Beverly Hills that I had prerented in New York sight unseen from Garson Kanin, who co-owned the building with his brother, screenwriter Michael Kanin. (I was friendly with Garson and his wife, Ruth Gordon, in England long before *Funny Girl*.) They had bought it both as an investment and as a place where Garson and Ruth could stay when in California. The Kanin brothers' elderly mother also had an apartment in the building, a situation I later realized was not too agreeable to Ruth. The first thing I did was enroll Cathy at Beverly Hills High School. Then I went over to nearby Sloane's Furniture and purchased a few necessary pieces for our comfort. I had taken the apartment as furnished. However, the Kanins had left only bare necessities. The apartment itself was elegant and far exceeded my expectations. But it was absent of any personal touch. I rather liked the idea of lending my own style to it, especially since I had the money to do so, and because the apartment had been rented to me far below its market value.

The building was unique in that two wings, which faced a wide courtyard, were centered by a small tower that contained two duplex apartments with their own entrance. On the lower floor of my apartment, one entered into a reception hall that led to a beautiful high-ceilinged living room with log-burning fireplace. Off this room was a glassed-in, lanai-sunroom from which one could look across the courtyard onto the street. The dining room would generously seat eight to ten guests. The pine-paneled kitchen had a built-in dining nook. Up a few steps and set back from the living room was a den or office, small but useful. Upstairs there were two good-sized bedrooms and baths, and a master bedroom suite that had its own private terrace for sunbathing. It all seemed too good to believe. We settled in fast and Cathy started school. Letters from Leon were caustic. "I hope you're happy now with your dogs and all that sunshine!" Not a good way to win back my affections.

My first meetings with Dick Zanuck and David Brown were warm and welcoming (as they would always continue to be). Although considerably younger, they were, like Sidney Buchman, gentlemen of the old school. Dick was the son of the dynamic Darryl F. Zanuck, who had been with Joseph Schenck, a founder in 1935 of 20th Century-Fox, and chief of production for over twenty successful years. As one of the most powerful men in Hollywood, he did not suffer yes-men easily and was famous for his studio meetings with his underlings where he would snarl, "For God's sake, don't say 'yes' until I finish talking!" Having had enough of Hollywood by 1962, and believing that the passion had gone out of the Industry, he joined his French mistress in Paris and appointed Dick vice president in charge of production. The relationship between father and son was (as were most of Darryl Zanuck's close connections) stormy. The son inherited a lordly title to a dominion in ruins. With the catastrophe of *Cleopatra*, the studio was on the edge of bankruptcy. Not one movie was being filmed on the huge lot. Dick closed the studio down except for a bungalow, which he took over for his office.

"That's where I operated the studio for two years. It was me, a legal guy, a couple of janitors, and a guard at the gate. You could literally see the tumbleweeds [on the old back lots]." Except for his talent as a filmmaker, Dick was nothing like his father. Small of stature, he was big on ideas and ran his office not on fear and bombast, but with intelligent discussion and respect for the opinion of others.

David Brown had been the studio's story editor then head of the story department when, in 1969, he became Fox's executive vice president of creative operations. Dick's senior by eighteen years, David was a tall, slim, always impeccably attired man, with a jaunty mustache, a wide smile, and a twinkle in his eyes. Before his association with Fox, his had been a literary background as editor of both *Liberty* and *Cosmopolitan* magazines, well known then for their fine short stories (and his as a contributor). The two men teamed up later to coproduce. They were a dream partnership, really. I have always referred to David as a "Bloomsbury gent." He held writers in high regard and had an acute understanding of how to adapt a book to film. Due to the difference in their ages, one might suspect that David was a substitute father image to Dick. That was not what I observed. They were much more like two bonded colleagues.

For our first meeting the three of us had lunch at the studio commissary's executive dining room. Paul Newman sat at the next table (he had recently completed work on *Butch Cassidy and the Sundance Kid*). I admit that my eyes strayed from time to time to his table. I think he was the handsomest man I had ever seen—bar none. It was the depth of intelligence reflected in his face that contributed a lasting impression. Dick then escorted me personally around the studio with a stop on the previously used set of the Harmonia Gardens for *Hello, Dolly!* (the great scene where Streisand, as Dolly, comes down a seemingly mile-long staircase to be welcomed back). Dick and David had grand ideas for *The Survivors*. They wanted whatever contribution I could give, but let me know straightaway that a studio writer would do the final adaptation (this turned out to be John Gay). They envisioned a cast headed by Audrey Hepburn (who had just completed shooting on *Wait Until Dark*) and Gregory Peck, both under contract at the time to Fox. I could not have been more pleased with the substance of our meetings.

Meanwhile, I had the publication of the book and the subsequent publicity tour to deal with and to ready myself for the latter, which was to take me to twenty-one cities in twenty-five days ending with several additional days of appearances in Los Angeles. To make sure Cathy, the apartment, and the dogs were in good hands, I hired a housekeeper, Lucy Adams, a marvelous black woman who immediately became a family member. I also engaged Jay Schlein to help me with research on the new project and secretarial needs on my current, crowded agenda. Jay had worked as a secretary for various writers, including Garson Kanin, and his know-how was extremely useful. He was also crazy about Cathy and the dogs and had enlisted Lucy into teaching him how to cook.

Jay was gay and had recently been freed of concealing his sexual choice by the death of his elderly, conservative mother, who had been in his care for years. He was a minted breath of freshness, good humored, bright, and always helpful. His sister's husband was a well-known Hollywood agent whose top client at one time had been the irrepressible, Brazilian, singing-dancing star with towering fruited hats and raised platform shoes, Carmen Miranda. At one point, at the height of her career, she had been in danger of losing her American visa and her agent his handsome 10 percent. Marriage to an American citizen seemed to be the answer, and Jay was almost badgered by his brother-in-law into being the dupe. Jay finally refused under threat of exposing his homosexuality (which would have let the government know that the marriage was a facade). A year after this incident, the "Brazilian Bombshell" died of a sudden heart attack.

Letters arrived in a steady stream from Leon, sarcastic in tone but yet hopeful. He wanted us to unite for a time just as soon as all the work on the publicity of the novel was completed. He felt we should try to work things out and that he was sure we could do so—"if only your head isn't turned now and you remember the good things we did share and could go on sharing." In another, he closed with "I love you deeply and do not want to lose what we can have together."

Truman Capote's "nonfiction" novel, *In Cold Blood*, had recently been published and caused a huge controversy over its subject—the real-life mass murder of the entire Clutter family in Kansas—and its new "faction" category. The book was brilliant—Capote at the top of his form—and it had been on the best-seller list for months and was to be a motion picture. The publication of my novel, quite accidentally, fit right into the theme—mass murder—without actually being like it in any other manner. My prepublication reviews in the trade papers were good, but the book had only been shipped to stores that week. To kick off my publicity campaign I was booked on a nighttime television talk show hosted by the controversial Joe Pyne, who had a huge viewing audience. However, Truman Capote, without question, was the star guest, to be given a lengthy time slot after which I was to have three and a half minutes.

I met Capote only briefly in the Green Room before he went onto the set and sat down before the camera for his interview. While there, he did not engage me in conversation nor do I recall that he even glanced at my book, which was resting on a coffee table in front of both of us. As I watched his turn on the television set in the Green Room, it was impossible not to observe his growing dislike for Joe Pyne, who was a mean-spirited, confrontational interviewer who was deliberately attempting to push Capote into a heated verbal exchange—leaving little doubt that he was antigay (among many other things). By near end, Capote was a tough adversary, hard to get the best of. But there was a moment when he seemed about to stalk off the set. Just before going to break, Pyne picked up a copy of *The Survivors* from his prop desk and turned it to show the cover to Capote. "I don't suppose you've read this book as yesterday was its publication date," he said. "But it also tells of the mass murder of a family." Truman grabbed the book from his hands and stared for a brief moment at it.

"*The Survivors!*" he snapped with a slight lisp. "Of course, I've read it. It's the best gothic novel since *Wuthering Heights!*" The camera zoomed in for a close-up of the iconic Truman Capote holding up my book—which had a gray-and-black cover that was a clue to its noir content—and then cut to commercials. I was then rushed onto the set. Mr. Capote had already disappeared and I was never to see him again.

"Well, well! The best book since *Wuthering Heights*," the host said.

"Hardly," I smiled (rather weakly, I am sure). "Mr. Capote said 'gothic novel.'" Pyne decided not to go there and we went through a brisk three minutes of, "You're not English?" and then "Is *The Survivors* as gory as *In Cold Blood*?" Quickly followed by, "What's the matter with you writers? Not enough blood being spilled in Vietnam for you?" I think I held my own.

I returned to the Green Room where the publicity representative from Holt, Rinehart and Winston, who had accompanied me, was waiting. She was ecstatic. "I'm calling the office first thing in the morning to use Truman Capote's quote! That was just fantastic!"

A moment later one of the show's staff came in to tell me to pick up the telephone, there was a call for me. I could not imagine who it could be and feared some disaster at home. An excited man's voice—most distinctive—American, a touch of masculine bravado in it. "Miss Edwards, this is Rod Serling. I just saw you on the show and would like to meet with you as soon as possible."

I knew of Rod Serling from his groundbreaking television series, *The Twilight Zone,* but was unclear why he would be calling me on an unlisted telephone in a television studio. "I'm set to leave on a book tour," I told him.

"When?" he asked.

"Next Monday." This was a Thursday night.

"Tomorrow. Lunch."

"I can't."

"Three p.m., then?"

I explained my problem. I would love to meet with him (I now assumed he might be considering hiring me to write an episode for a new series that I had read he was developing), but I had a lot of things to take care of before I was off on my tour. He persisted. Well, if he wanted to come to my apartment, so I wouldn't have to travel someplace for a meeting—fine. He agreed. I gave him my address and telephone number and headed home. It had been a long, exhausting, and eventful day.

The next afternoon at near the appointed time, I glanced out my windows on the lanai to see parked in front of the building, the most extraordinary, fire-truck-red car, long body, lots of shiny chrome, the convertible top down. I had never seen anything like it. Custom made or European, I thought. The driver jumped out and stood staring up at the building. The sun was very bright and he wore sunglasses. I wasn't sure it was Rod Serling, but as he was making a beeline for the private entrance to the two penthouse apartments, it seemed likely. I watched as old Mrs. Kanin, seated on a bridge chair in front of her apartment, gave him the once-over. He must have taken the steps two at a time as my doorbell rang almost as soon as he disappeared into the building.

He looked to be a longtime resident of Southern California, skin tanned to light leather color, some pale spots around his eyes where he had worn his sunglasses (now removed). A short man, perhaps five foot, five inches as we were eye level and I was wearing flats. He was firm of body and handshake, wide of smile, a bit boyish as he swept his dark hair back from his forehead. The dogs were immediately all over him and when he sat down on a living room chair, Biba jumped up on his lap. He laughed and let her settle in with him. You would never have guessed this was the first time he had come to visit.

He lit a cigarette and told me he had spent the morning reading the novel and liked it a lot. Someone had sent him a prepublication copy, which he had just begun when he tuned in to Truman Capote's advertised television interview the previous night. From what we both had said (it seemed he believed Mr. Capote's praise, although I am quite sure Truman Capote had never read a word of the book before that astounding quote), he felt moved to contact me. Indeed, he was developing a new series and I seemed to be someone who might have a story he could include. Having now finished reading the book, he wondered if the film rights were available. I told him that they had been bought by 20th Century-Fox. He did not seem too disappointed to hear this and commented that it would make a good movie. We got on to other things—England, people he knew there (a few expats whom I also knew), and his car.

"What is it?" I asked.

"Excalibur. There aren't many of them."

"I can see why."

Cathy came bursting in with a friend. I introduced them to Rod and they went upstairs to her room.

"Would you like to take a ride in it?" he asked eagerly, a young boy showing off his latest toy.

"I think I would," I replied.

He advised me to fetch a scarf and when I returned, he grabbed me by the hand and hurried me out, past a disapproving Mrs. Kanin and to the car. I walked around it in awed admiration. No wonder it was called Excalibur. It was something King Arthur might well have fancied. He headed up toward the ocean at a clip as fast as traffic and the speed limit permitted. He was a confident driver, and he and Excalibur had obviously become fast, close buddies. He drove to a spot on the oceanfront where there were no buildings—just a wide, golden expanse of sand and the deep blue Pacific washing up on it in great frothy white waves. Something had happened between us. He swore later that he really had come to speak to me about possibly doing some writing for his company. But although we talked about everything imaginable, and seemed in harmony with views—political and philosophical—we never spoke about what had actually prompted that first call. He asked me if I had a guy in my life. I told him I was separated from my husband, who was in London. "And you?" I asked.

"Married with two daughters. But currently separated," he replied.

The tentative word "currently" caught my attention, but I did not question him further. There was no doubt in my mind that we were mutually attracted. I had not dated another man since leaving England (or even considered the idea during our life together). If there were danger signals, I closed my eyes to them. After all, I was leaving town just three days later for an extended trip and I thoroughly enjoyed his company. We had dinner together that evening at Armstrong Schroeders, which was on my corner and quite a popular restaurant. He came by the apartment on Saturday and Sunday and, to my extreme surprise, showed up at my flight's departure gate early Monday morning just before I was to take off on my book tour.

"See you in Chicago," he said after taking me in his arms and kissing me rather soundly. Chicago was only three days away.

· *12* ·

A Question of Adultery

$\mathcal{T}$he extended book tour was considered an enviable endowment bestowed singularly by a publisher on an author whose book appeared headed for success. This was not unlike a bank granting loans to people with excellent credit and considerable assets. My publisher had 50 percent of the book's purchase for softcover to Dell as a selection of the Literary Guild Book Club and for a condensation in *Cosmopolitan* magazine. However, Holt, Rinehart and Winston did not have a percentage of any stage, film, or foreign rights, except for Canada. They had already made in sub-rights well over thirty times my extremely conservative $5,000 advance. (I had received six figures from Dell alone and would not receive a royalty statement for six months with the accounting of and a check for the book's sales.) Lost in this loaded literary reward system were books by some excellent authors who had not had the luck of a spectacular debut such as mine. True, *The Survivors* was no *Gone with the Wind*, nor in my opinion could it be compared to the more recent *In Cold Blood*. But, if indications proved reliable, it had a chance to do exceptionally well in the marketplace.

My job was to help boost sales beyond current estimates. I was to be a live, talking advertisement, appearing on local and national television and radio shows, giving press interviews, signing books in bookstores, and appearing as a speaker at the popular book-and-author luncheons that were the fund-raising staple for women's clubs across the country. Most fair-sized cities had a local early-morning television show. Radio interviews were generally conducted either very early in the a.m. or in the evening (to catch the daily commuters and late-night drivers). The idea was to push your book, to intrigue, to sell yourself and your subject. Some very fine authors who I knew found this a difficult, often impossible, task. They were comfortable only with the written, not the spoken, word. My experience and training as a child performer had finally come in handy. I loved to face an audience and felt rewarded with the sound of applause. I was also an unrepentant storyteller at dinner parties and was not intimidated by a microphone, a camera, or a room filled with three hundred women (and a few good men) picking away at a lunch that was generally boring and tasteless in the hope of breaking their tedium with a bit of culture or amusement. To get their attention, I always told a funny story first, preferably one that involved their area that could connect in some way to my being there (I made a habit of reading the local papers before starting off for the day).

Although I had appeared on that one program in Los Angeles, my tour officially started in New York City where I stayed for two and a half days at the Plaza Hotel, with its marble floors, Grecian columns, and the rarified air of grander, past decades. There was still what might be called "a gentleman's bar" and the strong scent of expensive cigars. The hotel's famous nightclub, the Persian Room, featured a glamorous singing star, seen on the poster outside wearing a gown worthy of an MGM designer, sleek and silvery, a thief's ransom of diamonds about her neck and dangling from her ears (or good imitations). At the heart of the grand, ground floor (highly polished brass humidors placed about conveniently, great vases with massive floral arrangements vying for space), was the area called the Palm Court, with red-jacketed waiters and ersatz palm trees. I hated it (so damned American chi-chi!); I loved it (so damned American chi-chi!). My room was somewhat of a letdown—high ceilings, skimpy on furniture, and a black-and-white all-tiled bathroom that when you flushed the toilet must have sent a gushing sound several floors above and below it! But, hey! This was the Plaza New York and, like the Ritz in London, where the best people stayed. I appreciated the fact that my publisher had put me there.

A member of their publicity staff accompanied me on all my rounds. I recall that her dresses were too long, her hair too short, and that she constantly forgot if we were going uptown, downtown, east, or west. Late-night radio was the most tedious and the hosts generally quite rude, whereas daytime radio was lighter and often fun. My favorite television appearance was on the Virginia Graham talk show where the great opera diva, Beverly Sills, was the other guest. We had a lively on-camera conversation about pickles (her father's business)—in which we both agreed they were best bright green, firm, and crunchy. Finding a segue back to my book was not easy. "Funnily enough," I managed, "a London police officer, named Pickles, was a great help in my research for *The Survivors*." Miss Sills looked like she would fall off her chair to contain her laughter, but I carried on quite seriously about crime and the law in London, slid into a comment on the current rash of grisly mass murders being reported, and then explained that although my book was a suspense story and involved a mass murder and the search for the person responsible, it was first and foremost the story of the survivor of that heinous crime. People often forgot the survivors who were irreparably marked by such crimes and concentrated, instead, on the horrific deaths of those who had not escaped.

Although Rod had a copy of my schedule, we had not been in contact since my departure from Los Angeles. I don't know what I expected, but I experienced a sense of disappointment when he was not at the gate upon my arrival in Chicago. Maybe he had decided not to involve himself further. I could understand that. Everything had happened so fast. During the flight to Chicago, I had myself felt conflicted. What did I really know about Rod other than our mutual, immediate sexual attraction? We had talked endlessly about so many things—what we liked, what we did not, movies opposed to television, political beliefs (we were both what was most commonly referred to as "left wing"), our early lives—but can you know the truth about anyone in less than a week's time? We really had only skimmed the surface of who we were. And, not uncuriously, neither of us had discussed our present situations regarding our marriages and our relationships with our spouses. Neither of us had wanted to go there.

As I stepped into the waiting room of my arrival gate, I was greeted by a uniformed chauffeur holding a card high that read ANN EDWARDS (wrong spelling, I always hated the deletion of the final *e* in my first name). At my request, the publisher had replaced the publicity aide, who had scurried about like a demented nursemaid, with a car and driver. Maybe I just wanted a bit more privacy. Mainly, I had been an independent sort of person since childhood who had always been accustomed to looking after myself (and close adults, as well) and was impatient and inwardly cross when being fussed over. I had been in enough hotels in my life to handle checking in and out, and was not the least bit shy at introducing myself to a producer or host of a television or radio program. Also, any local chauffeur would know how to find a building in Chicago (or St. Louis or Atlanta—wherever) better than a scatty lady resident of New York City. As the expense was equitable, the publisher had agreed not to send the publicity woman on the road with me. Hereafter, I was to have a car and driver at my disposal in each city on my tour.

A note awaited me at the front desk of the imposing, old-world Palmer House. "We're on the same floor—just three doors between us. Call me when you arrive. Rod." I waited until I was settled into my room (comfortable but stodgy) and had at least put a brush through my hair before I picked up the receiver and dialed his room.

"Rod Serling, here," he answered, sounding a lot like the host of *The Twilight Zone.*

"I'm alone and rather frightened," I replied.

"Of what?"

"All those mysterious objects in outer space."

"I'd make it down to your room. But, after all, I've had the longer journey. I vote that you come to mine."

We were acting like kids. There had also been an element of childlikeness and impetuosity in our short relationship. Time, I thought, to begin acting adult. "I yield to the senior Senator in the House," I said. When I opened the door to my room, I could hear another door opening at the end of the corridor. Rod stood in the hallway watching me as I approached. Then he grabbed my hand and pulled me inside and wrapped his arms around me in a tightly held bear hug. The strength in his arms always came as a surprise, despite the knowledge that he had done some competitive boxing in his youth. He had doused himself with cologne, a pleasant male scent that he often used, but it did not completely mask the detectible odor of nicotine. Rod was a chain-smoker and the ashtrays in the room held the crushed out, burned ends of numerous cigarettes. He had been waiting, it appeared, a long while for my call.

There was a terrible joy in our reunion. He had a smallish suite. The door was open to the bedroom which featured a large bed covered in a patterned spread with a matching fabric headboard. A dark, striated marble fireplace dominated one wall of the living room. A lovely crystal chandelier glistened in the reflected lights of the city that shone through the expansive window along the outside wall. He had made a reservation in one of the noted restaurants in the hotel, but suggested (strongly) that it might be nice just to have dinner served to us here. I agreed. He ordered up a bottle of champagne—I assumed because it seemed romantic and celebratory, for when it arrived neither one of us consumed more than one glass.

I had wanted us to approach our rendezvous in a slower, evolving manner. By meeting me in Chicago, Rod had stepped over the line from a romantic liaison to an affair—adulterous for both of us. Seeing his glowing face with that whimsical half smile (half insinuating, half sheer happiness) weakened any objectivity I might have had. For a long time there had been a cloud of gloom whenever Leon and I were alone together. I had felt it strongly. Leon could laugh and he could love, but he was never able to forgive himself for having done so. After we had sex (and Leon was a generous lover if not in the more material aspects of his life), I would find myself feeling disturbingly uncomforted. There was something very Russian, very Dostoyevsky, about Leon. At times this could be intriguing. In all our years together I had not been able to penetrate the many veils that his true self hid. This had seemed a challenge to which I was committed—find the real Leon, release him from his self-imposed bondage. With Leon in Europe, I felt free to be me. Rod was all boyish enthusiasm. He saw the glass half-full, not half-empty. We made love with unrestrained passion and arose from it filled with laughter (we could, it seemed, find humor in even small things) and a robust appetite.

The cover on the bed had long been displaced when we finally ordered dinner delivered to the suite and ate it dressed in the white terry robes supplied by the hotel management (with a subtle note slipped into a pocket that explained politely that the robe could be purchased before departure if the guest chose to acquire it). We talked until midnight. I agreed quite willingly to stay the night with him. Rod asked the operator for a six a.m. wake-up call. I was to be collected by my driver at seven a.m. for a morning television show. After that I had a radio interview and a stop at one of the city's largest bookstores for a book signing. I then returned to the hotel to freshen up before speaking at a book-and-author luncheon to be held in a ballroom on the main floor. When I had left in the morning, Rod had gone back to sleep. On my return I found a note. "I'll be in the audience to cheer you on." I think this was one of the first times in my life that I had a measure of stage fright. This was quickly dissipated when I located him seated at a table toward the back with two men. They were, it turned out, two members of his LA staff, whom he had flown in for a meeting (as a "beard" I suspected, a message to my brain I should, perhaps, not have shoved aside). I noticed that some women stopped by his table for an autograph and he smilingly obliged.

I was to be one of two speakers. The other was director Elia Kazan, the embodiment of the auteur, whose films were famous for their sexual and social realism. Kazan had recently published a novel, *The Arrangement*. I knew from my schedule that I would be sharing the bill with Kazan and had discussed it with Rod. There was always a sense of apprehension when an expat was placed in a social situation with an informer—and there was no more famous informer than Elia Kazan, or one viewed with more contempt by the expats and left-wingers in general. I had met Kazan only once, in the early spring of 1947 on a Sunday afternoon at the Rossens' when they lived on Warner Drive in Westwood, a lovely section of Los Angeles that surrounded the UCLA campus. He was with his wife Molly and they were on the coast, as I recall, as Kazan was filming *Gentleman's Agreement*. Jule and Robbie Garfield were also guests. The conversation centered emotionally on the subpoenas to appear before HUAC that had arrived or were currently making their way to friends and coworkers and the fear their imminent receipt was stirring. Bob was demonstrably resolute in his position of never betraying a colleague and in his contempt for those who had done so. Kazan shared these beliefs with equal vehemence.

Something in the American credo ranks informing high among the dark list of activities—murder, incest, treason—that incense their moral values often to the point of vengeance. To inform on a friend, was to many, an even greater crime than to inform on your country. In the old Warner Bros. hard-core gangster pictures (Bob's and Jule Garfield's home studio), the stoolie always got his just deserts. The three men foreswore their silence. No names. No betrayals. Fuck the Committee bastards! Time would see Bob and Kazan buckle once things got truly tough.

I was sure that Kazan did not remember me from that brief Sunday afternoon encounter. I was just a young woman engaged to marry his host's nephew and until this encounter, our paths had not crossed. I believed I had rid myself of the bitterness to which so many of my fellow expats held fast. My agenda was to be as casual as our current situation demanded. Still, I admit, I had a heavy feeling inside me. Kazan had caused more harm in his naming of names than almost any other informer. Because of his fame, of the kind of deeply moving message films and stage plays he had directed, his betrayal was the most shocking of all. Also, he did not look at all like the vital middle-aged man I had seen at the Rossens' two decades earlier. He was smaller in all ways—shorter, thinner, his mass of dark, kinky hair now receding. He had been nicknamed Gadget (and called "Gadge") because he had been constantly in motion, energized like some kind of lifetime battery. He now had the look of an unhappy man. The leanness of his face had made his large nose more prominent than I remembered, and his dark eyes had retreated further into his anatomy.

We sat at a long table on a raised dais facing the room. The president of the organization that was sponsoring the event and another woman who was to do the introductions sat between us. At either end were two people who were to be presented with an award of some kind. We had been notified that each of us (Kazan and I) would have twenty-five minutes at the very most. We would hear a little rap on the table when our time was almost up. Kazan was the first speaker. He discussed his book, which was about a Madison Avenue advertising man who self-destructs, thus bringing down all those close to him. I could not help but see an autobiographical analogy in this. But then he went on and on and on. There was a rap on the table. A second one. Then a third. His talk was now fifteen minutes overlong. Finally, our host got to her feet when he momentarily paused, thanked him, and then announced that Mr. Kazan had to leave for another engagement and so he could not personally sign books after the speeches and awards, but that he had presigned a large stack that would be on a table outside the ballroom that would be available for purchase. Although he must have arranged his early departure, Kazan was momentarily startled. He quickly regained his composure, smiled as though posing for a camera, waved his hand to the audience, turned, and with applause following him, walked out through the partings of the two curtains at the rear.

The host leaned in close to me and whispered to me to please keep my speech to twenty minutes maximum or there would not be much time for book signing. I did the best I could. Rod left with his companions at the end of my speech. I was handed a note when I sat down to sign books. ("You were terrific," it read. "Rap three times when you get back to the hotel.")

That evening I would be seeing Kazan again, as we were both on a television panel discussion show that included four men with various political views and was hosted by Chicago's well-loved television host, Irv Kupcinet. Only Kazan and I had books we were promoting. The seven of us sat around three sides of a huge dark-wood table with individual microphones set up before us. Kazan was on an end seat. I was in the center. Kazan and I were told that we should place our books on the table in front of where we were seated and when we spoke the camera would zoom in to the covers when there was a logical time for doing so. The show ran an hour with commercials. On most talk shows, guests are wired to a microphone. But we had unattached stationary mikes—so we could move during these interruptions. I got up to stretch my legs during the last break (fifteen minutes to go) and did not realize—until it was too late—that Kazan's book had been placed over mine. I turned to get his attention. He gave me a broad smile. I was not amused. When I knew the camera was not on me, I reached down as inconspicuously as I could and slid his book off and aside. It nearly knocked over a coffee mug and caused a minor moment of confusion. But when I next spoke, the camera was spot on the front cover of *The Survivors*.

I stood talking to our host for a few moments after the show. Kazan was about to leave the studio as I made my way back to the Green Room. We came face-to-face. "Mr. Kazan," I said, "I outgrew one-upmanship games a long time ago. But I hope I never grow too old to combat rudeness." He just smiled and shrugged his shoulders. I stood aside and let him pass and then watched him scurry down the hallway.

On April 4, three weeks before I was to leave for the tour (prior to my meeting Rod), I had attended a gala dinner party of about sixty people, given by Harold Cohen, a producer. It was held under a tent on a grand estate that he had rented in Beverly Hills, having recently come out to the coast from New York to inaugurate his new film company. My former agent, Blossom Kahn, was now working for him, and I attended the affair with her. Sometime between courses, a rising buzz saw of voices cut through the enclosure. Then someone ran into the tent and screamed, "Martin Luther King has been shot by a white man in Memphis!" A chill went through me. "Oh my God!" I thought. "Just like John Kennedy! Why always do they target the good men?" When we had been seated, I had made no note of it, but suddenly I realized that there was not one black face among the guests and not one white one among the dozens of the serving staff. There was pandemonium. People were sobbing. No radio or TV had been set up in the tent. Guests ran into the house or to their cars to find out what had happened. The black staff completely deserted their posts. Cries of deep anguish echoed. Blossom, a small woman, grabbed my arm. She was trembling, fearful, she confessed, of some of the staff turning on the guests.

Just two days later, and three weeks before I was to arrive, Chicago had been under siege for twenty-four hours by rioters. Arson fires flared. There was mass looting. Ten people died before the governor sent in five thousand state troops to try to control the mayhem. My publisher had wanted to omit Chicago from the tour. Several days passed before the city appeared to have come to a peaceful resolve and, as they had obtained some prime publicity outlets for me there, a decision was made (with my approval) that Chicago would be included. The reality of the riots did not hit me until I was driven through the streets where burned-out buildings were grim reminders of the fierce confrontation between the fired-up, anti-Vietnam protesters and the gun-toting troops.

I had returned home from so many years abroad, to see my country shedding the blood of its own people. We were a land in turmoil and even now, one hundred years after the Civil War, equal civil rights for blacks had not been won. Hope rested in men like Robert Kennedy and Martin Luther King. And now the man who so hoped for "peace in his time" was dead. And we were still sending our young men to be wounded and to die in a foreign place facing an enemy that had not invaded the United States.

"What has happened to my country?" I thought. I felt a terrible sadness, a sickening in the pit of my stomach. Now, here in Chicago, as I viewed the burned-out wreckage of the riots, that sickness returned.

These were issues that Rod shared with me. He was not a "joiner"—that is, to political organizations. He had found, much as I once had in writing westerns, that he could get a message across against intolerance, bigotry, racism, and the futility of war in the form of stories set in outer space or "another dimension." After the Kazan confrontation we discussed the blacklist and how everyone who was concerned, Kazan included, were victims. He was passionate in all his views and beliefs, revealing a vigorous anger against the injustice of the blacklist. I did not look at him as a cynic, for he was equally vehement in his certainty that good could in the end overcome evil.

He accompanied me in the limo to the airport. We were both flying to New York for a much-anticipated weekend together at the Plaza Hotel. He had one carry-on bag to my mountain of suitcases, packed with outfits for all occasions. I had nineteen more stops in several climates, formal and informal appearances to make, and no time to have clothes cleaned or pressed.

"Sure you don't want to change your mind?" I asked, just before we got into my waiting limo.

"Not on your life," he replied.

My original intention in spending two days in New York before continuing with my tour (instead of remaining in Chicago over the weekend) was to give me an opportunity to see some of my dear friends with whom there had been no time before I had flown to Chicago. Now, as Rod and I entered the Plaza together, I knew my agenda had changed. This was to be a very private time of coming to know each other better. I was getting in deeper and I was not sure that was the right thing for us to do, but it seemed we could not help ourselves. There had been this need to cleave together.

My publisher had taken care of my reservation. Rod again had his own room on the same floor. We both had families to consider, children who might need to reach one of us. This time the hotel had upgraded my reservation to a small suite. Rod had a standard room, so he remained with me and checked his messages frequently. We had perfect spring weather. The Plaza was across from Central Park and we had lunch, supplied by a street vendor, as we sat on a park bench. We walked—not too far from the hotel as Rod had a trick knee (a piece of shrapnel was in it, a leftover from service in World War II) and it was not behaving too well. We could not get over the fact that we both had same-leg problems ("How often does that happen?" he laughed), and we made love—now in a more familiar way. Ideas, opinions, remembrances from the times of our lives were told as though they had happened yesterday.

He came from a Jewish home (his father had been a hardworking butcher) and grew up in the small town of Binghamton, New York. He had loved his life there, his parents, his older brother, the high school he attended. He felt deeply, small-town American. Life changed for him with his youthful wartime service, which interrupted his college education. He was with the paratroopers and had been given a Bronze Star and a Purple Heart. He did not go into how these were won. But he did tell me once about seeing a close buddy of his crushed to death. (This resonated strongly with me as I recalled my father having witnessed the death of two comrades killed by a grenade.) Rod's wartime experience had badly scarred him. He still woke up at night from nightmares, haunting images of what he saw, how scared he had been at times, how close to losing a leg, his life, and witnessing the horrifying deaths of both friends and foes. Twenty-five years had passed and he still could not forget. After the war, he returned to college, which is when and where he met Carol. His parents had been upset about the fact that she was not Jewish, but he was very much in love with her; they married, and later he converted to the Unitarian religion, which he explained was based on ideals and not idols.

I did not press him on his current feelings toward Carol and he, only once that I recall, brought up my situation with Leon. I was clear that we were separated, an ocean between us and divorce not yet a settled matter. "Do you want to go back to Europe?" he asked (perhaps meaning to Leon). I had to answer honestly that I wasn't sure what my future held.

"And your writing?"

"Next to my kids, the most important thing in my life."

"Tough for a husband to accept that."

"Or a lover?"

"No. Not this one, at least."

What do I remember most about that weekend? Well, we never once turned on the television. We held each other all night, both nights. We talked and talked and talked—serious talk, nonsense talk. We went to see an old film, *Brief Encounter*, adapted by Noël Coward from his play *Still Life*, at the small revival movie house near the hotel and when the lights came up, both of us had tear-streaked faces. The story and performances were moving, but we had not expected how close Coward's fictional tale of an adulterous affair of two married people would resonate our own. It had an unhappy ending—but maybe the right one for them. Neither of us said it, but we both knew our affair might very well end in the same manner. Instead of returning to the Plaza, we got into one of the horse-drawn carriages that parked alongside the hotel and had the driver take us through Central Park. It was crazy. It was pure corn for tourists. It was romantic. What we did not do was hide out. We held hands when we walked through the Plaza lobby. Rod's arm went around my waist when we crossed a street. Terms of endearment were exchanged, a close intimacy established. We made no commitments and accepted the small world we had made for ourselves.

Our flights left at approximately the same time but from different gates, so we rode to the airport together in the limo and clung together as we kissed good-bye in the terminal for anybody to see. No one seemed to have taken notice—or recognized Rod. When we disengaged ourselves, I broke away to follow the porter wheeling my suitcases to the check-in point.

"Hey, Red!" A shout uttered in Rod's inimitable voice (a reference to my hair, not my politics).

I turned and he waved. Then he was gone—but certainly not from my thoughts.

As my itinerary was arranged to accommodate the time of special venues, it did not follow a logical progression. It took me south, back up to the East

Coast, down to Florida, to Texas, the Southwest, Midwest, east again and over the border to Toronto, then to St. Louis, halfway across the country and over the border again to Vancouver, down the Pacific Coast through Washington, Oregon, California—San Francisco to San Diego—and finally, after three weeks in the skies and on the road, I was back to Los Angeles. Along the way I reconsidered what being an American meant. We were a much-varied society. I was amazed at how both alike and unalike the people of each state I visited were. It was more than their regional accents—which were many, their political views—which were right or left, seldom both in one state, and the marvelous diversity of ethnicity and color.

Certain incidents on that inaugural tour stand out in my memory even after all the years that have since passed. No blacks in the Southern states had attended the book-and-author luncheons at which I spoke, whereas in Pennsylvania and Massachusetts, two fine black authors shared the podium with me.

Pittsburgh is recalled because of a bizarre incident. A woman, obviously suffering mental problems, grabbed me as I came out of a bookstore where I had signed books. She was diminutive, under five feet, and almost skeletal, dressed abstractly, pieces of clothing hanging at all lengths from sharp bones. Her face was heavily made up, thick black lines encircling the clearest, cold blue eyes I had ever seen. She spat at me and I pulled back. She spat again. "Jesus is returning and those who don't believe will be struck by a nuclear bomb!" she hissed. The store manager and several bystanders moved between me and the woman, and my driver was immediately by my side to guide me into my waiting limo. I had never had anyone—mad or sane—spit at me before. It was an upsetting experience.

This was the spring of 1968—a presidential election due in November. The Vietnam War was not yet quashed. Lyndon Johnson had just announced he would not run for reelection. The country was challenged by disunity. Violence was in the air with the upcoming political conventions. What we did not need were outward displays of religious intolerance, or a growing discrimination among the silent majority. The woman in Pittsburgh was mentally ill, but I was suddenly conscious on my tour of people taking their anger out onto the streets.

I flew over our magnificent mountains and vast, still unpeopled, lands. It is only when you have lived in a small country like England, and an even smaller one such as Switzerland, that you become aware of the awesome size of the States. All of Europe could possibly fit inside our boundaries. That is a startling realization. My flights, when lowering for landings and rising for takeoffs, revealed the remarkable new cities of high-rises and mirrored buildings, new for me as the only other time I had made such an intense crossing of the States was at the age of four, in 1931, the Great Depression at its abyss. My father, with the reality of his sudden loss of status and funds, had piled my mother, his sister and brother-in-law, their two teenage children, and myself into the one commodity he still possessed—a grand 1929, shiny black Packard, purchased before the 1929 stock-market crash and formerly driven by our chauffeur. (Also left behind had been my beloved, cross-eyed governess, Josephine, and several members of our domestic staff.) I sat in the front between my parents (my father driving, my aunt Bea and her family in the back, my two cousins on the jump seats). This was a terrible time for everyone else in the car—but at my young age, I knew nothing about the situation we were in except that we (my parents and I) were together and we were going on a great adventure (or so it seemed).

That early car trip across America was the happiest memory I have of us as a family. To me, my father was like a commander of a ship. He was in total charge (no one else drove). He directed our route, where and when we stopped, and where we ate. People in small towns came out on the streets and walked around the Packard in awed admiration. On the road, my father sang in his college-cheer kind of voice, "Life's Just a Bowl of Cherries," "You're Just Too Marvelous for Words," "Mademoiselle from Armentieres," "Over Hill over Dale" (actually the Marine Corps anthem—but I always called it that), and "Fine and Dandy," which was from the Broadway show of the same title in which my uncle Dave had costarred. It was to Uncle Dave's house—at that time, pre–my mother and my residing with him—on a steep hillside in the Hollywood Hills—that was our destination. Uncle Dave had always been Marion's protector, and he had stepped forward to suggest he might be able to get my father work in some facet of the film industry. Until then, my mother, father, and I could stay with him and my aunt Theo. The rest of the passengers in the car (also without funds) were to be guests of an aunt of Aunt Bea's and my father's, my aunt Dean, Big Charlie's youngest sister.

Every morning before we set out, my cousin Dickie's job (he, who traveled on a jump seat) was to wipe the car of all dust so that the black finish shone—a hard task when we drove through the dust belt where there had been a drought and then a wind and the dust clouds were nearly blinding. My cousin Aline (on the second jump seat) was charged with cleaning the car windows. I don't know who financed the journey, but my father was the banker. We stopped at motels (which I thought were fantastic, like little playhouses). Farmers stood along the highways (no super ones then) selling what little produce they had for pennies. Marion put together bag lunches for us and managed some dinners in our rooms cooked on a hot plate that traveled with us. Aunt Bea (blonde and blue eyed, skin pale, still beautiful and strangely fragile looking although weighing in at over two hundred pounds) was, to my recall, in a state of near collapse for almost the entire trip.

Our grand vehicle took us from small town to small town, up two-way roads to the ones with a passing lane in larger cities. There was heavy traffic along a good part of our route. It seemed the whole country was traveling west in any kind of vehicle that would move. Hitchhikers lined the way. We never picked up anyone. A man who thought Dickie—sitting on a curb, resting as our car was being refueled—was a hitchhiker, told him, "Boy, hunt for cows, never catch any ride on a mule," a story my cousin would repeat for years.

We passed caravans of migrant workers with their barefoot children and their junk heaps; gaunt, hungry faces at broken windows; dead animals—once pets—deserted ("Look away, Anne Louise," my mother would whisper to me and clasp her hand over my eyes). When we pulled into gas stations there would often be a woman there, a baby in her arms, begging for milk money for her tot. Men came up to my father asking for a gallon of gas to feed a car that was ready for the junk heap (in both cases my father proved benevolent). Going through Oklahoma, Native Americans, donned in full costume, performed Indian dances near roadside restaurants and passed a basket around for contributions from those who gathered to watch (dignity gone, pride vanished). The one most memorable scene in my memory of the entire journey from New York City to Los Angeles (which took us well over a week), took place after we had driven all night through the desert (to avoid the heat and the possibility of the car overheating and breaking down). Dawn, the sun just rising, I awoke to a scene of utter paradise. Everything green and lush, heavily fruited orange groves on both sides of the road.

Suddenly, a migrant family came in sight, their car parked (stalled and out of gas) to the side of the road in front of us. They were all out of the car barely dressed in tatters, the children (three or four of them) shoeless, newspapers for glass in their old jalopy car windows, boxes tied to the roof. My father parked behind them and got out to offer help to the one male occupant. He returned to our car, took a container of gas we kept in the trunk, and went back to give it to the man. The children began to run towards the ground where there were fallen oranges, an elderly woman with them. They were ravenously biting into their found fruit when a state trooper's car passed us and pulled up in front of them. Two uniformed men got out, went over to the group, knocked the fruit from their hands, and forced them back to the car. They said something to my father, who returned to our car. The small amount of gas he had given them got the jalopy going—but who knew for how far. The troopers came over to us, looking through the windows inside. "Good day, ma'am," one said, tipping his hat to my mother, and then withdrew. Both officers seemed amazed at the shiny black, neat-as-a-pin, luxury vehicle. They asked my father some questions about it and then waved us on. We passed the jalopy thumping along just a short way up the road. We all waved.

That world had disappeared along with those history and literature has called "the lost generation." I suppose one should be glad of its demise when there was so much suffering and poverty throughout our land. Still, as I flew from city to city and saw and felt the enormity of the despair and disconnect between ordinary people and the government, the young and their elders, I wondered if some things might not have been better in those days, and if we—the people—had not tried harder we might well have had the best of both worlds. A certain innocence had been lost at the gain of creature comforts, better technology. But home no longer had the same meaning.

When I arrived back from the book tour, the dogs jumped all over me as a welcoming committee of two. Cathy had arranged a special dinner including candlelight and a dessert she had made. There were several reconciliatory letters from Leon and a loving note of welcome attached to a large bouquet of flowers from Rod.

• *13* •

The End of an Affair

$\mathcal{T}$he penthouse across the hall from mine on South Spalding Drive was occupied by Dominic (Nick) Dunne, recently divorced and the father of three
children, who was in the depths of a midlife crisis. Our apartments were co-
joined only by our upstairs decks that extended from the master bedrooms.
We did share the staircase leading to our front doors and the hallway that
separated the apartments. I have always made it a point to be casually friendly
but not make friends with neighbors, as I work at home and writing is a
consuming occupation that can easily be thrown offtrack by a neighbor who
wants to borrow something or simply exchange gossip or pleasantries. I never
answer the telephone when I am writing, but a doorbell, especially if I am
alone, is another matter. Somehow, its ring is like a call to arms.

On this particular Sunday afternoon, in the fall of 1967, I was by myself,
Cathy with friends, and Jay and Lucy on their day off, when the doorbell
signaled me to rise from my bed. I was perched on top of the covers working
in longhand on some pages for my new novel, research books on the floor a
hurdle for me to get to the door of the room. Then there was the apartment's
interior staircase to navigate safely in my robe, which was, since I was barefoot, an inch or more too long. I thought it might be Cathy, who occasionally
forgot her keys. It rang again, this time more urgently. "Maybe it's Rod," I
thought, and ran my hands through my hair to neaten it a bit.

I opened the door. There stood my penthouse neighbor, Nick Dunne,
obviously in a state of great agitation. Whenever we had met before (always
in the hallway), he had been dressed elegantly and groomed impeccably—
whether in tennis garb or evening clothes. Now, his shirt was buttoned un-
evenly and hung loosely over a pair of capri pants. His feet were bare in a pair
of well-worn slippers. Most notably, his thick, dark brown hair had been hand

169

combed in an absentminded manner. Only once had we spoken more than a brief greeting and that had been a somewhat uncomfortable conversation held in the hallway, wherein I suggested it was not a good idea, considering we both had children (his three—two boys and a girl—lived with their mother, but came on Sundays to visit), for the recognizable odor of marijuana to suffuse the hallway and couldn't he smoke it in the farther reaches of his apartment? Which, from that time, he apparently had done . . . for a while, anyway. Now he asked, "Can I come in?"

"Yes, yes, of course," I replied, recognizing by his state that this was not just a neighborly visit.

Once inside, he asked, "Can I sit down?"

"Please . . . I'm sorry. . . ."

Upon entering the living room, he collapsed into the nearest chair. "This is crazy," he said. "I shouldn't have rung your doorbell."

"Obviously you are distressed about something. Are you ill?"

"I thought I was going to kill myself," he said, seeming to crumble into the back cushions of the chair. "I was afraid that if I was alone a moment longer, I would do so."

A chill gripped me and I went immediately into reflex action. Just a few weeks earlier Joyce Jameson, a childhood friend of mine, now a fine comedic actress, had telephoned me late one night to announce that she had swallowed the contents of a bottle of sleeping pills. Her ex-husband, composer Billy Barnes, rang on my second line, which I also picked up while trying to calm Joyce. She had alerted him as well. I said, "Call 911!" Billy thought it better not to do so. She had just taken the pills—we had time. He whizzed over to me and we drove at a wicked speed over the hills to her house and spent several hours holding her under the shower, walking her in the pool, back and forth on the deck, emptying pots of black coffee into her until she finally came out of the stupor we had found her in when we had first arrived. Was there something in the sunshine in LA that drove people to such extreme solutions to their problems?

"Have you taken any sleeping pills?" I demanded of Nick, this time deciding I would dial 911 if he answered yes.

"No . . . no."

"Shots? Heroin? Cocaine?" He looked disoriented enough for that to have been the case.

"No . . . no. Everything just seemed so hopeless. I've been struggling against . . . suicide." His mouth quivered when he said the word. "I'm Catholic," he uttered as an explanation, leaning farther back into the chair and closing his eyes for a moment.

"You sure you haven't taken anything?"

"Yes . . . I mean no . . . no I haven't."

"There's coffee left over from breakfast. I'll reheat it, come with me."
I helped him to his feet. He was a well-built, short man, not too sure of his
footing. He took my arm and we walked slowly into the kitchen where I sat
him down at the corner nook. Our apartments were not reverse images, he
commented with some surprise. "Yours is larger," he said and took the mug
with the hot, black coffee that I brought to him.

"Look, if you want to talk, fine. I'll listen. Then I'll forget everything
you say. Okay?"

This brought a faint smile to his very Irish face. There was a line across
the bridge of his nose from the glasses he generally wore for his shortsighted-
ness and which he had not put on in his trip of desperation across the hall to
my apartment. Things probably looked blurry to him, which did not help in
his confused and troubled condition.

His wife, "Lenny," after a long marriage, had divorced him. She had
been the linchpin in his life. She was an heiress with large sums of money
at her disposal. He had dreams of becoming a top Hollywood producer and
being accepted into a society that had scorned him in his youth in Hartford,
where Irish Catholics were excluded from such circles. Lenny had been a
grand-style party giver. She invited the most glamorous and famous guests that
she could, and reports of their parties were leads in the social columns in New
York and Hollywood, where they moved for Nick to fulfill his ambition.
He had not been able to make his mark despite Lenny's loaded Hollywood
celebrity guest lists to their extravagant parties and he did not think he could
manage his life without her. Recently, he had been arrested for possession of
marijuana. "Put into handcuffs!" he said emotionally. He got off with a hefty
fine (paid for by Lenny). He was having a hard time just making the rent, was
spiraling downhill and he knew it. And—there was more—he feared he might
be homosexual (and he was Catholic).

Although more cohesive, he was shaking and still in a bad state. I got up,
fetched a bottle of scotch or rye—I forget which—and poured him a strong
drink.

He pushed it aside. "No . . . no! I think I'm becoming an alcoholic as
well!"

"Have you eaten anything today?"

"I can't remember."

I got up and went to the refrigerator and pulled out some makings for a
sandwich and ground some beans for a fresh pot of coffee.

"Lenny is the real thing," he was saying. "I was not," he said. "Our
friends turned out to be her friends. Once we separated, I no longer got

callbacks from them. They were supposed to be the right people who could help me get where I wanted to be—where Lenny wanted me to be."

"The right people?" I queried. "Who the hell are the 'right' people?" He looked visibly shaken at my bluntness and I switched the conversation to his kids (this was the day they were to visit but he had canceled), and when that was met with a great sigh followed by a clamping of his lips, I moved on to what kind of movies he liked—or wanted someday to produce.

"Something of worth," he replied.

Over an hour had passed and I was still sitting across from him at the kitchen table in my bare feet and robe. Soon Cathy would be home, perhaps with friends. A house full of young people was not what Nick needed. Yet, I did not think he should be left by himself.

"Look," I said, "think of someone you can call. You don't have to discuss the things we have just talked about. You just need to be distracted."

"I don't think I really would have done it," he said.

"I'm sure that's true. And you aren't going to do anything drastic. So who can you call? I'll make a deal with you. Whoever it is, the two of you come here later for dinner. Okay?" There was a telephone on the ledge of the nook and I handed it to him. "I can get you a directory, if you need it," I offered.

"I'll call Mart Crowley."

"He's a good friend?"

"Yes." Nick added that Crowley had been supportive since his and Lenny's divorce. Crowley had then been Natalie Wood's secretary and a hopeful playwright. His play, *The Boys in the Band*, recently had been given an acclaimed off-Broadway production while making theater history in its bold treatment of homosexuality. Crowley had returned to Los Angeles and had been helpful to Nick during his growing state of depression.

I left the room and went back upstairs to put on some slacks, a T-shirt, and slippers. When I returned, Nick was standing by the chair in the living room where he had first been seated and in which my smaller poodle, Biba, sat on her haunches, ears pointed, alerted to defend her territory, my large poodle, Sandy, guarding her right. "Mart is coming over," Nick said.

I scooted the dogs out of the way and we sat down, Nick in the chair, me on the couch facing him, the front door left open so that we could hear his friend when he came up the stairs to our hallway. That was about a half hour later and by then Nick had regained his composure, although a hangdog look haunted his large dark brown eyes.

The next morning there was a note under my door which read: "Dear Anne—I never knew a neighbor could also be such a good friend. Thank you, Nick."

My life was filled with its own confusion. Rod was still very much a presence, the flame still bright. There is a sense of renewal in a fresh relationship, the chance to start over once again. Down deep it is difficult to believe this, for there is always too much back baggage to carry with you. Rod and I each had personal issues to work out and neither of us pressed the other for a quick resolution. My relationship to Rod—now defined in my head as "the other woman"—was previously unknown to me, and one to which I was not adapting well. I had always been so moralistic about such alliances, had taken a strong feminist stand. There was nothing equal about being the other woman—the word "other" trumped it. Nor was it for his betrayed wife, who I was sure knew nothing about us. I did not believe that Rod had actually lied to me in the beginning, just twisted the truth. He and Carol were obviously having some difficulties. He had said they were separated. And neither of us at that time realized we were spiraling on fast track into an affair. Sex played its part. But the danger was our natural compatibility, how comfortable we were with each other, our shared understanding of the creative process. I believed that, against my better judgment, I was in love with him. He conveyed the same message to me.

On days when both of us were fairly free, he would collect me in Excalibur and we would head for the ocean. We knew every small restaurant on the patch of the Pacific Coast Highway from Santa Monica to a few miles past Malibu. Sometimes, but not always, we would spend an afternoon or an evening at the house in Malibu. I called it the mystery house. Rod (under oath, he stressed) never revealed to me who owned it, only that the owner, a single friend and colleague, was in Europe making films and pending final divorce dictates was leaving it empty. It was furnished in what I call "beach style"—lots of bamboo and white upholstery. The front windows where the living room and master bedroom were situated had floor-to-ceiling windows looking out to a deck and sand and sea. A housekeeper came in once a week but almost all personal belongings had been removed. I say "almost" because on the bedroom bureau was a photograph in a silver frame of a lovely little girl of nine or ten. The owner's daughter. That picture haunted me. Why had he left it? Where was that child? The story mind in me could not let it go.

I never saw evidence of anyone else using the house, and the housekeeper did keep small edibles and drinks for us in the refrigerator. We inhabited it when we were there. Moved freely through it. Spent afternoons or evenings on the deck looking out at the vast sea to the horizon. When the weather was good, night was the most beautiful. Just us and the stars and the sound of the water rising and falling onto the sand and then ebbing into silence. We spoke two or three times a day when we did not have a meeting planned. What we never discussed was the elephant in the room. This could not last forever. Either an end or a resolution had to come. We were both married with children, although in my case my children were grown and Leon's distance and my insistence that we were definitely to view this as a separation, was less inhibiting. Considering my long absence, I did not expect Leon to remain celibate. I am not sure what his expectations were of me. But I knew I could not publicly flaunt an affair, nor be dishonest to him. There was no way I wanted him to find out through an outside source who might have seen Rod and me together. I wrote him that I was seeing someone but did not say who it was. I added that it was a caring relationship but that I was not sure it would ever go any further, which was the truth. He did not acknowledge the information, ignored it completely, but his letters immediately changed from sarcastic missiles to ones of hope for our reconciliation. ("Don't forget the good times we have shared, the help we have been to each other," he wrote in May '68, "the reawakening to a sexual unity.")

Rod's status was a different matter. Away from LA, in Chicago and New York, we had just been two people fresh with love, learning what we could about each other. We still were infatuated with each other. But, once we returned to Los Angeles, our relationship had taken on a clandestine aura. If we did meet in the city, a member of Rod's staff was present and his attitude was friendly and yet detached. The first time this occurred I informed Rod that this was not my style and found it demeaning. Why meet anywhere that we could not be ourselves? I understood his need not to bring undue pain to Carol, especially if he was unsure of where we were heading. He was apologetic, the gentle touch, a kiss on my eyelids. "Look, you owe me nothing but honesty," I told him. "I should think that you owe Carol that as well."

"I can't leave Carol right now," he replied.

"And I never have, nor never shall, ask you to do so. I did believe, mistakenly, it seems, that you had made a decision otherwise before we met." I suggested we stop seeing each other for a time. The next day he called to arrange a private evening in Malibu.

There was no doubt now in my mind that Rod, although strongly attracted to me, still loved Carol. It is possible that someone can love two people at the same time, but when there is a history and children involved, the outcome is loaded. I had appeared in his life at a time when he had experienced great changes. Although critically successful in his pre-Hollywood years when he was gaining a reputation as a writer of fine television dramas, he had not earned a great sum of money. Then Hollywood called, and in the past few years he was transformed by his own unique talent into one of the very few celebrity writer-producers, recognized in public, lauded by his peers, and rich beyond anything he might have imagined for himself. Carol had shared those earlier, tougher years with him even before his good fortune in New York and he was fully conscious of her contribution as a mother and as a helpmate to him in his career. Indeed, I admired and respected him for this. Yet, here I was in a situation that I had vowed I would never enter into, that I believed was demeaning, for me, for any woman. However, I did not want to make a decision or usher him into one that either of us might regret, for in many ways we were good for each other both creatively and in supplying what was apparently currently missing from both our lives.

What saw us through this period were the demands of our current projects, his more multiple and complicated than mine, but no less engaging. The book I was writing—a political thriller set in Paris during the recent student riots—had been contracted as the first novel of a three-book deal for Coward, McCann & Geoghegan, my new publishers (a switch made, because Thomas Wallace, who had bought *The Survivors* for Holt, Rinehart and Winston, had taken over as editor in chief for C, M & G). My protagonist was a famous Russian ballet dancer whose defection in Paris coincides with the protests. The character was loosely based on Rudolf Nureyev who, in 1961, had defected at Le Bourget Airport in Paris with the help of the French police and then gone on to dance with a Parisian ballet company. The story's background required mounds (and months) of research to ensure as much accuracy as possible. I also had to brush up on my French, which had never been good and would never get better! All in all—not an easy load. Jay was a godsend. He seemed to know when to be available and when to get so involved that I didn't know he was in the apartment. He was a terrific sounding board, and—as I had a homosexual character in my story—he was able to tell me when I had it right and when I had it wrong.

For the first time in my life, money was not an issue, which helped because Cathy would be entering university in a year's time. Michael had been on a full scholarship at Berkeley but was about to start a career, he hoped, in some facet of the political arena. His eyes were set on becoming a member of senator Robert F. Kennedy's staff. Kennedy was presently campaigning to win the Democratic nomination for president. Earlier, when Lyndon Johnson made his stunning announcement that he would not run for another term, vice president Hubert Humphrey had entered the race along with senator Eugene McCarthy of Minnesota. Senator Kennedy had not declared his candidacy until mid-March. As the brother of the country's assassinated past president, John F. Kennedy, he had national sympathy in his favor. But his political objectives were not viewed kindly by Wall Street and the business world as he stood on a ticket of both racial *and* economic justice, nonaggression in foreign policy, and decentralization of power and social equality. Only forty-two, his youth, debating skills, and passion had quickly won him the popular support of young voters. His speeches were lively and laced with a brash candor. Michael (still not old enough to vote) believed strongly in Kennedy's ideals, and he and his peers and cobelievers were, after all, the future. I could not help but feel that Kennedy's nomination and election were essential to our country—most especially because it looked as if Richard Nixon would be the Republican candidate. I respected the two other Democratic candidates, but I did not think either of those men had the ability or smarts to win against Richard Nixon, who was bound to use every dirty trick in the book to overcome his opponent.

I had a vivid memory of Nixon on the campaign trail in 1952 when he was Dwight Eisenhower's vice presidential running mate, for this was the last election I had voted in before leaving home for my unexpected long residency in England. I also recalled his disingenuous televised "Checkers" speech to rebut charges that he had taken payoffs from California businessmen during his term in office. Checkers was the name of a cute cocker spaniel (who shared the camera with him) presented to the Nixons for their daughters: the message being that gifts given to him by men seeking his patronage had nothing to do with graft but were extended in true friendship. *Sure!* Going further back— there had been his disgraceful vicious denigration of Helen Gahagan Douglas when she ran against him for a Senate seat.

The Republicans had the long, costly war in Vietnam, for which they blamed Lyndon Johnson, as a weapon. But Robert Kennedy had become connected to his countryman's pain—blacks, Latinos, returning veterans, the farmworkers who were vastly underpaid, and young people who needed financial help to gain a college education. Among liberals, a great fear had lodged itself. Robert Kennedy represented a last hope for the nation they so loved. His momentum was in high gear when he arrived in Los Angeles in early June having just won the California Democratic Primary, a crucial defeat for his closest Democratic contender, Eugene McCarthy. It looked like nothing could stop his bid for the nomination.

In the early dawn of June 5, the sun not yet fully up, my bedside telephone rang. It was Michael to tell me, in a voice near to breaking, that Robert Kennedy was dead. Around midnight of the previous evening he had been shot in the head at close range as he made his way from the Ambassador Hotel Ballroom (where he had addressed many hundreds of his supporters), through a crowded passageway with employees and what was assumed to be a pack of devoted fans, to the hotel kitchens to greet the serving staff. Upon being hit, he had fallen immediately to the floor, blood streaming from his wound, and had been taken by ambulance to the hospital. A short time later Robert Kennedy was pronounced dead. The assassin was a twenty-four-year-old Palestinian, Sirhan Sirhan, who might or might not have shot him due to his support of Israel, or was just a crazy person.

The country was once again in mourning for a man who offered great ideals, who died too early to see his dreams become reality. ("Let the dream not die," Robert Kennedy's one surviving brother, Ted Kennedy, said at his funeral.) Michael had lost his hopeful leader but was asked to be the aide to former New York congressman Charles Goodell, chosen by that state's Republican governor, Nelson A. Rockefeller, to fill Robert Kennedy's Senate seat. Michael was not sure how good a fit this was, for Goodell was a Republican, although he had been considered pretty much a liberal and he was a strong advocate in a withdrawal from Vietnam. (As a senator, while Michael worked for him, Goodell's liberal views came to the fore. After serving out Kennedy's unfinished term, he would gain the nomination of both the Liberal and the Republican Parties in the next senatorial election, a first in Washington politics.)

I had given Michael money as a graduation gift to buy a car. He purchased a shiny red two-passenger British MG coupe sports car, in which he crammed his belongings into the small space behind the seats and in the minuscule trunk, and took off by himself to drive cross-country—king of the road—to his new life in Washington, DC. That car would prove to be a bonding agent for Michael and the senator—for Goodell did not drive, and he and Michael zoomed about DC and over highways together in his little two-seater for several years while Michael honed up his skills as a speechwriter and campaign manager.

One morning Jay came up from his office to my bedroom-cum-office.

"You said no interruptions or phone calls but . . ."

"But what?"

"There is a man calling from Florida. It's about your father. . . ."

"He's had an accident?"

"The man is a jeweler. I think you better speak to him."

Jay left and I picked up my line. It turned out that my father was buying a $2,000 diamond engagement ring and had informed the store owner that I would pay the bill, as I was in charge of his finances. This was difficult for me to process. An engagement ring? Two thousand dollars! And I was in charge of my father's finances? Well, I did, indeed, send my father a monthly amount to help cover his expenses, for he was not well enough to go back on the road (or ever would be). He also had a monthly Social Security check and a small stipend from the Veterans. That was the extent of his income. Although my father and I seldom spoke, I thought I might have heard from my aunt Bea (who seemed to know more than I did) if he had a serious lady friend. At first I thought it was a scam and said so. The jeweler was indignant and put my father on the line.

There was that bravado in his voice. "How are you, darling! [no pause as he continued] Yes, I have met a wonderful woman and we want to get engaged and to do it properly. She is a very fine lady," he assured me.

"If you want to get married, I certainly will not stand in your way," I replied. "But I will in no way pay for a diamond engagement ring when you could not even pay for my mother's funeral! The answer is no!" I was immediately sorry I had mentioned the last, but anger and resentment were building inside me.

He kept talking, repeating what a fine lady she was and how he knew I would be pleased to welcome her into the family.

"The answer is no," I repeated and hung up.

A half hour later, the "fine lady" was on the telephone. She hardly had finished a greeting when she began berating me. *How could I treat my father this way? A man who had taken such good care of me throughout my life and who had trusted me with his sizeable fortune for me to invest for him, and now would not let him have access to it!* She had a high-pitched Boston accent. "You, dear lady, have been lied to," I finally managed when she took a breath. "I know my father can be charming and convincing, but he has zilch. He has certainly not supported me throughout my life. He has been a compulsive gambler. Probably, he still is. We don't talk much." I then told her the amount I sent him every month and said if she still wanted to marry him, I would not stop the payments, but unless he was ill and needed special care I could not be counted on for a penny more. "*I am sure that you are the liar—and a bitch!*" she shouted into the phone, and then the fine lady hung up.

The short end of it was that they never got engaged or married and my father, when he called or wrote, never mentioned the incident to me again.

Returning to Los Angeles after so many years had taken some acclimation and compromise on my part. I adjusted well to the physical changes (as one had to do with any major city in the world after an absence of nearly twenty years)—the luxury tower apartment houses stretching along Wilshire Boulevard to Santa Monica, the citification of Westwood Village, which was still just a college conclave when I departed, and the massive glass-and-mirrored corporate buildings standing butt to butt that had replaced the once vast back lots of MGM and 20th Century-Fox studios, the area newly christened Century City. The era of the giant movie lots with their replicas of ghost towns, Paris streets, London's creepy alleyways, and other fantasy-inspired foreign lands had vanished as films were now shot largely on location, audiences able with the huge growth in travel to have seen the real McCoy so that mock-up imitations cheapened the appearance of the film. Movie stars no longer reigned supreme, their big-screen allure diminished with the advent of television. The city had been unwrapped of its earlier glamour.

Still, the sun shone down benevolently on its worshipers as it always had. The Hollywood sign had not been pried from its position on the Hollywood Hills, and Beverly Hills and the surrounding upscale area seemed almost untouched, certainly unaware of the battlefield east Los Angeles—only twenty miles away—had become with gang clashes between Latinos, blacks, and the lawmen who seemed to beat and shoot before full knowledge of a crime was known.

I had lived in gentrified Beverly Hills for most of my youth, my small life centering on a corner that was now occupied by the modern, much-expanded Chasen's. There had been a family "scandal" in the mid-1940s that had altered the close relationships between my uncle Dave and his siblings. Not that familial love was gone. It was aplenty. But he had a new home which no one came to. Here is the reason told to me by Marion, who had been told firsthand by my aunt Theo, neither of whom were given to exaggeration.

One afternoon when the kitchen workers in Chasen's were preparing for the dinner guests and the restaurant was closed, my aunt Theo decided she wanted to talk to her husband about something and crossed from the small bungalow behind where I had lived with them as a child and which was still their home, and entered by the rear kitchen restaurant door.

"Where is Mr. Chasen?" she inquired of the kitchen staff.

Silence prevailed. Finally, someone said, "In his office."

Theo headed for the back stairs. "Dave," she called out.

"I'll be right down," he answered.

There followed a shuffling sound, and Theo started up the stairs, then paused—startled to see a nude blonde woman apparently dragging her clothes and scooting across the hallway to the linen closet that was positioned opposite Uncle Dave's office. He stepped out into the hallway as the linen closet door slammed shut. His appearance was somewhat in disarray. Theo kept on coming, pushed him aside, and opened the linen closet door. An attractive woman stood huddled against the shelves, her clothes held close to her body to cover her nudity.

The woman was Maude King Martin, a beautiful blonde divorcee with a teenage daughter. She was the receptionist/manager at the new beauty salon in Saks Fifth Avenue where, on the same floor, Uncle Dave and a partner had recently opened an elegant lunchroom. Uncle Dave closed the door to the linen room again as Theo fled in tears and fury downstairs, out the rear door where she had entered, across the back area to that sweet little bungalow we all had called home, and packed her bags and moved to her close friend Ruby Keeler's house, where Uncle Dave finally went to soothe her and apparently ask for forgiveness. Man being man, blonde beauties being blonde beauties, he had made a fatal error in judgment and according to the family hotline, had apologized. "How could you!" Theo claimed to have shouted. "And in a restaurant with workers right on the premises and me practically next door!" She could not be placated.

They had been married over twenty years and she had struggled with him in his early days of vaudeville (where she supported them on her dancer's salary) and had been by his side helping with their first effort, Chasen's Southern Pit, built in the bean field facing Beverly Boulevard and behind their home. They cooked in a tiny kitchen (my mother helping as well—creating recipes—giving Theo a hand in the preparation and serving). Theo was adored by all our family to whom she always opened her home and her heart. The humiliation seemed too much for her to endure, and within three weeks she had filed suit for divorce.

Theo did not drive. So, on the day she was to appear in the downtown courtroom to ask for a divorce, she took a taxi and met her lawyer in the courtroom. The whole procedure took less than an hour. Uncle Dave agreed to all of her demands—which were few, for she asked only for support and gave up all claim to the restaurant, the house, and property, which had all become places of great sadness to her. Moments after she had gotten into a taxi to ride back to the apartment she had rented in Westwood, the vehicle was sideswiped by a small truck and the driver lost control of the wheel, careening into a telephone pole. Theo was thrown out onto the road. Seriously injured, she was rushed by ambulance to the hospital, both legs broken in several places. She was never able to recover fully, as pneumonia set in, and she died. It was a tragic and unfortunate sequence of circumstances. Our family was bereft, Uncle Dave filled with grief and guilt. He eventually married Maude, who let it be known that no member of the family was welcome to their new home in Bel Air. That was eased in later years but for the most part, family members met Uncle Dave elsewhere, most times at the restaurant where he kept fairly long hours. Everyone in the family, including Marion, blamed Maude for what had happened. No one seemed to take into consideration the fact that Uncle Dave was hardly the innocent party and that my beloved aunt Theo had acted too rashly.

I was in my early teens when Uncle Dave married Maude. My mother had joined my father in Dallas, Texas—the location of the company he was then working for. I had stubbornly refused to join them. Marion was torn. But I was in my mid-high-school years and had a life of my own that I was not willing to desert, being active in young creative circles, knowing now that writing for theater or films was what I wanted. Inez Russin, a first cousin of my mother's, lived in a one-bedroom apartment in Beverly Hills and worked as a secretary at MGM. It was decided that I could stay with her, a wonderful compromise as she was a fantastic lady of whom I was very fond (and who had, in fact, once lived with us).

My uncle Dave, with his crinkly red hair and wide, endearing smile, had been a surrogate father to me when my own was not around. He was the light in my difficult early years: funny when I needed to laugh, loving when I needed a hug, and someone to say, "Things will be all right." A great mime, he would pass his hand over his face, when I might be sad, changing his expression from tortured grief to wild joy. It was at the house on Rosewood that Ruby Keeler had taught me to tap-dance on the linoleum floor of the small kitchen, W. C. Fields (whom I called Uncle Claude) brought me bouquets of dandelions and let me beat him at Ping-Pong on the table that was set up on the back lawn, and that fine comic and character actor, jolly, foxy Guy Kibbee, would come to my defense when Marion would declare, "Anne Louise, time for bed!" and he would plead, "Ah, come on! Give her one more hour." My childhood "friends" were some of the most famous and most talented actors of the 1930s, although I was not aware of their notoriety at the time. Theo and Dave had no children of their own and, I suspect, I filled the cavity they might have felt. They were there for me from the age of four to ten, at which time my mother and I moved out and she and my father reunited. Still, even (or maybe especially so) after Aunt Theo's exit and demise, Uncle Dave remained a major presence in my life.

After he and Maude were married, we had a standing date one day a week. He usually ate his dinner at the restaurant at five p.m. before the doors were opened for the evening trade. Cracked crab on ice was a favorite of mine and although it was not always on the menu, there would be a beautifully prepared plate of it waiting for me. He would ask me about school, my friends, any problems I had that I would like to talk about. He was my confidant. He gave me my first wedding reception—a dinner for fifty guests held in the banquet room upstairs in the restaurant. "Anne Louise," he had said, "Jimmy Stewart is to be married soon and is having his dinner here—and it will be the same menu as you are having." Although invited, Maude had not attended either the wedding ceremony at the Rossens' Westwood home or the dinner reception at the restaurant. The standoff with the family remained. Maude was resentful, and who could blame her? What occurred was far distant and it was certainly not her fault that Theo met with such a tragic and early end. Still, she remained distant from her husband's family and had not been won over even by the time I had returned to Los Angeles; Uncle Dave was now in his seventies and not too well, having undergone recent surgery for a slipped disk in his spine. I called him frequently and saw him whenever it was possible. Not long after the engagement ring incident we spoke and he said to me, "Come to the restaurant at five p.m. We'll have dinner."

There was cracked crab on ice. We sat alone in one of the red leather booths in the empty front room, which would soon be alive with the sound of happy voices and redolent scents. His hand shook slightly, and he walked with some difficulty. He had aged considerably, was frail and smaller than he had been. His red hair was brushed with gray, his shoulders rounded, but when he smiled an aura of brightness lighted the dimly lit, ghostlike room where framed photographs of the Hollywood players who had been his friends and companions through the years lined the walls.

"Your father could have climbed the highest mountain," he told me. "Don't blame him. Blame the crazy world he grew up in. He was never prepared for life and still doesn't know how to handle it. He's like a lost kid in a forest where it's always night."

He took me into the kitchen later and had a helper wrap up some bones for me to bring home to the two poodles. When we parted, he held my face between his hands. "Marion was always proud of you," he said, "as I am now." He kissed me on the forehead and escorted me out front where a staff member in a car waited to drive me home.

He died in 1975. Shortly after, Maude called, warm and conciliatory, to inform me that Uncle Dave's will, which was written a number of years before my mother's death, included a provision for a small income to be provided for Marion. She said I must come to the restaurant when I was next in LA and she added, "It was all so long ago."

The one disturbing element about returning to Los Angeles was that, despite the memories it evoked, the relationships and friendships it vivified, it did not feel like home. This was curious, because most of the American writers in self-exile that I knew always talked about one day "going home," and considered themselves living as outsiders in their host countries. There were good reasons for this. Before the blacklist the greater percentage had settled into what they thought was their earned lifestyle. They owned homes with swimming pools, had nannies to care for their children, joined clubs, and were looking forward to the rewards they had reaped for their future. Once in Europe, having lost their status, their homes, their identities, they set their goals for recovery, a return in some triumph. They thought of themselves as patriots and remained mostly in the company of their compatriots. They were all movie folk, after all, and in the movies the good guys won and the bad guys came to a bad end. Joe McCarthy would be brought down in months, then next year, then—some year—and they would get their comeuppance. A growing fatigue set in, fenced by resentment, often bitter. Exile was a punishment, even if self-imposed. So they all clung together, drawing comfort from the mutuality of their experience and feelings. I, too, had been visited at times by these same emotions. The difference was that nothing in my life had been settled before I left for Europe. It had, in fact, been in utter disarray. I was, therefore, open to finding a place for myself and my children wherever fate might take us. Now I was not sure if it was Europe that I missed or the group therapy provided there by my circle of compeers.

We were never immigrants. We held fast to our American identities and to our citizenship. Voting was a pledge of honor—and allegiance. The only member of our coterie known to me who had rescinded his American citizenship was Leon. Given his history, one could rationalize his decision—at least I tried to do so. Born in Canada, he was first a citizen of that country. Shipped to the United States as a young boy, he yearned to be a part of the family and the land in which he then lived. After Pearl Harbor he applied for and received American citizenship and joined the armed forces. However, Canada, unlike the United States, allows dual citizenship. So, when he was named before HUAC and blacklisted, his career in the States suddenly ended, he reactivated his Canadian citizenship, thus forfeiting his American citizenship and any chance of ever reclaiming it. This act did enable him to find work immediately in Great Britain. Canada was bound to Great Britain as a dominion, "equal in status, in no way subordinate to each other." It is a sovereign nation as is Australia, with a prime minister and a governor general but one that also pays allegiance to the British Crown (which for over fifty years has been Queen Elizabeth II).

The matter of Leon's relinquishment of his American citizenship had always disturbed me. It was all part of the enigma that was Leon. He had reaped the harvest of the best—and the worst—that the United States had to offer, and he had retained the essence of the country's beliefs. He still, after all these years, considered it home despite the fact that he could not, by American law, once having forfeited it, reclaim his citizenship. This had a strong bearing on our relationship, for it meant the greater portion of our lives, if we did not divorce, would be spent in Europe. He did have the option of living in Canada, or any other one of Britain's dominions. But, at that time, there were only two major arenas for moviemakers—the United States or Europe.

While I was working on my current book in Beverly Hills and trying to make decisions regarding my relationship with Rod, Leon was hopping back and forth from London to Madrid, preparing the latter as a location for a film, *A Talent for Loving*, that he was coproducing with Walter Shenson. He had never given up trying to get me to return, and during the late summer of 1968, he went into full gear. Every week there were wrenching telephone calls, cables, and letters. There is no denying that I was moved by them. We had been separated for over a year. A lot had happened in my life in that time. There was Rod. But I knew by now that whatever we had together was not to be a lifetime relationship. There was a kind of desperation in Leon's actions, and I was feeling a heavy guilt that I could not just end everything. Aside from my ambivalence over my situation with Rod, the question remained if I really wanted to return to Europe to live. That was a major hurdle for a reconciliation with Leon as he could not live or work in the United States. I spoke and wrote to him about this. In a letter he replied,

> I agree with most of what you say regarding "roots," involvement, etc. Again these are vast areas for discussion and exploration. There is one point you raised that I think you should be clear about. The question of my reverting to Canadian nationality. I did *not* want to do this. It was not my choice. After all, for all practical purposes I was and still am, an American. I believe this was the most serious conflict I ever had with Kathryn. It would have created a break if I hadn't compromised. And since I felt (you will probably not believe it, but it is so) that our relationship was more important than anything else . . . and since it became almost an obsession with her and created all sorts of emotional upset, I compromised. I wanted to fight the thing through from wherever I could. I knew this could only be an erratic incident in the history of the country, if only from the knowledge of the histories of other countries. But she was so nervous and fearful, what with the hounding by the office in London [referring to the need for a working permit and a permanent visa], etc., that I gave in. And I honestly feel that this was a factor in the subsequent tragedy [Kathryn's affair with Carl and her suicide] arising from guilt regarding the incident??? [The three question marks are Leon's.]

Our relationship was caught up in a war between our incompatibility on one side and our shared experience with the HUAC years and having to start anew in a foreign country—granted, one whose language was English—on the other. Leon was well known in Britain's movie colony as an expert in many areas, production and technical, especially with music, sound, or language; he was seldom out of work. His pay was not on a par with the "big guys"—the directors and producers who were able to package their own projects—and as he kept his financial matters highly exclusive from me (I would say secretive), and as I now had my own resources (which I did not do likewise), I did not take this situation further. It troubled me that he had few close friends among the expats. I brought them into our lives and he could not avoid their presence. He never enjoyed social home gatherings, which I encouraged. He had, more or less, parted ways (at least on a personal basis) with Carl, and his mentions of him in letters had become almost vitriolic. In many ways I thought that the more distance he placed (or Carl did) between the two of them, the better they both were for it. This same bitterness had entered into his frequent telephone calls to me. After one emotionally searing exchange, I asked him not to call me again.

A few days later I received an express letter: "A relationship to be anything," he wrote, "cannot be one sided. And that is why I said to you, yesterday on the phone, that I would stop annoying you with phone calls and cables. I'm sure there's nothing more annoying and irritating to anyone than an attempt at communication without a synchronous receiver. I do not beg, nor am I a supplicant. If you are sincerely convinced that you no longer feel for me and that our future together is nil, then say so and I will stop bothering you. My concern for you and the kids I cannot obviate and eradicate . . . this will always be. Either you feel it or you don't. End of paragraph."

Then, in the very next paragraph he writes: "I have a home in Madrid waiting for you [where he was preparing the film for shooting]. This is a lovely, three-bedroomed, three-bathroomed apartment with a modern kitchen (even including a garbage-disposal unit) . . . immaculate, completely equipped . . . on the fifth floor of a brand-new apartment building with a lift and a swimming pool on the roof. I have a woman, Aurora, who cleans and cooks dinner. . . . Again, as I told you on the phone, if you can and feel like coming, I will send you the ticket or the money, whichever. I got this large a place with your coming in mind . . . it is waiting and I am waiting . . . the final decision is yours. *Nothing* would make me happier than to meet you at the Madrid airport. But you must do what is best for you, in terms of both your health and your emotions. Take care and God bless. You still have all my love. L."

Well, of course, the "home" he had waiting was a temporary place to hang our hats, and perhaps our hearts. It would only be ours for the length of the shooting of the film. Then where would we be? Back to square one.

All of this was transpiring while Rod and I were having our own issues to deal with. I was hesitant to discuss Leon with Rod and he, in turn, could not talk about his own situation. We were slowly withdrawing from the intimacy we had. The affair was coming to an end and both of us knew it.

The last time we met was in early May, a time that can be—and was that day—spectacular in Malibu where our affair, a little more than twelve months

young, had begun. The ocean was splashed with sunlight, soft waves undu-
lated toward the beach. We both knew we were meeting to say good-bye. We
talked about inconsequential matters. I was perched on the couch and he was
seated across from me in this glass-fronted, modern living room that looked
out on a glorious blue sky and white-frosted, rolling waves. Suddenly, the sun
shifted and a sharp beam of light came through the windows and lay between
us like a bar to a gate being lowered. He got up and helped me to my feet and
held me in a bear hug for a long time.

We rode mostly in silence back to my apartment in that crazy red car
of his. At one point he pulled off the road. "Do you forgive me?" he asked.

"Why?"

"I took a piece of your life," he replied in a dramatic manner.

These were words exchanged by the lovers in *Brief Encounter*, the film
we had seen together in New York. We both caught what we had done and
broke out laughing. When we finally reached Spalding Drive, we sat quietly in
the front seat of Excalibur a few moments while he held my hand. Finally, he
broke the silence. "We'll always have New York," he said with a small smirk
on his face. He was referring to the early rush of love between us, the seeming
innocence of it all then. I told him not to get out of the car to see me to the
door as it was still light. As soon as I stepped onto the sidewalk, he called out
to me, "Hey, Red?" I turned.

He waved, and I waved back and then made my way as quickly as I could
across the front courtyard to the door to the penthouses. Once inside my
apartment, I went over to the lanai windows that looked out onto the street.
Excalibur was still there. I stood for several minutes watching until finally, in a
sudden grinding and whooshing, it bolted forward with a roar of its powerful
motor and was immediately out of sight—if not sound.

· *14* ·

Judy, Judy, Judy!

$\mathcal{T}$he end of an adulterous affair can affect the participants in many disparate ways. In the case of Rod and myself, I believe we reacted very much in the same fashion by throwing ourselves into the creative work that had always had first claim on our lives. *Miklos Alexandrovitch Is Missing* (the story of the Russian ballet dancer who defects in Paris) was in its editing stage. I was ready to go forward and had decided on the themes and setting of the two remaining books of my three-book contract. Both had European backgrounds, for which I would have to do considerable foreign research. I chose as my immediate project *Haunted Summer*, a fictionalized version of Lord Byron and Mary and Percy Shelley's summer of 1816 together in Switzerland, during which Mary wrote *Frankenstein* and Byron his epic poem, "The Prisoner of Chillon." My story and characters were clear in my head, as was the way I planned to approach them. The book was to be written in the first person as though Mary Shelley was the narrator of her own life. I now wonder how I had the nerve to step into her shoes and—so to speak—write with her pen in my hand.

The work to follow *Haunted Summer* was tentatively titled *Post Mortem* and would be the novel I had waited so long to write, set among the expats in London during the McCarthy years. I put Mary Shelley, who was long in her grave, first as I was still not fully prepared to rake up the ghosts of the more recent past, or to expose—however much fictionalized—the lives and feelings of McCarthy's survivors who were close friends.

My agreeing to deliver each of the books in two years meant I had a heavy schedule for the next four years. Also, neither book could be successfully written without my returning for long periods to both London and Switzerland. Cathy had decided to do her first university year in Switzerland at Leysin, to obtain an International Baccalaureate diploma which would, when completed, give her a one-year credit to most European universities if she chose to continue her education abroad, as well as to schools in the States. Her choice also figured into my selecting *Haunted Summer* as my initial project. She did, however, have her last year at Beverly Hills High School to complete.

I don't know what I would have done without Jay. Never before had I the luxury of a secretary who could transcribe my handwritten pages at the end of a writing day (usually about three p.m.) so that I could edit them the following morning. Jay was also a brilliant organizer and a steadfast researcher, could drive me where I needed to go (I don't drive), and always managed to crowd in household tasks, like taking the dogs to the vet, as well. He was a one-man staff. He agreed that if my decision was to return to Europe, he would accompany me, for he had never been abroad and felt that now in his late forties it was time he spread his wings and saw a bit of the world.

Leon and I were corresponding, but my letters contained no mention of the subjects and backgrounds of my two new projects. I was fearful that he might use this as an added reason as to why we should reconcile. I did not feel that my presence on the same continent should invite any such outcome, but Leon was persistently adding logs to the fire—an English school would be a good choice for Cathy. London was no farther from Washington, DC, for Michael to travel to see me than was Los Angeles. I had left behind close friends who were always asking about me and when I would return. Sidney had spent four days in London, having dinner with Leon three of the nights, and talked endlessly about how much he missed my help on his new project. Actually, I had heard from Sidney and was clear that I did not want to work on any film project—at least while I got my new career as a novelist established—and he had been supportive of my decision.

Mary Shelley had been of strong interest to me for a long time. About five years earlier, I had attempted a short story dealing with her mother, Mary Wollstonecraft, famous for her *Vindication of the Rights of Woman* and staunch believer in free love. She had a child out of wedlock before her marriage to William Godwin, revolutionary, writer, publisher, whose great work *Political Justice* influenced the intellect of the youth in his era. Mary W. died shortly after their daughter Mary's birth. Godwin remarried a Mrs. Clairmont (whose daughter Claire would become Lord Byron's mistress). The Godwins' London home had drawn young men of revolutionary spirit, such as the poet, Percy Shelley, with whom Mary eloped (although he was married and the father of two children). In the short story, I had dealt mainly with Godwin and his two wives during an earlier time. Now I wanted to carry the story forward with Godwin's daughter, Mary, and his stepdaughter, Claire. The idea that these two stepsisters had been the lovers (and in Mary's case, wife) of two of the greatest and most controversial poets of their time was compelling.

The last time I was in Klosters, I had taken the rather long train ride to the brooding castle of Chillon with its grim underground chambers where evidence remained of the wall chains that once had manacled prisoners left to starve and die. Chillon haunted me. It was there, in the summer of 1816, that the runaway lovers with Byron, Claire, and Dr. Polidori, an enigmatic infatuate and drug supplier of Byron's, had often spent their nights exchanging self-composed horror stories and Mary's *Frankenstein* had been created. My first sketchy outline of *Haunted Summer* had been written shortly after the publication of *The Survivors*, but I could not get a proper handle on it and had put it aside and moved on to *Miklos* instead.

Over time, I had made, re the McCarthy-era story, copious notes in my journals, recorded memories of conversations, descriptions of people and places—my observations on the changes and confrontations between the members of our group. Since Bob Rossen's death, I had known the story would start with the death of the protagonist (which is why I had given it the working title *Post Mortem*) and then would flash back to his early Hollywood years, Washington, DC, during the HUAC hearings, and then to the great wave of talented Hollywood writers and directors who had washed up on the shores of Europe. It seemed ironic to me that less than two decades earlier, Hollywood had been the safe harbor for European filmmakers a step away from being victims of the Holocaust. Except for the technical artists (camera, sound, etc.) who had not been allowed into the unions of their crafts, these men and women had been brought into the studios, and their cinema style incorporated into what would be called film noir and had greatly influenced Hollywood's steady output of dark detective, murder, and horror stories. Now it was the reverse. The invasion of American film artists to Europe had given birth to Italian spaghetti westerns and epic dramas (the latter much in the style of Cecil B. DeMille).

I missed Europe: the age of it, the beauty of its architecture, the culture that changed whenever one crossed a border. There was always something new to see, to learn—and something old to discover; history that came alive. What I liked best about Los Angeles (and Beverly Hills, although an incorporated city, is just a section of LA with no visible division except a corner sign that indicates you are either leaving or entering one or the other) were the Spanish/Mexican architectural influences, presently being replaced street by street with modern buildings. Most of the seedy artifacts like the Garden of Allah apartments and the motels along with restaurants in shapes of derby hats and giant hot dogs were gone, as were nut burgers (no meat served) and the flashy drive-ins with girls in skimpy costumes that had proliferated in the earlier days of the movie industry, captured so well in Nathanael West's *The Day of the Locust*. Lost were the glamorous nightclubs like Ciro's, the Mocambo, and the Trocadero where the great stars of an earlier, more glamorous Hollywood had once graced such spots with their regal and splendiferous selves. Perhaps odd, but the detritus of those years still held a spell over me.

Growing up, I had been an avid biker and with my high school buddy, Greta Markson (an aspiring actress), spent every Saturday we could pedaling our way to the beach from Beverly Hills and back again, the wind in our face as we raced down the least traveled streets, each time trying a new route. Everything about Los Angeles, especially my corner that was Beverly Hills, was familiar to me. Each street I now turned down (on foot or in a car) brought back memories. I had old friends with whom I had never lost touch. Still, I had been away for a long time and had lived in such a different world from theirs that the adjustment was difficult at times. Political activism was now in the hands of a much younger generation. This was the time of the flower children, LSD, and other hallucinogenic drugs (which had also been part of the Shelleys' and Byron's generation); the time of civil unrest and protest (as was the background of *Miklos*). The years of the blacklist were not yet forgotten (certainly not by its victims)—but it was not a part of current life—especially among older liberal Hollywoodites who had escaped the sharklike jaws of HUAC. What irritated me most were the younger members of the Hollywood colony who treated former victims, now returned "home," as though their experience (which had caused them such great losses—a divorced mate, financial ruin, a career upended, their identity stolen) should be worn as a badge of honor. How crazy was that?

The expats I knew who had returned to California were trying desperately to bury those dark days. This was difficult when they still found doors shut to them (their credits too far in the past—their names not yet restored on more recent work). It did not help to be confronted every day by the very people who had betrayed them—who were doing very nicely, thank you! Harold and Ruth Buchman were in LA. Harold was trying to find a writing assignment with not much success. He had depended on Sidney for years, and his brother had extended a hand whenever possible—hiring Harold for a first draft of a proposed project at times. This had caused considerable sibling resentment on Harold's part. He had hoped to make it back on his own once in California, but it was not happening. Joyce Jameson (not a HUAC victim) had recovered (at least temporarily) from the throes of her depression and was now in love with the actor Robert Vaughn (nominated for a supporting Oscar for *The Young Philadelphians* and having given a fine performance in the recent *Bullitt*), who was extremely bright and politically active. I enjoyed his company and was pleased that Joyce (truly a better talent than her career offerings supported) seemed happy. We had shared our teens, our dreams, and many of the difficulties that our individual, complicated childhoods had involved. Despite our physical distance, Joyce had always looked to me for counsel (through voluminous letters when I was abroad). I never felt quite adequate to the task, for Joyce needed professional help, but I did step up to the plate and tried my best. Joyce had a bit of Marilyn Monroe in her (she would later play her in a Broadway takeoff) mixed with a natural intelligence that she had abused—and that the troubling circumstances of her life had caused. Joyce was always looking for someone or something to save her— a lover, a friend, fame, religion (later she was addicted not only to pills, but to television evangelical preachings).

As Christmas 1968 approached, and Rod and I no longer seeing each other, I decided to give a Christmas Eve party to cheer myself up. Michael would be home for the holidays and we three would be together, something I much looked forward to. The day before the party, I cooked up a storm. I had invited somewhere between twenty-five to thirty guests. A Mexican theme dominated the food to be served (this was Los Angeles, after all!). I made a huge pot of the now-famous Chasen's chili along with pots full of other re-membered recipes. Lucy had recently married a fine gentleman, who mixed a great margarita and took care of the bar.

We were a rather giddy group that included friends from disparate parts of my life. Besides Joyce, Robert Vaughn, Harold and Ruth, Bill and Betty Graf were present. The Grafs had been at my wedding to Leon, and Bill had only recently returned to the States after the international success of his film *A Man for All Seasons*. There was also another old friend, actor Jack Kruschen (nominated for an Oscar for his role as the neighbor and doctor in *The Apart-ment*), Nick Dunne, Jay, of course, and many more new and old friends. Both Cathy and Michael played host with me. As the midnight hour neared, I asked Michael to go upstairs and bring down a box of small gifts I had tagged for each of my guests. He did as asked and suddenly raced down the staircase, empty handed, and grabbed my arm.

"You have to come upstairs," he ordered, his voice in control, but with a sense of urgency.

"What is it?"

"Biba."

That was our toy poodle. "Biba?" I repeated inanely.

"She's under your desk and either she has a furry mouse or she has just delivered a pup and she is in great pain."

I must have looked dazed, not quite understanding what he had said.

"Please come with me," he added sotto voce.

So I followed, making as graceful an exit as I could so as not to gain anyone's attention. I entered my bedroom, where my desk was located, and stopped in awed surprise. Biba was, indeed, under my desk—which was an elongated, Spanish-style dining table that I had converted for my use as I could spread many pages out on it. She was whimpering and writhing—a tiny, apricot ball of fur trembling beside her. Thank God—it was alive, as was Biba. The whole thing was a complete mystery. The dogs' vet had told me that Biba had been spayed and that, anyway, a dog of Sandy's size would never attempt sex with a dog of her minuscule proportions. However, since Biba was never allowed off the leash when outside for fear of the heavy traffic, Sandy had to be the father. And, as she was a furry ball herself, I had not been aware that her stomach was swollen with pup—although she had been acting a bit churlish lately and when I thought about it, had some trouble going up and down the stairs.

I immediately started dialing vets from the Yellow Pages as it seemed that Biba had yet another pup to birth and could not do it on her own. However, this was Christmas Eve; no replies. Finally, I reached a live person and calmly explained the situation—as it seemed, to no avail. I became more dramatic. I knew it was a holiday, but our little dog had delivered one pup and we thought she had another but could not do it without help. I started to cry. "She could die!" I could not contain myself and sobbed mightily. Worn down, the man acquiesced but explained that as he lived in Santa Monica, it would be at least twenty minutes before he arrived. I put Michael back on and the vet told him what to do to make Biba as comfortable as possible until he got to us.

When the vet finally appeared at the door, there was a rush to greet him and escort him upstairs. He pulled back and shouted furiously at them, "Is this some sort of Hollywood joke?" for he had recognized one or two of his escorts as Hollywood players. He turned to leave but someone grabbed him by the arm. "This is not the least bit funny! It's Christmas Eve and I've left my family. . . ," he said as he attempted to break loose. A slight man, he was almost carried up the steps. He paused only for a moment as he took in the reality of the scene before him and then demanded everyone but Michael depart the room. My son—with absolutely no medical experience—was to be his assistant. Biba was gently lifted onto the top of the cleared desk, a clean, doubled sheet now covering it, as the vet prepared to perform a surgery to bring the reluctant pup forward and out into the world.

All's well that ends well, as Shakespeare wrote. Biba had a second female pup (ascertained by the vet who joined the party, got pretty drunk, and seemed to have a very good time). She was weak but alive, and her progeny were settled into a small basket lined with a heating pad turned on low, Sandy crouched beside it. Biba could not yet nurse so the pups were fed from an eyedropper. We named the firstborn Chrissy, the second—Noel. It turned out that Biba was a terrible mother. She truly hated Noel. One day, when she was quite recovered, she pushed the tiny creature down the staircase. Thankfully, Noel seemed none the worse for the fall. But as soon as was possible I gave her to my hairdresser, a dear man who had just lost his dog. Chrissy was a hardy sort and survived her mother's abuse and, in fact, followed Biba wherever she went. She grew to be much larger than her mother, and about half the size of her father. They were quite a curious trio.

In the weeks leading up to the Christmas Eve party, I had not been feeling too well. Since it was holiday time and we three united, I decided to put off seeing a doctor until the festivities were over. On New Year's Day the Grafs gave a party. As it was somewhat open-ended, I decided I would go but leave early. They lived in a glamorous new tower building above Sunset Boulevard, their apartment overlooking the city from ocean to mountains to downtown. I was happy for them, pleased to be there (they had always been favorites of mine). Suddenly, I felt dizzy, weak; a pain stabbed through me. I made it into the nearest bathroom where I collapsed (in a pool of blood I was later told). The next thing I knew I was in an ambulance on my way to hospital where I was rushed into Emergency. I had suffered a massive hemorrhage and after tests were conducted, was told I had a tumor in my uterus the size of a grapefruit.

The doctor who had delivered Cathy sixteen years earlier (and actually had taken care of me when I was a young woman), a man in whom I had great trust, was still in practice. I had the hospital call him. He told me I needed immediate surgery. It meant removing my uterus and ovaries. After examining me, he explained carefully what this involved and asked me if I approved. I did. Everything was arranged for early the next morning. At dawn, a hospital executive appeared by my bedside, clipboard in hand.

"From your record, I see that you are married? Is that correct?"

"I am currently separated from my husband. He lives in London."

He then informed me that my operation could not be performed until my husband signed a release form agreeing that he gave permission for my uterus to be removed and understood that I would not, therefore, ever be able to bear another child. To say I was stupefied would be an overwhelming understatement.

"This is a hospital rule?" I asked numbly.

"It is the law of California."

"I need my *husband's* permission to save myself from maybe dying?" I cried out in fury. "This is *my* body, *my* uterus! No one has the right to tell me what I can do with it!"

"Please control yourself," he managed. "It is the law. I can't do anything about it. Now if you can tell us how to get in touch with your husband . . ."

"Does California law give a wife the right to say yea or nay to an operation on her husband's prick?" I shouted.

"Mrs. Becker . . . please . . ."

"Anne Edwards. I'm Anne Edwards!"

"Can we reach Mr. Becker on your behalf?" he went on calmly.

"Let me see where it says in the California book of laws that a wife has to have her *husband's* permission. . . ."

"I assure you it is a law. Now where can we . . ."

I cannot to this day believe I did it. But there was a plastic pitcher filled with water on the bed tray, and I picked it up and threw it at him. Water splashed all down the front of his starched white hospital jacket. He jumped up and dashed out of the room, never to return. However, my own doctor was soon by my side.

"Look, Anne," he said in his best "trust me" voice, "you can call the governor and petition the state Senate later [something I had threatened to do] but right now, I need to have Mr. Becker's acknowledgment that he agrees to your surgery. Where can he be reached?"

Jay called Leon in London but had a hard time getting through. Finally, they connected. Leon called the hospital—as incensed as I was about the situation. The hospital insisted on written approval. And so Leon sent a telegram—which I saw—avoiding the word *permission*—stating that he understood his wife was in urgent need of surgery to remove her reproductive organs and that he agreed with her that it must be done. *Yahoo! Leon!*

Three days after the surgery, Leon appeared by my bedside. He had been given a visa by immigration to enter the country for a short stay due to my illness. This was the first time since he had left for England, in 1952, that he had been allowed to return. He remained with me until I was released to go home, about two weeks later, and then stayed with me in the apartment for another week as I had suffered some complications. When you are as weak and sick as I was during that time, vanity has little place. Leon truly tended to me, made sure in the hospital that I received immediate attention. When I came home he did all he could to make me comfortable. For the first time, I actually did look on him as a husband. He had come through for me, picked up and left the work he was doing, and conquered his own disturbing emotions of being treated as a foreigner in a country that he considered to be his homeland.

I did, indeed, write letters to the governor, who was none other than Ronald Reagan. I received rather murky replies from an assistant informing me that the matter would be turned over to the proper committee—*committee?* That appalling law was eventually repealed sometime in the 1970s.

By early March, back on my feet and on my own again, I realized that Leon had assumed that we were now reconciled (my fault, I fear) and was pressing me to join him in Madrid where he was still shooting *A Talent for Loving*. I was torn in having to make a decision both by gratitude for his coming to my aid and guilt that I had accepted it unconditionally, without setting any boundaries. He wrote me a letter.

> As you know, the apartment I have here [in Madrid] was always meant for you to share with me. There is a maid to take care of all household tasks. You can take it easy. . . . Yes, we have been apart for almost two years. You have been on your own. But the few weeks we were together after your operation should have shown you that we could, and certainly in my opinion, should, cohabit.
>
> There is Cathy, as you say. But Jay and Lucy can look after her as they did when you were on the book tour. She is sixteen—a very mature, intelligent sixteen, I might add, with her head in the right place. She also has her good friend Bridgette and Bridgette's family, who are close by. And we are talking about three weeks, not an elongated period and she has plans, which you have approved, for her to be more or less on her own this coming summer. . . . I will take care of all your travel arrangements and you can be safely returned to LA before her graduation.
>
> There are problems on the picture but you will like most of the cast and crew (you already know how difficult Topol [one of the stars] has been). Walter [Shenson] is here and his wife, who you like, will also be joining him. ILYVM (you know what that means) [I Love You Very Much]. LEON.

After much deliberation, I decided that I owed it to both of us to join him in Madrid and see if time and recent happenings had altered our relationship for the better.

Instead of going directly to Madrid, I flew first to New York for two days to meet with my editor there, then to London for the same purpose as all my books were to be published in Great Britain by Hodder & Stoughton and the editions would vary in small ways.

I had not yet removed my raincoat nor caught my breath (those evil stairs at Lennox Gardens) when the telephone rang. It was Mickey Deans, who was with Judy in London. Bobby had told him I would be in town for a few days. He gleefully announced that he and Judy were going to be married two days later. They had taken a mews house walking distance from Lennox Gardens, and were broke ("temporarily"). He was now Judy's manager and working on her "comeback." Judy was resistant, back on the pills, and had locked herself into the bedroom (the tiny mews house was built as all such homes had been, as staff quarters backing the main house on an alley or cul-de-sac. Judy's bedroom was small and upstairs over the garage). Would I come over? I asked to speak to Judy. He insisted I just show up. I finally agreed to do so as soon as I could.

When I arrived a few hours later, Judy was in the living room. I was shocked at her appearance. She was pathetically thin, her face gaunt, her eyes filled with fear as if she was waiting for something terrible to end.

"Diana Dors, James Mason, Ginger Rogers," she said, almost before acknowledging my presence. "I don't know why Mickey's invited all those people. I've been through too many weddings. I don't want a Hollywood premiere. I just want a marriage." She grabbed Mickey's hand. "I'm going to be Mrs. Michael DeVinko!" she said with pride. An afternoon paper was opened on the coffee table with a picture of the two of them. Mickey had released a guest list to the press and sent telegrams (due to the shortage of time) to his invitees.

Shortly after my arrival, Mickey left the house on an errand. Judy and I were alone. "You'll come to the wedding, Anne Louise?"

I said that I would, of course. "Do you love him?" I asked.

"I do, I do! He hasn't deserted me like all the rest."

She looked truly ill. "Can I make you some tea?" I offered. I glanced toward an open door to a small kitchen. "And maybe something to eat?"

"No, no. Just sit here with me. He loves me, you know."

She was convincing herself, and I did not think it was my place to cast doubt. She was in a pitiable state. I could not see how she could get through the large wedding that Mickey had planned. "I'm sure he does," I said.

"We're going to Denmark! After."

"For a honeymoon?"

"An engagement. A theater as large as Carnegie Hall. Bumbles [Dawson, a designer] has made me a gown. Mickey has handled everything. The orchestra, the arrangements. He says they love me in Denmark. They loved Hamlet, too! Look what happened to him!"

Between Judy's situation and my jet lag, I had trouble getting to sleep that night. About three a.m. the telephone rang. It was Judy.

"Mickey's downstairs on the couch having sex with a man," she whispered. "You have to come over."

"It's the middle of the night, Judy. Maybe you're wrong. Maybe he just fell asleep on the couch."

"No, no! I saw them!"

I explained that I couldn't go out at this hour. I kept the conversation going on for a short time—small talk. Finally she said, "I heard a car. He's leaving." Then she hung up.

Leon rang me early the next morning to tell me, quite excitedly, that he was flying up to London late that afternoon to join me. He had some work that had to be done. It would take about three days. He would change my ticket and we could then fly together to Madrid. I told him about Judy and the wedding and he said we would both attend but warned me not to let Judy's problems weigh too heavily on me.

Our reunion went exceptionally well. During the day, we both had things to do and people to see. We dined at one of our favorite local restaurants. He was full of stories about the company and production of *A Talent for Loving*, and had plans that he hoped I would like for some short side trips outside Madrid. He was caring, thoughtful, and loving, the gloom that often had followed his happy moments absent.

The grand ballroom at Quaglino's, where Judy and Mickey's wedding reception was held, was a bizarre sight. Mickey had invited something like three hundred guests, and the room he selected was tremendous. No more than forty or fifty people were present (at least half appearing to be members of the media) and seemed lost in the room's vastness. Connecting tables bearing large ice statues (one was a lion's head closely resembling Leo, the MGM symbol!), magnificent mural displays, and silver servers and platters containing an enormous amount of food lined one side of the room. They were manned by at least thirty uniformed waiters. Photographers' flashbulbs exploded like firecrackers on the Fourth of July. Judy was overwound, appearing shrunken in a blue chiffon dress, too sheer and too short, that revealed her bony knees and her skeletal frame. Around her narrow shoulders was a dyed-to-match boa that reached the floor and that, to avoid tripping over it, she kept tossing over one shoulder as if it were the wires of a microphone, an action she often did on stage. She wore a blue band over the top of her head with pearls that dangled from it onto her forehead. If Bumbles was responsible, she must have thought she was designing a costume for *Guys and Dolls*.

However delusional Judy might have become, she was far too intelligent not to know in her heart what a horror the whole thing was. She clung to Mickey and beamed down from the rim of the room's empty bandstand where a many-tiered wedding cake had been bizarrely set up on a table—obviously for a photo op, as gathered below were a host of photographers clicking away as the wedding couple posed to cut a slice. Although I recall the singer Johnny Ray being in the room, only a very few, well-known personalities—mostly English—attended. At one point Judy pulled me aside. "I think at least Ginger could have come," she said tersely. (Ginger Rogers was starring in *Mame* in the West End.) "Mickey purposely arranged the time for when the theaters would be closed!"

Judy finally sat down (she looked as if she would collapse otherwise). She was all alone in a long line of unoccupied reception chairs. Mickey was mingling with the press, giving details of their upcoming trip to Denmark. I went over and sat down next to Judy. "It will haunt me forever," I later wrote in my journal, "Judy with a desperate giggle like a distortion on a sound track of her old Rooney MGM films, grabbed my hand, her nails cutting into the flesh of my palms, holding on long after she had said, 'I'm so grateful you came. Please stay till the end.'" There was no wonder left in those wide brown eyes. Leon approached and she tightened her grasp on my hand. "Don't leave," she bit out. She started talking—reeling off the words, really. She wanted to write a book—maybe one with her poetry.

When the time to part arrived, she grabbed my hand again. "It will be different now," she said as she walked Leon and me to the doors of the empty-ing room, Mickey by her side. "I have Mickey now."

He told us that Denmark was only the beginning of her new career. He had lined up the best venues for her in Scandinavia.

I ended my entry in my journal for that day with the comment: "Mickey plans to take over her career as Ethel and Mayer and Luft did. I cannot see how she will survive it."

A studio car met Leon and me at the airport in Madrid. This was not my first trip to Spain, having spent a glorious time on the coast for the filming of *A Question of Adultery*, but I had not gone inland. My view of it through the car window as we headed for the apartment Leon had prepared for our reunion was not inspiring. Madrid, which is the capital of Spain, is a landlocked city, dead center of the country. The outskirts are on a desert plateau. Roads were rutted, dust flew about like volcanic ash as the car's tires bounced about on the asphalt. Leon had warned me of the horrid extremes of the climate. On this day, the temperature must have been above one hundred degrees. There was mile after mile of small tract houses to pass before the car entered the city, which sat on higher land. Then, suddenly, the ground began to rise and the city of Madrid, like the Emerald City of Oz, dazzling in the strong sunlight, spread out before us.

• 15 •

The Emerald City of Madrid

$\mathcal{L}$eon pridefully led me to the front door of the handsome apartment house on Avenue Generalissimo Franco. In a letter to me when he had rented the flat, he had written: "It is a lovely, three-bedroomed apartment (in an elevator building) with a modern kitchen (even including a garbage-disposal unit) . . . immaculate, completely equipped . . . on the fifth floor . . . with a swimming pool on the roof. . . . I got this large a place with your coming in mind. . . . It is waiting and I am waiting." Leon did not lean toward extravagance, so I knew that securing a place of such luxury in a high-rent section of the city underscored his wish to have me back. The gesture moved me, and I waited anxiously as he opened the front door to the building and we entered into the colorful Spanish-tiled hallway and made our way to the lift (the driver having deposited our suitcases just inside).

A note—in Spanish—was taped to the door. Leon translated. The management was sorry for the inconvenience but due to the recent power outage, the lift was not working and tenants would have to use the stairs. We both glanced soulfully at our luggage. It would have to be carted up five flights! Leon said we should just take the lightest (my makeup case and his briefcase) and he would get the superintendent of the building to manage the rest. So up we climbed, and as all the apartments had high ceilings, it was a mighty climb. When we reached the fifth floor, we rested a moment before he turned the key in the lock and pushed the door open.

We were greeted by a fetid stench and dense darkness.

The electricity was off and apparently had been for at least forty-eight hours (gathered from the note on the door of the elevator). Leon took out his trusty old Zippo wartime lighter and led the way to the kitchen where he knew there were some candles and a window to let in some fresh (if steamy)

199

air and the strong light of the afternoon sun high in an azure blue sky. The garbage disposal had backed up. When we turned the water on in the sink, it sputtered out and was the color and consistency of coffee dregs. All the drapes and shades in the apartment had been drawn to keep out the heat. With the power outage, the air conditioning was not functioning. The place was stifling. We opened all the windows and I went from room to room spraying each with the small cologne dispenser I kept in my purse. Still, the place did not smell like the house of Chanel.

Leon was red faced with despair.

"It doesn't matter," I tried to assure him. "New York and LA get plenty of power outages." I heard someone pounding on the door.

"Señor Garcia!" Leon said gratefully and let the gentleman in with our baggage. Unlike Lennox Gardens, at least there was a superintendent to mount the steps with heavy parcels! Señor Garcia was an imposing figure, not much taller than me but surely weighing well over two hundred pounds. He took out a large patterned cloth from his pants pocket and wiped the sweat from his jowly face. "I get fan," he beamed, his two upper front teeth noticeably missing. Down he trudged again to return with the fan, which we assumed must be battery charged, and then, as he put it down when he returned, shook his head and made a hopeless gesture. "No electricity," he said.

Luckily, by evening, a cool breeze had risen. We were both so exhausted from the travel and the heat in the apartment that we fell asleep as soon as our heads hit the pillows. Some time during the middle of the night we were startled awake by the sound of multiple motors—dishwasher, air-conditioning, garbage disposal all starting up at the same time as the lights came on. By morning, Aurora, the maid Leon had hired, arrived. Leon was right. She was a gem and a very nice woman. She promised to have the apartment in order by the end of the day. Observed in daylight, it was quite comfortable and attractive despite the furnishings being what I had named "postwar Moderne," seen in newish French apartments as well. Fabrics were in glaring patterns, woods were light. But the rooms were large, the two bathrooms modern, and the view looking across the Avenue Generalissimo Franco intriguing with its fine old buildings.

Leon took the day off so that he could show me around "the neighborhood." We had a long, leisurely lunch at a charming cafe. We drank a full carafe of red wine. He seemed happier, more lighthearted than I remembered him being. His dark eyes shone. His voice had a lift to it, and when he smiled (which was quite often) the shadows so often clouding his face disappeared. He took my hand and held it across the table. "Thank you for coming home," he said. He thought our troubled past had been obliterated, and for the time I decided to let it go at that.

He had hired a car and after lunch we took a tour of the city. I was more impressed with the sound of Madrid than its architecture. Madrid was the noisiest, most boisterous of the cities I had known. Pop music blared through open windows. Cars honked their way through traffic. Tires screamed as motorists stopped short, or revved up. I did become infatuated with the Madrileños. They were people of a joyous nature who had a sense of individual importance, of self-dignity. A majority were poor. All of them had suffered much in the course of their civil war, World War II, and the long road to recovery, to which Anglo-American film companies had greatly contributed.

A Talent for Loving was being made at the *Estudios Sevilla* in Madrid, with some location work in nearby sites. There were three more studios in Madrid, and they were as busy as Hollywood's motion picture factory once had been. Anthony Quinn was shooting a movie on a nearby stage to *Talent*; Orson Welles (whenever he showed up) on another. For fifteen years Madrid (and Spain) had been the center for American/European production. Bob Rossen was credited with its debut and the growth that had resulted from a deal that he had made with Franco in 1952 to shoot *Alexander the Great* in Spain. American production companies with large-scale dramas to shoot followed suit. There were vast, fairly unpopulated areas a short distance from Madrid that were perfect for filming war, western, and adventure movies. Except for technicians and laborers, many of these early companies had employed American expats in key posts (except for actors whose careers had ended with the blacklist for, as they were recognizable, they could not get a pass by taking an assumed name). How odd was it that men and women who considered themselves dedicated liberals could have so easily done business with Franco's Spain? Extremely! For the American dollars that were paid to the Spanish government for the right to film on their land and in their studios were, during those years, being used to prop up the generalissimo's dictatorship.

I was sorry to never have asked Bob about his feelings and motivations in being in business with Franco when he had been such an outspoken critic of the regime, especially during the time of the Spanish Civil War, when he considered fighting with the Lincoln Brigade against Franco (as some American writers had done)—not that he had ever been in the physical shape to participate in any army! By the midsixties, grand Anglo-American epics like *Alexander the Great, Spartacus, Lawrence of Arabia, 55 Days in Peking*, and others of their genre had tapered off. Still, filming in Spain saved American dollars and—as the rationale went—Franco's influence in 1969 was also waning, as was his health, and he was preparing to "step back and let his protégé Juan Carlos, grandson of former King Alfonso XIII, take over in the event of his death." (On Franco's death in 1975, Juan Carlos became king, restored the monarchy, and successfully oversaw the transition of Spain from dictatorship to parliamentary democracy.) However, there was no way to avoid the fact that while the generalissimo was alive, Spain was a dictatorship. I don't think Leon felt any more comfortable with this than I did. But the film colony appeared exempt from much government control. In fact, with divas like Quinn and Welles afoot, the production companies had their own disruptive power figures to deal with. I was never on those sets, but I am sure they could not have been as troubled as was *A Talent for Loving*, nor Welles or Quinn as outrageous as Topol, the Israeli actor who recently had been a big hit in the lead role of Tevye in the London musical production of *Fiddler on the Roof* (played by Zero Mostel on Broadway). After Topol had agreed to do *Talent*, he was signed to appear as Tevye in the film version of *Fiddler*. Not yet a household name, proximity to such acclaim had already turned his head, for it was to be his next film. By the time of my arrival in Madrid, it was evident that the director, Richard Quine, had lost the power battle between them. The cast included the actor Richard Widmark (who appeared as though he walked onto the wrong movie set, so quick were his exits when he completed a scene); the fine stage actress, Genevieve Page; the elegant, dashing Cesar Romero; and Quine's third and current wife, singer Fran Jeffries.

As happens with film companies, the participants—actors, director, producer, cameraman, and their families—form a tight group, which can often be quite pleasant. Aside from Widmark's indifference and a hopeless script, the major problem in *Talent* was that Topol was a loose cannon. Despite his wife's constant attendance on the set, he chased after every young woman who had a bit or extra role (the younger they were, the better he seemed to like them). Angry mothers and threatening brothers, uncles, or fathers appeared at the gates of the studio wanting to have at him. It was Leon's task to pacify them. To add to this, the Quines were constantly quarreling. Fran Jeffries was a singer, not an actress, and did not like her role, especially the scarcity of her scenes. By the end of shooting, she had filed for divorce (they had been married about a year). At one point, Quine went missing for five days and the assistant director and Leon took over. Widmark, at fifty-six one of Hollywood's most durable stars, appeared on the set when called for and then made haste for his dressing room to remain behind a locked door until required to return to the stage. That left Cesar Romero who was a "peach of a man," if one dare use such an old-fashioned phrase. He was warm, fun, intelligent, a truly good human being and, with his classic Latin good looks, a joy to behold. He remained unruffled by the chaos around him, and I never saw him even once lose his cool or his professionalism. Cesar was the one light in the entire holy mess that was the making of *A Talent for Loving*. When he was not scheduled to work, the ambiance truly got dark on the set.

Walter retreated to London shortly after my arrival, leaving Leon as negotiator and peacemaker, attempting to keep things rolling in what must have been the most dysfunctional film set in cinema history. I was present almost daily as Leon thought I might be helpful (mostly to keep Fran Jeffries occupied, I suspected). I greatly respected his diligence and understood why he was never between jobs. Leon could be counted upon, and his knowledge of so many facets of filmmaking was a great asset when producing a movie of wide scope, with star players, on a tight budget. Working hours in Madrid were controlled by the sun, custom, and a need to save energy (physical and artificial). Temperatures in Madrid can rise dramatically midday. The whole city seemed to shut down between noon and four p.m., including the studios. At four, work would commence until nine or sometimes ten p.m., when restaurants and nightclubs really came alive. Very often members of the company (excluding Mr. Widmark) dined out together. Cesar Romero (who often was addressed as "Butch" but not by me) and I clicked. We shared an offbeat sense of humor and an overview of the mad happenings on the set (never, I must add, involving his participation). In the parlance of society, Cesar was a confirmed bachelor. Remarkably, perhaps due to strong studio control (he had been at 20th Century-Fox for much of his film career), his homosexuality, though well known in the industry, was not public knowledge. Frequently called upon to escort a single female star to a premiere or other publicity function where he would be photographed with one of these glamorous ladies on his arm, his fans viewed him as a sophisticated man about town. Nothing in his attitude or appearance hinted at his sexual orientation.

At sixty-three, when he appeared in *Talent*, he was well over six feet, his posture remarkable, his physique that of a man twenty years his junior, his dark, thick hair handsomely streaked with gray. Both his hair and his famous mustache were always impeccably trimmed. What you saw first, however, was his wonderful smile, which said "I'm a happy man and I'm glad to be alive." Suave and sophisticated though he was, there was not an ounce of pretension about him. He had Cuban parents, but he had been born in Manhattan and had started his career as a ballroom dancer. He loved music, and when he chose where we (the members of the company who had joined for an evening) were to go, it was always someplace where there was good Spanish dance music, establishments that did not always serve the best food.

I still loved to dance and often attended dance classes for exercise. But my leg problems made me fainthearted on a public dance floor. I politely resisted when Cesar first asked me to try the tango with him. He would not take no for an answer and swept me onto the dance floor. His hold was strong and supportive, and I knew I could trust him not to let me fall. The next day on the set, he drew me aside and helped me to master the basic tango steps while avoiding placing too much pressure on my bad leg. Between takes, when I accompanied Leon on location, Cesar would sit with me and talk.

His great love had been the actor Tyrone Power, who had died suddenly of a heart attack at the age of forty-five a decade earlier in Madrid while he was filming *Solomon and Sheba* (he was replaced by Yul Brynner). I knew that Power had been married several times so I assumed he was bisexual. But the odd thing was that Judy Garland, as a very young woman before her first marriage to David Rose, had been madly in love with Tyrone Power and followed him to Mexico where he was making a film, only to find him with Lana Turner in "a love nest." Of course, when the studios ruled Hollywood, the sex lives of their stars (their properties, really) were whitewashed by teams of publicists, hired for just that purpose.

Cesar had his own curious faith called "liberation theology," a combination of Marxism and Christianity, which held that religion and communism were compatible (although Marx wrote most famously that "religion was the opiate of the people"). He tried to explain this to me, but I admit I found understanding it daunting. He believed in a utopian society and that what Christ would have created, if he had lived, would have been a kingdom that bore a strong similarity to Marxism.

Despite, or maybe because of, the problems with *Talent*, my reunion with Leon had been successful due largely to my involvement with his work. I had put my writing aside. I was there for him when he needed to let off some steam or discuss the day's latest snarl. The picture was not going well, and he knew it. The original concept had been geared to satiric comedy (which is perhaps why Topol, who spoke with a distinctive Israeli accent, was cast as a Mexican general). But Quine was not comfortable with the genre, so the satire was not funny and the script was so twisted that it was hard to get the story or characters straight. Leon's hope was that it might come together in the cutting room as had happened to the Beatles movie *Help!*, when he and Walter had thought it should have been called *Helpless*. (For the record, *A Talent for Loving* did not obtain a theatrical release for twenty years and was dismissed with sharp criticism and departed abruptly from theaters.)

What did I learn about Spain and its people in the short time I was there? Well, they drank more beer than wine. The Prado was so badly lighted that the great art that hung there could not be fully appreciated. Spanish women were more powerful in business than one would expect, especially in a country that was a dictatorship and where men seemed to rule their households. I was amused to find painted on the door of ladies' lavatories in several restaurants a woman's gloved hand holding a red rose, men's room doors decorated with a black top hat and a silver-topped black cane—à la Fred Astaire. I refused invitations to the barbaric bullfight contests (which received full coverage on the government-controlled television, the gore not censored for children). In fact, there was little else to watch on television other than bullfights. The generalissimo's portrait remained prominently displayed in both private and public buildings (including the hallway of our apartment house). The workers with whom I spoke to at the studio were more materialistic than I expected. There were soul-crunching slums in certain districts (but then, as I had spent time during my first marriage in the southern states, Alabama and Mississippi, as well as Texas, I was no stranger to the inhumanity of slums).

"*Viva la Muerte!*" had been the strident battle cry of Franco's Falange Party in the civil war (paradoxically translated "Long live death!" in English, but surely meant "to the death"). However, Franco's rule was dying, as was the man. Madrid (which is the only Spanish city on which I can comment) seemed to be celebrating the wake before the death of their generalissimo and of his national party.

Before I departed, Leon and I made short-range plans. His secretary Leigh would work with a real estate company in Switzerland to find us a small chalet in Gstaad on a six-month rental, the lease to begin in June. Gstaad had been a compromise choice of residence. I would miss Salka in Klosters, but I would be close to Chillon and to the library in Montreux, which had a fine archive on the period I needed to research. Gstaad was also a short train ride from Leysin, the university to be attended by Cathy (now desiring to be called by her full name, Catherine, an invigorating wake-up call that my daughter was no longer a girl but a young woman with a strong identity of her own).

In Gstaad, Leon would have the pleasure of rekindling his years-long friendship with Yehudi Menuhin, who had a full-time residence there and had also founded a music festival held during the summer in a church in nearby Saanen. *Talent* would be wrapped up by June and Leon would have the best part of the summer with me before heading to Denmark, the location of his next project.

Tax laws in Britain had grown progressively difficult with an enormous chunk of one's earnings (if either a British citizen or a legal resident) being eaten away. There was a loophole that lessened the bite if the taxpayer spent six months plus one day out of the country. This is what Leon desired us to do. The way he configured it (or his accountant had done), we could achieve this by one or both of us spending the time required in Gstaad and for the lease to bear Leon's name. Never clever in such matters, I had no idea how this setup might affect my own tax situation, except for the fact that I could not be subject to double taxation. What I knew instinctively was that a marriage should not be regulated by tax considerations or for one's life to be measured in dollar bills. After an emotionally testing afternoon of disagreement on this matter, I gave in to Leon's scenario and therefore cannot blame him for what became a rocky start to the reconciliation that my time in Madrid had engendered. Once again we would be apart for long periods of time, which I felt was not a foundation for marital harmony. What sweetened the plan was that Cathy could come "home" on weekends, I was deeply involved in my novel, and had Jay, who was most enthusiastic about being in Europe, to help me in my research and transcriptions.

I returned to Beverly Hills and, with Jay's help, packed up the apartment ready to be placed in storage. Cathy left California directly after her graduation for London where she was to spend several weeks at Lennox Gardens to see friends before joining me in Gstaad. By that time, with Jay's help, I would be set up in our new—if temporary—home. I did not fly across the ocean unaccompanied. Our three poodles rode in the cargo section in the lower half of the plane. (They presented still another problem for me to ever return full-time to London, as Britain had a six-month quarantine for all dogs entering the country and I knew I could not subject our pampered pets to such a trial. "Oh, well," I thought in a cavalier way, "I'll have to deal with that later.")

Leon's company took care of my flight ticket and, as they received a substantial discount from Iberia (the Spanish airline), I flew on one of their new jumbo jet carriers from Los Angeles to Barcelona where I was to transfer to a smaller craft taking me to Geneva (a distance about equal to that of LA to San Francisco). I had two hours between planes. The first thing I did was to check with the airline how my dogs were doing and to make sure they made the connection with me. I was informed they were fine. About thirty minutes before flight time, I was paged. Somehow Air Cargo had misplaced the crates with my animals in them. But they wanted to assure me that if they weren't found in time for my flight, they would be placed on the very next available one.

"Then they are *here* at this airport?" I said, trying to keep my cool.

"Si, si." In Air Cargo, it seemed, but they were not sure which crates they were in.

I tried to remain calm as I knew the Spanish anger hotly when they are confronted, a situation that could only make matters worse.

"Take me to Air Cargo," I managed with some control.

Oh, that was not permitted.

Unable to contain my anger a moment longer, I raised my voice. "I want to see the *agente de policia immediatamenta!*" I shouted in my limited Spanish, with visions of my three dogs suffocating in their crates and possibly being sent to some foreign shore where they might never be found—or worse! to be eaten!!! I turned away and shouted again, "*Policia!*"

"Señora! Por favor!"

A representative of the airline, a short, square, flustered gentleman with a ludicrous Groucho Marx mustache, was swiftly by my side. "Take me to Air Cargo!" I managed in my best deep-voiced, dominatrix imitation. I think the man had visions of my pulling out a whip from my over-the-shoulder bag, for he grabbed my arm and with a stammering of Spanish—not one word of which did I understand—steered me out a side door, across a field, and into a large Quonset hut–style building. "Air Cargo, señora," he announced, glancing up at me with utter disdain as we entered the steaming interior. There were hundreds—maybe thousands—of crates piled up one upon the other. I took a long step forward and called out—*loudly!*—"SANDY! BIBA! CHRISSY!" Immediately, I was answered by a chorus of barking dogs, their barks familiar to my ears! Still, I could not yet tell where the sounds were coming from. I stepped forward several more paces and then started to stride down the center aisle between the crates and suitcases. "SANDY! BIBA! CHRISSY!" Closer now, the barks accompanied by pawing on wood. Very close. And then I saw their pink noses poking at the airholes in three crates of various sizes (to accommodate their different sizes).

I insisted on walking them across the field to where my connecting plane now sat, ready to be boarded. The airline allowed me to fly with Biba (who was so upset she seemed to be having a fit until—once in flight—I was able to calm her) on my lap. Sandy and Chrissy, still barking their indignity, were put into cages in the cargo section. When the plane landed in Geneva they were brought to me (now out of their crates) and we boarded the charming mountain train that travels from Geneva to the villages above. The Swiss seemed to have no problem with dogs riding with their families.

In the late 1960s, Gstaad in the summer was a small Alpine village of about two thousand residents, not yet invaded by supermarkets, elegant boutiques, souvenir shops, and hordes of tourists, although once the ski season started after Christmas, its inns and small hotels required early reservations. I had loved Klosters, but Gstaad immediately took hold of my heart and robbed me of my breath. Set like a gem in a valley of the Bernese Oberland, surrounded by mountain lakes, lower mountains with towering mountains behind them, and the awesome Diablerets Glacier, its frozen tip blinding in the summer sun and a beacon in the winter, one became overwhelmed with the natural beauty that abounded. The Swiss as a people, although churchgoers, are not religious zealots. I attribute it to the magnificence of the terrain. How much closer can one get to heaven than the peaks of its glaciers and the gently sloping lower mountains carpeted in the summer—when I arrived—with a brilliant display of wildflowers? When church bells pealed, the clearness of the air gave them a pleasing, echoing sound like a chorus of well-tuned sleigh bells.

The town's one, long commercial street banded the lower mountains. On it was a fabulous bakery, a grocery, a unique multilanguage magazine-newspaper-bookstore and stationer, Cardineau's, which was operated by a red-bearded, eccentric, intellectual Englishman, John (whose selection of reading matter would have pleased Voltaire), his charming Swiss wife, Monique (who worked while he read), and her elderly mother, Madam Cardineau (wife of the original founder and a fixture behind the cash register). As they carried books and newspaper in many languages, it was a meeting place for all foreigners living in or near Gstaad. Main street also contained several ski, shoe, and clothing shops, two banks, the post office, and a number of outdoor cafes (some fronting an inn or small hotel of which there were several). At that time, the ski runs were beyond the business section. (There was also the limited membership Eagle Club at the top of the ski run as well as a *gemutlichkeit* indoor/outdoor cafe.)

The house that Leon's secretary, Leigh, had leased for us was two blocks from the heart of the town and in what might be called "the flats." The mountain train ran about two hundred feet behind us: quiet, no black smoke, a musical whistle that could well have inspired Rodgers and Hammerstein. The small cafe backing the train station was a favored gathering spot, and watching the trains arrive and depart along the winding tracks to upper regions was a form of genuine entertainment; one would not have been surprised to hear the Trapp family from *The Sound of Music* singing an appropriate song as it slowly diminished from sight.

There were no slums or "bad places" to live in Gstaad at that time. Every street was clean, all the houses I ever saw kept pristine—at least their exteriors. In the higher reaches of the village, the chalets were larger and a bit grander and had closer access to the one *grande dame* hotel—the Palace, perhaps the most elite hotel in all of Switzerland due to the exclusive, highly acclaimed, and famed boy's boarding school, Le Rosey, which was located just outside Gstaad. Attending the school were the sons and heirs of many world leaders and some of the world's richest families who stayed at the Palace when they came to either visit, register, or collect their offspring.

Homes in every section of town were built of wood in the chalet style, and ours was quite a handsome new construction. We could watch the trains come and go on our large rear terrace. Built on three levels, the lowest floor (which you walked down to) was set up as a separate (and quite commodious) apartment. This was Jay's to occupy and he was thrilled with it. The house, which we leased furnished, also had a "cave" for entertaining with a built-in counter bar, a sound system, several pine tables and chairs, and a space that might be called a small dance floor. The upper and main part of the house contained three bedrooms and three baths, a sweet-smelling wood sauna, and a large, open, interconnected space that was sectioned off into living room, dining room, and kitchen.

Our nearest neighbor was Lisette Prince, heiress to the Armour fortunes and a brilliant photographer who had fallen in love with a rather dashing ski instructor. (Their incredible wedding, which I attended, was memorable—rustic Swiss crossed with American high society.) In the higher reaches of town were the homes of Elizabeth Taylor and Richard Burton, David Niven, Sean Connery, Julie Andrews and Blake Edwards, Yehudi Menuhin, and Karim, the young Aga Khan who had attended Le Rosey as a boy. What impressed me more was the number of literary talents who lived nearby—William Buckley and John Galbraith, among them. Gstaad had a literary history, begun when Ernest Hemingway, forty-plus years earlier, had written *A Farewell to Arms* at a table in the small front tavern of the homey Rossli Hotel. This roll call of famous residents might suggest that Gstaad was a stuffy, pretentious place. Gratefully, it was not. Later, that perhaps changed. But when I lived there no one paid much attention to the celebrity of some of its inhabitants. In summer, Liz Taylor strode down the main street in jeans, little makeup, and a scarf tied over her hair. Sean Connery did not bother with his toupee, and Julie Andrews was followed by a gaggle of yipping dogs. There were those starchy characters who liked to align themselves with the rich and famous. I recall a pretentious Greek columnist who could have been cast in an old Preston Sturges movie, so over the top was he. There was also a suspicious-looking American with Hitchcockian resemblance who had the amazing power to turn up at the bank whenever one of the town's Yanks went in to make a deposit. Most of us were quite certain he was a spy for the Internal Revenue Service.

Leon and Catherine arrived not long after I did, and Michael soon joined us during a short break in his working schedule. It was great being a family again although I had the feeling (later confirmed) that Catherine and Leon had not gotten on too well in London, something to do with her dating choices, I believe. I thought he should have spoken to me first before confronting her, a matter of disagreement between Leon and myself. Shortly after, Leon left for Denmark for work on his current film, *Welcome to the Club*, a satire about American servicemen and USO entertainers in postwar Japan. The script was not much better than his previous production, but I remained as removed as was possible from making any comments. The short time he had been in Gstaad had not been unpleasant, however. He found some tennis partners and there had been some magical musical evenings spent with Yehudi Menuhin and his family.

A week or so after his departure, I received the tragic news that Judy had died in her London mews house. I was prepared to fly to England when I was informed that her body was to be shipped back to the States for burial.

All I could think of was the sad time in London when she had called me in the middle of the night to tell me Mickey was downstairs with a man having sex on a couch. And then, on my last visit with her, how terribly frail she was, her face hollow, her eyes huge, her frame shrunken. I remember coming away, feeling quite ill and thinking that must have been the way Anne Frank looked toward the end of her young life, for Judy had been so small, so shrunken that she had seemed a child. These were hard images to block out. When I was in Madrid, she had gone with Mickey to Copenhagen and I had received a letter from Hans Vanghilde, a Danish radio personality, that followed me to Spain. Mickey had given him my London address as someone who might be helpful. It seems Judy had suffered a breakdown during her concert appearance in Copenhagen. Mickey had gone on the next contracted stop on their tour and left her in Hans and Grethe Vanghilde's care. By the time I received the letter Judy had returned to London with Mickey.

Toward the end of the summer when I joined Leon in Denmark, I met the Vanghildes and experienced their genteel kindness and felt, that at least for the short time Judy had been with them, she had been in the company of good people. Hans was a sensitive man with a homely quality about him. Of sturdy Scandinavian stock, when we met he was dressed in rough, well-worn tweeds. He spoke fluent English and had a wonderful chuckling kind of laugh. He had met Judy only once, for an interview for his program, before he and his vivacious wife had been made her keepers while Mickey went off and left her behind.

The Vanghildes (with four welcoming children and huge Lassie-like collie jumping about) invited me to their home for tea. We sat talking until darkness was hard upon us. Hans played the entire radio tape he had made with Judy (and that had been edited some time before airing). There was an evident empathy that passed between them.

Halfway through Judy broke off what she was saying and confided, "I've worked very hard, you know, and I've planted some kind of—I've been lucky enough I guess to plant a star—and then people wanted to either get in the act or else they wanted to rob me emotionally or financially, whatever. And then walk away . . . [re her fame]. You're only surrounded by people who are not truthful and who are using you." (Her voice on the tape had an unfamiliar sound to it. I made a note in my journal that "the throb is there, but it is harder, more brittle, a dried branch that could crack easily under the slightest pressure.")

"If you're unaware as I am," she continued, "and you're a woman, it could get pretty rough sometimes."

Nothing could have been rougher than that week she spent with the Vanghildes, certain that Mickey had deserted her, for he had departed the hotel leaving her an envelope containing fifty dollars and the unpaid hotel bill (taken care of by her sudden hosts). She was having trouble walking, refused to eat, and without her pills must have been going through a disorienting and painful withdrawal.

"Do you know who I am?" she had asked Grethe.

"Yes, of course. You are Judy Garland, a great star—so great that in a couple of moments you can give ordinary people something they will never forget," Grethe had replied. "Please—say that again," Judy asked in a wisp of a voice. And Grethe did.

The Vanghildes told me that when Mickey finally returned to collect her Judy was in high spirits, "almost hysteria." She and Mickey quickly got into the rear seat of the chauffeured limousine he had come in. The Vanghildes waved their good-byes as the car pulled off, but "Judy was so tiny that even the back of her head was not visible in the car's rear window."

A few weeks after Judy's death, and following a very public funeral in New York, Bobby called me. He and Mickey were flying from New York to London the next morning to spend two days there before coming down to Gstaad to see me. They must talk to me. Could I put them up? Frankly, I was not too keen on Mickey as a houseguest, but Bobby was my father's kid half brother and we were joined by blood and a part of the same dysfunctional family. I had no idea what they needed to talk to me about but assumed it must have to do—not with Judy—but their own topsy-turvy relationship. I said as much and added that if that were the case that I would have nothing to do with it, for I was fearful that Mickey might be trying to lure Bobby into some pie-in-the-sky scheme.

"No, no!" Bobby assured me.

"What, then?"

"We'll talk about it when we see you," he insisted and was gone.

Leon was still in Denmark when they arrived a week later. From their attitude toward each other, I assumed (correctly as it turned out) that for now at least they were once again lovers, Bobby very much the protective member of their relationship. In his youth, although tall and big boned, there had not been much flesh on those bones and what there was—was pasty white. Asthma and a rare blood disease had plagued his early years along with the emotional injuries he had suffered as the unathletic son of Big Charlie. My father, with his athletic prowess and his short career as a soldier, had—however briefly—at least won their father's praise ("love" is not a word one could associate with my grandfather). Bobby was unable to compete in any sport and was rigorously protected by his mother against any possibility of being placed in harm's way. Yet, except for his spare body, he was undeniably Big Charlie's son, tall and blond, the same square chin, crooked nose, and deepwater blue eyes. What he possessed, that my father had not, was a true intelligence and a gladiator's will to survive. He fought and won his freedom by receiving a scholarship to Pomona College, located a short distance from Los Angeles, despite his mother's attempts to keep him close to home in Portland, Oregon.

His health would never be robust, but his transformation had been almost immediate. We saw quite a lot of each other during his first year at college. He came to Los Angeles whenever he had a free weekend. He had lunch with me at MGM where I was working in the Junior Writer program. Although we were both underage, he escorted me with much élan to the Mocambo nightclub situated on glittery Sunset Boulevard. Along with Ciro's, the Mocambo was a favorite of Hollywood's top players. We sat at the bar and sipped fruit-flavored-and-decorated cocktails and danced shoulder to shoulder on a small dance floor with movietown's famous (and infamous) stars. Giant birdcages containing exotic, wildly colored birds hung from the lighted ceiling. The room was scented by massive floral bouquets. Laughter was high pitched, the atmosphere heady. Bobby was fascinated with Hollywood and its celebrities, but he never cared to become involved in the industry. Social causes, poor people's needs, the emotionally crippled were of greater relevance to him.

Sometime around his junior year, he had the strength to come out of the closet—not an easy step in a conservative school like Pomona in the 1940s. Quite soon his appearance took on a more macho look. He worked out and added weight and muscle to his generous Swedish frame. Shortly after graduation, he shaved off his blond hair (which he had always loathed) and—bald headed (a look he maintained)—moved to New York and, refusing to take money from his mother (my "aunt" Edith), lived in humble circumstances while employed in a low-level job with the city's social services, where he was now a moving force. I admired him for what he had accomplished. No two men seemed less likely to be lovers than Bobby and Mickey.

How then to explain Bobby's relationship with Mickey Deans? The obvious is, of course, sexual attraction. Mickey was a flytrap for lost souls. But Bobby (now self-renamed Robert Jorgen) had found his—or so I had believed. He was a reformist and somewhat of a utopian who believed there was a good person inside everyone (except Big Charlie!). I had concluded that both these elements plus sex had been responsible for the fact that here he now sat on the sun-filled rear deck of my chalet in Gstaad, a consoling arm around his lover's shoulders, as Mickey—in his slick, con-man glibness—explained his need to see me.

Had I received a letter from a London law firm regarding Judy? he asked. No, I had not. Well, I would, for she had given me her personal papers and writings, the last referring to her poetry and several attempts she had made at an autobiography. I recalled the time she had told me that she wanted to write such a book but that Sid "owned her life." I had said that was nonsense, no one but she "owned her life" and that she should start by speaking into a tape recorder whenever memories of happenings and people who had affected her life came to mind.

"I should," she had replied. "You're right, I should." She had not mentioned it again to me.

"I have a publisher interested," Mickey said.

"A publisher?"

"For a book about Judy and our last year together. He has offered a generous sum."

He leaned forward, edging closer to me. I could not look into his eyes as he wore large, dark sunglasses. "You see, there's been a problem having to do with Judy's burial." He began to explain, one hand now on the arm of my chair. He believed that Judy Garland was the greatest entertainer of her time and should be buried in fitting style. So, upon his return to New York with her remains, he had signed a contract with Ferncliff Cemetery in Westchester County, New York, where other "greats" like the composer Jerome Kern and Broadway producer/librettist Moss Hart were interred. Ferncliff's manager had assured him that "Judy would be its greatest star." He had thus agreed for a special niche to be built in the cemetery's marble mausoleum. The cost was $37,500. Judy's coffin was transferred from Campbell Funeral Home in New York City to Ferncliff, where she remained in a temporary crypt (actually a file drawer—two bodies above, two below) as work on a permanent resting place was put aside to be completed when he could pay the outstanding bill. He had not been able to raise funds, so Judy remained where she was and this hurt him to the quick (so he said). "It's wrong. It's *very* wrong," he added as he adjusted his glasses and slid back, and away from me, in his chair.

The publisher was offering him a sum that would take care of Judy's burial and then some. The problem was, writing was not one of his talents (he played a credible piano and was a master talksmith). He wanted my help and since he had just discovered that I was the recipient of Judy's papers, it seemed we should collaborate on what "he was sure could be a best-seller."

Mickey certainly did not lack for gall or swagger. It did not seem to bother him that his grandiose ideas had created this appalling situation. I did not hesitate in telling him that I would in no way consider collaborating with him on a book. He continued his pitch. Finally, to save further confrontation, I got up and walked back into the house. Bobby followed me.

"Poor baby," he said with a nod to Mickey sitting, brooding, on the deck. "He has all of Judy's debts to deal with along with this ugly situation at Ferncliff."

"Judy's debts!" I countered. "Who do you think created a good hunk of those debts? Mickey used Judy, just as he's using you and trying to use me. Maybe he can get away with it with you. But you can bet your life on it—not me!"

"You've got it wrong. Mickey was trying to help get Judy back on her feet," he insisted.

"Back on her feet? What? To stand on a stage, a wraith, all alone, like she did in Copenhagen, dying as she performed, badly disoriented? Judy needed someone to take care of her, not someone who would siphon off her last strength to support *them*! Judy was an American phenomenon. Perhaps the greatest entertainer of the twentieth century. She was also flesh and blood, a woman, a much overused, exploited woman, devoured by leeches like Mickey and all the other tacky men in her life."

"You're overreacting," he cajoled, a familiar vein in his forehead twitching, but his chin set, his voice firm.

"No way, Bobby! Forget it!"

Dinner was disastrous. They departed the next morning. Two days later three large cartons containing Judy's papers—old contracts, her Screen Actors Guild card, her passport, letters and her writings—mostly poetry—and numerous tapes, arrived. I had no idea what I should do with them. I asked the law firm to contact Judy's daughter, Liza, who was in Hollywood filming *The Sterile Cuckoo*, to see if she wanted them. Several months passed before a member of the firm wrote back to say that Liza's answer was, "No."

I brought the boxes back with me to the States when I returned two years later, and kept them under lock and key. Mickey collaborated with a writer on a tell-all book. Five years after Judy Garland's death, I wrote and Simon & Schuster published my book, *Judy Garland: A Biography*. The first edition concluded with a small section of Judy's poetry. I don't know why, but the poetry was pulled from all future editions. It never had been included in the British edition. During my work on the book, I went to Ferncliff and was shocked to find that Judy's remains were still in that file drawer (so much for Mickey wanting to write his book to pay for her burial. The bill was still outstanding plus steep interest charges). I was in correspondence with Frank Sinatra at the time re his memories and association with Judy. In one letter I wrote about the state of affairs at Ferncliff, whereas Judy remained in a drawer with a nameplate reading—"Judy Garland DeVinko." Several weeks later the manager of Ferncliff wrote me stating that Mr. Sinatra had paid the outstanding bill and that Mrs. DeVinko would soon be given a proper burial. At Sinatra's request, I did not include this information—or this disturbing backstory—in my book. Upon the publication of *Judy Garland: A Biography*, I sent all the material originally in the three boxes to Judy Garland's legal firm in New York City.

• *16* •

Swiss Interlude

$\int$witzerland was at present my Shangri-la. Gstaad attracted the rich, power-ful, and famous. Yet, at heart, it remained a mountain village. Cowbells rang and echoed through the passes. Large tin containers on the milk wagon jangled as it bobbed along the cobbled mountain streets on its way from the *Molkerei* to the hotels and restaurants. Fresh summer breezes carried the evergreen scent of pine. The glaciers glistened in the sunlight like ornaments atop a circle of massive Christmas trees. Villagers were solid, hardworking folk amazingly tol-erant of the multinational strangers who invaded their peaceful community. An enigma existed here as well. For although countrified, Gstaad was the host to some of the world's most sophisticated people as well as being far ahead of London and other cities I knew in technical equipment and service.

Unlike Klosters, Gstaad had not attracted any of my expat friends, al-though it was a part-time home to a small group of film folk who were keen on winter sports and the absence of paparazzi. I found myself somewhat iso-lated, perhaps by my own making. The problem with my leg made me fearful of skiing and après-ski gatherings bored me. I am not at my best with small talk or gossip. I withdraw into myself at such get-togethers. Ever the writer, I become the observer. Dialogue lodges in my brain as if on a mental disk. I missed the most remembered refrains—or those to be placed on file. There was a hole that "we three" had occupied for so many years. My love was not diminished, but I had to accept the reality that both Catherine and Michael were now adults with lives independent of mine. However, loneliness did not overcome me—even with Leon's long periods away. I had my writing, Jay was ever present, Catherine just a short distance by train. I rather quickly made a few new friends, and my house appeared to be on the stopover for numerous old American friends on European tours. If I had one wish, it would have been that Michael was not at such a distance. But he was currently speechwriting and campaigning for hopeful candidates in the coming state elections.

Jay, quite open in his sexual orientation now, had made a connection with a cultured group of gentlemen of his like who pivoted around Chalet Coward in Les Avants, about an hour's drive from Gstaad. Noël Coward spent the spring and summer in this his beloved retreat, shared with his longtime lover, Graham Payn, who had first entered Coward's life at the age of fourteen back in 1932 when he auditioned for a role in Coward's *Words and Music* by singing "Nearer, My God, to Thee" while doing a tap dance (quite a "feet"!). Noël was so startled that he hired him on the spot. Payn was Coward's protégé for the next decade and had cast him in numerous plays to sing, in his strong baritone voice, many of his romantic songs, in hopes that the young man would become a star. That was never to be, possibly because Payn, although talented and good looking, did not have the ambition, which had first been his mother's and then Coward's. With Payn in his early twenties, and two decades Coward's junior, the two men began their lifetime partnership as a couple. Payn presided over their homes and was dearly loved by Coward, who called him "Little Lad."

Born with the century, Coward was sixty-nine, Payn, a dapper man of fifty, still extremely youthful in appearance. He possessed a dry wit, clever enough to keep up with Coward and their close circle of adroit companions who, when winter approached Les Avants (no member being even mildly inclined toward snow sports), followed the sun with the couple from Chalet Coward to their second home, Firefly, in Jamaica. But some of their members remained in Les Avants, to Jay's great joy. The town (a village much like Gstaad) overlooked the city of Montreux, with Chillon and an excellent library close by for me to do my research. Jay accompanied me there once or twice a week. Montreux was a jazz center with many jazz clubs and fine dining restaurants frequented by nearby residents of Les Avants and Vevey, which included Coward, Payn, and members of their entourage—Cole Lesley (Coward's secretary, collaborator, confidant—and later—biographer), and whoever was his guest at the time. I had a somewhat tenuous connection to this traveling group of players through Jay, who met them within a month of arriving in Switzerland.

I never knew (nor inquired) how Jay, for a time, at least, became a fringe member of Coward's household. I assumed he had become acquainted during evenings when I had decided to remain overnight in Montreux to return to Chillon early the next morning. I had bought him a silver Volkswagen Beetle that was easy to shepherd through the often narrow mountain passes. Before long he told me he would be going into Montreux for the weekend, adding— a bit later—that he had spent time at Chalet Coward and had become friends with Cole Lesley, a charming man, who did come to Gstaad upon occasion. After Jay's new acquaintanceship began, his attire grew impressively more fashionable. He wore a blazer, with a cravat and matching pocket square, when we ventured into town to have dinner. For Christmas he received from a mysterious sender (not revealed to me) a smart, Asian-style lounging robe. Years later, at a party Elaine Dundy gave in London, which Cole Lesley and I both attended, he asked about Jay. I had to convey the sad news that he had died. Cole said, "I was truly sorry to have lost touch with him. We had some memorable times together. I was very fond of Jay." I wanted to say, "and he of you," but I just smiled.

The imminence of Coward's seventieth birthday had become a national celebration in England. His old shows and reviews with his music were currently occupying London's theaters. He was, however, in declining health and spent what time he could in Les Avants (and later at Firefly) painting (an avocation Payn shared with much talent) and to conserve his lagging energy. I had not met Noël Coward, but I was a great admirer of his special oeuvre. Among Judy's letters in my inherited boxes was a warm, flattering, and gracious one he had written to her after her famous 1963 Carnegie Hall concert. With all the moving about, the near homelessness she had endured, the lengthy hospital stays, and hard times, she had kept few mementos. She obviously had treasured Coward's letter, I was sure, as such praise from a man she so admired must have meant a great deal to her. I thought he might like to know that. I wrote him a short note explaining how I happened to have possession of his letter, adding that I thought he might be warmed by the knowledge that Judy had kept it with her until the end of her life.

Coward swiftly replied. Knowing that the letter had been held so dearly by Judy Garland—"one of the world's greatest entertainers"—had "brought tears to an old man's eyes." We had a small exchange of letters after that. I wrote to congratulate him on his investiture as Knight Bachelor the following February, the honor long overdue—many thought because of his homosexuality. However, he was a great friend of the Queen Mother and of Princess Margaret, as well, and loved being in both their company. Whatever the reason for the delay, he now had "Sir" as a title and I was not sure how I should address him. I wrote:

Dear Sir (?)
Dear Sir Noël (?)
Dear Sir Noël Coward (?)
Dear Sir Coward (?)
    Please excuse the ignorance of a girl from the Colonies, but I am not sure how to correctly address you.

He replied:

Dear Madam
Dear Ms. Anne Edwards
Dear Mrs. Anne Edwards-Becker
   Dear me! Owing to my ignorance of proper American etiquette, I am not sure how to address YOU. [Then he continued:]
Dear, Dear Lady:
   I accept your kind words with deep gratitude.
   [He signed the short letter] Yours, Noël Coward.

A parade of good friends visited me in Gstaad throughout the summer months, among them the author-screenwriter Vera Caspary, who at seventy had more vitality than any of the young people Catherine brought home from college. Short and spunky, she hiked for miles accompanied by other guests (I was not much on walks over a mile!). Vera was marvelous company. She always had a good story to tell (the stories seeming to be amplified with each retelling). The Chicago doctor who had delivered her was a Doctor Frankenstein (a fact that stimulated her interest in my current work in progress). In her youth, Vera had been an editor of a dance magazine and the pseudonymous author of mail-order pamphlets on how to dance "by following the step patterns within" (her invention). She had also had a stint as a fortune teller in a Gypsy tearoom before writing her first novel, *The White Girl*, which was an instant success. Best known for having created *Laura* (as a play, then a novel, and finally as a film that would become a classic), her career as a screenwriter, mostly at 20th Century-Fox, had brought her a dozen fine credits including *A Letter to Three Wives*, *Three Husbands*, *Give a Girl a Break*, and *Les Girls*. She was known as a pitch artist—a writer who could go into a producer's office and in fifteen minutes or less could sell a story she created on the spot. Her success, she claimed, was due to the fact that she always based her stories on the same framework—three women caught up in a predicament that was not solved until moments before the closing credits. Her trick was to place each story in a different setting, and give them a surprise twist. Three was the magic number, she insisted, never two or four. She claimed she sold the studio a story idea titled *Three Coins in a Fountain* in five minutes—just by placing three girls in Rome to find their true loves, who meet at Rome's legendary Trevi Fountain where each makes a secret wish and throws a coin into its waters. Vera's contribution to the film went uncredited.

A spirited woman with glacial blue eyes and a determined chin, Vera had a sharp mind and an inflexible will. She did not suffer prigs or pretenders easily and was quick to lash out at them in a voice containing a scratch, as though being stretched too far, and often in uninhibited language. An early fighter for women's rights, she believed in free love but, after eight years, had married her longtime lover, Igee (Isador Goldsmith)—only recently deceased. At 20th she had rebelled against the lack of air-conditioning in the Writers Building by working at her trusty typewriter in the nude (and soon got an air conditioner as the male writers in the studio lost too much time seeing how she was getting along). I greatly admired Vera's candidness and honesty. She was a good friend, loyal, understanding, and not reticent in contributing her true feelings and advice, always given with an attitude of "this is what I think—do with it what you wish."

Although not blacklisted, Vera returned to the novel form, as her openly expressed left-wing views still made her unemployable in Hollywood. She loved my present story *Haunted Summer* ("the Dr. Frankenstein connection," she laughed, "and all that young fucking!") and accompanied Jay and me to Chillon several times. She and Jay bantered back and forth on our road trips. Of whether Jay and Cole Lesley were lovers, she said: "Of course, a skinny, unattractive man like Cole Lesley is attracted to Jay. He worked for and among some of the most famous of Hollywood's philistines [referring to his previous associations with Garson Kanin, Ruth Gordon, Katharine Hepburn, Carmen Miranda, and Tallulah Bankhead] and he is fresh fruit to a gay Englishman like Lesley, especially since Jay falls to his knees as soon as he hears an English accent!"

No one could replace Salka's dear friendship (and guidance) in Klosters, but Vera's lively stays with me in Gstaad were much appreciated. Work on *Welcome to the Club*, Leon's current film, kept him in Denmark for all of the summer and most of the fall. I had spent two weeks with him in Copenhagen and he took several weekend breaks in Switzerland. Once she was settled at Leysin, Catherine did not come home every weekend, but when she did she often brought friends. I was possessed by my work on *Haunted Summer*, driven by my need to deliver the completed manuscript to my publisher by the spring of the coming year. I had the company of Jay and some new, interesting friends. Yet, my life was absent of elements that remained important to me. I deeply missed being a part of my old group of expats and writing buddies who, when they traveled to Switzerland, chose Klosters over Gstaad as a place of respite. My reconciliation with Leon had been less successful than I had hoped it might be, chiefly because he was seldom there to share with me the experience of everyday life. I came to understand how army wives must feel.

We were living separate lives and, in my case, there were no ties of family and home to bind us. Switzerland's property laws allowed foreigners to buy property only for a one-year period between two seven-year, nonpurchasing periods. That time slot was approaching, as was the expiration of the six-month lease on my current rental. I suggested to Leon that we might do well to look for a suitable house, if we could buy it at a good price. He agreed, with seeming enthusiasm, that we should have a real home and that Gstaad was an excellent choice. With the help of a real estate agent, I started a search for properties in our price range. One, Chalet Fleur-de-Lis, strongly appealed to me. The next time Leon was in Gstaad, we toured it together and agreed that it was the right place.

As most structures in Gstaad, Chalet Fleur-de-Lis adhered to the Swiss village fashion dating back to the nineteenth century (and probably much earlier), in which the exterior of buildings had a sameness, a kind of ski-lodge look that was not exactly ugly, in fact, was rather charming (especially in the warm months when a profusion of bright-colored geraniums bloomed in window boxes), but allowed no building to stand out. The view, however, from the generous windows facing front, was spectacular with the village below like a Disney fantasy, in the distance the tall mountains and the ice-tipped glacier. When I first saw the chalet, the lower mountains were carpeted in brilliant shades of wildflowers. But one could imagine the transforming beauty when in winter Gstaad became a glistening white wonderland.

The interior had capacious rooms, with high ceilings and wood beams. There was a handsome, solid staircase of light wood. The sound factor in the living room (or salon, as it was called) was perfect for a piano. A long balcony overlooked the front and would be lovely for spring and summer lunches, especially when outfitted with pots of bright flowers. And there was a complete apartment on the lower level with a separate entrance, perfect for Jay. Best of all, the place was in excellent condition with an up-to-date kitchen and bathrooms. Except for some personal decorating touches, no great outlay of money had to be spent in renovations.

Directly below us on the mountain where Chalet Fleur-de-Lis stood was Yehudi Menuhin's chalet compound with its private yoga building. I confess to imagining musical evenings held when he was in residence (which did not occur).

Chalet Fleur-de-Lis was close enough to walk down to the village. The return trip would be a steep climb, however, so I did not envision myself trooping back on foot or bicycle. The property was owned by an English family, meaning we could purchase it with pounds (my contribution coming from my British earnings) and not lose anything on a money exchange. Leon and I agreed that I would be responsible for the down payment (50 percent of the agreed sale price of forty-seven thousand pounds) while Leon would take care of the monthly mortgage payments on the loan for the remaining sum. The deal could not be closed until the following year, and our current lease expired at the end of October. The owner, a Mrs. Maitland, kindly allowed me to rent the chalet (which was not presently occupied) until the time when a sale could be put through and executed, the outlay to be deducted from the sale price. She was also happy to leave the piano and some of the furniture that, if we chose, we could buy at the time of final purchase. For Leon the chalet would provide a financial base, which demanded only a small amount of Swiss taxation and gave legitimacy to his tax situation in Great Britain. For me it would be a home.

With Jay's help and additional assistance from local workers we moved into Chalet Fleur-de-Lis in mid-October. The first snows of the season had turned the outside world into a dazzle of brilliant white during the day, the sun still shining high in the azure sky. We had, I felt, bought ourselves a parcel of paradise. The next morning I awoke to the sound of a lashing wind whipping around the corners of the house. I could barely see through the broad windows of the room as my new world was veiled in a thick, gray mountain mist that brought *Wuthering Heights* to mind. Had I made a terrible mistake? I admit to having some thoughts that it was possible. Then, about noon, the sun finally emerged to renew and reinforce my enthusiasm.

Jay maintained his privacy, but we generally ate our meals together and he was always a part of any gathering I managed to put together. Cole Lesley joined us once and Jay, not usually so forthcoming, was wildly entertaining, doing an imitation of Carmen Miranda while holding with one hand a flowering plant on his head as he gyrated with great agility to a record of one of the Brazilian Bombshell's famous songs, aping her inimitable accent. We were joined by a new friend, Dale Witt, a unique American woman, recently widowed and an architect of some note.

Dale and her husband had made a fortune by successfully combining their talents—he as a builder and she as the architect—to create huge tracts of medium-income houses in Florida at the end of the Korean War, increasing their success in the decades that followed. They had worked such long hours during those years that they were left with little time for vacations or just that special time together. Then he had died of a sudden heart attack. It was only then that Dale realized just how much money they had accumulated. So furious was she that it had cheated her of the years together in which they had planned to explore the world once their children were grown, she turned the business over to a management team, sold her house, bought a seaworthy yacht, took a month of navigational training, and with three of her children (the fourth and oldest, a son attending an American university, remained behind) and a staff of two—neither experienced sailors—took off from Fort Lauderdale traveling eastward to Johannesburg, South Africa. Dale's prejourney nautical studies had not left her time for the matter of bringing a boat of that size into port. She crashed into the dock, left the boat there, and hired a safari crew (to see—not hunt—wildlife) to take her and her brood through the wilds of South Africa. After several months of travel, she realized her three younger children had to return to school. Thus her choice of Gstaad, Switzerland, with Le Rosey and several other fine schools nearby.

When the foreign right to purchase property law came into effect, Dale bought land on the very top of our mountain and designed a spectacular house with a 360-degree sash of nonreflecting window glass circling it. To reach the house, a funicular had to be constructed. One had to park one's vehicle below to be carried upward to her unique private ski lodge in the sky. I don't know how she was able to get the Swiss (normally a conservative people) to grant her permits for such an unusual house. But Dale was a most beautiful and determined woman (becoming a female architect in the States in the 1940s had not been an easy task either!).

I would have many adventures with Dale in Gstaad and beyond. Dale and Jay got on famously, Dale and Leon—not so.

Early one Sunday morning in January, Catherine and I were seated across from each other at the small kitchen table when Jay advanced, shouting up the stairs, "Give it to me! Biba! Give it to me!"

Our smallest poodle streaked into the kitchen with Jay in hot pursuit. She circled our table and then, as Jay went to grab her, scooted underneath it and out the other side into the connecting laundry room, Jay finally closing in on her.

"Give it to me!" he ordered as he swooped her up in his arms. I now could see that Biba had something grasped between her jaws.

"What is it?" I cried out, unable to clearly identify the object but guessing it was a bone of some sort.

Jay pulled Biba's jaws apart, grabbed the item, dropped Biba to the floor, and held it up in the air.

"MY TEETH!" he bellowed, as Biba darted under the table again. Catherine and I stood up somewhat aghast. Jay was holding a well-gnawed set of false dentures.

"Oh my God!" he cried and then clasped his free hand over his mouth. By now Chrissy and Sandy had come on the run from another part of the house to see what all the noise was about, adding to the confusion with a foray of arrival barks.

In all the time Jay had been with me I had not been aware that the even, white, toothy smile he exhibited was dentist constructed. Nor, for that matter, had Catherine and I think most other people. We were to find out later that it had been crafted by the artistry of one of Beverly Hills' most famous celebrity dentists (Clark Gable's false teeth being his best kept secret—to the public, but not the cognoscenti).

Jay put them down on the table, Biba quivering beneath it. I lowered my gaze to study this *dentilabial* work of art, now resembling a jawbone of a prehistoric man found in some ancient digging.

"They are ruined! Ruined!" he cried in exasperation and collapsed into a chair. "And it's Sunday!" He clasped both hands over his mouth this time.

I had to agree, the teeth were a mess.

"There is a dentist in Saanen," I added, trying to be helpful. "This is an emergency. I'm sure a dentist would go into his office, even on a Sunday, for an emergency."

Catherine had been silenced by her astonishment until now. "I don't think a small town like Saanen would have a dental laboratory," she said.

"Oh my God!" cried Jay again. "It could be days—a *week*! I can't be seen like *this*! *Toothless*!" He exhibited an exaggerated, cadaver-like, pink-gum smile.

"How did it happen?" Catherine asked.

"When I was in the bathroom, she knocked over the glass on my bed table that I keep them in at night. When I came out—there she was—*the little bitch*—chewing on them as if they were a *bone*!"

"I'll try to call that dentist in Saanen," my daughter said sensibly and was instantly on the telephone with a directory assistant. In less than an hour we were in the dentist's office. The teeth were beyond repair, but he took a full-mouth impression and promised to send it express to a laboratory in Bern. Jay refused to leave the house for the five days it took for the new set to be delivered to Saanen. Biba kept her distance from Jay during this time. But, once his new teeth were installed, she jumped up onto his lap, stretching her snout close to his face to sniff at them. Jay grabbed her and put her down on the floor with some force.

"They are not a bone, you thieving bitch!" he said in a tight voice.

Previous to this incident, Jay (who, by the way, loved dogs) had always favored Biba, and she had followed him everywhere and had slept on and at the foot of his bed. She must have yearned to get ahold of those teeth for a very long time before making her bold move. Jay's bedroom door was now locked to her. She slept in the hallway just outside his room and still followed him around. However, Biba could be a charmer, and she was difficult to resist as she had such a winning way about her. Soon he relented and they were friends again. Nonetheless, his bedroom remained off-limits to her.

Shortly after the first of the year, Sidney arrived in Gstaad and stayed at the Palace. He was there ostensibly to talk to Elizabeth Taylor about starring in a film, *Les Maison sous Les Arbes* (*The Deadly Trap* in English). He was producing and cowriting the screenplay with René Clement, who would direct. The role he wanted her for was that of an emotionally fragile woman who becomes inadvertently involved with an industrial espionage scheme and is, with good reason, in fear for her life. Sidney had worked with Elizabeth on the beleaguered film *Cleopatra*, cowriting the adaptation with the book's author. Filming had been interrupted, delayed, and then seemingly abandoned when Elizabeth became gravely ill. Sidney came back on the script when production restarted in Rome, Richard Burton now cast opposite Elizabeth's Cleopatra as Marc Antony. The two entered into an adulterous affair, which became a worldwide scandal. The production suffered more lengthy delays and cost the nearly bankrupt 20th Century-Fox such severe financial problems that they had to shut down for a time. Eventually three more writers and Joseph Mankiewicz, the producer, reworked the screenplay, building up Burton's role. Despite the acrimony between the studio, the writing staff, and the stars, Sidney had retained a friendship with Elizabeth.

Having personally experienced Sidney's simpatico manner with women, I am certain that during those rough times, he must have been a buffer between the studio and Elizabeth. Since that fiasco Taylor and Burton had married, appearing together in a number of films, her role in one, *Who's Afraid of Virginia Woolf?*, winning her an Oscar for her performance. She had just completed shooting *The Only Game in Town* in Paris opposite Warren Beatty. The Burtons were well known to be having marital problems and were apparently in Gstaad to attempt a reconciliation. The fact that Sidney's film had no role for Burton might or might not have dissuaded Elizabeth from taking the role in which Faye Dunaway was eventually cast. More likely it was the story, about industrial espionage, not a subject that held much interest for Elizabeth (nor did it to the general public when it was finally filmed and released).

Sidney was most generous with his time, and it was a joy to be with him. On the third night of his stay he asked me to join him at the Burtons' for dinner. They had inquired if he was alone. He said he was but that he had a good friend in Gstaad. "Bring her along," he claimed they had chimed. Of course I accepted, although I had no idea what to expect.

"Will it be a dinner party? I mean other guests?" I asked.

"I'm not sure. Their style, however, is relaxed and Liz said she would do the cooking."

We were the only guests. Liz cooked while our host drank, getting drunker by the glass. I ventured into the kitchen to help my hostess who, in fact, seemed to have things under control. This was a weekend and she had no staff. There was, however, a prepared casserole ready to slide into the oven and a tossed salad chilling in the fridge. Her ebony hair was tied back into a ponytail and she wore only a touch of makeup. Her natural beauty and her astonishing violet eyes transfixed me. She wore a casual, deep purple, silk velvet lounge outfit and two diamond rings that commanded their own attention.

"Are you having an affair with Sidney?" she asked in that trilly voice of hers (not yet lowered from alcohol and cigarette abuse).

"Oh, no. Sidney's a good friend."

"They are the kind you have to watch out for," she warned.

When the casserole was heated through, she removed it from the oven and then, dinner delayed for Richard to have another, and another drink, put it back an hour later. It was after eleven p.m. when we finally sat down to eat.

"Elizabeth made me what I am today," Burton sneered sarcastically. His wife ignored the remark.

Our hostess drank very little and was sober throughout the entire evening. She was also warm, funny, and amazingly tolerant of her husband's intoxication. There was little doubt of Burton's ability to hold his liquor. He stood without wavering and spoke without slurring his words, even as his sharp tongue whipped them out in a marvel of educated language and unique composition. His tone, however, grew harsher and his attitude toward his wife was more than once—cutting—piercing, really.

Sidney joined me for Sunday brunch at Chalet Fleur-de-Lis and remained through dinner, both meals served on trays in front of the fireplace, which he helped to keep aflame by feeding it logs from the wood box while he told me of his newfound love for a Czechoslovakian woman, half his age, very lovely and intelligent, who was having a difficult time due to the political problems in her country, which remained since 1948 a Soviet-dominated state. To remarry at his age—and with her comparative youth—seemed wrong minded. Yet, if they wed, they could live comfortably in Cannes and she would be protected by his American citizenship.

I could offer him only the advice he had once given me: to follow one's heart, not one's head. I had not done so and had married Leon, which I now felt had been as hurtful a union to him, as it had been—and still was—to me.

"Are you planning to remain in Switzerland?" he asked.

"That had been the plan."

"I've only been in Gstaad a few days," he offered, "but I can only envision it as a stopping-off place for anyone other than its countrymen—and women. It would stifle me. There is no dialogue to be had. It is detached from the world and the people who make your life and mine vital. If you decide to stay in Europe, you should consider the South of France—even as a second home. It is a true international community. Think of the great art and artists." He began telling me of the latest exhibits he had attended; a meeting he had with Picasso; a confrontation he endured ("very stimulating!") with one of France's young, new, modern artists. There was always an interesting film and crew shooting at the studios in Nice. And then, of course, many of our expat friends had moved from London to the South of France. English taxation was partially responsible. But the sun, the ocean. "It feels more like California to them. Thank heavens only as a habitat, not its habits. Creative people need solitude when we are at our craft, but we also need a city so we can exchange ideas, recharge, and be initiated back into the chaos of real life."

I told him that I had finished work on *Haunted Summer*, except for some last-touch editing and would be sending off the manuscript to the publisher in a week or so.

"Have you been thinking about a new book?"

Until now, except for Jay, I had not discussed *Post Mortem*. I now revealed the theme and the major characters (leaving aside, I am ashamed to say, the one I planned to base on him). "No one has yet written about those of us who left home to continue our lives and are still adrift after all these years."

"It's time someone wrote that story," he agreed. "I'm glad it is going to be you."

The night sky was filled with a full galaxy of stars when he finally departed. There was the scent of new snow in the air. This was *the* season in Gstaad. Thousands of ski tracks would be crisscrossing the slopes and the town would be swarming with tourists. "Good for business," old Madam Cardineau would say as she rang up one sale after another of foreign-language books, papers, and magazines on her cash register. It was, however, the time when I least liked Gstaad.

It had to end and I knew it. Each morning I awoke and told myself I would call and tell him that very day that our marriage had been a mistake. It disturbed me that it would have to be in the evening when Leon was home alone after a frazzled day in one of Shepperton's editing studios. He seldom went out on a weeknight. He would have fixed some eggs or opened a can of sardines. Leon loved good food, but he never bothered to cook for himself. It was as though he thought he didn't deserve a proper dinner unless someone was there to share it with him. I often joked that he had married me so that once in a while he got a real home-cooked dinner. When we spoke on the telephone when we were apart, I usually asked what he had done about dinner. "Oh, I scrambled some eggs."

"That's all?"

"Well, I had a big lunch with the crew," he would reply.

Somehow, it made me feel guilty as all hell. Then—defensive. After all, he was as responsible as I was for the distance between us. Sidney had told me, "What Leon wants of you—and is afraid to ask as you would no doubt refuse—is for you to say, 'I don't care about your taxes—or my career. I want to be with you.' And then for you to follow through, move back to London, into Lennox Gardens, and be free to accompany him to wherever his work takes him."

Sidney was right. If Leon had demanded I play housewife and camp follower, I would have refused. He was also correct in saying that in my case, Gstaad—as a year-round residence—offered little stimulation. I decided that I did not want to go through with the purchase of Chalet Fleur-de-Lis and, more importantly, that I had to end my marriage. I considered it my failure as well as Leon's, and was ready and willing to take the blame. Still, it took me weeks before I had the courage to confront him with my decision, doing so on the telephone when he told me he would be down the following weekend and be able to stay for several weeks as he was between assignments. I had thought so long on what I planned to say and believed I had phrased it as kindly as was possible under such circumstances.

I was shocked at his response, although I don't know what else I could have expected. His voice was cold, steely. If I filed for divorce, he would contest it and file his own brief citing desertion on my part. That would mean a long delay—years, perhaps, and relieve him of any financial responsibility toward me. I countered with my intention of not asking for any financial aid whatsoever from him—no settlement, no alimony. He would be free and clear of any liability where I was concerned. "The problem is, you are not concerned," he replied—and hung up the phone.

I notified Mrs. Maitland's representative that I would not be activating our proposed bill of sale and that I would be moving from Chalet Fleur-de-Lis in thirty days and that she could have access to show it during that time, and of course, keep the deposit of 10 percent of the sale price that I had given in good faith. (Chalet Fleur-de-Lis was sold almost immediately upon my notice to quit, to Julie Andrews and Blake Edwards.)

I had decided that I would take Sidney's advice and move (with Jay and our canine family) to the South of France. Where was a big unknown. Then Jules Dassin called. He was actually looking for Leon, and when I told him my current situation, he said he knew of a house that was for rent in Beaulieu-sur-Mer, as is. *As is?* It had been used as a location for a film and needed some cleaning up. The owner lived in Paris and rented it out for that purpose when she didn't have an occupant.

"You'll find a lot of the old group nearby," he added. "There's been a steady march of expats from London to these sunny climes this year."

That cinched it for me.

The town of Beaulieu-sur-Mer was almost equidistant to Nice and Monte Carlo, beautifully set on the Mediterranean coast. I called the owner in Paris. If I would do the cleanup, she would lease the property—which had a "gracious main house, a cottage for staff, several hectares of land, an orange grove, and private access to the shore by an underground stairway." It was completely furnished. Very grand, she added. Five bedrooms, three fireplaces, an elegant master suite, and a view all the way to Somerset Maugham's villa at the tip of St. Paul de Vance and over the Mediterranean to the horizon.

Somerset Maugham?

Well, of course, he died sadly five years earlier. But the villa was quite a noted historic site. Oh yes, and I had to agree to retain the couple and their young son who lived in the cottage. The wife took care of the house, the husband the grounds. And she wanted to be paid in dollars.

The rent was . . . ?

Four hundred dollars a month on a year's lease, *as is*—and an extra one hundred dollars for the services of the couple. She expressed a photograph of the exterior and grounds of the house—the *Villa Roquefille*. I could not believe my luck. It looked to be sheer heaven.

· *17* ·

On the Riviera

$\mathcal{I}$was on my way to Beaulieu-sur-Mer, all my portable belongings crammed into Dale's spacious American station wagon, leaving just enough room for her to see out the rear window when we were on the road. The vehicle, with its wood sides, drew long glances from cars passing from the opposite direction, as most were much smaller (and more practical) European models. Dale had bought the car at the US Army PX in Frankfort where she purchased most of her supplies at cut-rate prices as her husband had been a major in the reserves. She also had a small Fiat but used "Gertie" (her name for the station wagon) for hauling her purchases from Germany to Gstaad. Gertie was not easy to manipulate around some of the narrow roads in the Alps, and things had a way of shifting when one had to navigate the steep inclines and downhill reverse action. But Dale was an excellent driver and was blissfully happy at the wheel. Jay would follow us in three days in the silver Beetle with his possessions, the typewriter, boxes of my scripts, supplies, and our poodle family.

April is a spectacular time in the Alps, rivulets of melted snow streaming down the lower mountains, flowers of a brilliant mix of colors only nature could create carpeting ground level, the glacier shimmering in the glare of the spring sun. Dale seemed as excited about my move as I was. Mme Jeanette de Boussieu, my new landlady (who lived in Paris) had sent me a portfolio of photographs, interior and exterior, of Villa Roquefille that had truly overwhelmed us. My new home was not quite a chateau, but the pale pink, handsomely constructed, art deco stucco facade was as stunning as any movie-star estate in Hollywood. The grounds were magnificent: sloping lawns, an orange grove, several well-located, exterior terraces, and a concealed underground staircase below the grove with thirty-nine steps (just like the Hitchcock film!) that led to the coastline of the Mediterranean.

The foyer as you entered was impressive with a many-faceted crystal chandelier, terrazzo floors, and a wide, sweeping staircase that led to the second floor. The master suite was situated across the entire front of the house. Dale translated the dimensions of the bedroom into American figures. To my astonishment, my bedroom had a ceiling eleven feet high, twenty-six feet wide, and thirty feet long. There was a comfortable sitting area in front of the fireplace and a chaise lounge near the bed (when one wanted to greet visitors in one's boudoir, I assumed). A door connected the bedroom with a gentleman's dressing room that included a single bed, a sink for shaving, and a very impressive built-in wardrobe for his attire (one knew this was for the man of the house, as a horizontal bar divided the hanging space for shirts and trousers). Go through another door and voila! You had entered a lady's toilette (very Jean Harlow—mirrored dressing table and a painting on the wall of a coyly concealed lady holding a sheer blue scarf). Another door opened into a Roman-style marble bathroom, with a recessed tub that would have pleased Cleopatra. Five more bedrooms, three additional bathrooms, a walk-in linen closet, and a back staircase completed the second floor.

The salon and dining room on the ground floor were separated by a unique two-way stone fireplace. Behind the dining room was a "morning room" (I could not help thinking about the "morning room" in Daphne du Maurier's *Rebecca* where the new Mrs. de Winter hid a broken piece of china in a desk drawer). That room would be perfect for Jay to use as an office. My landlady enclosed no photograph of the kitchen but proudly noted that there was an American refrigerator and a six-burner range. This photo gallery that I was sent went a long way in raising my spirits at a time when my second marriage was crashing and I had no idea what my immediate future held for me. At least I now knew I would be living well—and at a price that was less of an outlay than my apartment in Beverly Hills had been. Having never previously visited the Cote d'Azur, I was struck by its resemblance in many ways to Southern California—the palm trees that stretched their narrow trunks into the sky, the deep blue of the Mediterranean waters that rimmed the coastline for miles and miles; the cliff-hanging houses painted in pastels, their red-tiled roofs fiery beneath the sun. It was as if all the Impressionist paintings I had always loved had suddenly come alive. It came to me that the scenic beauty of the Pacific Coast Highway that curved with the sea in Southern California shared so much with this part of France that it felt familiar and, for this time in my life—familiar was good.

We had a marvelous journey. The drive should have taken about six to seven hours. But, considering the weight of our baggage, Dale went at a rather slow speed, concerned that if, by some ghastly misfortune we had an accident, the car—as weighted as it was—could well flip over. On the narrower roads, no one was able to pass us and, at times there was a parade of cars lined up patiently behind Gertie as we lollygagged up and down the mountain roads. Incredibly, no one honked at us (as drivers certainly would have done in the States). Although, when two motorcycles whizzed past, the leather-clad drivers each lifted one hand in a rather impolite (and familiar) gesture. We stopped for lunch en route at a charming roadside restaurant. Outside there was a large water tank filled with live blue trout which, after we selected the ones we wished to have, were cooked (just barely) over an open fire, then deboned and served with a delicious lemon-and-caper sauce. We sat at a table near a window, the midday sun sharply reflecting through it massaging our road-tired shoulders and backs. We lingered. No hurry. Mme de Boussieu had expressed the house keys to me along with a signed contract and a list of local merchants. Genevieve and Gerard (the domestic staff) and their seven-year-old son, *petit Gerard*, were in residence in the house behind the main house and had been notified of my imminent arrival.

I had the new Michelin Guide and, once again on the road, read off all the restaurants in the near vicinity of Villa Roquefille. Rather than unload the car and dress for dinner, we decided we would pick something up from another roadside restaurant and bring it with us. We approached our destination about seven that evening. Never had I seen such a spectacular view as met our gaze when we started down from the *Grand Corniche*, the night-fallen Mediterranean awash with ripples of white foam, a full moon, and a sky crowded with luminescent stars reflecting upon it. We drove along the coast, the city of Nice now behind us, until we came to a sign announcing that we were entering Beaulieu-sur-Mer. Dale pulled into a restaurant called the African Queen (I mean, who could resist *that!*). She insisted on my staying in the car with all my belongings while she ran in to get something to bring to the villa for our dinner. She reappeared less than five minutes later. "How could anything be cooked in such a short time?" I asked.

"They're not cooked. I got two lobsters and a bottle of chilled champagne!"

So off we drove again—my new home now only a half mile ahead of us. Creeping up the steep incline that was the start of the lower Corniche until we came to the first hard turn in the road. There it was, lighted as though for a gala party. The property was gated. I opened it with a key marked "*exterieur.*" The scent of orange blossoms perfumed our way up the path to the front door. To our right was a large patio with tall french doors that obviously led into the living room, but as the shutters had been drawn we could not see inside.

Another key opened the front door. "Hello!" I called out as we entered the foyer. Facing us was that grand staircase. Brightly lit as the house was, I could see clearly into the living room, which was on my right. We both stopped short and stared. Boxes were everywhere, papers piled high. Ashtrays were filled with dead cigarette butts. Empty beer cans were littered about. "Maybe the former occupants haven't moved yet," Dale reasoned.

"There were no former occupants. Just the film crew who, I was told, did not stay here, but used the premises for location shots."

"Did you ask what else they used them for?" Dale said as she walked into the room and held her nose as she pushed aside the piles of debris.

It came to me now—*as is!* The place was filthy.

"Hello!" I shouted again. No reply.

We made our way into the kitchen—a vast room, much like a huge farm kitchen—a stove that made my old stove when I arrived in London resemble a child's plaything. Indeed, there was an American refrigerator, and in the center of the room a large wood table literally stacked high with more empty beer cans and refuse. The double sink was filled with food-encrusted dishes and when I opened the refrigerator, the remains of food left there at least four weeks earlier were covered in a disgusting gray mold. I quickly slammed the door shut.

"Genevieve!" I cried. No reply. I told Dale to sit down. "I'm not sure I want to," she said with distaste.

"Well I'm going to find Genevieve!" I started for the door from the kitchen that looked likely to lead to the cottage she and her family occupied (as shown on the map of the premises that had been enclosed with the keys and was quite a nice abode).

Genevieve was a *huge* woman (today we would call her obese and think we were being polite). Her husband came to her armpits and could have been lost in the folds of her skirt. Neither of them spoke a word of English. I have no idea why I had not asked whether they did in my letters to Mme de Boussieu, mainly because my landlady had written to me in English, and the one time I spoke to her on the phone, she was English literate (with a charming French accent). This had caused me to assume that her staff spoke at least some English. From the tone of Genevieve's voice, I could not help but know that she was raging mad and that she would have nothing to do with the condition of the house. "*Obscenite!*" she shouted over and over, and then ranted on. What I got was that she would have nothing to do with cleaning up after the *cochons!* (pigs). (These would be the film crew who had used the premises as a location.)

Dale suddenly appeared by my side with the bag containing the two lobsters and making some gestures (as though in a game of charades) that they needed to be boiled, handed the sack to her. Genevieve's thick, dark brows nettled, she opened the bag gingerly, squinted into it, and then with a shriek, threw it away from her and shut the door in our face.

Welcome to my new home!

I suggested to Dale that we go back into town and see if we could book a room at La Reserve, in the downtown section of the town, which I knew was one of the finest hotels on the Cote d'Azur (only foreigners refer to the southern coastal towns of France as "the Riviera," I had learned years before). It also had a three-star restaurant. Dale would not hear of it. "I'm starved. First we boil these lobsters and open the champagne. We'll eat out on the terrace." We found a pot that looked relatively clean, filled it with water, and when it came to a rolling boil threw them in (or rather, Dale did. I was squeamish about it). We also located a champagne opener. In the dining room there was a handsome breakfront filled with fine crystal and china. Plenty of champagne glasses there and it looked like the *cochons* had never removed anything from it—drinking beer from a can had been more their style.

We opened the shutters and turned off most of the lights in the house (the rest of the place was just as filthy but the grandeur that lay beneath it could not be concealed). Then we sat out on the patio under a deep blue, silken sky, lighted by diamond-like stars and a moon that hung in the dark sky like a magnificent, perfectly rounded pearl. We decided that for tonight we would only clean the areas where we would sleep. I had brought my linens, which was helpful. Dale said she would tackle the master bathroom. We had found cleaning equipment and products under the sink in the kitchen—and in the closet off the kitchen there was a substantial-looking vacuum cleaner. It was nearing eleven p.m. For a moment I stepped out on the bedroom terrace. The view was the superlative of spectacular. Across the waters, a light beamed, casting a shimmering line straight to the shoreline beneath our villa. It was most likely a lighthouse. Still, in my research on the area, I had discovered that Somerset Maugham had done his writing in such a tower room—often at night. Of course, Mr. Maugham had been dead for many years, but the idea that this light could be from the room in which he wrote some of his greatest novels regenerated my energy. (I don't believe in ghosts. Still, there is something to be said about *signs*. I liked to think this was a welcoming one from Mr. Maugham himself.)

Suddenly Dale let out a piercing scream. I ran into the bathroom. There was this most elegant lady, on her knees, her hair pinned back neatly into an upsweep to keep it from falling down on her forehead and her neck. To my puzzlement, one of her arms was up to the elbow in the toilet.

"Whatever you do, don't flush it!" she ordered. The rubber glove she was wearing had twisted and caught in the turn of the toilet pipe.

"Are you in pain?" I asked stupidly.

"On a scale from one to ten, give me a twelve," she replied.

"Oh my God! What shall we do?"

"*He* won't help. Call a plumber. We have to take the toilet apart." She was calm now. "First pour me a glass of scotch—you'll find the bottle in my hand luggage."

It was obvious that she was right. But the toilet was bolted to the marble floor and probably had been for at least forty-five years. Then what would we do about the flood of water that would then flow forth? "Maybe I can loosen those bolts," I offered weakly.

"We need plumbing tools. Please, the scotch first, then call a plumber."

After I had poured her a full tumbler of scotch, I opened the phone directory. Midnight was almost upon us and it seemed my chances to find a willing plumber to come out at such an hour were slim. Also, my French was extremely limited and certainly not equipped to make much sense as to why I was asking for plumbing help at this hour, considering we did not have a flood. And even if the man (I could not conceive France having lady plumbers) spoke English, how did one sound sane when explaining that a woman had her arm caught in a toilet pipe?

There were numerous plumbers listed in Beaulieu-sur-Mer. I started to dial the first one. "Crying is good," I thought, recalling the time in Beverly Hills when we needed a veterinarian on Christmas Eve. More likely he would not speak English. Before leaving Gstaad, Jay had come up with the helpful information that over three hundred English words that ended in either *tion* or *sion*, although accented *à la français*, had identical meanings. I had the list in my pocketbook along with a small English/French dictionary. After glancing at the list, I made a quick vow to begin French lessons as soon as we were settled. My eye went down the page:

"Accusation, accumulation, admiration, affliction, application, attention, celebration, collection, continuation, collaboration, classification, fornication . . ." Forget it! I would just have to wing it. The phone rang and rang. I was about to hang up when, on the other end, a man's sleepy voice said, rather angrily, "*Hallo?*"

I shouted into the phone, "*Attention!* Boom! Boom! Boom! *Explosion!* Villa Roquefille! *Tout de suite!*" (A tourist phrase meaning right away or immediately.)

He said, "*Oui! Oui!*" and hung up.

I thought I had successfully communicated with him. But then I realized I had not given him the address. I called back. No answer. I dialed several other *plumbiers*. No answers.

What I did not know at this time was that Villa Roquefille was the most famous house in Beaulieu-sur-Mer. No, not a whorehouse. It had belonged to Mme de Boussieu's lover, who was the town's greatest hero and martyr during World War II. Remember those thirty-nine steps leading underground to the sea? On the seaward side there were three locks, presumably to hold back the sea. But the middle one (constructed during World War I, I believe) was actually a dupe, with an amazing hidden door that—when approached by sea—could not be discerned—no cracks or openings visible to the eye. It had to be unlocked from the inside, meaning a cohort had to be waiting. During the occupation, Jewish refugees had been secreted from Italy up the coast on the darkest of nights (a blackout in effect during wartime) and had made it through that magical door, climbing the steps in pitch-black darkness (the door to the sea locked, the entrance concealed by thick brush) then guided through the orange grove, veering right to a path on the edge of the rose garden. Beyond that point, the terrain was nettled in overgrown shrubbery and brambles that had to be traversed to reach the back of the property, which was a steep, almost perpendicular cliff leading to the upper Corniche. In that rocky escarpment, small caves had been carved out, their openings covered over as had the steps. The refugees had to climb up that precarious edifice in darkness and silence. Three or four poor souls were held in each cave for days, sometimes weeks, until the Resistance felt it was safe for them to move up and over the top of the Corniche to continue on to Switzerland and safety. Some made it—some did not. Mme de Boussieu brought them whatever meager food she could from her own small rations, the Germans having stripped the orange grove for their own use. Her lover was eventually arrested by the Vichy government and hanged in the center of the town as a warning to all "foolish patriots."

Villa Roquefille was sacred to loyal Frenchmen from the area who had survived the war. It had been a call to arms that brought my *plumbier* so quickly to my door that night. It was also why Genevieve was so furious that the film crew—the *cochons*—had so desecrated the premises.

However, this was still unknown to me when the plumber arrived in record time. As soon as he entered the house, he appeared to have second thoughts. I was wearing a light-cotton robe and was in my bare feet. When I tried to get him to come upstairs with me, he was sure I had invited him over for sex and there had been no "Bomb! Bomb! Bomb! Explosion!" He turned to leave as quickly as he could. I grabbed him by the arm. Then I cried, the tears running down my cheeks as I pulled him toward the staircase. I never saw a more terrified man. Finally, he followed me up the stairs, crossly mumbling. (I learned later it was a moderate curse, something like "Fuck all bitches!")

When he walked into the bathroom, Dale now three scotches the better, he stopped short and stared in utter astonishment. He kept mumbling as he worked to disassemble the toilet bowl and tenderly, *most tenderly*, the pipe where Dale's rubber glove had become twisted and still painfully bound her hand. When she was free I suggested we go straightaway to the hospital as her hand looked just awful and she had a fever. However, she fell asleep on the big bed almost as we helped her to it. Her hand was badly bruised and swollen. I watched over her for an hour or so, the *plumbier* remaining downstairs in case he was needed. Finally, as she was talking feverishly in her sleep, I woke her up and with that kind man's help, managed to get her into his truck and to the hospital where her hand was put in a cast. She had badly broken a wrist bone and a dislocated a finger as well as having endured painful skin abrasions.

The sun had replaced the moon by the time we returned from the hospital. Thankfully, Genevieve had cleaned up some of the mess and had mellowed into a more cooperative attitude. We were on our way to a livable situation. Once the trash and dirt was removed, the interior of the house was warm and comforting as well as being quite handsome and luxurious. I later learned that Mme de Boussieu (who had moved to Paris shortly after her lover's death) had found it difficult to rent the house to full-time local residents. At the same time, she was loath to sell it and so had turned to film companies for it to be hired out as a location. To the French the Villa Roquefille brought back dark, painful memories; to me, that history was uplifting as I realized how many lives had been saved.

Jay arrived three days later, as planned. Dale had extended her visit for another week so that her hand would be strong enough to drive the station wagon back to Gstaad. One morning I was standing at the far end of the bedroom terrace, which overlooked the road that went by the villa, and saw Genevieve getting onto a moped. She put the thing in full gear. It revved up in a monstrous sound. It was a curious sight. A portion of Genevieve's much-padded *derrière* hung over each side of the seat as she zipped down the hill in a flash—full steam. A half hour later she returned. I heard the rear door slam, and shortly thereafter she trudged up the stairs with a tray of darkly brewed coffee, thick cream, fresh crescents, butter, and jam. (Although the Queen of Speed on her moped, Genevieve was a tired foot soldier off her vehicle, her considerable weight an impediment to fast action.) Her early-morning trip was to the *boulangerie* where on my account ("the rich American lady") she also bought bread for lunch and double the amount for her family, and did the same thing at the butcher and charcuterie shops. It was tradition, I was told. And though, of course I knew this was not true, I decided to let it go as I did not think the hundred dollars she received monthly for her services (as arranged by Mme de Boussieu) was fair pay, even given the fact that the cottage in which she and her family resided was rent-free.

Genevieve and Gerard finally got the house in shape. *Petit Gerard* fell in love with our poodle family and kept them running and scampering up and down the grounds—exercise they had never experienced before. There were always bowls of flowers from the garden in the main rooms and fresh-picked oranges in a large dish on the kitchen table. Genevieve had a warm spot for the dogs and although I tried to stop her, she continued to bring home from the *boulangerie* day-old sweets for them, served with saucers of cream. "Cream is for cats," I told her. But the dogs were quite happy to lap up the cream, and she just smiled triumphantly. The warmest spot, however, Genevieve reserved for Jay.

I don't think she knew anything about homosexuals and if she did, certainly did not realize that Jay was one. Late one night, sometime after eleven, I was reading in bed when I was jarred by a commotion in the far end of the hallway outside Jay's "suite," which consisted of two connecting bedrooms, so that he could have a private sitting room. Jay had on his sophisticated Asian robe while Genevieve's fleshy body was barely covered by a flimsy nightdress. She was pulling on his arm. The dogs were in a dither, Biba snapping away at the hem of her ludicrous garment, Chrissy running around in circles, and Sandy barking (if I understood dog language, I would venture to say that he was egging his family on to further attack this strange creature).

"What is it?" I managed.

Jay pulled himself loose and shooed the dogs away. Genevieve turned and, sobbing quite dramatically, ran down the back staircase, the kitchen door slamming behind her as she exited the house.

In a declarative voice, Jay explained: "When I went to my room, there she was *splayed* on my bed! Her breasts spilling out of that obscene nightdress like two mammoth, rising yeast bowls of dough! No pretty sight, I'll tell you! Can you believe it! How the hell did she get there? And in a nightdress? She came down from her house in a see-through night dress! It's insane!"

"She's got a crush on you," I said, trying to control my desire to laugh.

"Well, she better get over it fast!" he said and turned on his heel—the dogs dutifully following behind him—and entered his room, not shutting his door until the poodles were safely inside. It took me very little time to adjust myself to life in Beaulieu-sur-Mer, perhaps due to the many likenesses it shared with Southern California: the gracefully curving coastline, the whiff of the salty sea the gentle summer breeze brought, the palm trees swaying in the soft-blowing wind, and the buildings—so many in the pastel colors so dear to California architects. The coastal highway wound itself just below our villa, weaving along the edge of the sand and sea much as the Pacific Coast Highway snaked its way from San Diego past Santa Monica, Malibu, up to Santa Barbara, and beyond. The younger Frenchwomen wore huge sunglasses (now popular), and sunbathed near nude on the decks of private hotels (well, at least, breasts exposed and wearing a bikini bottom that looked more like a G-string). As the hotels were on the sea and at ground level, their shiny, oiled, tanned bodies could be looked down upon from the windows and terraces of homes built into the cliffs.

Dozens of small seaside villages dotted the coast from Monte Carlo (east of Beaulieu) to Cannes (westward). We were situated less than a half hour's car ride from Monaco and Nice, both of which had glorious outdoor weekly markets that were dazzling in their array of food and flowers. Cannes and Antibes were an extra thirty-minute ride (providing one did not drive during the heavy traffic hours) along one of the most glorious coast roads, equal—but not quite in my memory—to California's magnificent Pacific Coast Highway. The best time to traverse this route was from noon to three p.m. when the French always stopped work to enjoy a relaxing lunch. What was strikingly different in the landscapes of Southern California and the South of France were the Corniches, where cliff-clinging villages had been built centuries earlier. I was fascinated with the old graveyards, well kept, many grave sites marked by porcelain flowers. I tried to plan some excursion, if only for a few hours, on one day of the weekend. I particularly liked market days, when we could buy a freshly baked loaf of bread and tomatoes that smelled redolently of the earth and sun. I can still remember the glorious taste of that humble meal, sprinkled with salt and a pinch of fresh pepper.

On weekdays I put in my usual long hours of writing. But on the weekends, with Jay at the wheel, we took to the highway and the narrow, curving, rather dangerous upper roads. Jay was a supercautious driver, seldom reaching the allowable speed. The French not being as polite as the Swiss, we were always being honked at, which did not bother Jay in the least as he kept to his snail's pace. Often a driver would shout out offensive epithets. We learned very quickly that we were in a German car—and in this part of France, anti-German vitriol that had built up during the Occupation twenty-five years before had not been squelched.

I was deeply into my current book on the lives that had been thrown asunder by the blacklist. This novel had obsessed me to a degree that no other previous work had done. I had remained in close touch with Bob Rossen's former secretary, Eleanor Wolquitt (now living in New York), and she had become irreplaceable in terms of research, traveling to DC to obtain copies of testimonies of friendly and unfriendly witnesses during the years that HUAC had such a manic hold on our country. I had renamed the book *Shadow of a Lion* (a Shakespearean quote) as I felt *Post Mortem* gave the false impression that the fallout due to the blacklist had ended, when I knew it had not.

I did not close my mind to the book on those weekend outings, for so many old friends and expats had relocated to the South of France. As in London, they hung together. Most remained bitter toward Hollywood and their expulsion during the McCarthy period. Suspicions festered—who had secretly named names; animosity flared—at those who had regained a foothold back in their profession, be it in Europe or in the States. Afternoons and dinner were often shared with them. Nearly twenty years had passed since they had been forced to leave home. They carried the past with them in unlocked areas of their minds and their hearts. Small incidents, words, names could bring forth a swell of emotions and recollections. The monkey still clung to their backs; the elephant remained in the room. I vowed I would not let that happen to me. Shifting what talent I had into writing books, not film scripts, had helped me to refresh my priorities. Now that I was writing about those times I had to chain my emotions. "No sliding back!" I would tell myself and try to abide by my own decree. This was difficult, however, when we were gathered together. All someone had to say to start a good two hours of dragging out the past was, "Did you read the reviews on Kazan's new movie?" Or, "Well, that *son-of-a-bitch-Reagan* is going to run for a second term as governor of California!" (Reagan had notoriously betrayed the entire membership of the Screen Actors Guild when he was its president by giving names of his constituency to the FBI and the Committee.) They had not integrated into the life of the people of France; their current political, economic situation was seldom discussed, nor were the French films that were being made by French companies right on their doorstep at the Nice Studios, unless someone like Jules Dassin (and so one of them) was involved. (He was, in fact, filming *Promise at Dawn*, the project that Sidney and I had once worked on.)

There was plausible reason for this. The French liked Americans—especially the tourists who helped rebuild their businesses and bank accounts. But they seldom opened the doors to their homes to those of us who were now living in their cities and towns. When in their company, you lunched or dined in restaurants. They came to your home—but never seemed comfortable in doing so . . . even when they were fluent in English. They also had little patience for those who did not speak their language correctly. That would include me—as I never could get the right accent and often mixed my tenses.

With the parade of Hollywood expats who I saw and welcomed to Villa Roquefille and with my deep involvement with *Shadow*, I had very little extra time. Catherine came down from Switzerland whenever she could, often bringing a girlfriend, or as on one memorable weekend, a group of six or seven of her chums—male and female—who I found stretched out on mats all over the living room one Saturday morning. It was glorious to see her and to spend time with young people who were set to devour the world in one large gulp.

Catherine was a beauty—if I as a mother have the right to say so. In California she had adopted a somewhat gamine look—short-cropped hair, trim clothes. Now she was a full-bloom flower child, her mahogany tresses shiny, loose and long, her skirts full and filmy. Still, her straightforward approach to life had not changed, nor had her work ethic, nor the uncommon common sense with which she could surprise you.

Hardly a week went by that I did not have guests. Vera flew over and stayed for weeks, working on a novel of her own in two upstairs rooms across the hall from Jay. They got along famously. Neither ever let the other get away with anything. "Stop being so polite to me!" she once ordered him. "That's what happens to me when I am in the company of an old woman who is too vain to put on her glasses to look where she is going!" he once retorted. She laughed raucously.

Vera and I would take long walks together along the shore, talk about the problems we were having with our work, and exchange opinions on just about anything that took our fancy. Confiding in Vera was comfortable. She looked at things with a clear eye, no mist or sugarcoating. "If you can't communicate with a man and the sex has lost its fervor, what else is left?" she said of my decision to divorce Leon. "You have a career. You are independent of his support. I've known Leon for years. He's like the blindsided captain of a ship who steers it into an iceberg and then expects everyone on board to go down in the deep waters with him. He's entombed himself in that apartment of his with steps that could lead to a scaffold. It's his penance. But it damn well should not be yours!"

Vera's presence was more bracing than the salty winds that came to shore off a rolling sea. I loathed to see her return to the States but Paul Jarrico and his new lady, Yvette, came shortly after her departure and brought with them a fresh wind. Yvette was French, formerly married to a Czechoslovakian, politically involved in his troubled country's postwar problems. Putting aside Paul's inclination to speechify, he was a very likeable character. He had been nominated for an Oscar for his screenplay of the lighthearted Ginger Rogers film *Tom, Dick and Harry* (1942, directed by Garson Kanin) as well as producing—on a shoestring—*Salt of the Earth* (1953), an iconic left-wing movie about the hardships of Latino mine workers in New Mexico, an impressive endeavor as almost all members of the company were either unprofessional actors or blacklisted filmmakers. Gaining an American release was impossible at the time. Yet, because of its unique history, the film had gained stature abroad and in private showings in the States. Certain that one day he would be famous for what he considered his contribution to cinema, the trunk and backseat of his car (which seemed the only permanent home he had at the time) was piled high with every paper that carried his words. There were hundreds of letters from "famous people" to him, and reams of notes he had made on his day-to-day doings and thoughts. There was only room in the front seat for the two of them. Yvette accepted this with good nature and by taking a minimal amount of her own belongings.

My old friend Lester Cole spent a weekend with us that first summer. He remained bitter, testy at times, but he had a new love, Kay, an attractive American divorcee, an intelligent, amiable woman who seemed able at times to gladden his moods from gloom to cheeriness, and when in the latter state, Lester could be extremely warm and entertaining. Harold and Ruth Buchman were now living in Cannes, as, of course, so was Sidney. Friends from London, John and Harriet Collier, lived up the coast a bit in a villa that Napoleon supposedly had bought for his sister, quite a bawdy lady as the story went. John was one of the few English writers who had been blacklisted in Hollywood, where he had immigrated in the midthirties having already become a critically acclaimed short-story writer in England. He notably contributed to the screenplays of *The African Queen*, *I Am a Camera*, and *Her Cardboard Lover*. He had a terrific story mind, very offbeat. A short bulldog of a man with bushy black eyebrows and a wry smile, he often took pleasure in belittling himself. He was now reflective of his Hollywood years. "I sometimes marvel," he wrote, "that a third-rate writer like me has been able to palm himself off as a second-rate writer." But he did regard himself a fantastic chef and insisted on having these big gatherings where he did all the cooking, always finding some exotic fish or animal body part that was seldom served (for good reason). Once nearly all the guests came down with food poisoning (I was laid up for a week after that meal), and on another occasion only an hour after dinner had been served, John had to be rushed to the hospital with such strong stomach pains he could not stand up.

Jules Dassin had a residence in Lausanne, Switzerland, and offices in Paris. But he shot most of his films at the Victorine studio in Nice—seldom bringing Melina Mercouri (now his wife) with him. Melina devoted much of her time as a political activist and campaigned diligently against the ruling junta in her native Greece. Her passport had been confiscated, her citizenship revoked, and she had been forced into becoming an exile from her beloved country. The similarity of their situations had initially brought them together. Sadly, now it seemed to be placing a wedge between them. Mainly, I suspected, because Jules had turned away from his activism to his work as a producer and director, while Melina had distanced herself from acting and had become more deeply involved in the political chaos in her native Greece.

One morning Jules rang me. He was working on postproduction of a film at the Victorine and having serious problems with the quality of the sound mixing. He once again wanted to get in touch with Leon and hoped he might be with me in Beaulieu, as he had not been able to reach him in London. I told him that we were now permanently separated and that I did not know where he was. "I thought you two had pulled it together," he mused.

"I'm afraid not. How's Melina?" I asked.

"She's fine, but we're having some difficulties of our own at present. I always seem to be coming in the front door when she's leaving through the back." We consoled each other for a few minutes, and then he asked if I would have dinner with him at La Reserve (a fairly midway point for the two of us). It was a Friday night and I was free. Jay could drive me there and I could take a taxi back (not an expensive fare).

I had recently read an article about Jules that said something to the effect that he was "a man still in search of a country and a cohesive artistic style." Bea (his ex-wife) had told me once that he was always looking to morph into a new persona, never sure of who he really was or who he wanted to be. His parents had both been Russian immigrants who had settled in Harlem which, at that time, had separate black, Jewish, Irish, and Italian ghettos. Everyone seemed poor, and the groups were constantly fighting each other. The elder Dassins had eight children and they were hardly able to keep their family fed. "We were so poor, it was ridiculous," Jules once said. "There was always the problem of eating. And it was cold . . . it was always so cold."

"You know," he also said to me, very seriously, when we happened to be talking about Vivien Leigh just after her tragic death in 1967. "I am the only man I know who understood Scarlett O'Hara (Vivien's most famous role), for she was a woman's creation, after all. But that line—'I'll never go hungry again—nor will any one of my family'—I understood that. Sympathized with that. I felt the same way when I was a young man. Still feel that way. It makes you ambitious—but it also makes you insecure, fearful."

When I first met Jules he was in his forties. He was now in his midsixties. He looked tired and older than his years and somehow had the aura of defeat about him, something of course that Scarlett O'Hara never had, and since he had done reasonably well in Europe, adding rather than subtracting to his preblacklist status, it seemed odd. He was genuinely glad to see me. We were seated at a rather secluded table in the elegant dining room of La Reserve. Our waiter spoke English quite well, but Jules always addressed and answered him in French. We talked about a variety of things—the business (films), my books, his concern for his children (now adult). Suddenly, he asked me, "You were close to Bob Rossen, weren't you?"

I explained the relationship.

"I always wondered how he could face his kids after he had named names, betrayed his friends. What kind of a role model is that for a son or daughter?"

"Stevie, his son, had the most trouble with it," I admitted. I recalled how Bob was always telling Stevie to face down those who tried to bully him. Stevie was a sensitive youngster—not a fighter, really, and Bob wanted his son to be more of a macho man. "I believe that Bob thought the fact that he had given in to the Committee, not fought his battle, was a greater betrayal to his son than to those who he had named."

Jules sat across from me thinking about that for a long time. He took a deep breath, cast his gaze somewhere in the past for a moment, and then turned back and stared hard at me. "That's one of the saddest stories of the consequences of the Committee's bullying tactics that I have ever heard," he said in a soft voice, moist with emotion. "There can't be anything worse than if a man's children think he has betrayed them."

He insisted on driving me home. Our conversation grew lighter, perhaps superficial as we glided around the curves of the seafront highway. He got out of the car to escort me to the door.

Not long after our dinner, his son Joe, who had been a singer, died of a heart attack. Jules suffered one himself a few months later but recovered. I never was able to get that moment out of my head when we were discussing Bob Rossen and a father's betrayal to a son and how deeply Bob's family situation had affected Jules. I wondered if he hadn't felt his leaving Bea for Melina was also a betrayal to his children—or perhaps that his son had thought it had been. I made a mental note for my book to investigate the effect the blacklist had on the children whose lives had been upturned (including my own) and who thereafter carried the engraved stamp on their deepest, darkest, interior feelings of their parents' decisions during the early days of the blacklist and of HUAC's brutal gavel.

· 18 ·

Going Home

$\mathscr{B}$eyond the sealed shutter doors of the living room, the wind whipped across the patio and rattled the front gate. This was November, the time of Le Mistral, a dry cold, northerly wind that blows in squalls toward the Mediterranean coast of southern France. I had been told that it could reach a speed of 180 kilometers an hour and leave towering, aged palm trees bowed and broken, sands and roads littered with debris, and rooftops shed of tiles. Residents of the Cote d'Azur made a fairly mass exodus to calmer, less depressing places—for the rain and mist that preceded it, and then the untempered wind itself, affected one's state of mind as well as one's business, many of which closed for the entire month of November.

I sat, legs up, on the sofa, a blanket over them, Biba quivering on my lap, Chrissy and Sandy (growling under his breath) on the floor beside us. I could hear the click-clicking sound of Jay's nimble fingers on the typewriter in the morning-room-cum-office. Genevieve (making her presence known with her grumbling) had deposited some groceries on the kitchen table and then slammed the door hard after herself. Dale had tried unsuccessfully to persuade me to bring Jay and the dogs to Gstaad for the month. Truth was, I had welcomed Le Mistral. I was not enamored with the gray skies, the lowering clouds, the sea that had turned to slate, and, especially, the need (in case of breaking glass) to live behind locked shutters and to have my days brightened only with artificial light. But the upside was that I could fully concentrate on my work. Visitors were few, and those who did come left as swiftly as they could once they realized no sun could be promised for the day following their arrival.

The dark soul of my novel was upon me. I had to find answers to all the questions that crowded my thoughts. I had named my protagonist (and

244

antihero) Max Seaman (yes, with its homophonic in mind) and it was through him that I meant to convey to a reader the cataclysmic damage rendered to the men and women who had gone before the Committee, both those who had defied it and those who had caved in. They were all victims, as Dalton Trumbo had said.

I was exhausted this day. Le Mistral had blown fierce, turning more bellicose by the hour. I had been up all night wrapped in a blanket on the chaise lounge in my bedroom, writing. I managed a few hours sleep in the early morning—which could not reveal itself to me with all the shutters tightly sealed. I had edited the six or seven pages of lined yellow paper that contained my scrawled and marked-up handwriting that Jay was now transcribing on the typewriter, although I could not imagine how he could read my scribblings at all, never mind at the speed at which he was copying them.

The clicking stopped. A few moments later he came into the living room and stood by the fireplace, the fire now down to glowing embers. He held the pages to his chest, hands crossed over them. "I don't think you should read these until tomorrow morning," he said.

"Why?" I asked, somewhat surprised as Jay seldom made such suggestions.

"You need a good night's sleep to clear your head a bit."

"What does that mean?"

"You shouldn't be quick to change anything. This passage says it all. I understand Max now. I feel sorry for him, for his loss. You know, my heart was pounding as I was typing. I felt in a small way a part of something important. What you are writing is important." He walked over and put the pages down on the cocktail table in front of the sofa. "I'll make some coffee," he announced and went into the kitchen as Biba jumped off my lap and followed him in.

We sat across from each other at the kitchen table, caressing our hot-brewed mugs of coffee between our swallows. Genevieve had left a yeast-scented bread loaf and several croissants along with some sliced ham, milk, cheese, and a half dozen eggs, several of which were apparently cracked, as their contents were oozing through the paper sack that held them, most probably the cause of her ill humor earlier. Despite Le Mistral's wrath, *boulangers* in town had kept their ovens baking. I was sorry to have missed the sight of Genevieve tightly gripping the handlebars of her moped as the vehicle was accelerated ever faster by the winds on her way into town and the brassy fight she must have fought to make her way back against them.

Jay pulled the last cigarette from a pack and lit it. He made a show of not crumpling the empty packaging and stuffing it into a pocket. A ruse, but I did not miss the fact that he smoked well over a pack a day. Early on in our relationship I had tried hard, without nagging, to get him to cut down, with no success. I watched him now as he inhaled deeply and then struggled to stifle a cough.

"Are you okay?" I asked.

"Fine. I could use a few good days in the sun," he replied in a gravelly voice once he had stopped coughing.

He did not look fine. He had lost weight in recent weeks, and his cheeks were sunken. I had been concerned about his cough, which had begun to sound deeply imbedded in his chest, and had suggested he see a doctor in Cannes whom Sidney had recommended. His refusal was brusque. I reluctantly let it alone. I knew he was finding Beaulieu a bit lonely without the stimulation of the group at Chalet Coward, who were now wintering in the islands.

"It's none of my business," I ventured, "but have you heard from Cole Lesley lately?"

"I had a card," he answered tersely, "forwarded from Gstaad. He obviously lost our new address."

I was about to suggest he might like to take a week's vacation to Jamaica. Certainly he was due more than that as he hardly ever took time off. But he continued. "He wrote something like—'sky is blue, sun is great, Noël in painting mode.' On the other side was a copy of a painting Noël had done of the island. No invitation. And I don't go where I'm not invited." Coughing overcame him again and he turned away.

By nightfall, Le Mistral's energy had slackened. I suggested we call and see if the African Queen was open for dinner. He was instantly enthusiastic. The restaurant was on a stretch of the coast just down the hill from us known as "Petite Afrique." There were several other restaurants all with good food and one that was quite exceptional. Wagons of seawet fresh seafood were stationed on their patios for inspection and choice, many varieties totally unfamiliar to me. However, no one was seated outside, for Le Mistral had not been stilled. There remained a brisk wind that caused all the storefront canopies to flutter with a thudding sound. The sea remained unsettled; the many-splendored lights of the row reflecting on the agitated waves. Boats, docked at the far end of the marina, swayed in their berths.

The African Queen was our favorite restaurant. The ambiance was more California than the South of France. Movie posters of Humphrey Bogart and Katharine Hepburn, in their iconic roles as the alcoholic river captain and the maddening spinster traveling down river in Africa during World War I in the film for which the restaurant was named, decorated the walls along with fishnets and marine objects. The clientele was young, full of spirit. There was a singer who accompanied himself on the guitar, his repertoire current and fairly new American hits translated quite freely into French. The piece most requested seemed to be "Raindrops Keep Fallin' on My Head," the popular song from the movie *Butch Cassidy and the Sundance Kid*, played and sung in such a unique fashion that, although lively and charming, might not have been recognized by the song's composers, Burt Bacharach and Hal David. The place was warm and cozy. Voices were spirited. A guest at the African Queen could linger as long as they wished. The bill was never presented until the diner requested it. And, indeed, we lingered, for Jay was never at a loss for a story to tell. This evening he was looking back at his life before coming to Europe, on how difficult it had been to be gay when he was young, how much he resented having been the sibling elected to live with, and take care of, his mother as she aged, because he had to keep his personal life so locked up that it took on a sleazy feeling. He had hated that. He still could not let the memory die.

Within two days, the sun rose golden, the roads were cleared, and at Villa Roquefille Gerard had swept the patio and terraces of fallen leaves and branches. Best of all, I was able to open all the shutters and could see daylight once again. The last week of November was approaching and with it, the American Thanksgiving. I made plans and invited guests to celebrate with Catherine (who was taking the long weekend off from her studies), me, and Jay (whom my friends considered a family member and always included in their gatherings). I tried to persuade Michael to fly over, but he was in the very last days of a political campaign he was managing. My expat friends came from all directions of the Cote d'Azur and Catherine was bringing a French fellow classmate; we would be thirteen in all.

Procuring a turkey was not an easy task, and finding cranberries and pumpkin for the usual holiday favorites—cranberry sauce and pumpkin pie— no less daunting. The first American-style supermarket (so advertised with much to-do) had opened on the coast highway just the other side of Nice, so Jay and I drove there to see what we could find. The place was gigantic with a distinctive circus feel to the decor. Dozens of flags lined the road leading to it. Rock music blared forth as you entered. People had come to see it as they would have gone to—well—a circus! The French were accustomed to shopping for their food supplies at stores that specialized in different categories— the *boulangerie*, charcuterie, and so forth. The supermarket introduced a new way of obtaining their household and cooking needs under one gigantic roof. There were crowds at every display, aisles were blocked with wagons. The largest group of gapers and tasters was gathered suspiciously around a massive display of wine—not bottled, but in cardboard containers, a first at that time in a country where wine is revered as no place else on earth.

In the international food section I found canned pumpkin and small tins of cranberry sauce, the latter produced in Great Britain and bound to be closer to jam and very sweet. The market appeared to have every fowl known to man, case after case of the packaged winged wonders. But no turkeys ("*dinde*"), which are not indigenous to France. Still, I had been told that they were being newly bred in some part of the country, obviously not the South of France. I finally located a butcher in Nice who was doing a brisk business in supplying turkeys to the American colony in the area. The birds were on the small side, the largest he had weighed between twelve to thirteen pounds. I bought two of them ("plucked and beheaded, please"). I liked the idea anyway, as then there would be four legs for those of my guests who were hooked on drumsticks.

I doctored the cranberry sauce, toning down the sugar content as best I could with lemon juice and chunks of oranges—a bit of brandy poured in for a little nip. I made two pumpkin pies topped with crème fraîche and two rich, delicious Boston cream pies (my mother's recipe—and definitely an American invention). Believe me, no one went hungry. I have always held that Thanksgiving (and Christmas, as well) should be a shared, all-in-one family kind of meal, so I had Gerard bring in the patio table to extend the dining table. With a board and some padding he managed to make the two tables connect and level. The sideboard had to be moved into Jay's office to make room. We then placed it, front facing into the dining room, against the opened double doors so that it could be used to serve from.

Dinner, ready at six, was a huge success. Catherine's guest, however, had found fowl served with a fruit sauce "most exotic" and had no idea what a pumpkin was—or even its French translation, "*citrouille*." When told that it was a kind of squash, he commented, "How unusual American cookery is! Fruit with the main course and a vegetable for dessert!" As he took two helpings of everything, I assumed he approved.

All in all, it was a memorable Thanksgiving and somewhat of a wake-up call. For the hours of that day, I forgot that I was an American in a foreign country. I had felt comfortable, whole.

Catherine would be returning for Christmas, and I wanted to spend as much time as I could with her. So, on the Monday following Thanksgiving I set a rigid work schedule for myself and accepted no interim social engagements. Eleanor Wolquitt had gone to the Congressional Library in Washington on my behalf and had sent me transcripts of Bertolt Brecht and other writers' appearances before the Committee, of which good ole Harry S. Truman had said, shortly after turning over the presidency to Dwight D. Eisenhower: "The House Un-American Activities Committee is the most un-American thing in America!" Reading these gut-grinding transcripts demonstrated how right that gentleman from Missouri had been.

That morning, the sun just rising in a peaceful blue sky, I started work on a key scene toward the end of the novel where Max, whose life is closing in on him, flies to Washington from London to search out answers to the many questions he had about his testimony there a decade earlier, the one in which he had brought himself to believe that to survive he must betray his friends. He goes to the Congressional Library and takes out the transcript of his appearance. Once I had settled in on my chaise, yellow pad and several pens on the ready, the words seemed to flow directly from my brain to the paper. I wrote that Max sat down with his transcript

> in that scholarly place . . . his hand on top of the nineteen pages (only nineteen pages!) that represented his entire testimony. Just sat there with his hand resting that way. What was that—a caress? Who the hell did he think he was comforting? And why had he just sat that way never reading the transcript he had come all the way to Washington to read? Irrational—totally irrational. The ground was slipping from under him. . . .
>
> And yet he had not felt bad when he left Washington. That was the odd thing. He had in a way even felt comforted. There had been a demonstration of young people in Washington at the same time he had been there. And he had left envying them. They cared. They felt akin to this country. Dissent passionate enough to march itself right up to where the heart was. "Beat for us a while. Listen to our voices," was the message their attitude revealed. They cared. They belonged. This was their country and they were still young enough to fight for it their way. They were still hopeful that it could be what they dared to dream it could be.

A lot of what I personally felt was scrawled on the pages of that yellow lined pad. In my youth, I had written protest letters—hundreds of them—to senators, congressmen, newspapers, guilds, and unions. I joined organizations that seemed to be for what I was for—the Anti-Nazi League, charities for the victims of beleaguered nations—I signed petitions for the integration of blacks into the schools in the South—and for the right for all people of all races who were citizens of the United States to vote in our elections. Incredibly, these actions (which seemed the least I could do) were mostly accountable for the Committee's interest in me . . . that, and my close relationship to Robert Rossen. Guilty by association had become the Committee's mantra.

I still cared just as my creation Max Seaman had cared, but I was no longer politically activated enough to become involved. Guilt infused me. Anger—at myself—tasted bitter. I was no longer young (in my forties), nor resident of the country of my birth, I missed my nonaction. But idealistic dreams belonged to the young, I rationalized. They were the future. Shit! Age had nothing to do with it!

When I finished writing that day, I knew I had to go home—not just for the time it took to write a screenplay or sell a book. I had to reroot myself. Home meant America to me. But where? Any place but the Southern states and Texas where as a first-time married woman (all of nineteen to the age of twenty-three) I had been exposed to a bigotry for race—black and Latino—that had made those years the darkest of my life.

Of all my American expat friends still living in Europe, only Sidney seemed to have truly put down roots. I knew he loved America and was just as certain he would never return to live there. Yet, although he had a home in France, he surrounded himself with Americans and American projects. Few of the friends that I had met at his home were French. That was the enigma that was Sidney. I guessed that I knew him as well as anybody (even his brother, Harold, who seemed to be a man living on the edge of the sea, unable to ever wade in to test the waters). Still, there were times that I felt I did not know Sidney at all. Falling back on my own experience in psychoanalysis, Sidney appeared not to have lost the guilt of his childhood—the accidental shooting death of his sister. I think he wanted to be somewhere that would not bring up those memories. Well, he was dear to me and that was all that I could concern myself with—that, and to return his friendship in whatever way that I could.

Shortly after the publication of *Haunted Summer* there had been a flurry of interest in the book for films. Raymond Stross was now the leading contender. He was remarried to Anne Heywood, a beautiful actress whom he liked to think he had discovered. As Violet Pretty she had, however, been a beauty queen and played small parts in several British films and television. Raymond had taken over her career and cast her in more international films where her costars were American actors. Her recent film had been *The Fox*, adapted from a D. H. Lawrence story and in which she had given a strong performance (opposite Sandy Dennis) as the dominant half of lesbian lovers. Raymond wanted my novel so that Anne could be cast as Mary Shelley, a role he felt would give her career another big lift.

Raymond owned a new, American, pink Cadillac, one of the largest models they were then manufacturing. He had obviously imported it, as it had an American left-hand drive, which would have been on the wrong side for Great Britain but fine for the rest of Europe. Which, as he and Anne were making a second home in Switzerland, it apparently did not matter. They were extremely late to arrive because once Raymond had turned onto the High Corniche the car was too wide for the narrow roads and he had to back up and take a different route. They were staying at La Reserve. He called upon arrival to tell me that he would be further delayed, as he had crashed the Cadillac into another vehicle when he went to park. It reminded me of the one time he came to see me in Beverly Hills before I left for England to work for him. He had driven his rental car over the curb and straight up onto my front lawn.

If his driving ability had not improved, Raymond had. Before anything else, I noted with great happiness for him that his stutter was only slightly noticeable. His attire was far more conservative, and no one could doubt that he was utterly in love with his beautiful wife. Yet this was a more mature caring. Anne was his equal, not his charge. She had dark hair and striking eyes that had years of close observance behind them. She was also charming and well spoken. I liked her immediately. I told him straightaway that any negotiation for the rights of the novel had to be done with my agent. Of course, he agreed, explaining that what he wanted was to discuss the adaptation with me, which he thought should more deeply center on Mary Shelley and show the strength she had as the leader of the runaway artists—Percy Shelley, Byron, and his mistress, Claire. I countered that the story would be best told as an ensemble piece and to alter Mary Shelley's character would be to alter history. These discussions were left up in the air. After all, he had yet to finalize a deal for the rights, and even when that was done, I was not at all sure that I wanted to write the screenplay.

He brought me news of all that was going on (from his point of view) in Britain's film industry, which he claimed had been nearly devoured by American interests. It was almost impossible anymore to make a film that was for a British audience. A project had to appeal to an international distributor and, to do that, one of the stars had to have international appeal. He was, it seems—if he did obtain the film rights to *Haunted Summer*—considering the idea of casting the rock star Mick Jagger as Byron. Nothing Raymond ever said caught me off guard. But, I admit, I paled a moment at that idea. When thinking about it in later years, I decided that Mick Jagger might well have given the movie a contemporary feel that would have brought a dab of modern-day reality to the story. Byron, Shelley, Mary, and Claire were brilliantly talented young rebels during a season of rebellion, a time not so different from what was happening currently throughout the world. Driven from their own country (how familiar did that seem!), they sought solace in writing, sex, drugs, dreams, heightened perception, and the supernatural (Haight-Ashbury and Woodstock—in the 1960s—as a comparison comes quickly to mind).

In the end, another producer acquired the rights. The cast was young and talented, but the film was a great disappointment to me. Early on, I found something wondrous about my characters being brought to life on a screen—small or large. Yet there is a measure of discomfit along with wonder. One's written pages are now seen and made to animate through an adaptor's eyes. A director puts in his take and the actors portraying your characters still another. I can't speak for other authors, but in my case, I have a special vision of my characters. I can hear their individual voices in my head, understand their motivations—what they would and could do and what they would never attempt. In later years, when I was writing the biography of Margaret Mitchell, author of *Gone with the Wind*, I came upon correspondence between Mitchell and David Selznick, the iconic film's producer. In one letter he inquires who she might see as the dashing Rhett Butler. Mitchell replied, "Jack LaRue." Now, LaRue was of Italian descent and had made a name for himself in many early Hollywood films as an ominous thug or gangster and was a character actor, not a leading man. He did have dark, impressive looks and a sexuality that perhaps could perk up a young woman's nipples. Mitchell's seven-year work on the book had given her a deep understanding of who she thought Rhett Butler was—in fact she knew, guiltily, that she had modeled him after her abusive first husband. Her loathing and fascination of him had been hard to dispel. In her mind, Rhett was dangerous—a threat—yet sexually exciting, and he was rich (which her first husband was not). Selznick, wise filmmaker that he was, knew it was Rhett's charms, not his darker side, that would appeal to a movie audience—who he thought, with this project, would be overwhelmingly female. Polls taken at the time proved that readers chose Clark Gable from the start and, of course, Selznick ended up casting him in the role. To this day, Rhett Butler will always be Clark Gable to those who view the film. He was not to his creator.

Jay was truly sick. He had continued to lose weight, and now he was coughing up blood. For several weeks he had adamantly refused my pleadings that he should see a doctor. Just one week after we had sent the final manuscript of *Shadow of a Lion* off to my editor in New York, he collapsed at the top of the staircase on the bedroom landing and fell halfway down. I called for an ambulance, and he was taken to hospital in Nice and diagnosed with an advanced case of lung cancer. After a week, I brought him home. Sidney suggested an oncologist in Cannes who was known to be one of the best in all of France. Paul Jarrico and Yvette had broken up, and he was staying with me at the time. He drove us into Cannes and Sidney met us at the doctor's office. The oncologist explained to me—Jay's x-rays clipped to a board along one wall—just how serious was his condition. The lung had to be removed, and there was no way of knowing until then how far the disease had spread to other parts of his body.

He took the grave news like a major, although his mouth was drawn into a straight white line and, when I took hold of his arm, I could feel the quickened beat of his pulse. We left the office and drove to Sidney's flat. Jay made it clear that he did not feel comfortable having the operation in France. Not that he thought French doctors were unqualified. "If the cancer has spread," he said, his voice cool and collected, "I don't want to die abroad." Paul drove us back to Beaulieu. The next day Jay called his sister in Los Angeles and explained the situation and that he wished to return to Los Angeles and for her to do some research on oncology surgeons. Within two days everything was arranged for him to return to California. The next hurdle was how to get him safely returned. He would have to fly from Nice to Paris, change planes from the domestic building to the international wing for the last leg of the journey—a long hop, nonstop, to Los Angeles. Jay was entirely too weak to handle this on his own, even if Air France had allowed him on board without someone to accompany him, as he looked extremely ill. Paul offered to fly with him. He was anxious to get back to California and see what he could do about restoring his credits. He had good friends (former expats, Tiba and George Willner) living in Ojai, a fairly short drive northeast of Los Angeles, with whom he could stay. However, he did not have the money for a ticket. I was happy to oblige and Jay seemed to welcome the idea.

Twenty-four hours later, I stood at the gate of Nice Airport as Paul wheeled Jay down the ramp to board their plane. Jay had said, "No good-byes!" And had added, "Never forget that you gave me a new life and that I've loved every minute of it!" On my return to Villa Roquefille, only Sandy and Chrissy raced down the stairs to greet me. Biba was lying in front of the door to Jay's room. She would return there every night to sleep as long as we were resident. It was uncanny.

Leon called when he heard about Jay to tell me how sorry he felt. Actually, the two men never did get on. In fact, the evening before his departure, Jay had told me in a hard voice, "You must not go back to *that* man, whatever you do!"

"I'd like to come down to see you," Leon was saying. "I know we parted with great bitterness. But before we cast off our marriage, let's be civilized and talk about it."

I reminded him that he brought on the animosity by declaring I had deserted him.

"I was deeply wounded at the time. Let me come down. We can talk about it like two intelligent people."

I said no, my mind was set. He just kept talking and finally wore me down.

"I won't press. I just want us to be sure that this is the path we both want to take. I never said I didn't love you. I do. I'll come for the weekend. Just two days."

"On one condition," I finally agreed. "You cannot stay here."

He arrived that Friday. Two painful days followed. He had not made a reservation at a hotel. By the time of his cool departure, caused by my refusal to even consider a reconciliation, I knew we would never see each other again and that he would, as previously decreed, seek the divorce on grounds of desertion.

Catherine joined me at spring break, bringing Wendy, her roommate at school. The sounds of young voices in the large house were cheering. I had heard from both Jay and his sister (who gave me a more detailed and realistic report of his progress). The surgery had gone well, but the cancer had spread. The doctors were hoping that with treatment Jay could be given some added time. His letters were optimistic. He sent me a photograph of himself smiling, wearing his spiffy Asian robe while a good-looking hunk of a male nurse stood behind him.

The silver Beetle remained parked in the garage. I decided to ship it to him, hoping he might see it as a positive goal. Jay had loved driving that crazy car. I wrote that it would take a month before it arrived in Los Angeles (actually in the port of San Pedro) and that maybe his brother-in-law could arrange the pickup. When it was finally delivered, Jay sent me a telegram: BABY DELIVERED LIKE NEW AND SHINY CAN'T WAIT TO TAKE HER FOR A SPIN LOVE YOU JAY. (He never was able to get behind the wheel, but in my head I can see him riding along the Pacific Coast Highway, breathing in the scent of salt on the sea and ignoring the horns for him to drive faster and not to hog the road.)

I suffered a true case of postpartum once *Shadow* was with my editor. I had not felt so grievous a loss on completion of my first three novels. *Shadow* was different. I had put so much of myself into it. I was not sure I could ever reach so deep again. There was also my responsibility to my colleagues and friends to deliver a book that was truthful to their history. My editor at Coward, McCann & Geoghegan was most enthusiastic and between the two of us (missiles flying back and forth across the ocean like homing pigeons) meticulous care was given to the editing of every page of the manuscript. I had one great dilemma. I had started the book in Madrid and had promised I would dedicate it to Leon. By now, communication had completely broken down between us. It was a strange thing to do, especially with our breach. Still, a promise is a promise. The acknowledgment page thus reads: "For Leon." In retrospect, it seems right, for I believe we were both victims—politically and maritally—and that there had been good times—just not enough of them.

My lease on Villa Roquefille ended on June 1. I could renew it if I so wished. I did not. Every guest should know when it is time to leave—even a country. Catherine now chose to finish her college years in New England and had applied to several schools and was waiting for replies. The plan was that we would return to the States and spend the summer together. Where? was still the question. I wanted to be close enough to her school for her to travel home on weekends if she so chose. I did not want to live in Hartford, Boston, or any other large New England city. It had to be a small town with no personal history attached.

Catherine finally ended my indecision by conceiving a rather mad idea (the apple does not fall far from the tree!). She tore out a large map of New England from my atlas and tacked it to a kitchen wall. Then she tied a scarf over my eyes, took a bookmark, and pushed a tack into the end. "Turn around a couple of times," she commanded, helping me to do so. "Stop!" she called out. "Now, hold out your hand with the bookmark in front of you and walk forward." I did as she asked.

The tack had amazingly landed between three towns that appealed to me due to their history and their connection with the arts: Woodstock, New York (scene of the youth and music rebellion), Stockbridge, Massachusetts (home of Tanglewood and the summer residence of the Boston Symphony Orchestra), and Williamstown, Massachusetts (with a fine college and art collection). I wrote to the chamber of commerce in each town, although I was not sure that towns still had them! I asked about their community and the names of real estate agents. I received only one letter in return, from an agent in Stockbridge. I instantly replied with a list of my rental needs and the added information that I had three dogs. She answered that she had the perfect house for me to rent. It was on Christian Hill in the historic section of town, dogs welcome, a short walk from town, and would be available on June 10. It had been built in the early nineteenth century as a schoolhouse and was near the Daniel Chester French House, where the American sculptor had kept his studio and where he had carved the famous seated marble figure of Abraham Lincoln that adorned his memorial in Washington, DC. I agreed to a one-year lease with an option at the same price for another year to follow.

Now came the tough part. I had to pack up everything I had including all the files that Jay had kept for me, my small library of books, and all the paintings, furnishings, and tableware I had collected throughout the years I had been abroad. Decisions, decisions, decisions. I needed help to get everything sorted out. Someone told me that a young man working for the actor Dirk Bogarde (who lived on the Cote d'Azur) was looking for employment, that Bogarde was on location making *A Death in Venice* and this fellow was not happy in France and wanted a position that would fill in until he got a visa to immigrate to the United States.

His name was Alex Cortez. He was from the Philippines and of Asian and Spanish heritage, a truly beautiful young man in his midtwenties, slim, tallish, dark, expressive eyes, ink-black hair, and light bronze skin. He had immigrated first to London to finish his education, done some modeling, and then worked in a restaurant to keep body and soul together. He had a passion and a talent for cooking and was hired as a cook by a British couple who had a second home on the Cote d'Azur. When they sold the house to return to England, he had gone to work for Bogarde. With the actor away for a long stretch, Alex decided to move on.

He was bright, could type passably, and brought me some Asian-style hors d'oeuvres he had made to prove his ability as a cook.

"I'm leaving for the States in ten weeks," I told him. "It's only a temporary job to help me organize. I'm a writer, I have mounds of papers, research, and books among other things. I can't see myself throwing any parties during that time where your abilities would be an asset."

"I want to go to America," he blurted out. "I'm working on a visa. If I please you, maybe you would take me with you as an assistant. It would make it easier for me to obtain a visa."

"You want to accompany me to the States?" I asked, stalling for time to digest this.

"Yes, and allow me to work for you there."

"As a cook?"

"Well," he grinned, showing a mouthful of perfect white teeth. "I can type and file. Mr. Bogarde is also writing now. I helped him copy his pages. And I am a good organizer."

We were sitting in the kitchen and I was munching away at a flavorsome cocktail-sized egg roll filled with shrimp. "What is it you want to do in America?" I asked.

His broad smile returned. There was pride and intelligence in his face. "I plan to start the first gourmet Asian fast-food chain," he said.

Seated across from me was a potential émigré with a dream, a throwback to earlier men and women bound for America because they believed their dreams could be fulfilled there; men like my grandfather, Big Charlie. Dreams were often changed by circumstance, but everyone has the right to go in search of his or hers.

Of course I hired him. He moved in the next day to occupy the rooms that Vera had always used when she was with me. I simply could not give him Jay's former suite.

· 19 ·

Last Call!

"Just try it, Genevieve," Alex would say as he presented her with a beautifully plated dish of tiny seafood dumplings.

"Poison!" she would spit back and turn away.

Alex had arrived at Villa Roquefille the morning after our interview, bringing with him a battery of woks, steamers, bamboo accoutrements, and a shopping bag filled with special spices, jars of Asian preserves, and a five-pound bag of rice. There was, from that day forward, a pot of steamed rice kept on the back burner of the stove, ready to eat or use in a recipe, memorized or created on the spot, as he owned no cookbook (at least not one that I had seen). The kitchen was immediately his domain, to Genevieve's furious rumblings. She refused to wash the dirty dishes and pots from his cooking or to eat anything that he had made, no matter how hard he tried to tempt her to do so. Alex was, in fact, of an easygoing nature and added a needed light touch to the atmosphere of the house, still feeling the absence of Jay. He was also a superb cook—a chef, really—and happiest when he was in the kitchen whipping up a meal.

He had overrated his typing skills (which put me back to work on the typewriter when necessary), but more than made up for it in his organizational abilities. He also drove a car, which I rented for our use during the remaining time we would spend at the villa. He went through all my papers with me, boxed and numbered them, and then entered what was in them into a ledger. Catherine finished classes a week before I had set the date of our departure on the Italian liner *Michelangelo*, departing from Nice at noon on May 27, a Saturday, and arriving in New York the morning of May 31. A car had been booked to take us to Stockbridge (a three-hour ride) and reservations made at the highly rated Red Lion Inn (substantiated by the reviews from magazines enclosed in the agent's correspondence to me) until the house on Christian Hill was available. She also had found a "doggie hotel" nearby the inn where our poodle family could board until we took possession of the house.

Before Catherine joined me, I wanted to have a good part of my packing done so that we could enjoy a few days seeing the parts of the Cote d'Azur that I had missed or wished to visit once again. Dale was also coming down for a weekend before the house was too filled with boxes, crates, and suitcases. The one great thing about our traveling by ship was that each passenger was allowed a very large baggage weight, and as there would be three of us going first class (Catherine and I sharing a large outside cabin, and Alex a smaller inside one), I would not have to ship anything separate.

Deciding what to take and what to dispose of during a major move is not an easy task. I had carted everything I had in Gstaad to Beaulieu and still had furniture and other household goods in storage in California which I planned to transport once we were settled. I tried to be sensible in my choices and ruthless in my disposal (Genevieve worked as a willing taker by my side, which I suppose made things easier). I thought about Paul Jarrico and his car heaped with personal papers. I would hold on to only those that I felt needed to be kept as a record—my final drafts of books, unpublished stories, things related to my family history, and a few large envelopes of letters and photographs. Sorting through my relatively small library was more difficult. I packed several boxes of the books I could bear to part with and Alex took them into Nice to donate to the American Library there. I gave all things electrical to Genevieve, as I did not want to have to deal with converters. Still, the numbered boxes now occupying a good portion of the living room grew.

I was almost euphoric when Dale arrived and I had reason to put aside the cleaving, chaos, and disorder for a few days. We had decided to just tootle around the area, stopping wherever we felt drawn to do so. She had the small car—perfect for two women with only a couple of changes of clothes and for investigating some of the small villages on the High Corniches. There were only short stretches between them and each had its own special appeal. It was on this short tour that I came to appreciate why the Cote d'Azur, putting aside the sister palm trees of Southern California, had felt familiar to me from the start. Whatever vista I looked to, seaward, the mountains, down the small roads of ancient villages, past flower gardens and flower stalls, I had seen before in the great paintings of the French artists of the last decades of the nineteenth century and the early ones of the twentieth—Cezanne, Manet, Matisse, Monet, Utrillo, Dufy, Pissarro—their canvasses glowing with the images we now drove past, painted in the uniquely fierce light of the South of France. The azure skies, red-tiled roofs, and silvery olive trees swathed in luminous sunshine and dramatic shadows.

We started out early in the morning. With Dale at the wheel, we headed up the Moyenne Corniche to the fortified medieval village of Eze and perused its ancient streets with their high stone walls and roads made of red brick, worn to a pale rusty color through the centuries. The town was perched precariously on narrow rocky cliffs. We had a morning coffee in a restaurant that hung over the side of a great cliff, seemingly without support, and sat at a window that looked down to the coastal towns below as the sea rolled in soft waves out to and over the horizon. We left before the onslaught of tourists arrived and drove westward to Saint Paul with the sun lighting the whole countryside and the glare on the sea so strong that it was best not to look sideways or down.

Saint Paul was also an ancient fortified village, perhaps the most intact example in the South of France. We were not stopping there to see the thousands-year-old ramparts, but to walk around the village and have lunch in the glorious courtyard at La Colombe d'Or, which was famous for their amazing collection of art obtained at the end of the nineteenth century when artists like Monet, Cezanne, and others of that era, not yet making a fair living from their work, lived in the area and traded paintings for food. The spectacular private collection now hung on the walls of the warren-like rooms of the main building. It was there that I had a simple salad with the most succulent, sun-toasted tomato I had ever eaten and for dessert, rich red strawberries served with ground black pepper. We had chosen an outside table on the tree-shaded terrace because we were aware that if you ate inside, you would have gapers leaning over you to look at the incredible art display.

Our next stop was Vallauris, a town famous for some five thousand years for its clay works and where Picasso, who lived for ten years in the Villa Galloise, then on the outskirts, had begun his love affair with ceramics—and with the town itself. In the ancient chapel he painted his enormous fresco, *War and Peace*, not at all, with its grotesque and bloodied figures, what the townsfolk expected. Once seen (and we stood there a long time studying it), it is difficult to erase from your memory. We walked the narrow streets, lined with galleries and shops where dozens of potters plied their trade and sold their work. Finally, we entered the Madoura pottery works where many of Picasso's pieces were on display—the originals at a high cost. I was enamored of a glazed white pitcher, its unique design in black, signed by the artist; and I deliberated its purchase. The high price, and the fact that I had vowed not to bring back anything more for us to pack, stopped me. At this time, Picasso was ninety-two (he died one year later) and it was doubtful that he had any more works forthcoming. Still, it was enough for me to enjoy his unusual pottery on display—especially after that walk in and out of so many shops showcasing other potters' art pieces—for one understood why there was only one Picasso and what a genius he was.

After a light supper at an outdoor café we spent the night at a quaint inn (six or seven rooms at the most) in a nearby village. When I awoke the next morning it was to a great deal of sound and commotion. I ran to the window (small, like one to be found in an attic room). Below, on the cobbled courtyard, a farmers market had been set up and was, even at this early hour, enjoying a heavy business. Dale and I dressed quickly and went down to join the market crowd. I was used to the huge open markets in Monaco and Nice. This one was minisized compared to them. But it was one of the finest I had ever shopped at. One had the feeling that everything had been picked only hours before, for the displays of fruits and vegetables were still touched with the fresh early-morning dew. We bought more than enough to eat as a picnic lunch somewhere on a side road on our return to Beaulieu.

My parting with Dale was difficult. We were both choked with emotion. She promised to come see me in Stockbridge as soon as it was possible for her to make a trip to the States. Right now she had a massive new project that involved a hotel, spa, and condominiums on an island in the Turks and Caicos that still did not have boat or air service to the mainland.

A friend drove Catherine down at the end of school, the car jam-packed with her possessions. The living room now looked like a loading dock. Our plan was to travel east along the coast with Alex the following day to Monte Carlo (Monaco), Menton (France), and over the Italian border (less than a three-hour drive), staying one night someplace on the Italian coast before returning. We talked like two young girls way into the night. I woke up a little later than planned. I was not yet dressed to go down for breakfast when I heard Genevieve screaming. Catherine raced down the stairs and into the kitchen, me following on her heels. Genevieve was sobbing, the excess flesh on her arms flapping as she heaved with each new outburst. Alex was attempting to find out the cause.

It was Sandy. Gerard had found him on the grounds lying on his side, apparently unable to move, the two other dogs yipping and barking. Out we went as fast as we could. Sandy was whimpering—the other dogs barking as they ran around us. I got down on my knees and stroked his head. He looked up at me with his large brown velvet eyes. He trusted me and the whimpering stopped. I could see no blood anywhere on his underside or on his light apricot fur that always made people turn to look at him, so handsome did he wear it. I thought hopefully at first that he might have only broken a bone. Alex helped me raise him up. He could not move or stand, and we gently laid him back down again. Catherine went in and called the vet while Alex carefully lifted him and held him in his arms. He was a hefty dog—weighing over fifty pounds. We got him into the rear seat of the car. Catherine, having reached the vet, returned with a blanket, covered him with it, and then sat in the back next to him while I sat in front with Alex.

Together, Alex and I carried Sandy into the vet's office and placed him on the steel examining table, Catherine fast by our side. After the long, trying minutes while he was being examined, the vet informed us that Sandy had suffered a heart attack and stroke. Most of his body was paralyzed. Catherine was crying, and I had a hard time holding back my own tears. Sandy had always more or less been Catherine's dog. He had been with us for nearly eleven years, had stood at the window in Klosters waiting for her to come home from school when she was a youngster. The vet was moved by our sadness, but he had to tell us the truth. There was no other recourse but to put Sandy down. Catherine let out a sobbing, "No!" and held on to me. I asked the vet to leave us alone for a few moments. When he returned, both of us having regained our composure, we each stood on one side of the table on which Sandy lay and stroked his head as he was put to rest. Never before had either of us experienced death. In Sandy's case it came most peacefully.

The trip down the coast was canceled by mutual assent, and Catherine and I kept ourselves busy with the work of preparing for the longer journey.

Sidney came to see us off. The previous day, a service had picked up the baggage that was to be stored in the ship's cargo. The last box was marked 42! We each also had two smaller suitcases to be delivered to our cabins. We arrived early just to make sure all of this went smoothly. Biba and Chrissy were to travel in the kennel on the top deck, but we were able to keep them with us until the ship was at sea. "You're doing the right thing," Sidney assured me as the ship's bell rang and the shout of "Last call! All ashore who's going ashore!" repeated in Italian, French, and English, echoed throughout the massive ship. I watched him descend the gangplank. We exchanged an enthusiastic wave (not royal at all!). He saluted—which rather amused me. There was fruit and a bottle of champagne in our cabin from the ship's captain, and two beautiful floral bouquets, one from Sidney and one from Dale. The three of us went back up on deck to watch as the ship churned the waters and we were finally at sea. The day was magnificent: warm breeze, the waters calm. I could only hope that Sidney had spoken the truth.

I had sailed on Dutch, English, and French ships. This was the first time on one flying the flag of Italy. There was constant confusion. The first safety drill was utter chaos. And the dining captain never knew what table we were supposed to sit at for our meals. I finally asked for a private table for the three of us. It was never really private because the maître d'—a slender, slightly balding, dark-haired man—was constantly at our table making sure . . . well, I was not exactly sure of his purpose, until Catherine said, "Mom, he has his eye on you."

After a meal, when I went up on deck and had settled comfortably into a lounge chair with a book—he would suddenly appear at my side to lean over to ask in a manner (in Italy anyway) obviously meant to be seductive, "Is there anything I can get for you, madam?" The morning of our third day out, I answered a knock on my cabin door and there he stood, a sweater I had left in the dining lounge just outside the restaurant folded like a napkin over his arm. "I believe this is yours, no?" he smiled.

"Yes, thank you," I said, took it from him, and went to close the door. He took a step inside. I assumed that this was not a first for him. He most probably thought I was a rich divorcée (first-class passage and an Asian assistant) or widow and had the idea that as such I (and others before me) might be glad to be "entertained."

I planted my feet more securely on the rug, put my hands on my hips, and glared at him. "You know the large Russian gentleman with the mustache who looks a lot like Stalin and is traveling alone and sits at the next table to mine?" I asked in a strong, declarative voice.

"Si . . . si?"

"He is a friend of my husband's." I took a deep breath. "Mafia."

"Mafia!"

"You come one step further into this cabin, and if I were you I would . . ."

The door was open and as fate would have it, that same Russian gentleman was passing by in the corridor. "*Dos vadanya!*" I called out to him. Actually, it means "good-bye" in Russian, but they were the only words of Russian that I knew. The man turned, smiled, and paused a moment, while the maître d' made a quick exit down to the opposite end of the corridor.

For the rest of the voyage, the maître d' avoided speaking to me, even in the restaurant.

The sea was smooth, the days filled with sunshine and gentle breezes. I cannot swim and have a fear of water. Yet, I have always loved boats (big ones only!) and the feeling of being so cut off from the rest of the world. I was exceptionally weary when I boarded the *Michelangelo*, but with each day at sea, the weariness waned. Catherine was having a pleasant time, as there were many young people and activities for them on the boat. We both visited the kennels three or four times a day. Alex managed to get us a private tour through the ship's kitchens—a fascinating experience. The nighttime entertainment was better missed than attended, but I did meet some nice people, and the Russian gentleman and I became almost pally as he turned out to speak English well and was on his way to a Midwest university to teach Russian literature—which just happened to have been my major in my last year at university.

Suddenly, it was the night before we were to dock in New York. Shortly after midnight, Catherine sound asleep, I went up on deck. My head was filled with thoughts about returning to the States, this time with no strings attached to pull me back to Europe. The ship had put on speed. I could hear the engines rev up. There was a chill in the air, and I held myself tightly in my own arms. It was like I was holding my whole life to my breast. It was the one thing that was wholly mine. I thought I might have abused it from time to time, maybe not treated it with enough respect or held on to the best moments long enough. But I had never given up hope for better times, appreciated what I had been given—my two beautiful children, my love of the written word—or slacked in my attention to them. That had to count for something.

And now—was I really going home? One of the last things I had packed was my favorite dictionary, the cover worn badly, the last pages loose. It had been close at hand for me to use for over twenty years. It went where I went. My constant companion holding the entire English language between its covers. I had looked up home and transposed the most meaningful definitions (there had been eighteen) into my journal.

"Home—4.a. An environment offering security and happiness. b. A valued place regarded as a refuge or place of origin. 5. The place, such as a town, where one was born or has lived for a long period. 7. The place where something is founded or developed; a source."

I was seeking all of those—especially security, happiness—a source of creativity. And, yes, home meant my place of origin. I hoped it would not be simply a refuge. More than any time I could recall, life seemed to be leading me back to my roots, which I now knew did not mean a specific house or town.

That night as I stood looking out across the dark sea, I remembered the time so many years before when I had held my two children's hands as we looked out over a similar scene. I told them we were on our way to a great adventure. It had turned out to be just that. But adventures do end, and where does one go then? I whispered it to myself: "*Home.*" I thought I could see the lights from shore, but they turned out to be another boat in the distance going along a horizontal course.

I came back up on deck the next morning after immigration had stamped our passports. Everyone was crowded against the railing wanting to get a photo or just a good look of the Statue of Liberty, which was straight ahead and fully visible. Never had I felt freer. I knew not what was ahead for me. For that matter, no one can foresee their own future. I was full up with plans. I had returned in time for a major presidential race and would get into some part of it and fight for the candidate of my choice. That idea excited me. I held no grudges or resentments. Writing *Shadow of a Lion* had somehow placed the McCarthy years, and my life as an expat, into the past, a part of my personal history. I had the curious feeling that I had never really left home. I had taken it with me, along with my book that held almost every word in the English language.

Catherine and Alex had joined me on deck. Alex was jumping up and down. "Lady Liberty! Lady Liberty!" he kept shouting and waving as we passed her by. We went up to the kennels and took Biba and Chrissy back to the cabin with us as we waited to disembark. Finally, the motors stopped. The moment I stepped off the gangplank, a wave of wonder flooded over me. This was not another visit home, this was a final return. Wherever I went from this day forth, home went with me.

> *Home tomorrow yet no one awaits me*
> *It has no front or back door.*
> *Sky for roof,*
> *Earth for floor.*
> *It is the wide country where I was born*
> *And will be forever bound.*

Index

About the Author

Born on the East Coast, at the age of four **Anne Edwards** moved with her parents to Hollywood, where she spent most of her childhood and young adult years, first as a performer, then as a film writer. The event of McCarthyism and the Hollywood blacklist in the late 1940s and early 1950s caused her to leave home and find work abroad. Fate placed her in London, where she spent the major part of the next two decades.

Her return was a second act few of her colleagues enjoyed. She very quickly became a best-selling author, first of novels, then of numerous critically acclaimed biographies that include Vivien Leigh, Margaret Mitchell, Katharine Hepburn, Sonya Tolstoy, Queen Elizabeth and her sister, Princess Margaret, Princess Diana, Maria Callas, and two volumes on Ronald Reagan (*Early Reagan* and *The Reagans*).

She gained much media attention as the author of the much-discussed and never published (due to estate problems) sequel to Margaret Mitchell's immortal novel *Gone with the Wind*. She is also a past president of the Authors Guild.

She finally has returned to California, where she lives with her husband, author and musical theater historian Stephen Citron.